Law, Ethics, and Integrity in the Sports Industry

Konstantinos Margaritis
University of Crete, Greece

A volume in the Advances in Business Information Systems and Analytics (ABISA) Book Series

IGI Global
DISSEMINATOR OF KNOWLEDGE

Published in the United States of America by
IGI Global
Business Science Reference (an imprint of IGI Global)
701 E. Chocolate Avenue
Hershey PA, USA 17033
Tel: 717-533-8845
Fax: 717-533-8661
E-mail: cust@igi-global.com
Web site: http://www.igi-global.com

Library of Congress Cataloging-in-Publication Data

Names: Margaritis, Konstantinos, 1984- editor.
Title: Law, ethics, and integrity in the sports industry / Konstantinos Margaritis, editor.
Description: Hershey, PA : Business Science Reference, 2018.
Identifiers: LCCN 2017048744| ISBN 9781522553878 (hardcover) | ISBN 9781522553885 (ebook)
Subjects: LCSH: Sports administration--Moral and ethical aspects. | Sports--Moral and ethical aspects. | Sports--Economic aspects. | Sports--Law and legislation.
Classification: LCC GV713 .L38 2019 | DDC 796.06/9--dc23 LC record available at https://lccn.loc.gov/2017048744

This book is published in the IGI Global book series Advances in Business Information Systems and Analytics (ABISA) (ISSN: 2327-3275; eISSN: 2327-3283)

British Cataloguing in Publication Data
A Cataloguing in Publication record for this book is available from the British Library.

For electronic access to this publication, please contact: eresources@igi-global.com.

Advances in Business Information Systems and Analytics (ABISA) Book Series

ISSN:2327-3275
EISSN:2327-3283

Editor-in-Chief: Madjid Tavana, La Salle University, USA

MISSION

The successful development and management of information systems and business analytics is crucial to the success of an organization. New technological developments and methods for data analysis have allowed organizations to not only improve their processes and allow for greater productivity, but have also provided businesses with a venue through which to cut costs, plan for the future, and maintain competitive advantage in the information age.

The **Advances in Business Information Systems and Analytics (ABISA) Book Series** aims to present diverse and timely research in the development, deployment, and management of business information systems and business analytics for continued organizational development and improved business value.

COVERAGE

- Big Data
- Geo-BIS
- Legal information systems
- Statistics
- Business Models
- Forecasting
- Data Analytics
- Decision Support Systems
- Management Information Systems
- Data Strategy

IGI Global is currently accepting manuscripts for publication within this series. To submit a proposal for a volume in this series, please contact our Acquisition Editors at Acquisitions@igi-global.com or visit: http://www.igi-global.com/publish/.

The Advances in Business Information Systems and Analytics (ABISA) Book Series (ISSN 2327-3275) is published by IGI Global, 701 E. Chocolate Avenue, Hershey, PA 17033-1240, USA, www.igi-global.com. This series is composed of titles available for purchase individually; each title is edited to be contextually exclusive from any other title within the series. For pricing and ordering information please visit http://www.igi-global.com/book-series/advances-business-information-systems-analytics/37155. Postmaster: Send all address changes to above address.

Titles in this Series

For a list of additional titles in this series, please visit:
https://www.igi-global.com/book-series/advances-business-information-systems-analytics/37155

Analyzing the Impacts of Industry 4.0 in Modern Business Environments
Richard Brunet-Thornton (University of Economics, Czech Republic) and Felipe Martinez (University of Economics, Czech Republic)
Business Science Reference • ©2018 • 410pp • H/C (ISBN: 9781522534686) • US $215.00

Protocols and Applications for the Industrial Internet of Things
Cristian González García (University of Oviedo, Spain) Vicente García-Díaz (University of Oviedo, Spain) B. Cristina Pelayo García-Bustelo (University of Oviedo, Spain) and Juan Manuel Cueva Lovelle (University of Oviedo, Spain)
Business Science Reference • ©2018 • 356pp • H/C (ISBN: 9781522538059) • US $215.00

Social Network Analytics for Contemporary Business Organizations
Himani Bansal (Jaypee Institute of Information Technology, India) Gulshan Shrivastava (National Institute of Technology Patna, India) Gia Nhu Nguyen (Duy Tan University, Vietnam) and Loredana-Mihaela Stanciu (University Timisoara, Romania)
Business Science Reference • ©2018 • 321pp • H/C (ISBN: 9781522550976) • US $215.00

Harnessing Human Capital Analytics for Competitive Advantage
Mohit Yadav (BML Munjal University, India) Shrawan Kumar Trivedi (Indian Institute of Management Sirmaur, India) Anil Kumar (BML Munjal University, India) and Santosh Rangnekar (Indian Institute of Technology Roorkee, India)
Business Science Reference • ©2018 • 367pp • H/C (ISBN: 9781522540380) • US $215.00

Corporate Social Responsibility for Valorization of Cultural Organizations
María del Pilar Muñoz Dueñas (University of Vigo, Spain) Lucia Aiello (Sapienza University of Rome, Italy) Rosario Cabrita (University Nova de Lisboa, Portugal) and Mauro Gatti (Sapienza University of Rome, Italy)
Business Science Reference • ©2018 • 328pp • H/C (ISBN: 9781522535515) • US $215.00

For an entire list of titles in this series, please visit:
https://www.igi-global.com/book-series/advances-business-information-systems-analytics/37155

IGI Global
DISSEMINATOR OF KNOWLEDGE

701 East Chocolate Avenue, Hershey, PA 17033, USA
Tel: 717-533-8845 x100 • Fax: 717-533-8661
E-Mail: cust@igi-global.com • www.igi-global.com

Editorial Advisory Board

Table of Contents

Preface xiv

Section 1
Legal and Ethical Issues in Sports

Chapter 1
The Redefinition of Fairness in Sports Since the Arrival of Comparative Fault Tort Reform 1
Rodney J. Blackman, United States Sports Academy, USA

Chapter 2
Sport and Antitrust Law 23
Alena Redkina, Kutafin Moscow State Law University, Russia
Igor Ponkin, Kutafin Moscow State Law University, Russia & The Russian Presidential Academy of National Economy and Public Administration, Russia
Olga Shevchenko, Kutafin Moscow State Law University, Russia & International Association of Sports Law, Russia

Chapter 3
Blow to the Head: The Legal and Ethical Implications of Chronic Traumatic Encephalopathy (CTE) in Professional Sports 54
Dino Sossi, Columbia University, USA

Chapter 4
International Sport Business and Global Sport Governance 83
Efthalia Chatzigianni, University of Peloponnese, Greece

Chapter 5
The Legal Validity of E-Sports as a Sport 101
Reyhan Mir, Independent Researcher, Spain

Chapter 6
E-Sports at the Olympic Games: From Physicality to Virtuality....................... 124
Renata E. Ntelia, Institute of Digital Games, Malta

Chapter 7
Physical Education and Religious Freedom: The ECtHR Perspective 144
Konstantinos Margaritis, University of Crete, Greece

Section 2
Case Studies

Chapter 8
"Body Culture": A Spiritual Echo of Olympia and the Fragmented Nature of Physical Education in the Modern-Day School in Greece................................ 157
Konstantina Gongaki, National and Kapodistrian University of Athens, Greece

Chapter 9
Legal, Ethical, and Integrity Issues in Sports Industry: The Russian Experience 169
Igor Ponkin, Kutafin Moscow State Law University, Russia & The Russian Presidential Academy of National Economy and Public Administration, Russia
Olga Shevchenko, Kutafin Moscow State Law University, Russia & International Association of Sports Law, Russia
Alena Redkina, Kutafin Moscow State Law University, Russia

Chapter 10
Problems of the Fight Against Doping in Professional Sports: On the Example of Russian and World Experience.. 202
Anatoly Peskov, Russian International Olympic University, Russia

Chapter 11
The Emergence of Sports Law in Kenya 241
Asha Mikinyango, Mount Kenya University, Kenya

Compilation of References 263

About the Contributors 301

Index 305

Detailed Table of Contents

Preface.. xiv

Section 1
Legal and Ethical Issues in Sports

Chapter 1
The Redefinition of Fairness in Sports Since the Arrival of Comparative Fault Tort Reform 1
Rodney J. Blackman, United States Sports Academy, USA

Tort reform advocates take varying dispositions regarding whether or not comparative fault tort reform has sufficiently compromised the ethical practices of sports industry practitioners. It follows that two of the best place to look for evidence supporting or refuting such claims is in the laws that govern sports and the sports cases that have been brought before the courts regarding the rights of individuals within the communities in which those individuals exist. Consequently, the aim of this chapter is to provide an overview of the role of comparative fault tort reform in sports cases. Examination appears regarding how that role has factored into meeting societal demand calling for a re-definition of fairness, as well as changes in the ethical codes of sports practitioner acumen.

Chapter 2
Sport and Antitrust Law..23
Alena Redkina, Kutafin Moscow State Law University, Russia
Igor Ponkin, Kutafin Moscow State Law University, Russia & The Russian Presidential Academy of National Economy and Public Administration, Russia
Olga Shevchenko, Kutafin Moscow State Law University, Russia & International Association of Sports Law, Russia

This chapter explores the relationship between sports and different types of competition, legal and actual possibility to apply competition, particularly antitrust, laws to sports, primarily to the sphere of professional sports and sports industry. The commercial and non-commercial components, yet linked to the interests of profit, in modern professional sports entails certain applicability of competition law to the field of sports. However, excessively strict application of antitrust laws can lead to devastating consequences for all types of sports or sports in general. Therefore, it is important to take into account specific characteristics of the sport sphere (more than any other sphere of activity). This is important when deciding on the application of competition law to this sphere or withdrawal of this sector from the application of competition law. Nature and inherent specific features of professional sports activities and sports in general have a significant impact on the application of competition law. Economic competition in the field of sport is atypical. The authors give their definitions of "sport," "competitiveness in the sport," "commercial competition in the field of professional sports," "autonomy of sports," "sports monopsony," "sports monopoly," and "sports oligopoly."

Chapter 3
Blow to the Head: The Legal and Ethical Implications of Chronic Traumatic Encephalopathy (CTE) in Professional Sports..54
Dino Sossi, Columbia University, USA

Chronic traumatic encephalopathy (CTE) is a degenerative disease that has begun to be discovered in various deceased professional athletes across sports. The pathology of CTE involves repeated traumatic blows to the head. Due to the longitudinal and cumulative aspects of this disease as well as the high financial stakes involved in professional sports, its discovery has led to many important issues that need to be investigated. This chapter explores some of the legal and ethical implications of CTE in professional sports.

Chapter 4
International Sport Business and Global Sport Governance 83
Efthalia Chatzigianni, University of Peloponnese, Greece

The purpose of this chapter is to introduce some fundamental concepts and principles that are associated with modern sport business in the framework of international organization and global governance. In the opening section, a discussion on terms related to the international organization and governance of sport and sport business will be presented along with relevant issues that have emerged in the modern international sport context. Then, an overview of sport business activity in the field of global sport will take place, followed by a brief presentation of several aspects of contemporary sport business in order to demonstrate the diversity and importance of international sport business stakeholders to contemporary global sport. Topics include corporate sponsorship, media and social media, and information and communication technology. The chapter will conclude with a discussion about the impact of modern sport business on global sport governance as the main goal of this chapter is to convey the message and highlight aspects of the significant impact of international sport business activity on the global governance of sport.

Chapter 5
The Legal Validity of E-Sports as a Sport 101
Reyhan Mir, Independent Researcher, Spain

The chapter aims to investigate the e-sports phenomenon and analyze its legal relevance and validity with the traditional sports world. The chapter looks to provide the current framework of the e-sports field and its potential to be a sport, followed by the legal challenges it faces towards being possibly recognized as one. The second segment of this chapter additionally looks into the regulations currently in place as well as analyzes the minimum changes required in order to ensure the growth of this field. The chapter eventually concludes by analyzing the possible future for the field and suggestions to help facilitate its development.

Chapter 6
E-Sports at the Olympic Games: From Physicality to Virtuality 124
Renata E. Ntelia, Institute of Digital Games, Malta

The chapter follows a comparison between e-sports and physical sports in terms of their formal properties as games. Through this approach, it is argued that e-sports differ essentially from physical games due to their spatiality. Specifically, it addresses how the virtual space of e-sports undergoes a different process of production from that of physical space in the sense that it does not adhere to social rules and the power of the hegemony, but rather to the code of the machine. This results to a negation of the physical body of the player, which is in dialectical antithesis to the spirit of the Olympic Games unlike any physical game.

Chapter 7
Physical Education and Religious Freedom: The ECtHR Perspective 144
Konstantinos Margaritis, University of Crete, Greece

Freedom of religion has been constantly characterized as one of the foundations of a democratic society. On the other hand, the significance of physical education in the development of children's overall personality is beyond dispute. Thus, the question that arises is, What happens in a case of a conflict involving the above? The aim of this chapter is to provide an answer on the basis of the case law of the European Court of Human Rights. In particular, the fundamental cases of Dogru vs. France and Kervanci vs. France will be examined, as well as the recent case of Osmanoglu and Kocabas vs. Switzerland. Through the analysis of the cases, useful conclusions will be drawn on the possible impact of religious freedom on physical education.

Section 2
Case Studies

Chapter 8
"Body Culture": A Spiritual Echo of Olympia and the Fragmented Nature of Physical Education in the Modern-Day School in Greece 157
Konstantina Gongaki, National and Kapodistrian University of Athens, Greece

"Body culture," a modern term in Western Europe, owes its philosophical content to ancient Greece and especially to Olympia. Altis turned out to be a creative place for presence and mixture of cultural elements of a set of people that through this exchange of ideas gradually conquered its first characteristics as a nation. Philosophically, the ideology that was cultivated formed the reflection of the deepest background position which the classical culture identified with coexistence of the opposites. The physical perfection of the Olympic model was reflected in art as the symmetry of Kouros, with a transcendent and spiritual dimension, idealizing the human body. The Olympic athlete reflects harmony and symmetry, the most complete form of the perfect citizen, the concept of moral beauty, as it is defined by Plato and Aristotle. But sport that is provided by the school in Greece today, instead of being an integral part of mainstream education, as it was in antiquity, represents a compressed and therefore inadequate education tool. Sport in Greek schools operates within an oppressive organization framework that is basically imposed because of competition. As a result, the final aim of sports "education" is to teach discipline and physical efficiency with the view to ultimately promoting an organized performance industry. But this obsession, about wanting to be first, in addition to being a source of personal stress, only achieves is to develop the student's personality with competition as the prevailing principle. Moreover, this pursuit of personal affirmation through sports ranking depreciates personal value and the individual as a whole, whilst breeding insecurity and the need for personal recognition through unsafe means. What's more important, instead of being the best tool for bearing social life and reducing egocentric subjectivity, it inflates egocentrism and creates human beings susceptible to individualism. In this way, a type of "one-dimensional man" is cultivated, which Marcuse describes as the most dangerous of all because it destroys society's cohesion by deconstructing man's perception of coexistence.

Chapter 9
Legal, Ethical, and Integrity Issues in Sports Industry: The Russian Experience 169
Igor Ponkin, Kutafin Moscow State Law University, Russia & The Russian Presidential Academy of National Economy and Public Administration, Russia
Olga Shevchenko, Kutafin Moscow State Law University, Russia & International Association of Sports Law, Russia
Alena Redkina, Kutafin Moscow State Law University, Russia

This chapter focuses on the issues of the sports industry. Since sport, in addition to its other aspects, is a fast-growing industry, the chapter considers the importance of sports industry for the sector as a whole. The chapter shows the basic elements of sports industry structure, together with the peculiarities of Russian sports industry legal support in general and in some particular directions. The authors give definitions of "sports industry," "sports product," "sports entertainment product," "professional sports," "professional athlete," "sports ethics," and "sports integrity." Being a good basis for sports business development, the legislation of the Russian Federation in the sphere of legal services for business and commercial activities within the sports industry takes into account sports-specific features and its principal functions enabling professional sports sector to provide benefits to economy and society. However, there is still space for further development.

Chapter 10
Problems of the Fight Against Doping in Professional Sports: On the Example of Russian and World Experience....... 202
Anatoly Peskov, Russian International Olympic University, Russia

Doping became, as many experts note, not only more diverse, highly specialized, and efficient, but also dangerous for the health of athletes. One of the main factors that allows athletes to escape responsibility is corruption. The author pays particular attention to research and new technologies in the field of sports medicine, including generating new kinds of doping. The chapter also examines the practice of international standard on granting exceptions on therapeutic use of drugs. The author suggests reconstructing the existing system of criminal and administrative law to develop new enforcement mechanisms in the fight against doping to impose a ban on the testing of new drugs on professional athletes.

Chapter 11
The Emergence of Sports Law in Kenya 241
Asha Mikinyango, Mount Kenya University, Kenya

Sports law is a relatively new topic in Kenya. Once played for recreational purposes and entertainment, sports have become professionalized and commercialized. This evolution led to government intervention to prevent a conflict of interest. The government in Kenya created and regulated the infrastructure supporting these sports, as well as provided dispute resolution mechanisms for arising issues. This infrastructure included both the legal and structural frameworks of the industry. The government intervention ran through the legislature and the judiciary. Through the legislature, the government created laws to regulate the sports industry. The judiciary adjudicated issues demanding judicial treatment. Sports have grown into a highly competitive industry with global pervasiveness. This chapter will discuss regulative and structural frameworks within the sports industry by highlighting the legislation primarily providing sports law. The chapter then highlights contemporary issues as well as make recommendations on the same.

Compilation of References 263

About the Contributors 301

Index 305

Preface

Sports clearly play a significant role in society, presenting a multilevel field of interest. This being the case, sports is hard to be accurately defined. In an attempt to, sports means all forms of physical activity which, through casual or organized participation, aim at expressing or improving physical fitness and mental well-being, forming social relationships or obtaining results in competition at all levels (Council of Europe, 2001). The aforementioned definition sets the framework and the aim of sports. Sports include physical activities, not to the exclusion of others, as will be explained below, in a casual or formal perspective, referring to both amateur and professional sports. Hence, the aim of sports is manifold reflecting health, societal and economic aspects and promoting a unique philosophy which combines the competitive spirit with the sense of entertainment.

Of course the concept of sports is not new. Depictions of physical activities have been discovered that are dated back to the prehistoric period (Barber, 2005; Voros, 2007). Geographically, that evidence is extended from Mesopotamia to Egypt and North America through a variety of civilizations (Blanchard, 1995). In particular, sports such as wrestling in various forms, running and swimming seemed to be significantly popular in several instances. Specifically, sports events could have a ritual perspective as the funeral games in Sumerian or the Mycenaean civilization. In other cases, sports were just a proof of strength and stamina among soldiers or a way of worshiping gods.

The most popular sports event that keeps its glory up to nowadays is the Olympic Games. Dated to 776 B.C., the Olympic Games were held periodically every four years in honor of Zeus. A multi-sport event, the Olympic Games gathered the best athletes from every city state throughout Greece in a highly competitive athletic environment. Together with sports, artistic events were taking place related to poetry and drama, highlighting a perfect combination of body and spirit. The level of competition strengthened the meaning of victory; the winner brought honor not only to himself, but to his race and hometown respectively as he proved his virtue and physical constitution (Goggaki, 2004).

Preface

In modern times, the concept of sports has dramatically changed. It is not far from real to argue that professional sports are a multi-billion business. Millions of people around the world are somehow involved, from players and officials to managers and journalists and of course fans who constitute the basis of the whole system. Sports events such as the FIFA World Cup or the modern Olympic Games attract international investors; the latest summer Olympic Games held in Rio de Janeiro in 2016 were expected to bring in a total of 9,3 billion dollars in marketing revenues, whilst the 11 global sponsors bankrolling the tournament had a combined market value of over 1,5 trillion dollars (Chapman, 2016).

In this environment, several issues of integrity inevitably arise. Major scandals of corruption have been disclosed that challenged the effectiveness of sports institutions. A recent example is the FIFA corruption scandal burst in 2015, leading to several officials and corporate executives being arrested, indicted for racketeering, conspiracy and corruption (US Department of Justice, 2015). In the same line, doping scandals in sports are considerably increasing. In a recent example, several Russian athletes were banned from the 2016 summer Olympics because of a doping scandal including relevant state authorities.

Apart from the traditional aspects, the concept of sports has been extended covering video games and forming a new category: esports. Growing as a cultural phenomenon and eventually a sports event, esports have emerged into sports business (Taylor, 2012), providing a fundamentally different framework, since they do not require physical activity. Nevertheless, official esports tournaments have been incredibly increased during the current decade. In addition to the above, there has been an official request to the International Olympic Committee for information on how esports may be included in the Olympic programme, whilst esports has already been determined to be a medal event in the 2022 Asian Games.

This complicated system surrounding sports inevitably needs to be regulated. In this regard, sports law touches upon an assortment of interrelated areas of law, including competition, taxation, employment, even constitutional and administrative and latterly EU (Davis, 2001). Furthermore, for dealing with the complexity of sports law cases, a specialized quasi-judicial, independent body has been established, the Court of Arbitration for Sports (CAS). According to Rule 61, par. 2 of the Olympic Charter, CAS enjoys exclusive jurisdiction on disputes arising in connection with the Olympic Games; any other dispute linked directly or indirectly to sports may be submitted to CAS after an arbitration agreement to this has been concluded between the parties or if the jurisdiction of CAS appears in the regulations of a sports organization.

All the aforementioned establish an ethical dimension to sports. The concept of ethics contains a system of moral values which as opposed to law is much broader in principle and much harder to be defined. However, the prevailing ethical approach is tested through practice and is accepted by the vast majority. In that sense, ethics have a complementary role to law; people, who act within the established ethical standards, act as if bound by a rule, following a precedent. Therefore, in several cases an ethical approach could prevail over a formal rule to people's conscience.

Arguably, sports can be explored through different angles by using different methods and tools. The book titled "Law, Ethics and Integrity in the Sports Industry" is a collection of chapters written by leading experts in sports from both an academic and practical standpoint. The academic diversity of the authors guarantees a multi-faceted analysis of the sports phenomenon. This comprehensive and timely publication aims to be an essential reference source, building on the available literature in the field of sports law and ethics in sports, while providing for further research opportunities in this dynamic field. It is hoped that this text will provide the resources necessary for scholars and practitioners with a broad interest in sports from a variety of disciplines.

ORGANIZATION OF THE BOOK

In particular, this edited volume is organized into two sections and 11 chapters. The first section contains analytical papers on matters of law and ethics in sports, whilst case studies with reference to particular legal orders are presented in the second section. An outline of each chapter will follow.

The collective conscience of society steers the soul and the shape of the law. This being his fundamental philosophical stance, the author focuses on the ethical shifts in sports law by analyzing the comparative fault tort reform in Chapter 1. Through case law and subsequent statutory amendments, the application of the doctrine in practice and the effect of sports ethics is illustrated. This paradigm leads the author to consider further developments which redefine the concept of fairness through a legal and ethical standpoint.

In Chapter 2, the authors explore the application of competition law with a particular focus on antitrust law, in sports. The regulatory scope of antitrust law and its applicability in professional sports is examined. Moreover, since the extent of such applicability is affected, according to authors, by certain specific inherent characteristics of professional sports activity, several contradictions arise which are explained under the prism of those characteristics. Their approach is supported with strong case law examples from a comparative perspective.

In the next chapter, the disease of chronic traumatic encephalopathy (CTE) is explored. The problem identified is the discovery of CTE in a variety of deceased professional athletes across various contact sports, with a particular emphasis on NFL.

Through a set of targeted questions, the author provides a comprehensive analysis of CTE and explains the dangers of NFL players to be affected by the disease. Finally, he proposes solutions for enhancing the means of protection for the NFL players.

Chapter 4 is dedicated to the interrelation between sports business and governance from an international perspective. In the first part of the chapter, the relevant terms are clarified, whilst in the second part, several aspects of sports business are explained in global context, such as corporate sponsorship, media and social media, IT and e-business. At the end, the impact of sports business activity in sports governance, where challenges concerning the ethical dimension of sports arise.

A very innovative topic that redefines the concept of sports is discussed in both Chapters 5 and 6, eSports. In Chapter 5, after explaining the growth of eSports industry and its huge potential, the author examines the recognition of eSports as sports from a legal perspective, by arguing in favor of such recognition and addresses the difficulties that still need to be tackled. In that comparison, the paradigm of several traditional sports is used concerning their organization and functioning.

Whether eSports can be identified as real sports from a philosophical point of view constitutes the author's main question in Chapter 6. By using the theory of play by Roger Caillois, the author argues that there are three major discrepancies between eSports and traditional sports: the production of space, the application of rules and the treatment of the human body. As a result, their possible inclusion in the Olympic Games will essentially change the event's nature to a large extent.

In Chapter 7, the author examines cases of conflict between two significant rights, the right to religious freedom and the right to physical education, by analyzing the relevant case law of the European Court of Human Rights (ECtHR). Since in all cases the Court has ruled in favor of the latter by justifying restrictions on religious freedom, the author explains the rationale of those decisions and their impact in society, highlighting the importance of physical education in the curriculum.

In the first chapter of Section 2, the author develops the philosophical content of "body culture" and the approach of the educational system towards physical education in Greece. After explaining its background from Ancient Olympia, the author acknowledges the main parameters related to the lack of interest on behalf of the Greek state to cultivate sports culture. By examining the most significant of them, the author draws conclusions on the effects of the State's aforementioned absence to the development of students' personality.

Chapter 9 provides a case study of Russia. The authors analyze particular aspects of the sports industry and its functioning in Russia. In particular, after identifying and defining the relevant key terms, the authors provide an insightful view of the commercial activity regarding the industry of sports, from a legal perspective. In that sense, the ethics and integrity of the complex sports system in Russia is highlighted, as well as the interrelation of the factors participating in the sports industry.

In the following chapter, the author addresses the significant problem of doping in sports with a particular interest to the case of Russia. In the light of one of the biggest doping scandals in sports history, the author examines the reasons of doping in such a massive scale in Russia and scrutinizes the mechanism of doping control worldwide. In addition, the author provides a historical background of doping, explaining the concept of the sports competitive policy during the Cold War and its implications to athletes.

Finally, in Chapter 11, the author explores the emergence of sports law in Kenya. Through a historical background from the pre-colonial period, the special characteristics of Kenya as a case study are revealed. Moreover, the author analyzes the current legal framework and underlines significant issues in Kenyan sports law relevant to employment, gender inequality and corruption. Closing the chapter, several measures for improvement are proposed in order to modernize the country's sports law and supervision mechanisms.

The abovementioned classify *Law, Ethics, and Integrity in the Sports Industry* a product of interdisciplinary research in the field of sports. Therefore, scholars and practitioners with a broad interest in sports from a variety of disciplines, general legal audience having interest in sports law as well as scholars interested in institutional aspects of sports and ethics, academicians, researchers, advanced-level students and sports officials will find this book useful in furthering their research exposure to pertinent topics in sports law and ethics in sports and assisting in furthering their own research efforts in this field.

Konstantinos Margaritis
University of Crete, Greece

REFERENCES

Barber, G. (2005). *Getting Started in Track and Field Athletics: Advice & Ideas for Children, Parents and Teachers*. Victoria, BC: Trafford Publishing.

Blanchard, K. (1995). *The Anthropology of Sport: An Introduction*. Westport, CT: Greenwood Publishing Group.

Chapman, B. (2016). Rio 2016: The Richest Games in 120 Years of Olympic History. *Independent*. Retrieved January 22, 2018 from http://www.independent.co.uk/news/business/analysis-and-features/rio-2016-olympic-games-richest-ever-usain-bolt-mo-farah-a7171811.html

Council of Europe. (2001). *Recommendation No. R (92) 13 REV of the Committee of Ministers to Member States on the Revised European Sports Chapter.* Retrieved January 21, 2018 from https://search.coe.int/cm/Pages/result_details.aspx?ObjectID=09000016804c9dbb

Davis, T. (2001). What is Sports Law? *Marquette Sports Law Review, 11*, 211–244.

Goggaki, K. (2004). The Athletic Victory as a Value in the Pindaric Odes. *Nikephoros, 17*, 123–134.

Taylor, T. L. (2012). *Raising the Stakes: E-Sports and the Professionalization of Computer Gaming*. Cambridge, MA: The MIT Press.

US Department of Justice. (2015). *Nine FIFA Officials and Five Corporate Executives Indicted for Racketeering Conspiracy and Corruption.* Retrieved January 23, 2018 from https://www.justice.gov/opa/pr/nine-fifa-officials-and-five-corporate-executives-indicted-racketeering-conspiracy-and

Voros, G. (2007). *Egyptian Temple Architecture: 100 Years of Hungarian Excavations in Egypt, 1907 -2007.* Cairo: The American University in Cairo Press.

Section 1

Legal and Ethical Issues in Sports

Chapter 1
The Redefinition of Fairness in Sports Since the Arrival of Comparative Fault Tort Reform

Rodney J. Blackman
United States Sports Academy, USA

ABSTRACT

Tort reform advocates take varying dispositions regarding whether or not comparative fault tort reform has sufficiently compromised the ethical practices of sports industry practitioners. It follows that two of the best place to look for evidence supporting or refuting such claims is in the laws that govern sports and the sports cases that have been brought before the courts regarding the rights of individuals within the communities in which those individuals exist. Consequently, the aim of this chapter is to provide an overview of the role of comparative fault tort reform in sports cases. Examination appears regarding how that role has factored into meeting societal demand calling for a re-definition of fairness, as well as changes in the ethical codes of sports practitioner acumen.

INTRODUCTION

It is not unfair to say the world is an increasingly democratized world. The practice of some form of democracy, where individuals have an effective voice in their own societal affairs, has been given root on a global scale. In addition, democracy inherently suggests freedom. Not surprisingly then, notions of freedom have entered the social consciousness of individuals from many different countries. It follows that freedom begets the concept of fairness. Interestingly, the concept of fairness is often

DOI: 10.4018/978-1-5225-5387-8.ch001

considered first by individuals as the freedoms of the individual. As individuals perceive according to a natural tendency for self-centeredness, fairness then becomes what is fair for each individual, as viewed from each individual's own perspective. Accordingly, in democratized countries fairness is of increasing importance to the individuals that constitute the various societies of the world.

In matters of democratic governance, the collective conscience of a society directs the shape and manifestations of its laws. In America, this is observable through legislative or judicial actions which create effects that change the laws within individual jurisdictions. At times, changes observed in one jurisdiction are likewise adopted in other jurisdictions. Freedom for these societal shifts and their concomitant influencing of the rule of law is protected by the US Constitution. Accordingly, such freedom allows and provides the underpinnings for the establishment of societally accepted ethics, and ethical behavior. Ethics as a concept is representative of considerations regarding what is right and what is wrong. Ethical tendencies in a society are manifest in social norms, as well as legal governance. Ethics as reflections of societal determinations of right vs wrong, proper vs improper, or appropriate vs. inappropriate are continually being influenced by societal consciousness.

Given the historical popularity of sports in American culture, one particularly meaningful way to examine societal and legal shifts that point to ethical reflections of societal consciousness appears in the context of sports. Sports commonly include fundamental concepts such as following rules, scoring, committing fouls, and receiving penalties. In fact, these are essential to the nature of sports. Effectively, they also present commonly understood structures for unpackaging potentially confusing meanings and nuances of legal maneuverings and manipulations. In many legal matters, the sports paradigm is useful for identifying a more concrete articulation of the sacred and profane. The manifestation and application of the legal aspects of sports can thereby provide clear perspective on the American societal consciousness. Accordingly, this chapter will provide insight for understanding ethical shifts in sports over the past 40+ years, how the values attached to these shifts have been clarified, and consequently, how fairness has been redefined.

THE ADVENT OF COMPARATIVE FAULT TORT REFORM IN SPORTS

The law is a codified approach to human interactions. As such, the role of the law, at least in part, is to maintain the delicate balance between individual rights and community interests. Historically, until the mid-1980s, community interests were weighted more heavily, and perceived to be more important than individual rights. This was manifested in a variety of ways, notable among which was the establishment of, and adherence to the contributory negligence rule. Notably, contributory negligence summarily precluded plaintiffs from any and all recovery, if it could be demonstrated that they, the plaintiffs, contributed to their own injury in any way (Keeton, Dobbs, Keeton, & Own, 1984; Sells, 1994).

To properly understand how the contributory negligence rule and its preclusion of plaintiff recovery facilitates a balance tipped in the favor of community interests over individual rights, one would do well to consider two associated notions. First, when accidents happen, how often are people quick to attempt to appear innocent? Often, this appears as one party emphasizing the blame of others as a means to veiling, or at the least making it difficult to recognize their own fault. Also, secondly, when people are honest with themselves, how often do accidents happen that are only the fault of one party?

Add to these questions the uncertainty of judicial outcomes, the plaintiff costs of litigation (in the days before there were lawyers exploiting contingency clauses), and the relative lack of consistently successful trial attorneys – and, what remained was a proclivity for protecting community interests, among each member of the community. It is what people were conditioned to do. Efficiently and effectively then, the contributory negligence rule had a chilling effect on the number of plaintiffs that the courts were entertaining. Being attentive to others, sensitized to their needs, and their weaknesses – this was what made the most sense, rather than taking matters to court. It was *the right thing to do*, according to the ethical constructs of the time. People had the right to sue – it was just not standard practice within most communities. Members of society, at the time, generally sought to resolve their differences amicably, or honorably – according to the value systems of that time.

An additional residual of this social construct, however, was that certain imbalances appeared. Take, for example, a child – filled with curiosity, wonder, and a bit of mischief – who wanders into a dangerous area, where the full measure of said danger cannot be properly appreciated by this child. Predictably, yet unintentionally, the child unveils the brutal truth of said danger, and s/he collects serious, life-altering injury. Can that be *fair*? Is that what society members consider *the right thing*? As such, some accidents happened that just did not seem *right or fair*, and thereby such accidents did not neatly fit into any available proper places within the societal consciousness. The frequency and severity of such accidents also inevitably increased – and society members began to rethink the *that's life* mantra. *That's life* – *and, life isn't fair* were no longer acceptable answers. Not surprisingly, as older generations were replaced, and societal values shifted, changes in the law followed.

Enter the era of the individual. Demand for the recognition of increasingly sophisticated emphasis on individual rights commissioned lawmakers to make room for societal championing of individual rights. This paradigm change appeared in the form of a theoretical shift in tort law from contributory negligence as a complete bar to recovery to comparative fault theory, where blame is apportioned among plaintiffs and defendants. Interestingly, it should be noted that there are a handful of state jurisdictions (including the District of Columbia) that still adhere to contributory negligence as a complete bar to recovery. However, the role of contributory negligence as a rule has largely been re-shaped to fit into the comparative fault theory, as a tool for distributing blame according to the actions of the litigants. Effectively, this seismic shift occurred primarily in the 1970s and throughout the 1980s. Most notably, it came through judicial rulings and state legislative actions, subsequently understood in legal parlance as a major occurrence of tort reform (Cotten, 2013; Huber 1990; Judges, 1993).

Tort reform advocates take varying dispositions regarding whether or not comparative fault tort reform has sufficiently compromised the ethical practices of sports industry practitioners. Among the best places to look for evidence supporting or refuting such claims is in the laws that govern sports. In addition, it is noteworthy to also examine the sports cases that have brought before the courts questions regarding the rights of individuals. Accordingly, in the remainder of this section, notable cases which shaped the development of comparative fault tort reform will be examined in light of their contribution to legal and societal perspectives on fairness, ethics, and societal values. While many of the legal considerations presented here are overlapping, for ease in capturing illustrative information regarding the development of comparative fault tort reform, two cases are presented which address salient sports issues, and which are also relevant to the legal landscape of tort reform, namely those of supervision and assumption of risk.

In 1978, the *Gerrity v. Beatty* case required the Illinois courts to review supervision standards. The case fact pattern demonstrated that, in 1973, then 15-year-old Matthew Gerrity suffered severe injury while making a tackle in a football game conducted by the high school where he was a sophomore at the time. The plaintiff filed a multi-count personal injury action seeking damages from the manufacturer of the football helmet he was wearing. In addition, he sued his attending physician, the hospital where he received treatment, and the defendant school district. For purposes of this review, the focus of analysis will be limited to the portion of the complaint which alleged ordinary negligence on the part of the defendant school district for furnishing an ill-fitting and inadequate football helmet. The trial court dismissed this portion of the plaintiff's claim for negligent supervision against the defendant school district, on the grounds that an Illinois state statute precluded recovery unless the plaintiff demonstrated willful and wanton conduct on the part of school personnel. The willful and wanton bar was considerably higher than ordinary negligence, and thus, the trial court's dismissal of this claim.

On appeal, plaintiff Gerrity alleged that the school district carelessly and negligently permitted him to wear an ill-fitting helmet, refused to furnish adequate and proper football equipment, and provided the inferior helmet when it knew, or in the exercise of ordinary care should have known said helmet was not sufficiently suited to protect plaintiff from injury. In a distinctive ruling, the appellate court opined that public policy considerations argued rather strongly against any interpretation that would relax a school district's obligation to ensure that the equipment provided for students, in connection with sports activities, is fit for the purpose. Accordingly, the ruling of the trial court dismissing this portion of the complaint was reversed.

Historically, this was a timely ruling in favor of the adoption and application of comparative fault principles and rationale, even before the state officially adopted the doctrine. It was also important for clarifying the standard to which service providers would be held in Illinois. Interestingly, a short time after the *Gerrity* ruling, the state officially endorsed comparative fault rule through its legislature, as governing law for Illinois.

Moreover, the implementation of comparative fault rule was different according to state, in terms of timing, and the nature of the rule adopted. Accordingly, the timing of cases impacted the growing acceptance of comparative fault rule principles, which also affected the timing of adoption, as illustrated in *Gerrity*. Also, influential in the shift to comparative fault were certain legal issues which carried weight regarding the consideration of the importance of individual rights. One such issue was assumption of risk.

Moreover, it is noteworthy that the implementation of the comparative fault doctrine, by case law or by statute, greatly diminished the effect of the assumption-of-risk defense. However, in most states that have adopted comparative fault, assumption of risk is still a viable defense in some narrowly construed instances. Courts in many states have continued to entertain defense arguments for assumption of risk, given the rather sophisticated distinctions between primary assumption of risk, secondary assumption of risk, and contributory negligence. Prior to the adoption of comparative fault, the courts had no need to distinguish between differing types of assumption of risk. Courts in states that have adopted comparative fault are forced to inquire into which forms of assumption of risk are compatible with the comparative fault system in that state, and which are not. Nowhere is this better illustrated than in the California case of *Knight v. Jewett* (1992b), where defendant Jewett prevailed.

In Knight v. Jewett (1992a), Plaintiff Kendra Knight and defendant Michael Jewett, together with a number of other social acquaintances, attended a Super Bowl party at the home of a mutual friend. During half-time of the Super Bowl, several guests decided to play an informal game of touch football on an adjacent dirt lot. Each team had four or five players and included both men and women. The plaintiff and defendant were on opposing teams. No rules were explicitly discussed before the game.

A few minutes into the game, the defendant ran into the plaintiff during a play. According to the plaintiff, she told defendant that he was playing too rough, and that if he did not stop she was going to have to stop playing. She indicated that the defendant seemed to acknowledge her statement and he left her with the impression he would comply. The defendant claimed he recalled that the plaintiff asked him to play more carefully, but he did not remember her saying she would quit the game if he did not (Knight v. Jewett, 1992a).

On the very next play, the plaintiff sustained the injuries for which she sued. Her version of the incident was that her teammate had caught a pass and that as the defendant was running toward her teammate with the ball, he ran into the plaintiff from behind, knocked her down, and stepped on her hand. Witness testimony stated he kept running until he tagged the plaintiff's teammate, and that he tagged the ball-carrier hard enough that she lost her balance and sprained her ankle. The defendant, however, recalled the incident differently. He stated that his team was on defense on that play, and that he jumped in attempt to intercept a pass. He touched the ball but did not intercept it, and when coming down he collided with the plaintiff, knocking her over. When he landed, he stepped backward onto the plaintiff's right hand, injuring her hand and pinkie finger (Knight v. Jewett, 1992a).

The informal game ended with the injury to the plaintiff. She sought treatment thereafter, including three surgical operations, all which failed to restore the movement in her pinkie finger or to relieve the on-going pain of the injury. Ultimately, the plaintiff's finger was amputated. Plaintiff then instituted her suit against the defendant, seeking damages from the defendant on theories of negligence and assault and battery (Knight v. Jewett, 1992a).

The trial and appellate courts wrestled with summary judgment arguments, where the defendant argued that implied reasonable assumption of risk was applicable, and the plaintiff wanted the facts of the case more thoroughly reviewed. Accordingly, the appellate court ruled on two matters: 1) the factual dispute was immaterial to the issue of assumption of risk, and; 2) a requisite element of assault and battery is intent, and there was no evidence that Jewett intended to injure Knight. This was a case of an unfortunate incident, and echoes of mantras like *that's life*, and *sometimes that happens* were swirling in the courtroom (Knight v. Jewett, 1992b).

Knight took her case to the California Supreme Court, questioning the application of assumption of risk principles, in light of California's adoption of the comparative fault doctrine. Particular was the issue of the interpretation of a distinction between reasonable and unreasonable actions, as operative under implied assumption of risk. Accordingly, the California Supreme Court ruled that there was a portion of the assumption of risk doctrine, namely the reasonably implied assumption of risk, which could not be merged into the comparative fault doctrine, and thereby could still act as a complete bar to recovery (Knight v. Jewett, 1992b).

Was it *right*, or *fair*, that Ms. Knight lost her finger? Who is to say? The vagaries of fate have their own path. Still, the short story was that plaintiff Knight lost her pinkie finger, she sued, and she lost her lawsuit too. In so ruling, the California courts made an important distinction which amounted to the recognition that accidents do happen, and that sometimes they are no more or less than that – just accidents. Yes, what happened to plaintiff Knight was tragic, but defendant Jewett could not rightfully be blamed for the accident that it was. Was Ms. Knight just *sue happy*? No. She believed she had a good case. But – as demonstrated here, even the comparative fault doctrine has limits. The overall effect, in terms of this case and its bearing on the formulation of comparative fault, was that this case required the courts to make distinctions – to spell out what certain legal matters mean – and to draw lines. Accordingly, these lines worked to shape the general redefinition of fairness that was occurring.

ETHICAL SHIFTS ATTACHED TO COMPARATIVE FAULT TORT REFORM

In sports in America, injuries have been widely considered simply part of the particular game being played. The ethically relevant documentation about legal liability for injuries in sports and recreation that appeared before the late 1970s was brief, and typically formatted as a caveat to other more urgent issues of that time. This included issues such as justification for the need for recreation and sports programs, the goals of recreation and sports programs, programming models for recreation and sports programs, and the responsibilities of local government and other institutions for recreation and sports (Butler, 1976; Farina, 1973; Fitzgerald, 1948; Jensen, 1977).

Until the late 1970s, the nomenclature in popular literature and textbooks regarding legal liability for injury was loose, relatively imprecise, and generally nonchalant. The tone of popular literature intimated that lawsuits were unlikely events. Safety standards were only sparingly addressed, and the links between providing safe sports and recreation environments and the ethical nature of such practices was tenuous at best. However, growing dissatisfaction with legal principles governing sports and recreation activities, such as assumption of risk and sovereign immunity, led to common law challenges against practitioners' assumption that immunity doctrines and other legal principles could always cover their errs. As common law rulings and state statutory revisions through the 1970s and 80s began to limit the margins for practitioner error, the need for increased attention to participant safety began to infuse itself into the consciousness of both academicians and prominent decision makers in the sports industry (Bannon & Bannon, 1987; Bianco, 1994; Butler, 1976; Cotten, 2013; Farina, 1973; Fitzgerald, 1948; Hackbart v. Cincinnati

Bengals, 1979; Knight v. Jewett, 1992b; Mull, Bayless, & Ross, 1983; Nabozny v. Barnhill, 1975). Accordingly, this section will include illustrative examples of the connections between court rulings and changes associated with comparative fault tort reform. It will also provide information and explanation of concomitant changes in sports industry safety standards.

The 1985 case, *Sawyer v. State of New York* (1985) illustrates this well – in the context of vicarious leisure. Notably, in the mid-1980s vicarious identification with sports stars and attending and witnessing sporting events was becoming situated as an integral element of leisure in America. *Sawyer* was one of the first spectator injury cases where the plaintiff prevailed. A 13-year-old spectator, Joanne Davis, was injured by an errant flying hockey puck while watching a hockey game at a State facility. Davis' mother, Carol Sawyer, on behalf of her minor daughter, subsequently sued the State of New York seeking damages for the injuries to her daughter.

The facts revealed that the spectator was familiar with hockey, and the various protections that were afforded to spectators at hockey games at that time – however, in this instance, modifications had been made – a tempered glass protective shield had been erected to replace netting, and the net was drawn to the ceiling, leaving a large area behind the goals relatively unprotected. Ms. Davis was unfamiliar with the dangers associated with this modification, and was subsequently struck in the face by a puck that had been deflected by the goalie and travelled up over the protective glass, into the stands where the Ms. Davis was sitting. As a result of the accident, 13-year-old Davis received a through-and-through laceration to her upper lip, which required several stiches – and, the injury resulted in permanent scarring (Sawyer v. State of New York, 1985).

This case was also noteworthy for its address of contributory negligence. The New York court carefully examined and relied heavily on the reduction of the assumption of risk defense in comparative fault principles, and found that the State was negligent in not providing sufficient shielding of spectators from errant flying hockey pucks. The court also found that such negligence was a substantial factor in the occurrence of injury to Ms. Davis. In addition, the court found that the accident and the injuries sustained were not attributable to any culpable conduct on the part of Ms. Davis, so she could not be guilty of contributory negligence. Accordingly, the court awarded the plaintiff compensatory damages (Sawyer v. State of New York, 1985).

Subtly distinct from the vicarious leisure experience of attending a hockey game is an issue that was central to the development of comparative fault tort reform in the late-1970s – that of *vicarious liability*, where tortious liability can be transferred *up the ladder* to management and/or administrative authorities. At the same time, vicarious liability was growing as a central concern among sports and recreation providers. The case of *Tonjanovich v. California Sports, Inc.*, (1979) illustrates how important this notion is to organizations, institutions, and agencies which provide recreation and sports activities for their personnel, students, staff, clients, and visitors. This case also creates a clear connection to changes in the duty element of negligence claims in sports. While recreation and sports practitioners have a duty to both those who they supervise and serve, a part of their duty is to also protect participants from each other. Across America, the duty standard was being elevated to supervise the conduct of activities such that participants were not to fear negligence, recklessness, or assault and battery from other participants.

The undisputed facts in Tomjanovich showed that an incident began when there was a fight where blows were being exchanged between players for the Houston Rockets, the professional basketball team for which Tomjanovich played, and the Los Angeles Lakers. The facts of the case revealed that Tomjanovich was approaching the fighting players but was not directly involved in the fight. Subsequently, he was blind-sided when he was punched in the face by Kermit Washington, a player for the Lakers. The blow was of such force that Tomjanovich was left with a fractured skull, nose, and jaw. He also sustained a brain concussion, facial lacerations, leakage of spinal fluid, and some other less serious complications (*Tonjanovich v. California Sports, Inc.*, 1979).

At trial, plaintiff Tomjanovich alleged that Washington's attack was tortious and the Lakers were vicariously liable for negligence, recklessness, and intentional wrongdoing. He asserted that no matter how Washington's tort was characterized, the Lakers were liable under the theory of *respondeat superior*, where an employer can be held liable for the wrongful acts of their employees. The Lakers claimed that Tomjanovich was contributorily negligent and assumed the risk of injury. A federal jury disagreed – and found for Tomjanovich; specifically, they found Washington liable for battery, and that the Los Angeles Lakers were vicariously liable – the damages award assessed at over $3 million, of which $1.5 million was for punitive damages. Notably, this was *a jury award.* Or, put another way – peers of the citizenry offered this ruling, as punishment, to discourage other such failures, and to demonstrate the gravity of the societal shift in perspective that was underway.

The connection between this case and the shifting social consciousness is virtually unmistakable. The contributory negligence and assumption of risk arguments in Tomjanovich (1979) were affirmative, meaning the defense had to show a preponderance of evidence pointing to the contributory negligence and assumption of risk of plaintiff Tomjanovich. All the arguments of the defense were unconvincing in the Texas courts, especially in light of the plaintiff-friendly comparative fault rule adopted in Texas. In addition, the jury emphasized their ruling against the Lakers by attaching substantial punitive damages to their findings. Interestingly, a subsidiary effect of this litigation and other cases like it across the country was that, given the new genre of litigation under comparative fault rule, the cost of operating safe and efficient sports activities and services was also on the rise.

FLUID VALUE CLARIFICATIONS ACROSS JURISDICTIONS

Understandably, citizenry in different states have differing values and varying perspectives regarding comparative fault tort reform. In legal parlance, this has been made manifest through formula differentials for determining the assignment of blame. In this section, two illustrative cases will provide the background for comparative analysis made according to type of comparative fault formulations to which state jurisdictions have determined to adhere.

In Wisconsin, a state which adopted comparative fault officially in 1971, well before most other adopting states, the courts were asked to examine a product liability case in *Wussow v. Commercial Mechanisms, Inc.* (1979). The case arose from an injury sustained by 14-year-old Ronald Wussow, while he was playing in a public park in the village of Bangor, Wisconsin. The facts in the case indicated that young Wussow entered an unlocked tool and equipment shed in the park, where he spotted a pitching machine owned and used by the local school district as a training aid for its baseball team. The machine was equipped with an unguarded pitching arm used for throwing baseballs for batting practice. Although the electric machine was not plugged in at the time of the accident, it was left stored in a cocked, or energized position. When young Wussow tinkered with one of the pulley wheels, the pitching arm was activated, and struck him on the head, sustaining severe injuries – it struck with such force that it crushed the boy's skull in, impinged upon his brain, impaled in his head and remained lodged therein.

At trial, the lower court returned a verdict finding that 70% of the blame went to the product manufacturer, 10% to the village, 10% to the school district, and 10% to plaintiff Wussow. The case made it all the way to the Wisconsin State Supreme Court (*Wussow v. Commercial Mechanisms, Inc.*, 1980), where the Supreme Court tacked on punitive damages. Accordingly, this case is particularly illustrative of what amounts to a value shift suggesting that just because someone is partially at fault, this should not mean that they cannot recover. Further, this case was noteworthy for its contribution to the momentum, or traction being gained in the movement toward comparative fault rule. Accordingly, this case was recognized and representative across jurisdictions that distributing blame across each party that was at fault was a precise and desirable handling of fault. Moreover, it was considered more precise and desirable than precluding plaintiff Wussow from recovery just because he accidentally bumped a pulley wheel.

In addition to precise handling of blame, comparative fault tort reform has also affected the standards by which service delivery operators conduct their services. In sports, as the comparative fault doctrine has emerged, coaches and sports supervisors have become increasingly responsible for conducting activities safely. This has come to include instructing, managing, and disciplining player participants in such a way that co-participants are able to engage freely in competition. This also means to do so without unreasonable fear of injury, even in sports activities that are both energetic and require substantial physical contact between players (where such action would likely be considered assault and battery outside the competitive sports context). Not surprisingly, when the courts are asked to intervene in such matters, they are confronted with the problem of balancing the desire for spirited competition against the need to redress injuries sustained as a result of conduct outside the rules of the game.

In 1994, the Supreme Court of New Jersey was faced with questions regarding the application of an appropriate standard for recovery in the case of *Crawn v. Campo* (1994). The fact pattern indicated plaintiff Crawn was injured in a collision at home plate, where he was playing catcher during a recreational softball game. Defendant Campo violently slid into home plate, in direct violation of the rules of the recreational softball game, where the rule prohibiting sliding was meant to prevent collisions at home plate and possible injuries associated with such contact. Interestingly, as an aside – such rules, in addition to preventing injury, were being implemented because of a societal shift toward a popular new mantra: *Safety first*!

The trial and appellate courts in *Crawn* see-sawed back and forth regarding the standard of care, and the standard of recovery, understandably, in the event that the recklessness standard, which the plaintiff claimed, was relatively new at that time. The Supreme Court of New Jersey then ruled that recklessness was the appropriate standard of care, and decided that for conduct to be considered tortious during a sporting activity, it must be greater than mere negligence. Interestingly, this standard is not the same in all states (1994).

In its decision, the Supreme Court of New Jersey stated that a participant, while engaged in a sporting activity, is not liable in tort unless the participant's conduct rises to the level of reckless disregard for the safety of others, or an intentional act. The preference for a standard of care higher than mere negligence was due to the perception that injuries will occur in informal sports activities. The court agreed that this standard granted partial immunity to co-participants competing in recreational sporting events, but indicated that such immunity was appropriate. The justices also acknowledged two policy reasons behind this rationale: 1) promotion of vigorous participation in sporting events and; 2) avoidance of a flood of litigation of the type in *Crawn v. Campo*. A harness, of sorts, was thereby implemented, adding to the sophistication of the comparative fault doctrine, narrowing the scope of certain legal applications within the doctrine, and further shaping the doctrine, as a reflection of regional and jurisdictional value differences (Crawn v. Campo, 1994).

While these two cases presented in this section demonstrate differences across states, all the cases in this chapter suggest similarly that the emergence of comparative fault included variance, tertiary pathways, unique considerations here and there, and relative independence for dialectical manifestation. Yet, there are similarities as well. Collectively, every state follows one of four basic systems for allocating blame and damages – it is appropriate here to specify the differentials associated with these four systems:

1. Pure contributory negligence rule;
2. Pure comparative fault rule;
3. Modified comparative fault rule, and;
4. Slight/Gross comparative fault rule.

The pure contributory negligence rule is generally understood as a bar to recovery that exists where it can be demonstrated that the plaintiff, through their own actions, contributed to the negligence of the defendant causing injury or damage. While the majority of states have departed from this system, four state jurisdictions and the District of Columbia still adhere to it. Accordingly, those four states, in addition to the District of Columbia, are Alabama, Maryland, North Carolina, and Virginia (Blackman, 2002; Wickert, 2017).

Pure comparative fault states distribute blame on a pure comparison basis. In other words, even if a plaintiff is mostly at fault – as high as 99% at fault, s/he can still recover, and/or have payment reduced by the percentage of her/his fault. Twelve states follow this rule: Alaska, Arizona, California, Florida, Kentucky, Louisiana, Mississippi, Missouri, New Mexico, New York, Rhode Island, and Washington (Blackman, 2002; Wickert, 2017).

A majority of states follow one of two forms of the modified comparative fault rule, the 50% bar rule, and the 51% bar rule. Ten states adhere to the 50% bar rule, meaning a damaged party cannot recover if it is 50% or more at fault – but, if said party is 49% at fault or less, recovery is possible, although such recovery will be reduced by its degree of fault. These ten states are Arkansas, Colorado, Georgia, Idaho, Kansas, Maine, Nebraska, North Dakota, Tennessee, and Utah. The 51% bar rule prohibits recovery if a party is more than half to blame, but if blame is split 50-50, recovery is still possible, and reduced by its degree of fault. Twenty-three states follow this modified comparative fault computation formula, including Connecticut, Delaware, Hawaii, Illinois, Indiana, Iowa, Massachusetts, Michigan, Minnesota, Montana, Nevada, New Hampshire, New Jersey, Ohio, Oklahoma, Oregon, Pennsylvania, South Carolina, Texas, Vermont, West Virginia, Wisconsin, and Wyoming (Blackman, 2002; Wickert, 2017).

One state, South Dakota, follows the Slight/Gross comparative fault rule. This formulation requires a comparison, but only if the plaintiff's fault is slight, as compared to gross negligence of the defendant. Accordingly, the plaintiff is barred from recovery unless the fault of the plaintiff can be considered substantially less than the fault of the defendant. Interestingly, one other state, Nebraska, utilized the Slight/Gross analysis formulation as its original adaptation from contributory negligence rule to comparative fault rule, but subsequently revised its approach through legislative efforts, to its current adoption of the 50% bar rule (Blackman, 2002; Wickert, 2017).

MORE RECENT HISTORICAL CASES

Remarkably, adoption of comparative fault as the prevailing rule of law across states happened predominantly in a 10–20 year-span. There have been some modifications, as illustrated by the modification implemented in Nebraska, but for the most part, states have followed the formula originally devised when the decision was made for adoption. Some states adopted legislatively, upon notice of the trend, but most saw their courts handling cases calling for comparative fault tort reform, judicially, before adopting legislatively. Furthermore, there was often a dovetailing within the states' comparative fault adoption, where the majority of states also implemented some form of recreational use statutes, as a reflection of the Federal Tort Claims Act and individual State Tort Claims Acts. Primarily, these statutes provide guidelines for immunity provisions for landowners. State recreational use statutes have also effectively become a way for states to customize their comparative fault tort reform (Blackman, 2002).

While the cases presented thus far are illustrative of the paradigm shift to comparative fault, it is appropriate here to review some more recent cases that demonstrate how the same ideology that initiated the paradigm shift is still reflected in judicial decisions. For that reason, and to serve as further clarification of the societal re-definition of fairness, several more recent historical cases are presented in the remainder of this section.

In *Khachadourian v. State of New York* (2015), the facts revealed that the plaintiff was injured when he fell from a rope swing hanging from a tree in a public park. The plaintiff had intended to swing out from the tree and jump into a body of water. As it happened though, the rope broke, and Khachadourian sustained injury when he fell into debris at the bottom of the platform from which he was jumping. The plaintiff alleged that the State was negligent in failing to warn of the dangers of use of the rope swing, failing to prevent the use of the rope swing, failing to monitor or supervise the use of the rope swing, and failing to ensure the safety of the rope swing. Accordingly, this case turned on the duty element of negligence.

The defense argued for the application of primary assumption of risk, indicating that rope swings pose an obvious and easily avoidable risk of harm. The defense also noted that State statute recreational immunity precluded liability on a public entity for hazardous recreational activities. The court ruled that the assumption of risk defense was applicable and set upon determining if there were any conditions of exception regarding the recreational use statute immunity provisions. The issue before the court then became whether or not the State had constructive notice of the dangerous condition. In the end, the appellate court upheld the ruling of the trial court, and the State of New York was charged with constructive notice of the dangerous condition (*Khachadourian v. State of New York*, 2015).

Not surprisingly, the court also ruled the plaintiff had contributed to his own injury. According to the comparative fault formulation of the State of New York, the court split the blame 60-40, where 60% of the blame went to the defendant, and 40% remained with the plaintiff. The State would thereby be responsible for 60% of the damages associated with the plaintiff's injuries (*Khachadourian v. State of New York*, 2015).

In a similar landowner liability case, the recreation participant in *Hoosier Mountain Bike Association, City of Indianapolis, and Indy Parks v. Kaler (2017)* incurred a slightly different outcome. The case stemmed from an incident in 2011, when Richard Kaler was riding on a mountain bike trail owned and operation by the city of Indianapolis through Indy Parks. Responsibility for maintaining the trail was outsourced to Hoosier Mountain Bike Association, Inc. (HMBA).

While riding in approaching darkness, Kaler encountered a banked wooden turn on the figure-8 shaped trail. He failed to successfully negotiate the high-grade turn, and the 2-foot drop at the end of the turn. Kaler lost control of his bike and crashed. After the incident he rode his bike back to the trail head. Later that evening Kaler had dinner with family and friends, but in the night his discomfort was distinct enough that he sought medical attention in the early morning hours of the next day. He was diagnosed with a lacerated spleen and lacerated kidney. He was offered physical therapy but refused such treatment. Kaler seemed to recover well though, even participating in a 100-mile bicycle ride later that summer (Koslowski, 2017).

Kaler subsequently filed a premises liability claim against the city, Indy parks, and HMBA. Moreover, premises liability cases often deal with issues of duty. In this case, the city filed a motion for summary judgment that was denied by the trial court. After the trial court ruling, HMBA settled with Kaler and were dismissed from the case. However, the city, a governmental entity, appealed. Interestingly, the case turned on whether the plaintiff was contributorily negligent. According to the Indiana Comparative Fault Act, government entities are expressly excluded from claims that include the contributory negligence of the claimant. Kaler was found to be contributorily negligent. Accordingly, the appellate court reversed the ruling of the trial court and granted the city's motion for summary judgment. While Kaler took some relief for his injury from his settlement with HMBA, he lost the legal case (Koslowski, 2017).

A separate but related duty case arose in California. In *Doe v. United States Youth Soccer Association, Inc.* et al. (2017), the plaintiff was sexually abused by a youth soccer coach. The incidents of abuse happened when the plaintiff was 12 -years-old, and occurred over the course of a year, during 2011-2012. Accordingly, several distinct yet related issues were under review in this delicate and complex negligence case. Among these varied issues were matters of voluntary disclosure, special relationship duty, foreseeable abuse, duty to protect children, and the background check burden.

First, regarding voluntary disclosure, the coach lied on his application form, stating he had no prior convictions. Yet, in 2007, he had been convicted of battery against his spouse. The facts of the case revealed that the league administrators at West Valley Soccer knew or should have known that conducting a criminal background check would have identified an applicant who had lied on the disclosure form. However, the governing soccer authorities in this case, US Youth, Cal North, and West Valley Soccer failed to conduct a criminal background check to verify the coach's denial. At trial, the plaintiff alleged that these governing soccer authorities breached a duty to her in their failure to conduct a criminal background check on the soccer coach (*Doe v. United States Youth Soccer Association, Inc., 2017*).

To make this claim, the plaintiff argued that there was a special relationship between the plaintiff and the defendants. US Youth claimed otherwise, suggesting that they could not have a special relationship with the plaintiff due to a lack of physical custody and control. The appellate court recognized that the defendants had not duty to the plaintiff unless a special relationship existed. The court further indicated that a special relationship did exist, thereby rejecting this defense argument. Accordingly, US Youth was found to have a legal duty to exercise reasonable care in the selection and hiring of individuals maintaining the instruction and care of participants. The next consideration of the courts was whether reasonable care included criminal background checks of their coaches (*Doe v. United States Youth Soccer Association, Inc., 2017*).

Foreseeability was the issue in determining whether criminal background checks were included in reasonable care. Moreover, the climate of the youth soccer league at the time was one of the provision of activities exclusively for children. Unfortunately, such activities attracted sexual predators. The fact that there had been previous incidents of sexual abuse against participants led the appeals court to conclude that it was reasonably foreseeable that a child participating in such soccer programs would be subject to sexual abuse by a coach (*Doe v. United States Youth Soccer Association, Inc. 2017*).

Given this reasonable foreseeability, the court turned to consideration of the burden defendants had for requiring and implementing criminal background checks. The appeals court opined that the conduct of background checks would not have been overly burdensome. They could have done it. They should have done it. Of greater importance though, was the fact that criminal background checks would assist in the achievement of the consummate goal in society to protect children from sexual abuse. Consequently, the appeals court determined that the defendants had a legal duty to conduct criminal background checks on the adults who would have contact with the children in their soccer programs (*Doe v. United States Youth Soccer Association, Inc., 2017*).

All these more recent cases illustrate how the courts have sought to establish and operate within the boundaries for what is fair and what is not fair. For an unsuspecting rope swing enthusiast, responsible authorities are supposed to maintain proper care of facilities and equipment. For a bike rider taking one more lap before it's too dark to see, perhaps he should wait until another time, when visibility is increased, and danger is decreased. And for dangers that are foreseeable, service providers have an elevated burden. All these are for the good of society – and make living in society better. Such are fair protections, according to the comparative fault rule.

In the 40+ years since the majority of states have moved to adopt some version of comparative fault rule, the pendulum swing emphasis on individual rights has continued to flourish. This has been a reasonably accurate reflection of societal value shifts over the past several decades, and is generally representative of a re-conditioning of the American psyche –and sports are right in the middle of it. Other social phenomenon in sports support this assertion. For example, the Steroid Era in baseball was a purposeful burgeoning of the rights of individuals. In addition, the media has certainly had an impact on the proliferation of individual rights. Media partnering over the past few years and billion-dollar TV rights contracts are driving individualism deep into the construct and operation of both professional and college sports. Further, sports are increasingly considered an outward model of individuals' inward psychological lives (Antinori & Blackman, 2017; Ourand, 2017). Inescapably, this rise of individualism, in combination with the legal shift to comparative fault rule, these have re-shaped American ethics through a re-definition of fairness.

THE REDEFINITION OF FAIRNESS AND FUTURE ETHICAL CONSIDERATIONS

Safety First! This mantra is fully installed – and mothers across America are glad! Babies and young innocent youth are better protected – because they have to be. People have better lives, because other people are being held accountable – or so it is believed. With the abandonment of contributory negligence, it may fairly be said that, legal matters are more *fair* than they were. Accordingly, tracing the evolution of comparative fault tort reform suggests that what was once consider *fair*, or *fairness*, as a natural consequence of life, is no longer so. Beliefs, and values have shifted to say that people, individuals, should be able to get something when they have been wronged, even if they themselves are also partially wrong. Contributory negligence rule was too harsh – thus, with a new emphasis on *the me* in citizenry, new formulations were needed to determine what is *right*, and what is *fair*. The various comparative fault formulations presented in this chapter have illustrated this phenomenon. In addition, other conclusions may be warranted. Based on a trajectory of changes in societal perspective, this section will provide a forward look at the future of ethical norms in sports.

First, the legal advantages for plaintiffs in recreation and sports cases have increased. Fundamental fairness does not require an all-or-nothing rule which exonerates a negligent wrongdoer for even the slightest fault of her/his victim. Recognition of the harshness of contributory negligence brought judges and legislatures in most jurisdictions to abandon contributory negligence, except as a means for apportioning blame. Accordingly, the comparative fault doctrine is an acceptably less harsh formulation of culpability, in that it spreads blame across multiple wrong-doers. Clearly, this favors plaintiffs, and this is the new *fair* (Blackman, 2002).

Second, the availability of viable defenses to claims of negligence have been diminished, limited, or removed altogether. For example, assumption of risk, perhaps the best conceptual defense in sports and recreation cases and bar to negligence claims, has quietly been equated with the contributory negligence rule, and similarly abandoned. In addition, equipment manufacturers are increasingly being held strictly liable, and the applicability of waivers and warnings increasingly hinge on the precision of the language within the waiver or warning. Stadium operators' ability to protect themselves against spectator claims has been diminished, and immunities once available to practitioners, managers, and administrators have been limited. And – this is the new *fair* (Blackman, 2002).

Third, the duty of sports practitioners to their employees and participants has increased. When plaintiffs are given the advantages of the comparative fault system, and when viable defenses to negligence are limited, the natural by-product is increased duty for the sports providers. At the very heart of comparative fault principles is the imposition of increased responsibility on individuals who facilitate sports and recreation activities. This, too, is the new *fair* (Blackman, 2002).

Fourth, the vicarious liability of institutions, organizations, and incorporations which provide, or sanction sports and recreation activities and events will continue to increase. Under comparative fault principles, all parties eligible for blame are joined in suit, for the courts to apportion blame. With increased plaintiff advantages and decreased available defenses, corporate entities have increasingly been asked to stand behind their employees, volunteer staff, and the products they endorse through use. They are being held responsible for the actions and operations of all that is in their care – and this is the new *fair* (Blackman, 2002).

Fifth, the cost of creating, conducting, maintaining, and evaluating effective sports programs has, and will continue to increase. Where plaintiffs have been able to cash in, sports organizations have had to foot the bill. Increasingly, to absorb even the potentially high financial costs, new ways to transfer the risks associated with facilitating sports activities and events have been implemented. Accordingly, insurance is the most common method of financial risk management. Education, safety training, and job task training of employees, both paid and volunteer, have also become tangible ways to off-set costs. On-site risk management has also emerged as a means to mitigate costs – and all this too, is the new *fair* (Blackman, 2002)

Sixth, courts have increasingly relied upon precedent set in sports and recreation cases for rationale to support decisions in sports and recreation cases, as opposed to relying on precedent from cases not involving recreation and sports litigants. Early on, in the shift to comparative fault, non-sports cases were primarily used as precedent – there was not much else to go on – but this is no longer the case. Sufficient sports and recreation cases have established its own chapter, of sorts, in the application of tort principles. While all the basic rules of the law are applicable in sports and recreation cases, how they are applied now has significant history – and this too, is the new *fair* (Blackman, 2002).

Definitively, there has been evidence of necessary changes to accommodate this redefinition of fairness. Such evidence has come in the form of the establishment of sports industry safety standards, the formulation and implementation of accreditation and certification practices, the identification and development of risk management practices, as well as the implementation of alternative approaches to insurance (Blackman, 2002).

The connection between these changes to the development of the comparative fault doctrine has appeared in two fundamental ways: 1) the preservation of safety and protection of sports participants, and; 2) the protection of practitioners against the threat of liability. Still, injuries that are profound, permanent, or fatal can and do happen. These tragic accidents can be caused by the sub-standard behavior of practitioners, thoughtless other participants, faulty products or equipment, or some combination of all these. Risk is a basic factor of nearly all sporting events and activities. But incentive to limit the occurrence of accidents in sports and recreation is at an *all-time high*. And this too, is the new *fair*.

Concomitantly, in the future, legal matters in sports will likely increasingly be determined through the courts. This departure from the once held axiom that sports professionals should police themselves, for they know best about sports, suggests that less may be being done to prevent a general chilling effect on inclination to participate. Given the discovery of some less-than-trustworthy goings on, the courts are likely to be less hesitant to intervene – especially in sports at the professional level. How long then, will the present re-definition of fairness prevail? And what then will the next iteration of fairness look like? These are questions that will drive future research.

REFERENCES

Antinori, P., & Blackman, R. J. (2017, July 25). Contextualization of a shifting perspective regarding the steroid era. *The Sport Journal.* Retrieved from: http:// thesportjournal. org/article/contextualization-of-a-shifting-perspective-regarding-the-steroid-era/

Bannon, J. J., & Bannon, L. B. (1987). The insurance crisis: A dilemma for parks and recreation. In J. J. Bannon (Ed.), *Current issues in leisure services: Looking ahead in a time of transition.* Washington, DC: International City Management.

Bianco, J. (1994). The dawn of a new standard? Assumption of risk doctrine in a post- Knight California. *Whittier Law Review*, (15), 1155–1192.

Blackman, R. (2002). *Ethics and the historical development of comparative fault tort reform as applied in reported sports and recreation cases* (Unpublished doctoral dissertation). Indiana University.

Butler, G. D. (1976). *Introduction to community recreation* (5th ed.). New York, NY: McGraw-Hill.

Cotten, D. J. (2013). Liability of sports participants, sports instructors, and sports officials. In D. J. Cotten & J. T. Wolohan (Eds.), *Law for recreation and sport managers* (6th ed.). Dubuque, IA: Kendall-Hunt.

Crawn v. Campo, 136 N.J. 494 A.2d 600 (1994).

Farina, A. M. (1973). Legal aspects of recreation. In D. Gray & A. Pelegrino (Eds.), *Reflections on the recreation and park movement* (pp. 283–287). Long Beach, CA: William C. Brown Company.

Fitzgerald, G. B. (1948). *Community organization for recreation*. New York, NY: A.S. Barnes and Company.

Gerrity v. Beatty, 373 N. E. 2d 1323 (1978 Ill.).

Hackbart v. Cincinnati Bengals, Inc. 444 U.S. 931 (S. Ct. 1979).

Hoosier Mountain Bike Association, Inc. City of Indianapolis, and Indy Parks and Recreation, Appellants-Defendants, v. Richard Kaler, March 23, 2017. Court of Appeals Case No. 49A04-1604-CT-865. (n.d.). Retrieved from https://www.in.gov/judiciary/opinions/pdf/ 03231701par.pdf

Huber, P. W. (1990). *Liability: The legal revolution and its consequences*. New York, NY: Basic Books.

Jane Doe v. United States Youth Soccer Association, Inc., et al. H040688 February 22, 2017. (Santa Clara County Super Ct. No. CV 238994).

Jensen, C. R. (1977). *Leisure and recreation: Introduction and overview*. Philadelphia, PA: Lea & Febiger.

Judges, D. P. (1993). Of rocks and hard places: The value of risk choice. *Emory Law Journal*, (42): 1–142.

Keeton, W. P., Dobbs, D. B., Keeton, R. E., & Owens, D. G. (1984). *Prosser and Keeton on the law of torts* (5th ed.). St. Paul, MN: West Publishing.

Khachadourian v. State Of New York, 2015-039-440, New York State Court of Claims, Claim No. 121855. (n.d.). Retrieved from http://vertumnus.courts.state.ny.us/claims/html/2015-039-440.html

Knight v. Jewett, 11 Cal. Rptr. 2d 2 (1992b).

Knight v. Jewett, 834 P. 2d 696 (1992a).

Koslowski, J. (2017, July). Law review: Crash on challenging mountain bike trail. *Parks and Recreation Magazine*.

Mull, R. F., Bayless, K. G., & Ross, C. M. (1983). *Recreational sports programming*. Palm Beach, FL: The Athletic Institution.

Nabozny v. Barnhill, 334 N. E.2d 258. (Ill. App. Ct. 1975).

Ourand, J. (2017, June 26). Taking the pulse of ESPN: The sports media giant is on the defensive about declining subscriber base, layoffs, and executive changes. What happened? And, what's the plan for the future? *Sport Business Journal*.

Sawyer v. State of New York, 485 N.Y.S. 2d 695 (1985).

Sells, B. L. (1994). *The soul of the law*. Rockport, MA: Element, Inc.

Tomjanovich v. California Sports, Inc., No. H-78-243 (S.D. Texas Aug. 17, 1979).

Wickert, G. (2017). *Contributory negligence/comparative fault in all 50 States.* Work product of Mathiesen, Wickert, and Lehrer, SC. Retrieved from https://www.mwl-law.com/ wp-content/uploads/2013/03/contributory-negligence-comparative-fault-laws-in-all-50-states.pdf

Wussow v. Commercial Mechanisms, Inc., 293 N. W. 2d 897 (1980).

Wussow v Commercial Mechanisms, Inc., 90 Wis. 2d 136 (1979).

KEY TERMS AND DEFINITIONS

Assumption of Risk: Participants assume the risk of injury for inherent risks when participating n recreation and sports activities.

Community Interests: A collection of social interests which are protected by members of a community, benefit the members of the community, and promote the good of the community.

Contributory Negligence: A legal axion that precludes a plaintiff from receiving and sort of restitution if s/he contributed to their own injury in any way.

Individual Rights: Inalienable and other rights protected by the US Constitution, and generally perceived as associated with the freedoms of individuality.

Negligence: A legal term referencing the failure of parties with an obligatory relationship with others to practice reasonable behavior and restraint of behavior, whereby such failure produced injury to one or more others to who with an obligatory relationship exists. The four elements of negligence are duty, breach of duty, proximate cause, and damages.

Recovery: The restoration or vindication or a right existing in a person, as determined by court ruling.

Recreation: Activities practiced freely, for pleasure, restoration, exercise, play, or rclaxation.

Shift: Changes in attitudes and/or perspectives regarding individual or community matters.

Societal Consciousness: A general consensus among members in a society regarding normative and reasonable behaviors.

Supervision: The responsibility to watch over, lead, guide, direct, and/or protect others in her or his charge.

Vicarious Liability: Where the nature of the relationship between parties exists such that one party is responsible for the actions of the other party, even though s/he may not be physically present for said actions.

Chapter 2
Sport and Antitrust Law

Alena Redkina
Kutafin Moscow State Law University, Russia

Igor Ponkin
Kutafin Moscow State Law University, Russia & The Russian Presidential Academy of National Economy and Public Administration, Russia

Olga Shevchenko
Kutafin Moscow State Law University, Russia & International Association of Sports Law, Russia

ABSTRACT

This chapter explores the relationship between sports and different types of competition, legal and actual possibility to apply competition, particularly antitrust, laws to sports, primarily to the sphere of professional sports and sports industry. The commercial and non-commercial components, yet linked to the interests of profit, in modern professional sports entails certain applicability of competition law to the field of sports. However, excessively strict application of antitrust laws can lead to devastating consequences for all types of sports or sports in general. Therefore, it is important to take into account specific characteristics of the sport sphere (more than any other sphere of activity). This is important when deciding on the application of competition law to this sphere or withdrawal of this sector from the application of competition law. Nature and inherent specific features of professional sports activities and sports in general have a significant impact on the application of competition law. Economic competition in the field of sport is atypical. The authors give their definitions of "sport," "competitiveness in the sport," "commercial competition in the field of professional sports," "autonomy of sports," "sports monopsony," "sports monopoly," and "sports oligopoly."

DOI: 10.4018/978-1-5225-5387-8.ch002

INTRODUCTION

The scientific community has discussed the question of whether sports is subject to antitrust laws and to what extent. A simple answer has not been found. It also could not be found in principle. This section explores the scientific approach to the solution of this problematic issue.

The combination of commercial activities and sport led to the emergence of problems for public authorities authorized in the sphere of anti-monopoly activities implementation. It also generated a number of questions related to how the athletic competitiveness typical of sports events and competition in the economic sense can be interconnected.

The question about the extent to which sport can and should be subject to antitrust laws relates to whether sports organizations have the right, based on the principle of autonomy of the sports that are recognized by international organizations (including the EU [EU]), to set their own rules of realization of sports activities. This includes rules for the organization and holding sports events, which to some extent violates antitrust laws.

This section studies the approaches of some countries at the legislative level related to the decision of whether (or to what extent) professional sports can and should be subject to antitrust laws. In particular, special attention is paid to the study of the judicial practice of a number of countries on the issue. Because the study covers some countries with an Anglo-Saxon legal system where legal precedent is a source of law. And due to scientific interest to the positions of the judiciary set out in such decisions concerning various aspects of the problem issue under consideration and the possibility of such authorities to study each case individually, taking into account all of its extensive specifics.

Basic Definitions

Sport is a set of the following:

- Area of public relations and decentralized stratified system of institutionalized and regulated activities;
- Conducted in the competitive, educational, cultural, recreational, health or business purposes;
- Associated with organized or unorganized implementation by one or more persons or association of persons;

- According to certain rules and procedures;
- In the training form (including demonstrations) and/or in the form of coping yourself (passing physical test) or a match with an opponent;
- Physical actions, aimed at the development, achievement, expression and identification of a high level of morphological and functional and mental capabilities and achievements of the participants, their maximum productivity (technicality and/or achieving high performance standards) and/or the establishment out of the number of two or more competing parties (of individual or team members) the best one in the contest (the winner) (Ponkin, 2013, p. 142).

Competitiveness in the Sport

This is the form of social relations (including methods and mechanisms) realized in the field of sport. It is coupled with the goal of establishing more appropriate to a specific set of sports requirements to compete side (a participant of sports competition—athlete, sports team, playing squad/team of a sports club, a sports team). And it is ensured by by fixing and comparative (in comparison with the results of another party (the other participants) or to certain fixed parameters) assessment by actively participating third party (sports referee, referee board) of the effectiveness of actions of the competing two or more parties, followed by an exception out of the number of sides of those who showed lower results and/or non-compliance with the requirements.

Commercial Competition in the Field of Professional Sports

It is the applied in the field of sports topology of commercial rivalry mechanisms (objective presence of elements or conditions of competition). It is applied in the markets of sports and entertainment products and related intellectual property rights, sport services (provision of opportunities to use sports technical objects and others), sporting goods (sports clothes, shoes and souvenirs, sports tools, projectiles, accessories, equipment, and inventory), their manufacturers and/or suppliers. That competition is aimed at the conquest of a strong market position and the displacement of competitors and in the process of implementation of which each such producer and/or supplier, the company, has a definite place in the hierarchical structure ("stairs") of commerce under ordering in certain legal frameworks and within the business intercourse customs and exclusion of unfair practices.

Autonomy of Sports

Autonomy of Sports is the organizational and regulatory characteristic of sport (and at the same time the principle of the organization and functioning of the subjects of sporting relations). This characteristic reflects the decentralized organization of public relations in this field, the relative (i.e., within certain limits) regulatory creative and applied, institutional and structural, organizational and active, financial and economic, political and ideological autonomy and independence of the sphere of sport. That independence is from the public power systems (with the exception of lawful monitoring and supervision by the public authorities in the general order), as well as independence from political organizations, religious groups and business organizations, independence from authorization, interference and pressure from their side (Ponkina, 2013, pp. 69-70).

Sport Monopsony

Sport Monopsony is a special situation (the type of market structure of imperfect competition) that takes place at the labor market of professional athletes, determined by the nature of labor relations in the field of professional sports and characterized by the presence in one particular type of sport of one buyer (sports and labor resource) who establishes prices, and many sellers. In another meaning—a company with monopsony position in the market.

Sport Monopoly

It is a special situation (the type of market structure of imperfect competition) that takes place at the sports product market (including sports and entertainment products), characterized by the absence or substantial reduction of competition in the market and the presence of the dominant (or even unique) actor (seller, sports product provider). In another meaning—a company with monopoly position in the market.

Sport Oligopoly

Sport Oligoploy is a special situation (the type of market structure of imperfect competition) that takes place at the sports product market (including sports and entertainment products), characterized by the absence or substantial reduction of competition in the market and the presence of a very small number of actors (sellers, providers of sports product).

MAIN FOCUS OF THE CHAPTER

Features and Objectives of Competition Law in Relation to the Sport

In terms of absence of the economic component in the activity in the sphere of professional sports, competition law at the national level or the inter-state level (e.g., the EU), as a general rule, is not applicable. Even if such component is present, too strict application of the antitrust laws rules will most likely lead to devastating consequences for all types of sports or sports in general. Therefore, allowance and account of the specific characteristics of the sport sphere (more than any other sphere of activity) are very important when deciding on the application to this sphere of competition law or for the withdrawal of this sector from the application of competition law.

It is reasonable to allocate the following legislative approaches to the attribution of professional sports to activities that are subject to antitrust laws:

- Antitrust law does not contain specific provisions aimed at the regulation of activities in the field of professional sports (however, it is applied to such activities).
- Antitrust law contains specific provisions aimed at the regulation of the activities in the field of professional sports.
- Antitrust law contains specific provisions for the withdrawal of certain aspects or activities in the field of professional sports from its influence.

In some cases, there may be a combination of different approaches. However, it is a more common situation when anti-monopoly law does not contain specific provisions in relation specifically to the sport. Therefore, the basic functions in resolving disputes fall on the shoulders of the judiciary.

The objectives of the anti-monopoly legislation in relation to sports activities consist mainly to ensure free and fair competition. It also takes into account the specific characteristics of sport, including professional sports.

Domain Specificity of Sport From the Point of View of Competition Law

Cooperation between sport organizations is often considered (mainly by judicial authorities) an activity aimed at limiting competition or trade. It is violation of anti-monopoly legislation in because, in theory, sports clubs have to compete with each other rather than implement such cooperation (Farzin, 2015, p. 75). However, there are many reasons to prove the specificity of sport, exempting it out of the influence of the antitrust laws (at least concerning the products).

It is necessary to determine the directions of activities in the field of sport, in principle, which may be subject to antitrust laws. Furthermore, it should be noted that it may be mainly professional sports since little commercial activities are carried out within amateur sports, in any case, the commercial component is not as significant and has a substantially smaller volume.

The spread of the anti-monopoly law on sports to a certain extent (even if it is minimum) is inevitable as the regulation of professional sports requires a balance between competing interests and relationships of multiple parties in the process of sports marketing. The overall objective of the anti-monopoly legislation requires the protection of competition and the preservation of competitive markets. In relation to the field of professional sports and sports marketing, it is not quite clear what exactly should be the focus or what exactly should be considered by the relevant public authorities (Thorne, Berns Wright, & Jones, 2001, pp. 77, 80).

As noted by L. Farzin (Farzin, 2015, p. 75), despite the fact that material products do not exist within professional sports (for instance, import and export), the activity is still an important business area. Precisely because of the economic consequences of such activity, it should be consistent with the anti-monopoly legislation. At the same time, as it is noted by the researcher there are situations when such activity, due to its unique character, is derived from the application of antitrust laws.

The answer to the question of the principal applicability and the measure of applicability of antitrust laws to sports activities and other relevant activity in the field of sports is determined by the following factors:

- Implemented in this particular country model of sport autonomy; sport has a number of specific characteristics and exists in a variety of aspects and manifestations that are considered in different countries in different ways and in different combinations in the resolution of disputes relating to alleged violations of the anti-monopoly legislation;
- The specificity of a particular sport;
- Specific features of the organization and interaction (including subordinate) of sports organizations;
- Historical traditions related to sports in this particular country, as well as the role and importance of specific types of sports in the country;
- A significant impact of such legislation on sports and economic relations in the field of sport;
- It is necessary to take into account all the consequences of restriction of competition by sports organizations or the state intervention in these processes to all parties concerned, including sports organizations and consumers, and

despite the fact that such consequences for them can be diametrically opposed in their nature and importance;

- A clear boundary between professional sports and amateur sports or blur of such boundaries (professional sports is associated more with the business and economic relations rather than amateur sport).

However, according to Rizzo, in the implementation of sports activities it is not obligatory to respect the provisions of antitrust laws. Sport has an entertainment component; for those who directly engage in it (i.e., for the athlete) and also for a viewer. However, compliance with the antitrust laws by sports agents is inevitable due to the development of professional sports and the development of the related sphere of sporting events. The clash of sports competition with other forms of competition—economic competition opposes athletes to clubs in the extent to which the sporting events in which they participate impact significantly on their financial situation (Rizzo, 2001, p. 1).

The main emphasis in the topic under consideration should be on the professional sporting activity, which has a number of inherent characteristics that affect the application of competition law. Due to the presence of such characteristics, according to some judicial authorities of individual countries, perhaps such activity should be withdrawn from the application of these provisions. Among the main characteristics, the following are specified:

1. Combination of commercial orientation of professional sports with its role in the achievement of a number of non-commercial aims of high national importance, such as the importance of professional sports for the social sphere (for the economic development of the country, its separate regions, or districts), as well as the inherent to professional sports system accent on the effective creation of an attractive image of sport in general, positive propaganda impact of professional sports on attraction of children and youth to a mass sport;
2. Simultaneously implemented complex interrelations (intersectionality) of competitiveness (both in the field of play and in attracting sponsors and the attention of viewers and consumers of sports and entertainment products) and cooperation (in order to ensure compliance with the regulations issued by sports organizations) between different sports teams or sports clubs that is not quite typical for any other traditional business where the competition takes place under a little bit different conditions;
3. Ambivalent (for the purposes of anti-monopoly legislation) nature of the relationship between sports federations, sports leagues and sports clubs, and nature of the organization of sport. In certain situations, these organizations may be considered and stated as a single hierarchically-constructed organization

pursuing common goals and following the general rules. At the same time, these organizations are separate legal entities and have their own interests, including business;

4. The presence of specific monopoly and monopsony inherent in certain types of sports as a consequence of the specificity of sport, as well as appropriate rules of governing sports organizations in order to ensure correct and efficient organization and conduct of sporting events; sports labor markets, usually described as monopsony markets, are presented in only one buyer and many sellers of services; the number of sports organizations in specific sports is relatively small and their activities are interrelated in a complex manner that suggests their ability to unite and act as a monopsony in matters of employment and salary of professional athletes;
5. The unique structure of relations in the sports within which are integrated and connected by relationships of intersectionality competitive sports, recreational sports activities, sport as a form of culture, sports industry (including sports sponsorship, sports advertising, sports ticketing, transfer of rights to broadcast sporting events) sports marketing and others. Features of the complex interaction of these diverse areas and activities in the field of sport significantly affect the economic relations in sports.

At the same time, while studying a competitive situation on the professional sports market, there are often taken into account relationships that are realized in respect of a particular sport (except, perhaps, the relations associated with the production of sports goods and other similar). It is difficult to imagine the study in the context of competition law, interaction of hockey and football at the same time at the market of professional sports, for example.

It is necessary to consider the overall specificity of the professional sports organization system in the context of the subject studied.

Professional sports inherently involves the competitiveness between the athletes. Competition also exists between the sports teams through event ratings, as well as some of the economic conditions laid down by the governing bodies of sports federations. Professional sports fundamentally differ from any other areas of business in which a competition takes place. Among the determinants of clearly noticeable atypical economic (including commercial) competition in sports, the following should be specified:

1. No other commercial activity in other areas of public relations does not imply the need for cooperation between competitors in relation to specific issues (e.g., partnership of sports organizations to maintain and run an autonomous extra-legal normative order in the field of sports), while maintaining competition on

other issues, the intersectionality of such cooperation and competition. This unusual intersectionality is vital for sport ensuring the correct competition between the entities of the same level and the same nature. Professional sports federations and leagues consist of sports clubs, which are separate but interdependent economic entities. At the same time, to preserve a competitive balance between clubs, the professional sports federations and leagues set certain conditions for sports clubs superiorly. In order to maintain a competitive balance, sports clubs must cooperate with each other for commercial activities within certain areas. It is important to note that such cooperation of sports organizations, causing stability or even growth of their collective income, does not necessarily maximize the profit of each of the individual participants.

2. The specificity of sports and entertainment product (where a sporting event serves as one of the aspects):
    a. Integrated collective nature of sport product produced by professional sports teams and its flexibility (does not require translation or adaptation, being understood for the perception of representatives of all cultures), as well as the specificity of the nature of its main consumer properties.
    b. Personification of sports product of a professional athlete and professional teams, as well as a significant reduction (in contrast to other areas of business) of substitutability of sports and entertainment product provider (athlete, sports team) as a consequence of personification of sports and entertainment product.
    c. Such product cannot be produced by an organization operating solely on its own, and the quality and level of consumer demand for this product directly depends on the interaction between two independently-managed teams.
    d. Significant heterogeneity and subjectivity of parameters of sport product of a professional athlete or professional sports team in the perception of consumers of the product.
    e. Impact of the professional athletes' subjective and emotional sphere on the final quality of their sports product:
        i. Limitation and finality of sport product of a professional athlete and professional teams. The offer of sports product is limited because a professional athlete is able to perform at sporting events a limited number of times, as per unit time (e.g., within a year or a month), and in general for the whole his life, as well a sports team is able to play a certain number of games.
        ii. The volume of supply of sports product as a football match is objectively limited by such a banal fact as the limitation of the total number of seats in the stadium stands.

        iii. Impact of the environmental conditions on the final quality of the sport product of a professional athlete and professional sports team.
    f. Sports product is unstable and unpredictable because of environmental conditions: time of day, altitude, weather conditions, air and water temperature, humidity, pressure, wind strength, etc. (it does not subject to the control of marketers).
    g. An important determinant of the uncertainty of final characteristics of sport product and adds more uncertainty in the resulting characteristics of a sports product.
3. The number of teams competing with each other cannot be arbitrarily changed from the beginning to the end of the sports competition; in other areas of the business the range and the number of competing organizations may well vary according to the different kinds of circumstances.
4. Dependence of sporting and economic success of suppliers (athlete, sports team) of sports and entertainment product from other suppliers and the availability of permanent and radically different successfulness of one sports team:
    a. Sports teams may seek short-term dominance over its competitors but a sustainable competitive dominance of a team does not meet its long-term interests.
    b. Sports clubs are interdependent in their joint efforts concerning the organization of sports events.
5. Sports federations and sports leagues inherently have elements of the cartels but it is still atypical cartels:
    a. While in most other sectors the competitors are seeking to oust each other from the market, to capture as much as possible of its share to destroy competitors and become a monopoly, professional sports require cooperation between competing sports organizations and teams to get the final sports products and the economic success of sports organizations depends on the economic viability of its competitors.

Natural Monopolies in Professional Sport

In the business of professional sports, the sports clubs can act both as sellers and as buyers. This alone, obviously due to the specific characteristics of the sphere of sport, indicates the presence of both monopoly and monopsony in relation to different subjects. One example is a sports organization and athlete who may not have a wide choice of the employer at various conditions.

These monopoly and monopsony are created by professional sports organizations within the appropriate types of sports in very specific ways and on the basis of agreements between the teams. This is done to maintain a competitive balance between teams because the implementation of the real (classical) monopoly will lead, on the contrary, to the failure of the appropriate clubs (Farzin, 2015, pp. 77-78) and will not allow to achieve the production of truly commercially successful sports entertainment product.

The validity of the state recognition of the possibility of the existence and operation of the monopolies (sports federations) is determined by the following circumstances:

- This institutional structure is currently characterized by an autonomous extra-legal standard procedure in the field of sport (the rules of most national and international sports federations stipulate that their members may only participate in events they organize sports).
- An autonomous extra-legal standard procedure in sports is currently characterized by namely this institutional structure (the rules of most national and international sports federations stipulate that only their members may participate in sports events they organize).
- This institutional structure is currently the most effective way of organization of professional sports (substantial problems may arise in a situation where one of the parties in a particular sport believes that their interests may be represented by another, the new sports federation more effectively, that is why conflicts may arise sports organization within one of its type).
- Sports operates in market conditions that are different from the conditions in which business activities are being implemented in other sectors (see above), and the professional sports industry itself (inherently), is a complex of natural monopolies
- These conditions determine the provision for a consumer (and ensuring that consumer gets it) of a high-quality sports and entertainment product.
- These conditions are best for sports clubs to achieve their goals.

However, the presence of these conditions does not mean that the government cannot and should not seek to resolve this situation. Thus, the situation of oligopoly will not serve the interests of other strong parties that rely on competition to make the game exciting and unpredictable. The competitiveness on the game field will suffer if the coordination of activities outside the game field are not treated as well as activities in the more traditional areas of economic activity (Siekmann, Parrish, Verhoogt, Martins, & Olfers, 2005, p. 16).

Bourg noted that the uncertainty of sport performance (which is an important part of sports entertainment product) is not a consequence of the liberal functioning of markets in this area but the solidarity of the sports organizations (Bourg, 2004, p. 58).

Sports Rules and Competition Law: Interests of Sports Organizations and Government

As noted by Rizzo, there are controversial points regarding the interaction of anti-monopoly legislation and the norms issued by the sports organizations, in particular, with the rules of organization and carrying out of sports competitions. Too strict application of competition law can be the contrary to the objectives of ensuring fair competition between sports teams (Rizzo, 2001, p. 2), which the sports organizations who publish these norms containing some restrictions for such teams, seek to achieve. For example, according to Rocca, former deputy director general of the Directorate-General for Competition of the European Commission, the experience shows that the legislation in the sphere of counteraction to a restriction of competition and the rules adopted by sports organizations, as well as the development of sports in general, may not quite contradict each other (Rocca, 2005, p. III).

While the organizations engaged in sports management have important regulatory and economic functions, they are also responsible for ensuring the commercial success in the sport. It is necessary to distinguish agreements between sports organizations, which contribute to the implementation of sports interests only, and those that are primarily economic in nature. The first in this case cannot be subject to competition law, applying an objective, transparent, non-discriminatory, and proportionate way (Siekmann, Parrish, Verhoogt, Martins, & Olfers, 2005, p. 16).

In his 2001 report, Mario Monti, a former European commissioner for competition, said that the European Commission recognizes that there is a difference between competition in sport and competition in other areas of economic activity. Thus, the goal of the game in the sport is not to eliminate weaker rivals. There is interdependence between competing adversaries, as well as the need to maintain a balance between them, which is a specific characteristic for the sport (Monti, 2001, p. 3). Respectively, we can assume (and also the appropriate law enforcement authorities of the countries or international organizations adhere sometimes to this position) that the rules of sporting organizations that have an exceptionally sporty character and serve to achieve sporting purposes, should not be subject to antitrust laws. However, as it was noted by several authors, with the increasing commercialization of sport and the development of economic relations in this field, it becomes increasingly difficult to draw a clear boundary between the purely sporting rules and regulations and the nature of the activities that are implemented to achieve only the economic goals in professional sports (Lindström-Rossi, De Waele, & Vaigauskaite, 2005, p. 77).

Indeed, relevant public authorities pay more attention to the rules of sports organizations that deal with player transfers, the establishment of the salary cap for them and others (which are conditioned primarily by the specifics of a particular sport), taking into account the need to the counter of restriction of competition, free trade, and labor.

At the same time, according to some authors, the wider definition of the market, the less likely that sports rules or activities will be considered as having a significant impact on competition at this market (Siekmann, Parrish, Verhoogt, Martins, & Olfers, 2005, p. 16).

However, the judicial authorities of public power that allow these types of disputes often take a narrower approach to the definition of the markets in which the relevant sports activity takes place. Khemani (2002, p. 13) notes that professional sports organizations shall not impose undue restrictions or establish unreasonably strict conditions but they are entitled to create leagues and conclude agreements, which are necessary to ensure a reasonable balance between the teams, as well as, for the same purpose, to conclude international agreement.

Former European Commissioner for Competition Mario Monti, in his 2001 report, pointed to the position of the judiciary of the EU. According to it, the rules of the selection of participants for international sports events are inherently restrictive. However, they do not violate competition law regarding the prohibition of restrictions on freedom of service, if dictated by the inherent need of the organization of sporting events. Also, the rules that are strictly necessary to maintain a reasonable uncertainty in the results of sports competitions are not subject to competition law, as well as the agreements aimed at the redistribution of financial resources if they are needed to save the main cultural and social functions of sport (Monti, 2001, p. 3).

Rizzo (2001, p. 3) points out that it is difficult to determine the underlying markets in the field of professional sports for the application to them of antitrust laws. In fact, every major sporting event is a separate market. According to this researcher, two of the main areas can be schematically distinguished. The first relates to the economic competition for the sports spectacle and the second is related directly to the implementation of the professional sporting activity itself. In the first case there are all sports organizations and entities of professional sports compete: clubs, federations, and athletes, as well as other organizations operating in the field of entertainment, advertising organizations, and mass media. In this perspective, professional sports is clearly subject to competition law. Moreover, professional sports also contribute to the development of amateur sport, including financially. As it was noted by Van Miert's 1997 report *Sport and Competition: Recent Developments and Activities of the Commission*, professional sports is an economic activity containing some of the most important elements not inherent to the economic activity in itself, and which relate to its social and cultural role, as well as values for social integration (Van Miert, 1997).

It is important to note that the application of antitrust laws in the field of sports can be justified by the interests of protection of the sport sphere from unjustified restrictions of competition in this area created by the actions of the government by providing certain forms of assistance to subjects of economic relations in this sphere. The development of all sports, as a rule, is currently in the scope of interests of the government and despite the fact that the legislations of many countries contain restrictions precisely on the financing of professional sports, it can still take place but in indirect way.

Sports organizations tend to justify the close cooperation between them. For a variety of reasons, this can lead to restriction of competition. Additionally, as most frequent justification for their actions formally aimed at restricting competition, which fall under the anti-monopoly law, as L. Farzin (2015, pp. 75-76) noted, sports organizations say the lack of economic objectives of such cooperation but the practice of judicial bodies of different countries, including the U.S., shows that, as a rule, such an argument is not taken into account.

In view of the above, it is reasonable to conclude that the professional sports sphere can be recognized as a specific exception under the rules of competition (including antitrust) legislation to ensure a necessary blur of financial and economic differences between the subjects of professional sports and to ensure the organization of a unified professional sports system, as well as to improve the quality of sports product. And, basically, such an easing can be seen in the legislation of some countries as well as in the practice of some judicial authorities.

Labor Relations With Athletes and Competition Law

Quite often there are disputes related to the implementation of labor relations between athletes and sports organizations. In these disputes there are violations of competition law in the form of restrictions imposed by employers on the athletes, making certain conditions, which the athletes should match to be able to participate in competitions, as well as disputes relating to transfers of sports players. For example, additional restrictions and conditions imposed by sports organizations on the athletes while implementing the employment relationships with them may limit, in particular, their freedom of action and of movement, inter alia, by:

- The restriction of the possibility of players facing a unilateral breach of contract by clubs quickly receive compensation from employers.
- The restriction of the freedom of players to search for another job if, in their opinion, the employer treats them unfairly or unreasonably.

- The restriction of competition at the market by the group of dominant clubs who are able to finance large transfer payments for the most talented players and thus increase the value of the sports talents of players in the market (Szymanski, 2015, p. 1).

Sporting rules on the selection of players, as a rule, establish certain criteria relating to, for example, a certain age of players to participate in sports competitions. While sports leagues, teams, and associations of players adopt such rules and act in accordance with them, those individuals who have been found not to comply with these criteria may consider such situation, in fact, as a group boycott. As Shore (1990, p. 70) noted, currently the courts in the U.S. primarily apply to such regulations the criteria of reasonableness and recognize that some restrictions of this kind are necessary. Moreover, in a situation when the league or team challenges the legality of the application of such rules, when it was denied to make a deal or realization of certain activity, it is not a competitor in the truest sense of the word and even if restriction of competition will take place in this case it will be vertical that is less dangerous than the horizontal.

The question of whether the rules governing transfers of players are subject to antitrust laws is quite controversial. For example, according to the European Commission, at some types of sports the training of young sports players may be at risk due to the lack of rules aimed at ensuring that small clubs have the opportunity to be rewarded for their investment in the training of players, and such rules, if they are quite proportionate, should not be regarded as restricting the competition (Monti, 2001, p. 3). With the introduction of the mechanisms of financial fair play in football, the question arises, in particular, to what extent the establishment of the salary cap for players is related to the anti-monopoly legislation.

According to Jemson, regardless of the specificity salary cap installed for the athletes by sport organizations, these restrictions will always be in conflict with the process of competition. In a free market without salary restrictions, the optimal distribution of players will be reached when market forces will act in such a way that the players have been placed in those teams who assess them above all. With the introduction of the salary cap, clubs are faced with more complex processes of decision-making as to whether to sign the player, since it is necessary to take into account more factors. For example, with the introduction of salary cap, the question may arise of whether to buy a player with high athletic talents or two less talented athletes. Thus, preventing the free market processes, salary cap may lead to inefficient allocation of players between teams (Jemson, 2013, p. 10).

Studying the applicability of competition law to the relations between sports organizations and athletes, it is necessary to mention the judgment in the case of the German skater Claudia Pechstein disqualified for doping (this fact was disproved later as it was revealed that the samples were influenced by the features of the athlete's organism). The Supreme Court of Munich examined the legal recourse of the athlete mentioned (after referral to the International Court of Arbitration for Sport in Lausanne), ruling that the requirement of the International Federation of Skating to Claudia Pechstein to sign an arbitration agreement in favor of the International Sports Court of Arbitration was an abuse of dominant position at the market and grossly violated the antitrust laws (OLG München, Urteil v. 15. 01. 2015). This decision implies that the application of antitrust law to sport organizations creates a more effective guarantee of the athletes' rights in their relations with the dominating sports organizations.

Aspects of Professional Sports Which May Be Subject to Antitrust Laws

In general, the following activities are to be distinguished in the sphere of professional sports, which may be subject to antitrust laws:

- Contractual relationship of clubs with the athletes that set strict rules for their transitions to other sports clubs.
- Establishment of strict requirements by sports organizations for athletes and sports clubs to participate in sports activities (as well as the overly strict sanctions for violation of the rules stipulated by regulations).
- Establishment of the salary cap for athletes.
- Implementation of transfer activity (in some aspects relating to the relationship between sport clubs).
- Imposition of the arbitration agreement to the athletes, which may make it impossible for them to recourse to other remedies.
- Economic cooperation between sports teams is too close.
- Restriction of the range of organizations that have the ability to carry out the broadcasting of sports events (because of the exclusivity of each sporting event, as well as due to the fact that having sold the television rights to sports events organized during the season, a large sports organization may limit the ability to broadcast events on this type of sports for other broadcasters at all).
- Activities related to the selling of sports goods.

In the antitrust laws of some countries, the exceptions for certain sectors are provided, positioned as having special characteristics and special value to the public interest (energy, transport infrastructure, professional sports). The question of the realization of the rights for broadcasting sporting events and competition law is also to be noticed.

The collective sale of broadcasting rights for sports events by international and national sports organizations can also have negative impacts on the competition in the relevant markets. Thus, such contracts, due to the fact that they are a mechanism to fix prices, restrict the availability of rights for sports events, as well as strengthen the market positions of the largest broadcasting companies. At the same time, it limits the competition between broadcasters, as well as limits the choice of the consumer (Monti, 2001, p. 6). Back in the 1990s it was noted that the broadcast of sporting events had become an important economic sphere as sports programs, as well as some individual sports, are a key component for pay TV and they are inherently cross-border or international product wherein the relevant market is potentially competitive (Wachtmeister, 1998).

Sport and Competition Law in the EU

European policy in the field of competition is an integral part of the sustainability and competitiveness of the domestic market and its goal is to provide high-quality European goods and services sold at the lowest prices. Competition Law of the EU with regard to professional sports is of this article's most important topics for several reasons. One reason is the fact that the decisions of the relevant competent EU authorities because of their fairly broad scope may have materially significant implications for the development of even just a particular sport as a whole and lead to changes in rules of international sports organizations, which otherwise may violate the relevant provisions of EU law.

It also seems expedient to note that despite the fact that international sports organizations have the legal status of international non-governmental organizations and, accordingly, are not subjects of international law and the decisions of international intergovernmental organizations are not strictly mandatory for them, they are still taken into account anyway because they operate to a large extent at European markets also. At the EU level, the scope of application of competition law to the sport activity has mixed success because the interpretation of the provisions of such legislation often takes into account the specificity of sport that often involves withdrawal of the sport out of the legislation.

Among the main EU documents, which are of interest concerning the question of the study of the extent to which the activities in the field of sport is subject to antitrust laws at the level of the organization, are the following:

- Treaty on the functioning of the EU (its consolidated text), mainly Article 45 and Articles 101-106 (Treaty provisions are included in the competition law of the EU in general).

- Report from the Commission of the European Communities to the European Council with a view to safeguarding current sports structures and maintaining the social function of sport within the Community framework dated October 12, 1999 No. COM (1999) 644 final (so-called "Helsinki Report on Sport," where among other things the application of competition law to the sport sector is disclosed in detail).

The main focus of policies in the EU is done on the following activities:

- Fight vs. cartels;
- Prevention of power abuse by dominant companies in the market;
- Implementation of strict control of the merger;
- Control over the granting of the government help in various areas, which can lead to a distortion of the market situation.

It is obvious that all of these situations with which the EU fights could take place in professional sports (and may even be inherent to it due to some of its specific characteristics). Moreover, a very important role in the development of competition law with respect to the sports activities plays jurisprudence of the EU.

Among the iconic cases it may be noted the case of *David Meca-Medina and Igor Majcen vs. the Commission of the European Communities* (2006) the decision on which was made by the European Court of Justice in 2006. In this case, the European Court came to the conclusion that some of the anti-doping rules suggesting too strict punishment for the violation may lead to a restriction of competition and, consequently, to a breach of competition law.

The European Commission's practice in the application of competition law to the economic activity in the field of sport applies the following basic principles:

- Compliance with common interests taking into account the protection of private interests.
- Restriction of the activities of the Commission by only those things that are of interest to the community level.
- Use of so-called insignificance criterion, according to which the agreements of minor importance have no significant effect on the trade between EU member states.
- Definition of markets on the basis of common rules but taking into account the specific characteristics of each type of sport (Comité National Olympique et Sportif Français, 2006).

Van Miert stressed that the specific of the sphere of professional sports involves some restrictions of activities in this area, as well as the organization of sports and entertainment events, which should not take place in other industries or in other areas of services but at the same time such features of professional sports cannot justify the violation of the fundamental freedoms consolidated in EU law if the same objectives can be achieved through the use of less restrictive measures. At the same time, if we talk about how the principle of the autonomy of sports organizations is correlated, according to which they, inter alia, have a fairly broad rights for self-regulation of its activities, the implementation of the principle of autonomy of private sports organizations should not lead to a breach of the rights of individuals consolidated in the legal acts. Wherein the application of the legislation of the EU to the professional sports should not be directed at changing the national character of sporting activity by its excretion to a higher, regional international level thereby and should be carried out only in respect of economic activities in the field of sport (Van Miert, 1997).

Generally, the decision to leave the questions related to the restriction of competition for the mercy of sporting organizations to ensure the implementation of the principle of autonomy of sport is not possible for several reasons. Firstly, because of too many interested parties, sports organizations are not able to cover the interests of all the parties implementing such regulations from the inside. For example, the teams are ready to carry out self-regulation of competition between them properly to allocate resources accordingly. However, here this interest is in conflict with the interests of the players who are tend to have more freedom in the choice of the employer and are not interested in such artificial restrictions (Thorne, Wright, & Jones, 2001, p. 77).

According to Williamson, this peculiar economic feature of professional sports, which means simultaneous competition and cooperation of sports organizations, can be used as a sort of "Trojan horse" for the implementation of prohibited behavior, while the ability of traditional markets in self-correction and equalization unlikely to be able to influence the creation of cartels between sport clubs or leagues. Accordingly, the interference of the public authorities is important to ensure the protection of consumer interests (Williamson, 2015, p. 60).

AUSTRALIA

As a part of the subject presented, the experience of Australia is of a considerable interest. A basic legal act in the sphere of counteraction to restrict competition in Australia is the Australian Competition and Consumer Act of 2010 (Competition and Consumer Act, 2010). This act does not contain the provisions relating to sporting activities. However, it is important to note that it (and its predecessor in the legislation in this area) contains a number of provisions that aim to prevent restrictive trade practices. Just concerning the sports, the issue of trade opportunities in this sphere repeatedly arose in the Australian judicial practice. Therefore, further authors will examine some solutions that represent, according to the authors, the greatest interest in the study of the interaction of sports, sports law and antitrust law.

According to Johnson, the application of the rules relating to trade restrictions to activities in the field of sports in Australia, in particular professional sports, is implemented more responsive by the relevant authorities than in the U.S. and Europe. In this country, the interests of the players and the relevant sports organizations are balanced more effectively (Johnson, 2009, p. 1).

The following case of interesting. Despite the fact that the body that has considered it made a decision not in favor of the sports organization, it recognized the potential possibility of elimination of some activities of sports organizations in the field of professional sports from the application of antitrust laws because of its specificity and also the fact that even the restriction of trade by the sports organizations in relation to the athletes may not violate the interests of the athletes but, on the contrary, promote them.

High Court of Australia Decision (1971) HCA 71; (1971) 125 CLR 353 Dated 13 December 1971, the Case "Buckley vs. Tutty" (1971)

The defendant on appeal in this case was a professional football player. The appellants were William Buckley and the Football League, as well as Secretary of the Balmain District Rugby League Football Club. According to regulatory documents of the league, its rules extended to all its members and this league was also stated as an appeal court of a final instance for all disputes, including disputes that address issues related to potential misconduct.

Regulatory documents of the League also contained quite a wide range of rules related to the registration, retention and transfer of players. In particular, the athletes whose names were in the special lists of district clubs were forbidden to play for other clubs without permission obtained from the club, in the corresponding list of which they were recorded.

Moreover, according to the provisions of these regulatory documents, an athlete can take part in a match organized by the club only if he was firstly registered for this club. Accordingly, there was a situation in which athletes actually remained tied to their clubs and have not been able to register themselves for other clubs without going through the transfer procedures set in league rules and authorized by the first football club.

The defendant on appeal in this case has played for the Balmain's club for three seasons. For some time, his name was in the special list of this club and it did not suit to the defendant as he claimed that he wanted to continue to play professional football but in his opinion other district clubs could provide him with more favorable conditions. He wanted to terminate the relationship with the first club where he was originally registered. However, his request to transfer or remove his name from the list of the club was denied (Buckley vs. Tutty, 1971).

As one of the applicants on the appeal in this case said, such a system existed also to give football clubs an opportunity to plan their activities in advance and to create strong teams what in turn leads to an increase in the number of viewers and increase of revenue. The High Court of Australia considered that case from the point of view of ensuring compliance with the ban on trade restrictions. According to this body,

it is quite possible to say that a professional football player, who usually plays the game for a fee, is engaged in trade in the usual sense of the word but this is not essential. Such trade restriction implemented in accordance with the rules is contrary to public policy except the case when it is not justified by special circumstances or is not harmful to society. The High Court of Australia concluded that the desire of leagues and clubs to ensure that the teams put up for competition were strong and chosen as best as possible is legitimate in order to attract and keep the attention of the public in this competition and the players thus are provided with the best opportunities to develop and demonstrate their sports skills. Therefore, system maintenance, which will be provided by the stability of membership, to allow those who play for a particular club, to be trained as part of the team, develop team spirit and also the situations when the more powerful clubs will receive all the best players will be prevented, is lawful. However, the High Court of Australia did not recognize the above rules as reasonable and justified and considered that by that rules and unjustified restriction of trade is implemented (Buckley vs. Tutty, 1971).

The following decision of the Federal Court of Australia is of interest due to the fact that the relevant dispute arose because of alleged violations of antitrust laws in the implementation of activities on broadcasting of sports events.

The Decision of the Federal Court of Australia Dated 2 December 2009, the Case "Seven Network Limited" vs. "News Limited" (Seven Network Limited v. News Limited, 2009)

In this case the question was raised whether there has been a violation of antitrust laws in the following situation. Service provider and a provider of paid sports television channels acquired the rights to broadcast a number of major football events in the period since 2001 to 2006. The applicant in this case (is also a provider of related services) argued that these rights were acquired by the suppliers for the purpose of displacing him from the commercial activity in this field so that the defendant subsequently had the opportunity to dominate the market for supply of pay-TV to subscribers.

In particular, the applicant argued that a defendant's behavior violated the anti-monopoly legislation of Australia on several sectors of the market at once (such as pay-TV market in general and the market of paid television sports channels).

According to the applicant, the defendant carried out the specific actions to achieve the result of reducing competition at the market of paid television services, in particular, the market of paid sports television. According to the applicant, there have been violations of certain provisions of Australian legislation containing requirements to ensure that important public events, including sporting events, were also available for free viewing, not only in the pay-TV.

The court considering the case in the first instance dismissed the applicant's claim, the Federal Court of Australia upheld the decision of the trial court.

In particular, it was found that the purpose of the restriction of competition may indeed take place if appropriate actions are aimed at restricting competition at the existing market (Seven Network Limited vs. News Limited, 2009).

The Decision of the Federal Court of Australia Dated 6 September 1991 on the Case "Phillip Adamson and Others vs. the "New South Wales Rugby League Limited and Others" (1991)

The defendants in this case were 16 professional football clubs and the league, which exercises control over the competitions, which involved teams of these clubs, as well as approves the conditions under which athletes become and remain members of specific teams. In particular, some of the provisions of the document of this league provide that the players had to accept offers of employment from the first club requesting cooperation with them.

In the present case was raised the question of the extent to which such rules can be aimed at limiting the trade with violation of the relevant competition laws. In addition, players had the right to enter into contracts with the clubs only in accordance with their standard form (Phillip Adamson and Others vs. New South Wales Rugby League Limited and Others, 1991).

USA

According to Closius, professional sports originated in the U.S. in 1876 with the creation of the National Baseball League. It was not until 1972 that the country's legal system considered professional sports as a part of the entertainment sphere (Closius, 1985, p. 140). Among the basic legal U.S. acts in the sphere of counteraction to a restriction of competition, which extend to professional sports, accepted and act at the federal level, the so-called Sherman Antitrust Act can be mentioned (now included in Chapter 1 of Title 15, U.S. Code "Monopolies and combinations in restraint of trade" (Sherman Act)), the so-called Anti-monopoly Clayton law also now incorporated in the U.S. Code, as well as other specific provisions of the federal legislation such as article 1291 Chapter 32 of Title 15, U.S. Code, which addresses the issues of some tax incentives to sports organizations, as well as withdrawal from the application of antitrust laws of some agreements in the field of sport.

There is the significant decision of the U.S. Supreme Court.

"Federal Baseball Club of Baltimore vs. National League of Professional Baseball Clubs" Dated May 29, 1922

The U.S. Supreme Court came to the conclusion that it is necessary to remove baseball from the application of antitrust legislation. This judicial authority referred repeatedly to this decision when considering similar cases. In particular, when considering the following case in which the Supreme Court raised the question of the extension of the antitrust laws in the professional baseball (while taking into account the high national importance of the sport) (Federal Baseball Club vs. National League, 1922).

The Decision of the U.S. Supreme Court 407 U.S. 258 (1972) Dated June 19, 1972, the Case of "Flood vs. Kuhn"

The plaintiff in this case is a professional baseball player who has been "sold" to another sports club without his knowledge and without his prior consent and filed a claim for violation of antitrust laws after he was denied custody of his own agreement with another large league team since it violated the rules. The district court the plaintiff appealed to, examined the case at first instance, ruled in favor of the defendants and this decision was confirmed also while the case was considered on appeal.

The U.S. Supreme Court, having considered the case, came to the conclusion that it is necessary to follow a long tradition of withdrawal professional baseball from the application of competition law and that the reconsideration of this tradition is no longer the subject of the judiciary but the subject of the legislature and respectively upheld the previous decision (Flood vs. Kuhn, 1972).

In its next decision, the U.S. Supreme Court confirmed that the other types of commercial activities in the field of professional sports should not be withdrawn from the application of antitrust laws solely by analogy to baseball.

The Decision of the U.S. Supreme Court 352 U.S. 445 (1957) Dated February 25, 1957, the Case "Radovich vs. the National Football League"

The complainant in this case alleged that the defendants conspired to monopolize and control the professional soccer with violation of antitrust laws, in particular, according to the plaintiff, in their plot was to eliminate a rival league by boycotting the league and its players. Moreover, it was argued that each team used standard agreements with the players, which contained a ban on signing agreements with other clubs without the permission of the club with which the agreement was originally signed, bringing the violators of this rule in the "black list." In particular, the defendants brought the applicant in their "black list," preventing him from becoming player-coach in affiliated league and in general prevented him to be engaged in professional football in the U.S. The applicant argued that it is also led to a violation of antitrust laws.

Having considered the case, the U.S. Supreme Court separately pointed out that the rule concerning the elimination of professional baseball from the application of antitrust laws worked out in the case-law concerns only professional baseball and is not applied to the situation that has arisen in this case. In addition, as pointed out by the U.S. Supreme Court, even the volume of business organized at the interstate level within professional football makes it subject to antitrust laws (Radovich vs. National Football League, 1957).

The Decision of the U.S. Supreme Court No. 08-661 Dated May 24, 2010, the Case "American Needle, Inc. vs. the National Football League"

Thirty-two teams are included in the National Football League (NFL), each of which has its own name, colors, logos, trademarks, and related intellectual property, created the organization "Property of the National Football League" for the development, licensing, and sale of property. In December 2000 the teams provided an opportunity for the organization "Property of the National Football League" to provide exclusive licenses, after that the organization granted an exclusive license to Reebok International Ltd. for production and sale of hats for all 32 teams of the league (before that was signed an agreement with the applicant in the present case). When the plaintiff's license was not renewed, he filed a lawsuit vs. the defendants, claiming that they had carried out a plot on unlawful trade restriction. The defendants in this case indicated that they were not in collusion within the meaning of the relevant provisions of the legislation as the NFL and its teams in this meaning represent one single organization. The Court of First Instance ruled in favor of the defendants and this decision was confirmed in the proceedings on appeal.

Having considered the case, the U.S. Supreme Court came to the conclusion that such behavior related to the licensing of intellectual property is a concerted action that is not necessarily automatically subject to the so-called §1 of the Sherman Act, which prohibits the conclusion of contracts or participation in a conspiracy to restrict trade.

At the same time, the U.S. Supreme Court came to the conclusion that NFL teams are not characterized by uniformity in decision making and are individually different independently operated business and compete with each other not only directly on the playing field but also in attracting fans and the necessary personnel. As the U.S. Supreme Court pointed out, these teams are the suppliers potentially competing with each other at the market of intellectual property and when licensing such property, they pursue their own interests rather than the interests of the whole league. The fact that they have some common interests does not mean that their interests are necessarily identical.

However, the U.S. Supreme Court noted that football teams need to collaborate and such cooperation may not be subject to antitrust laws. In particular, all the league teams are interested in the success and profitability of the activities of the League and they must cooperate for the games that reasonably justifies the adoption of the set of collective decisions, however, the contested activities are not really are (American Needle, Inc., vs. National Football League, 2010).

The decision on the following case was made with taking into account the specific characteristics of the organization of professional football in the U.S. and it is interesting that the court sided with the sports organization with respect to which it was stated that its own rules and actions violated the antitrust laws.

The Decision of the U.S. District Court for the Eastern District of Pennsylvania State 550 F. Supp. 558 (1982) Dated November 5, 1982, the Case "Mid-South Grizzlies vs. the National Football League"

The task of the Federal District Court of Pennsylvania Eastern District in the consideration of this case was to define, in particular, whether the refusal of the professional sports league to accept as a member a qualified applicant (sports team) on a franchise in the area where no team of this sports league was originally housed is the violation of the anti-monopoly legislation or not. According to the applicant, such actions of the sports league could be considered as a boycott and restraint of trade. Federal District Court of the Eastern District of Pennsylvania concluded that the violation of the antitrust laws did not take place. So, the tribunal concluded that professional football is a unique type of business, in particular, for the reason that the professional teams of the sports league should ideally do not compete with each other too much outside of the playing field as it is unreasonable because of financial considerations. Accordingly, the decision of the NFL was motivated by considerations of reasonableness (Mid-South Grizzlies vs. National Football League, 1982).

The Decision of the U.S. Court of Appeals for the Ninth Circuit No. 594 F.2d 1297 Dated April 11, 1979, the Case of "Gregory P. Neeld vs. the National Hockey League and Others"

The lawsuit was filed by an athlete who had the vision in only one eye. The relevant section of the regulatory documents of the National Hockey League (NHL) provided that the player with only one eye or with the vision percentage of no more than a certain is not entitled to play for a club that is a member of the league. The applicant in the present case, in particular, argued that this situation is aimed at restricting trade in accordance with the anti-monopoly legislation as these rules prevented him from practicing sport as part of the league in any sport club. In that case, it was found that such a restriction of trade in the first instance was reasonable.

The U.S. Court of Appeals for the Ninth Circuit considered the case in the second instance and came to the conclusion that the contested provisions of regulatory documents of the sports leagues are not aimed at restricting competition or trade but dictated primarily by security considerations for both the applicant and those who will play with him and upheld the trial court's decision.

The U.S. Court of Appeals for the Ninth Circuit said that hockey is quite rough contact sport and even regardless the mask that can protect a healthy applicant's eyes, it will still be a danger to those players who will be on his blind side. In addition, as noted by the judicial authority, the league and its members in this case also have a legitimate interest not to be prosecuted for injuries that could potentially be caused to the applicant in the case and the other players (Gregory P. Neeld vs. National Hockey League, 1979).

The Decision of the U.S. Court of Appeals for the 2nd Circuit No. 670 F.2d 1249 Dated January 27, 1982, the Case of "North American Soccer League and Others vs. National Football League and Others"

The central issue for the U.S. Court of Appeals for the 2nd Circuit in the consideration of the case was the question of whether the agreement between the members of a league of professional sports teams (in this case, the NFL) to prohibit its members to carry out investments in relation to members of other professional sports league (in this case, the North American Soccer League) is violation of antitrust laws.

Considering the case, the U.S. Court of Appeals for the 2nd Circuit, in particular, pointed out that the success of professional football depends on a number of factors and the ultimate goal is to attract as many viewers as possible. To carry out such functions it is necessary to implement a specific joint economic activity, as a team owner cannot carry out activities in the field of professional football without at least one other competing team. Moreover, in order to successfully attract fans the competing teams should have similar characteristics in some respects.

However, as it was pointed out by the U.S. Court of Appeals for the 2nd Circuit, despite the fact that the members of the NFL have cooperated in many ways, each of them is a completely separate legal entity that has its own costs and revenues, which are not shared with other league members. Furthermore, it was separately observed that different teams' income and expenses can vary significantly, that is important in this case.

Also the U.S. Court of Appeals for the 2nd Circuit separately noted the interdependence of the members of professional sports leagues, the unique nature of the business activities carried out by them, as well as the limitations of the available directions for their capital investments.

The U.S. Court of Appeals for the 2nd Circuit noted that the performance of the NFL as a single business entity does not withdraw from the application of antitrust legislation prohibiting the restriction of competition the conclusion of agreements between its members for these purposes. Even the fact that such agreements may bring more benefit to the league does not justify fully their negative consequences (North American Soccer League et al. vs. National Football League, 1982).

It is worth mentioning Nathaniel Grow's point of view who notes that at present, while applying the rules of reasonableness to professional sporting activity in the resolution of disputes related to violation of antitrust laws, the U.S. courts use quite complex and subjective approaches in order to determine to what extent the impugned activities may negatively impact the competition in the field of sports and in other related industries. This is connected with the fact that, for example, the rules issued by sports organizations aimed at improving competition between the relevant sport agents, may adversely affect the market of trademark use licensing (Grow, 2015, p. 14).

CONCLUSION

Sports, especially professional sports, is a fairly large area of the business. Moreover, the scope of professional sports is mainly the show business industry, meaning that this area is associated with private business interests. The above cannot be reflected in the legal regulation in the sphere of sports, including the features of competition law (Ponkin, & Ponkina, 2014; Shevchenko, & Ponkin, 2014).

Most importantly, it concerns the possibility and features of the application of the provisions of competition or antitrust law to this activity. This raises a number of contradictions and difficulties. Since it is mainly a commercial activity, professional sports has a whole breadth of the specifics of sport sphere. This cannot be ignored as the incorrect application of these provisions by the competent authorities not only could have a negative impact on concrete actions of sports organizations, but also be detrimental to professional sports as a whole as it does not allow carrying out sports activities in accordance with its objectives and characteristics.

REFERENCES

American Needle, Inc. vs. National Football League, 560 U.S. 183 (2010).

Bourg, J.-F. (2004). Les sports collectifs professionnels en Europe: Quel modèle économique? In J.-J. Gouguet (Ed.), *Le sport professionnel après l'arrêt Bosman: Une analyse économique internationale* (pp. 43–60). Limoges, France: Presses Universitaires de Limoges.

Buckley v. Tutty [1971] HCA 71; (1971) 125 CLR, 353.

Case C-519/04P David Meca Medina and Igor Majcen v. Commission (2006) ECR I-6991.

Closius, P. J. (1985). Professional Sports and Antitrust Laws: The Ground Rules of Immunity, Exemption, and Liability. In A. T. Johnson & J. H. Frey (Eds.), *Government and Sport: The Public Policy Issues* (pp. 140–161). Totowa, NJ: Rowman & Allanheld.

Comité national olympique et sportif français. (2006). *Les incidences du droit communautaire sur le sport. Brochure d'information*. Retrieved April 29, 2016, from http://centre.franceolympique.com/centre/fichiers/File/brochure_impact_ue_sport_2005.pdf

Commission of the European Communities. (1999). *Report from the Commission of the European Communities to the European Council with a view to safeguarding current sports structures and maintaining the social function of sport within the Community framework N° COM (1999) 644 final of 10.12.1999*. Retrieved April 29, 2016, from http://eur-lex.europa.eu/LexUriServ/LexUriServ.do?uri=COM:1999:0644:FIN:EN:PDF

Competition and Consumer Act (2010). Retrieved from https://www.comlaw.gov.au/Details/C2015C00327

Consolidated versions of the Treaty on European Union and the Treaty on the Functioning of the European Union. (2012). *Official Journal, C 326*, 0001 – 0390. Retrieved April 29, 2016, from http://eur-lex.europa.eu/legal-content/en/TXT/?uri=CELEX:12012E/TXT

Farzin, L. (2015). On the Antitrust Exemption for Professional Sports in the United States and Europe. *Jeffrey S. Moorad Sports Law Journal*, *22*(1), 75–108.

Federal Baseball Club v. National League, 259 U.S. 200 (1922).

Flood v. Kuhn, 407 U.S. 258 (1972).

Gregory P. Neeld v. National Hockey League, 594 F.2d 1297 (9th Cir. 1979).

Grow, N. (2015). Regulating professional sports leagues. *Washington and Lee Law Review*, *72*(58), 14.

Jemson, T. J. (2013). *For the Love of Money, Football, and Competition Law: An analysis of whether UEFA's Financial Fair Play Regulations breach European competition law* (Dissertation submitted in partial fulfilment of the degree of Bachelor of Laws). University of Otago, Dunedin, New Zealand. Retrieved April 29, 2016, from http://www.otago.ac.nz/law/research/journals/otago065279.pdf

Johnson, J. (2009, January 7). Restraint of Trade Law in Sport. *Sports Law eJournal*.

Khemani, R. S. (2002). *Application of competition law: exemptions and exceptions*. Geneva, Switzerland: United Nations.

Lindström-Rossi, L., De Waele, S., & Vaigauskaite, D. (2005, Autumn). Application of EC antitrust rules in the sport sector: An update. *Competition Policy Newsletter*, *3*, 72–77.

Mid-South Grizzlies v. National Football League, 550 F. Supp. 558 (E.D. Pa. 1982).

Monti, M. (2001). *Competition and Sport the Rules of the game*. Speech presented at Conference on Governance in Sport, Brussels, Belgium. Retrieved April 29, 2016, from http://europa.eu/rapid/press-release_SPEECH-01-84_en.doc

North American Soccer League et al. v. National Football League, 670 F.2d 1249 (2d Cir. 1982).

München, O. L. G. Urteil v. 15.01.2015 – U 1110/14. (n.d.). Retrieved April 29, 2016, from http://www.gesetze-bayern.de/Content/Document/Y-300-Z-BECKRS-B-2015-N-02086?hl=true&AspxAutoDetectCookieSupport=1

Phillip Adamson and Others v. New South Wales Rugby League Limited and Others [1991] FCA 425; (1991) 13 Atpr 41-141; 103 ALR 319 (1991) 31 FCR 242 (1991) 38 IR 427.

Ponkin, I. (2013). On the question of the definition of "sport". In D. I. Rogachev, & O. A Shevchenko (Eds.), *Proceedings of the seventh International scientific-practical conference "Globalization of sport: the Olympic Games and international competitions"* (pp. 136-142). Moscow, Russia: Academic Press.

Ponkin, I., & Ponkina, A. (2014). Limits of State Intervention and Non-Intervention in the Sports Field. *Kutafin University Law Review, 1*, 92–105.

Ponkina, A. (2013). *Public administration and the autonomous institutionalization in the field of sports.* Moscow, Russia: Sports Law Commission of the Association of Lawyers of Russia, National Association of Sports Lawyers of the Russian Federation.

Radovich v. National Football League (NFL), 352 U.S. 445 (1957).

Rizzo, F. (2001). *Le droit de la concurrence au service de la specificité sportive.* Retrieved April 29, 2016, from http://www.revuegeneraledudroit.eu/wp-content/uploads/aj20011219rizzof1.pdf

Rocca, G. (2005, Septembre). L'application des règles antitrust aux règles sportives. *L'Observateur de Bruxelles, 62.*

Seven Network Limited v News Limited [2009] FCAFC, 166.

Sherman Act, 15 U.S.C. §§ 1.

Shevchenko, O., & Ponkin, I. (2014). On development of legal doctrine in the field of sport. *Teoriya i Praktika Fizicheskoy Kultury, 6*, 32–34.

Shore, C. E. (1990). Antitrust & Professional Sports' Eligibility Rules: The Past, the Present, and the Future. *Fordham Intellectual Property. Media and Entertainment Law Journal, 1*(1), 65–89.

Siekmann, R., Parrish, R., Verhoogt, P., Martins, R. B., & Olfers, M. (2005). *Professional sport in the internal market (Project Nº IP/A/IMCO/ST/2005-004).* Retrieved April 29, 2016, from http://www.asser.nl/media/2171/cms_sports_65_1_professional-sport.pdf

Szymanski, S. (2015, July). *The economic arguments supporting a competition law challenge to the transfer system.* Retrieved April 29, 2016, from https://www.fifpro.org/attachments/article/6241/Embargoed%20Stefan%20Szymanski%20Transfer%20System%20Analysis.pdf

Thorne, D., Berns Wright, L., & Jones, S. A. (2001, Spring). The Impact of Sports Marketing Relationships and Antitrust Issues in the United States. *Journal of Public Policy & Marketing*, *20*(1), 73–83. doi:10.1509/jppm.20.1.73.17279

Van Miert, K. (1997, November 27). *Sport et concurrence: Développements récents et action de la Commission.* Speech presented at Forum européen du Sport, Luxembourg, Luxembourg. Retrieved April 29, 2016, from http://ec.europa.eu/competition/speeches/text/sp1997_069_fr.html

Wachtmeister, A.-M. (1998, June). Broadcasting of sports events and competition law. *Competition Policy Newsletter, 2.* Retrieved April 29, 2016, from http://ec.europa.eu/competition/speeches/text/sp1998_037_en.html

Williamson, B. (2015, July). Premiership Rugby Union: Through the Antitrust Looking Glass. *The Competition Law Review*, *11*(1), 41–60.

Chapter 3
Blow to the Head:
The Legal and Ethical Implications of Chronic Traumatic Encephalopathy (CTE) in Professional Sports

Dino Sossi
Columbia University, USA

ABSTRACT

Chronic traumatic encephalopathy (CTE) is a degenerative disease that has begun to be discovered in various deceased professional athletes across sports. The pathology of CTE involves repeated traumatic blows to the head. Due to the longitudinal and cumulative aspects of this disease as well as the high financial stakes involved in professional sports, its discovery has led to many important issues that need to be investigated. This chapter explores some of the legal and ethical implications of CTE in professional sports.

INTRODUCTION

Chronic traumatic encephalopathy (CTE) is a neurodegenerative disease that has begun to be discovered in a variety of deceased professional athletes across various contact sports (Omalu, Hamilton, Kamboh, DeKosky, & Bailes, 2010; Rabadi & Jordan, 2001). These include boxing, ice hockey, mixed martial arts, soccer, and finally football, the main focus of this paper.

The pathology of CTE is believed to normally involve repeated traumatic blows to the head, usually through contact with other players when it occurs while playing sports (Gardner, Gardner, Iverson, & McCrory, 2014; Omalu, Bailes,

DOI: 10.4018/978-1-5225-5387-8.ch003

Hammers, & Fitzsimmons, 2010; Rabadi & Jordan, 2001). Due to the longitudinal and cumulative aspects of this disease as well as the high financial stakes involved across all major North American professional sports, CTE's discovery has led to the need to investigate many important related issues to safeguard players as well as the integrity of football and contact sports as a whole. This chapter explores a number of the legal and ethical implications of CTE in professional sports with a specific focus on the National Football League (NFL). It also informs this debate within broader medical, scientific, and sociocultural environments that contextualize these legal and ethical issues.

BACKGROUND: ALL THE WORLD'S A FOOTBALL FIELD

The National Football League (NFL) is one of the preeminent professional sports leagues in the United States. Its broadcasts are an important weekly habit for many and a common cause for celebration across the country as beloved local teams clash on the field.

The annual NFL Super Bowl telecast is an iconic event that garners incredibly high viewership and is normally among the top television broadcasts in the country and even across the world. For example, in 2017, 111.3 million viewers watched Super Bowl LI on Fox, although it should be noted that ratings have slipped over the past two years (Battaglio & James, 2017). The halftime show alone is a major production that features the hottest entertainers of the day. Recent shows included musical superstars like Beyoncé, Lady Gaga, Bruno Mars, Katy Perry, and Coldplay.

Weekly broadcasts of regular season games and playoff games leading up to the Super Bowl finale are also popular and have become an incredibly lucrative revenue source for the league. For example, CBS, Comcast, and Fox signed a $27 billion deal in 2011 to broadcast NFL games through 2022 (Berr, 2016). In addition, Walt Disney's ESPN paid $1.9 billion for the right to broadcast the iconic show Monday Night Football broadcast (Berr, 2016) that was earlier popularized on ABC starting in 1970 and arguably revolutionized the sport (Shapiro & Maske, 2005). Similarly, CBS and NBC signed a recent deal for $900 to broadcast games occurring on Thursday nights (Berr, 2017). As a result, negotiating television rights is a bitter battle that can cost broadcasters billions of dollars as proven by the steep deals mentioned above (Berr, 2016; Berr, 2017).

The NFL also demonstrates its financial clout through its partner organizations that make a great deal of money and gain valuable exposure through their association with the league. For example, fantasy sports league DraftKings reported that there was a 25% increase in players who signed up for its NFL services during the first couple of weeks of the 2016 season, signaling expanding interest in the sport (Tanier,

2016). Apparel giant Nike replaced Reebok as the official gear supplier for the league at the cost of $220 million per year for a five-year deal starting in 2012 (Bloomberg News, 2015). Although it is estimated that Nike may actually lose money despite selling official jerseys, experts believe being associated with the league helps the company's overall business by further marketing its iconic swoosh logo to television viewers blazoned on players' apparel in person on game days, during broadcasts, and seeing regular fans wearing jerseys in public (Bloomberg News, 2015).

NFL players like Tom Brady, the wildly popular quarterback of the highly successful New England Patriots franchise, have become global sports icons. Star players use this celebrity to endorse major products; Brady's portfolio includes watchmaker Tag Heuer, UGG boots, Under Armour apparel, and most recently Aston Martin automobiles (Forbes, n.d.; McIntyre, 2017; Nathan, 2017). Peyton Manning, the recently retired star quarterback of the Denver Broncos and Indianapolis Colts, has also stood atop the NFL's endorsements list over the past decade (Badenhausen, 2015). He earned $12 million in 2015 alone from endorshing Buick, DirecTV, Gatorade, Nationwide, Nike (previously Reebok), and Papa John's International (Badenhausen, 2015).

Player salaries also pay incredibly well. As of late August 2017, Detroit Lions quarterback Matthew Stafford is the league's highest paid player after signing a five-year deal averaging $27 million annually (Rothstein, 2017). This is just ahead of Oakland Raiders quarterback Derek Carr who signed a $25 million a year contract for a similar five-year deal (Rothstein, 2017). Compared to their peers, the NFL's most elite players earned $535 million in a combination of salary, bonuses, and endorsements over the year 2016, which is up over 37% compared to the previous year (Badenhausen, 2016).

Even NFL head coaches are millionaires. Although NFL coaching contracts are not disclosed, it is estimated that New Orleans Saints head coach Sean Payton and Seattle Seahawks head coach Pete Carroll make approximately $8 million per year as of January 2017 (Boyd, 2017), while Miami Hurricanes head coach Nick Saban may be the highest paid coach in any North American sports league at $11.25 million per year, although he coaches college football (Moriarty, 2017).

Due to a combination of its incredibly large global fan base, wildly popular players, regular prime time broadcast slots that have become appointment viewing for its passionate audience, growing presence in fantasy sports leagues, a public that wears its apparel all over the country, and generally broad reach across society, the NFL and its partners have become rich. For example, purchasing a franchise costs an astronomical amount. The Dallas Cowboys are currently the most valuable NFL franchise and are valued at $4.2 billion dollars (Ozanian, 2016). Current franchise owners are incredibly wealthy, topped by Seattle Seahawks owner Paul Allen from Microsoft who is worth $17.8 billion (Smith, 2015) and they will continue to prosper from owning a team. For example, it is projected that the entire league will gross $14 billion in revenue during 2017 (Florio, 2017). Teams recently split a pot of $7.3 billion in revenue, the equivalent of $226.4 million per team in 2014, an increase of 21% (Novy-Williams, 2015).

From this, it is clear that broadcast rights, merchandising and apparel deals, player and coach salaries, and franchise valuations have all increased greatly since the league's more humble beginnings. In short, the NFL is currently the dominant professional sport in North America. The league and football more generally play an indelible, even omnipresent, role in the cultural fabric of the nation as well as being a major moneymaker.

A CHALLENGING ISSUE RISES. THE DAWN OF CHRONIC TRAUMATIC ENCEPHALOPATHY (CTE)

Clearly from the above discussion, the National Football League (NFL) is in an enviable position in relation to other professional sports. However, the deeply disturbing deaths of former star players have begun to cast a dark shadow over the league, both presently and for its future. Chronic traumatic encephalopathy (CTE) has been clinically associated with some particularly gruesome developments and brought this disease to national attention as a consequence. A few particularly stark examples will be introduced here to demonstrate its impact.

A seminal case was the erratic behavior and eventual death of Mike "Iron Mike" Webster, the legendary Pittsburgh Steelers' center who played 17 years in the league and was a local legend. Webster formerly played center for the legendary Super Bowl champion Steelers team that won the league title four times over six years with its *Steel Curtain* defense (Dailey, 2006) that dominated the NFL during the 1970s and early 1980s (Breslow, 2013; Drenon, 2013; Kirk, Gilmore, & Wiser, 2013; Litsky, 2015; Silver, 2014). Unfortunately, this glory did not last. Webster's later life after his career came to a close was plagued by many sad incidents. Initially, his oral conversations rambled, he could not maintain focus, had trouble keeping jobs, and forgot scheduled meetings (Gordon, 2003). Later, when his condition worsened, Webster often slept in his car because he forgot his way home and even zapped himself with a police taser 10 to 20 times to calm his nerves down and cope with his uncontrollable shaking (Gordon, 2003). He became a recluse who suffered from hand injuries, herniated discs, and lived the remainder of his life in poverty before dying of a heart attack at the age of 50. He was later diagnosed with CTE.

Similarly, the beloved Junior Seau was a jovial presence with a sterling presence across the league who suffered from a similarly tragic fate. He was also a perennial star throughout his career, being named a 10-time All Pro linebacker and 12-time Pro Bowl selection (Pro Football Reference, 2017) while playing the bulk of his career with the San Diego Chargers. However, the end of his life was marred by atypical behavior and an untimely death at the tender age of 43 (Engber, 2012; ESPN.com news services, 2012; Fainaru & Fainaru-Wada, 2013; Fainaru-Wada, Avila, & Fainaru, 2013; Greene & Trotter, 2015; Schiavenza, 2015). Initially, Seau experienced difficulty sleeping and suffered from depression (Schrotenboer, 2016). Later, he was accused of assault by his girlfriend, allegedly drove off a cliff in an attempt to commit suicide, lost nearly the entire $50 million he earned in player salary, and eventually killed himself by shooting himself in the chest (Schiavenza, 2015). Like Webster, Seau was later diagnosed with CTE.

On a depressingly similar note, Kansas City Chiefs linebacker Jovan Belcher shot and killed his girlfriend and later took his own life in front of Chiefs' General Manager Scott Pioli and Head Coach Romeo Crenell, among others (Armstrong, Chinese, & Brown, 2012; Satriano, 2012; Vendel, 2012). These incidents involving Webster, Seau, and Belcher, as well as many other past NFL players, have been linked to CTE.

These tragic deaths as well as the subsequent diagnosis of CTE in the brains of these same athletes have collectively caused this once obscure disease to reach a relatively high profile across the general public. This includes being the focus of the motion picture *Concussion*, starring Hollywood powerhouse Will Smith. The movie also included other well-known actors like Alec Baldwin, Paul Reiser, Luke Wilson, David Morse, and Albert Brooks, as well as high-powered producer Ridley Scott (Scott, Facio, Wolthoff, Shuman, Cantillon, & Landesman, 2015). In the film, Smith profiled one of the key figures from the early days of the CTE fight, forensic pathologist Dr. Bennet Omalu, whose work is included in this chapter. From these developments and greater exposure of the problem, law suits have been launched, class action suits formed, and litigation pursued against the NFL regarding CTE.

Unfortunately, these legal issues and the ethical issues they involve have not been fully resolved. Due to the results of ongoing study of this disease and the evolving nature of possible future lawsuits, the legal and ethical implications of CTE on the league and its players is currently unsettled. Also, due to the deep pockets and omnipresent profile of the NFL on televisions, radios, newspapers, and the internet, issues related to CTE will likely remain in the news and broader popular consciousness for years. As a result of all of these loose and unexplored ends, a more in-depth examination of the constellation of issues regarding CTE needs to be conducted.

MAIN FOCUS OF THE CHAPTER: ISSUES, CONTROVERSIES, AND PROBLEMS

The main issues, controversies, and problems that will be explored in this chapter include:

- What are the historical roots of chronic traumatic encephalopathy (CTE)? How was it initially diagnosed? What sport was it discovered in?
- What is the current state of the science and medicine related to CTE?
- How did CTE become connected to NFL players, the league, and professional sports more generally?
- What are the longitudinal and cumulative aspects of CTE and their relation to the NFL and similar sports?
- What complications have arisen in connecting the evolving science of CTE and related issues that are currently unsettled concerning the business and legal affairs of the NFL as well as similar professional leagues?
- What are the past, present, and future legal and ethical implications of CTE on the NFL and professional sports more broadly?
- How can the NFL and professional sports acknowledge and cope with the realities of CTE to protect current players, improve the lives of retired professional players who are coping with the various impacts of CTE, and ensure the legal and financial viability of this sport in the future?

The NFL is a vital part of the North American sports landscape as well as its social and cultural life more broadly as described earlier. Also, the league earns billions of dollars of revenue each year for its owners, players, coaches, and related stakeholders who depend on the continued vitality of the sport for their livelihood. As a result, satisfactorily answering the questions posed above regarding CTE and its impacts is essential in preserving the integrity of the sport as well as ensuring its future viability. In short, if the public becomes disillusioned with the NFL, fans stop attending games, people forego watching television broadcasts, enthusiasts refuse to buy merchandise and apparel, and young people turn away from participating in football, the sport could be in deep peril.

WHAT ARE THE HISTORICAL ROOTS OF CHRONIC TRAUMATIC ENCEPHALOPATHY (CTE)?

Chronic traumatic encephalopathy (CTE) has been clinically defined in at least a couple of ways. For example, Rabadi and Jordan believe that CTE is representative of the long-term, cumulative neurologic consequences of repetitive concussive and sub-concussive blows to the brain, which may occur through participation in sports that involve contact to the head (2001). In addition, CTE has been defined more formally as the:

chronic cognitive and neuropsychiatric symptoms of chronic neurodegeneration following a single episode of severe traumatic brain injury or (more commonly) repeated episodes of mild traumatic brain injury. (Omalu, Bailes, Hammers, & Fitzsimmons, 2010 in Gardner, Gardner, Iverson, & McCrory, 2014, p. 86)

As a result, there is some agreement that CTE involves repeated traumatic blows to the brain.

Although CTE has recently garnered a high profile among fans and broader awareness across the general public, there are much deeper historical roots to the disease. For example, the term *punch drunk* was attributed to pathologist Harrison Stanford Martland in his early examinations of boxers (1928). In his landmark paper, Martland described a 38-year-old male who had boxed for 7 years, starting at the age of 16. A clinical examination of the same boxer 20 years after the initial onset of symptoms found that he displayed tremors, pyramidical tract dysfunction, and gait ataxia. Martland diagnosed the aged boxer as having *paralysis agitans*, more commonly known as Parkinson's disease (Martland, 1928). This study helped begin the formal conversation on how contact sports like boxing potentially negatively impact the brain.

CTE is initially diagnosed through an examination of the brain after the person who experience cognitive decline is deceased. Unfortunately, as Gardner, Gardner, Iverson, and McCrory state from their research, a clinical phenotype of CTE is currently unknown and cannot currently be diagnosed in vivo (2014, p. 89). As a result, to accurately study a brain for CTE, the patient must be dead to conclusively prove a clinical diagnosis of CTE.

Evidence of CTE has been found across a wide variety of professional sports. As stated earlier in this chapter, CTE has begun to be discovered in various deceased professional athletes in various sports (Omalu, Hamilton, Kamboh, DeKosky, & Bailes, 2010; Rabadi & Jordan, 2001). They include boxing, football, ice hockey, mixed martial arts, and soccer. As even casual fans would know, each of these sports unfortunately involves at least inadvertent trauma to the head for players (e.g., accidental collisions). From this, similar to football, there may be tentative connections between athletes playing these respective sports and CTE.

WHAT IS THE CURRENT STATE OF THE SCIENCE AND MEDICINE RELATED TO CTE?

Given that there has only been a relatively recent push toward researching chronic traumatic encephalopathy (CTE), the current state of the science and medicine related to this challenging disease is unsettled. In short, due to the fact that CTE as a subject of research has only been around for a short time, the research underlying it is necessarily underdeveloped. For example, only been 51 cases of CTE had been studied pathologically and published in medical literature in 2009 (Boston University CTE Center, 2017). Although this number had risen to 270 CTE cases as of late September 2017 (Boston University CTE Center, 2017), the absolute number of cases is still relatively small.

Efforts to establish a tentative connection between NFL players and CTE have also only been a recent phenomenon. For example, the groundbreaking paper "Chronic traumatic encephalopathy (CTE) in a National Football League Player: Case report and emerging medicolegal practice questions" was only published within the past decade (Omalu, Hamilton, Kamboh, DeKosky, & Bailes, 2010). Similarly, the effort to persuade former players and family members of the deceased to part with players' brains has only occurred for a short period of time. For example, former Harvard football star and professional wrestler Chris Nowinski formed the Concussion Legacy Foundation to help foster the study of brains (Concussion Legacy Foundation, 2015). He also has been instrumental in persuading the families of deceased athletes to donate their brains for CTE testing (ESPN, 2007). These types of important, deeply personal, and incredibly generous decisions by former professional athletes and their families is important to further studying CTE. Given all of this, more evidence that clarifies any possible link between athletes participating in the NFL and CTE needs to be collected to further develop the science and medicine regarding this disease to make it more conclusive.

HOW DID CTE BECOME CONNECTED TO NFL PLAYERS, THE LEAGUE AS A WHOLE, AND PROFESSIONAL SPORTS MORE GENERALLY?

As above, regarding the seminal work on athletes displaying *punch drunk* symptoms (Martland, 1928), the roots of CTE as resulting from repeated traumatic blows to the head was originally discovered through research on boxers. However, since that historic moment almost a century ago, CTE has become connected to NFL players, football as a whole, and professional sports more generally. This has occurred because of the efforts of various researchers (Omalu, Hamilton, Kamboh, DeKosky, & Bailes, 2010) as well as the efforts of former players and their families to share their brains for scientific study (Boston University CTE Center, 2017; Concussion Legacy Foundation, 2015; ESPN, 2007). Unfortunately, suspicious behavior, violence, and suicidal ideations that were in stark contrast to former football players' earlier lives helped draw attention to the possibility of the negative aspects of playing professional sports in the NFL.

WHAT ARE THE LONGITUDINAL AND CUMULATIVE ASPECTS OF CTE AND THEIR RELATION TO THE NFL AND SIMILAR SPORTS?

By its essence, the pathology of CTE normally involves repeated traumatic blows to the head. This usually occurs through contact with other players or collisions with various elements of the playing field (e.g., end boards in ice hockey, enclosures in mixed martial arts, heading the ball in soccer, or falling on hard playing surfaces, etc.). From this, CTE appears to have inherent longitudinal and cumulative aspects to it. Specifically, having the disease appears to involve being exposed to a number of repeated blows to the head over at least a minimal amount of time. For example, a recent study examined multiple prior concussions associated with symptoms in high school athletes (Mannix, Iverson, Maxwell, Atkins, Zafonte, & Berkner, 2014). From this, compared to older professional athletes, it appears as though even younger players who have experienced relatively limited traumatic brain impact could also suffer negative effects. As a result, it appears that there is a growing interest in studying any possible relationships between concussions and neurocognitive performance, even for young athletes, at least in guiding to return safely to the playing field (Mannix, Iverson, Maxwell, Atkins, Zafonte, & Berkner, 2014).

WHAT COMPLICATIONS HAVE ARISEN IN CONNECTING THE SCIENCE OF CTE TO THE BUSINESS AND LEGAL AFFAIRS OF THE NFL AND SIMILAR PROFESSIONAL LEAGUES?

Many complications have arisen in connecting the evolving science of CTE to the business and legal affairs of the NFL.

Professional football players could make a case of negligence against the league. They could assert that the NFL acted in a negligent manner by promoting their sport to the public as being violent as well as not effectively creating a committee to appropriately study issues related to brain trauma from the impact that occurs while playing the sport (National Football Players' Concussion Injury Litigation, 2012). Related to this, players could also assert that the officers appointed to this committee were unqualified and hence the league was again negligent, but in a different manner (National Football Players' Concussion Injury Litigation, 2012).

Due to the relatively recent emphasis on CTE as an area of concern with respect to the NFL, there is simply not a great deal of accumulated research on this disease as being potentially caused by a player participating in the league (Boston University CTE Center, 2017; Omalu, Hamilton, Kamboh, DeKosky, & Bailes, 2010). From this, the NFL could argue that mere awareness of preliminary studies regarding CTE did not mandate that it had a legal duty to warn its players about this type of research (Restatement, Second, Torts, 1965). In essence, the league could assert that it does not have a special relationship with its players nor does it have a special duty to warn them about any possible negative consequences caused by concussions (Restatement, Second, Torts, 1965). The NFL could argue this based on the idea that these players are simply employees of their respective teams and, as a result, the league does not owe them this type of legal duty to warn (*North American Soccer League v. NFL*, 1982). In contrast, NFL players could argue that the league does have a legal duty to warn them. This is premised on the idea that the NFL needs to warn them that their act(s) or omission(s) expose them to an unreasonable risk of harm. Due to not emphasizing possible harms from concussions, the league arguably did not provide its players with adequate and due care and puts them in a position where they could be found legally liable.

The NFL could also make the case that simply through playing the game, its players have made an assumption of risk, including the possibility of injury through their very participation (*Niemcyzk v. Burleson*, 1976). However, some believe that the league needs to have given actual knowledge of the specific risk of concussions and its aftermath to the players (Prosser, 1964; Restatement, Second, Torts, 1965). By not being fully forthright about scientific research, the NFL potentially prevented its players from making informed choices about concussion-related risks, subjecting the athletes to further long-term cognitive degradation and additional risk.

On a similar note, contributory negligence could come into play. This stands for the idea that damages from negligence cannot be recovered if the injured person contributed to his own injury. In short, the player may be at fault due to his own departure from prescribed standards of reasonable conduct. For example, a recent study found that 30 of 160 NFL players did not report, or under-reported, concussive symptoms (Associated Press, 2009). However, due to the wording of the current collective bargaining agreement, some players may feel compelled to withhold concussion information to preserve their contract status for the following year, which is currently not guaranteed under the collective bargaining agreement (CBA) (NFL Collective Bargaining Agreement, 2006).

The league could further argue that the NFL players' CBA may preempt any type of concussion litigation. Specifically, the CBA has a stipulation that in case of a dispute, any issue that needs to be decided upon must be submitted to arbitration (*Easterling & Easterling v. NFL*, 2011). Similarly, the Section 88 indemnification of the NFL collective bargaining agreement allows league alumni to receive annual payments of up $88,000 to help them deal with dementia (NFL Collective Bargaining Agreement, 2006). As a result, it could be argued that funds from Section 88 could potentially indemnify the league against civil liability that could occur in the future.

The presumed longitudinal and cumulative relationship between repeatedly suffering head trauma and having this occur over a specific period time to cause CTE complicates the current legal situation. From this, it correspondingly becomes difficult to connect playing in the NFL as the sole factor in causing CTE due to the great deal of time it takes for CTE to develop (Hanna, 2012). Professional NFL players presumably played for long periods of time in college, high school, and maybe even earlier where they could have suffered concussive and subconcussive impacts, which later led to impaired neurocognitive function as demonstrated through an eventual finding of CTE. Another complicating factor also directly complicating this already complex situation is that the average NFL career is relatively short; the NFL Players Association believes that it is only about 3.3 years in length (Statista, 2017). As a result, holding the NFL exclusively to blame for the neurodegeneration of its athletes becomes difficult to resolve given that it is not the players' only exposure to football-related contact.

The statute of limitations could also impact any potential legal judgments. As above, problems created by repeated trauma from participating in football can take a long time to manifest. This issue is complicated by wildly divergent time horizons for CTE. For example, the age where CTE has been discovered ranges from 25- to 76-years-of-age (Gavett, Stern, & McKee, 2011). Similarly, the average onset of CTE symptoms has been found to take approximately eight years after a player's retirement to manifest (Gavett, Stern, & McKee, 2011). This again extends the time horizons involved and challenges existing statutes of limitations. As a result, even if a relationship between repeated head trauma and long-term injury is established, this may not be proven until after the statute of limitations has come into effect.

It is also difficult to divorce any other previous concussive or subconcussive impacts to an athlete's head that may have occurred outside of football-related activities (e.g., if a football player played another sport involving head contact or suffered an injury from regular life events). If these types of incidents have already occurred, how is this additional trauma accounted for, if at all? For example, Dr. Joseph Maroon, a trainer for the Pittsburgh Steelers and NFL Committee member, argued that drug abuse, steroid use, and other substances caused the damaged brain tissues found in Mike Webster and other NFL players (Carpenter, 2007). From this, it could be argued that the tortious conduct of an actor must be a factual cause for the physical harm of another for the imposition of liability (Restatement, Third, Torts, 2002). Again, isolating playing professional football as the exclusive factor causing the head trauma that eventually contributes to CTE is incredibly difficult to find.

In summary, there are many complications that have arisen regarding the connection between the evolving science of CTE and how it relates to the business and legal affairs of the NFL.

WHAT ARE THE PAST, PRESENT, AND FUTURE LEGAL AND ETHICAL IMPLICATIONS OF CTE ON THE NFL AND PROFESSIONAL SPORTS?

The legal and ethical implications of CTE on the NFL and professional sports more broadly are not fixed to the present moment. They each have past, present, and future elements to them.

For example, there has been debate as to when the NFL knew about the potential problems relating to player participation in the NFL with any long-term impacts and possible neurodegeneration. Former NFL Commissioner Paul Tagliabue started the Mild Traumatic Brain Injury committee in 1994 (Ezell, 2013). As such, if additional evidence comes to light before this point in time regarding the NFL's knowledge of the possibly deleterious impact of playing the game on its athletes, it could put the league in a precarious legal and ethical situation if it did not inform its players about these findings. This could cost more than the NFL's initial $765 million settlement; some estimate that this total may eventually surpass more than $1 billion depending on how various factors impact this fluid legal situation (Wilson, 2015). From this, the NFL could become exposed to even more legal liability for damages from the time they possibly knew of potential negative impacts on its players without informing them of their findings.

Developments in the NFL and its brother or sister leagues could have cross-sport impacts. In short, any precedents set within one sport regarding settlements with its players or rulings against this specific sport could impact other sports in similar ways. It seems reasonable that a legal ruling in one jurisdiction regarding one professional sports league could become a binding precedent in another league with a similar fact situation. As such, how each sport deals with its respective players, players unions/associations, etc. may dictate how others are dealt with regarding settlements, penalties, or other rulings, etc.

Another ongoing legal issue that has plagued the league has been an ongoing dispute regarding insurance. More specifically, who is legally responsible for paying out any settlements, legal costs, future costs, or other related expenses for player health problems related to CTE? Recently, the NFL settled with six insurance companies for the expenses that resulted from the previous $1 billion concussion settlement (Kaplan, 2017; Zucker, 2017).

A further legal issue under consideration is the debate over whether any possible player injuries would potentially be covered by tort law or workers' compensation (Korngold, Farrell, & Fozdar, 2013; Parlour & Jones, 1980). Workers' compensation is commonly conceived of as a form of insurance that provides a couple of benefits; namely medical benefits and wage replacement to employees who have been injured while performing their employment duties (Parlour & Jones, 1980). However, in exchange for providing benefits, these same employees are prevented from seeking additional recourse outside the workers' existing compensation system and possibly more limited coverage than could possibly be provided through tort law. A future ruling finding that CTE and its negative impacts are covered under federal law and the prevailing collective bargaining agreement would prevent retired players from making claims under tort law (Korngold, Farrell, & Fozdar, 2013).

An additional legal issue is the idea of informed consent, which necessitates that both parties to a contract have fully disclosed everything that is judged to be of significance to the agreement under consideration (Schuck, 1994). This is a key constituent element of any contract (Schuck, 1994). Without full and free informed consent absent any form of coercion as characterized by the incredibly unequal bargaining positions of the very rich league and often poor players (Korngold, Farrell, & Fozdar, 2013), informed consent could become an issue.

From a broader perspective, the ongoing dispute between the NFL and its players regarding the impact of CTE arguably is creating a broader transition regarding the conception of the person in law and public policy. This is creating a contrast between *dispositionism* and *situationism* (Frontier Torts Project, 2013). The traditional media coverage of football focused on dispositionism, seeing players as being fully aware of the attendant risks of play like concussions and other forms of head trauma. Recently, situationism sees the league, its owners, and the sport as a whole to better comprehend the legal situation of concussions and CTE as well as long-term policy implications. The broader adoption of the transition to situationism may eventually become a determining factor in allotting compensation to players because it appears prima facie more sympathetic to their plight.

HOW CAN THE NFL ACKNOWLEDGE AND COPE WITH CTE TO PROTECT CURRENT PLAYERS, IMPROVE THE LIVES OF RETIRED PLAYERS WHO ARE COPING WITH CTE, AND ENSURE THE FUTURE LEGAL, ETHICAL, AND FINANCIAL VIABILITY OF FOOTBALL?

There are a number of ways that the NFL and professional sports acknowledge and cope with the realities of CTE. This includes initiatives to protect current players, improve the lives of retired players who are coping with different stages of CTE, and ensure the future legal, ethical, and financial viability of this sport.

For example, the NFL's recent settlement of a class action suit with hundreds of its former players (Wilson, 2015) is a tentative start toward a more transparent and mutually beneficial relationship between the league with both its current and former players who have retired. This settlement begins to help publicly acknowledge the possibility that there is a relationship between playing a high impact sport (e.g., football) and later neurocognitive degeneration (e.g., CTE). Although the league may not acknowledge legal or fiduciary liability for having players participate in its sport and none may ever be found depending on how the science, medicine, and law evolve, it appears as though there is some recognition of professional sports leagues in taking care of the broader medical needs of their former players through financial compensation or other reparations. Perhaps the NFL's initial settlement with its players can serve as the beginnings of a model for other sports that involve repeated impact to the brain and negative impacts on their health, later lives, and general level of well-being.

SOLUTIONS AND RECOMMENDATIONS

There are several major preliminary solutions and recommendations that are suggested from the previous issues regarding chronic traumatic encephalopathy (CTE) discussed within this chapter.

ALLOCATE MORE FINANCIAL RESOURCES TO THE STUDY OF CHRONIC TRAUMATIC ENCEPHALOPATHY (CTE)

By allocating more funding to formal CTE studies, ideally scientific and medical professionals will be able to develop their important work to help provide a more in-depth understanding of this tragic disease that has only recently gained wider attention from the public. Future research on CTE should be focused on its longitudinal and cumulative aspects as well as their relation to the NFL and similar contact sports like boxing, ice hockey, mixed martial arts, soccer, and analogous sports and activities. Ideally by mapping out the relationship between head trauma and the type of long-term neurocognitive degeneration demonstrated through having CTE, we can begin to understand how to prevent, or at least minimize, any negative short- or long-term impacts on NFL athletes and those who are involved in other professional sports where head trauma unfortunately acts as a part in gameplay, even when this contact is incidental or inadvertent.

DISCOVER A WAY TO DIAGNOSE LIVING PLAYERS WHO ARE AFFLICTED WITH THE BEGINNING STAGES OF CTE

An unfortunate limitation of CTE studies is that they are limited to the brains of deceased subjects. As such, the information that can be studied from their examination is more *summative* in nature at one fixed point in time; namely end of life. From this, this information is divorced from more *formative* ongoing insights regarding what is happening to players during their professional careers (or even earlier in their lives) as CTE damage is presumably worsening through repeated head traumas. Ideally this type of early career in vivo assessment can begin giving clues to provide more effective ongoing insight on, and treatment of, players who may be experiencing issues related to CTE. Given the current state of medical diagnostic capabilities, CTE can unfortunately only be conclusively discovered from the brains of deceased players and not in vivo (Gardner, Gardner, Iverson, & McCrory, 2014, p. 89). Any way to measure cognitive decline over the course of a player's career would presumably be useful in helping establish relationships between repeated head traumas and their possibly negative effects on long-term cognitive functioning.

DISCOVER AND FUND NEW TREATMENTS FOR CURRENT OR FORMER PLAYERS WHO ARE SUFFERING FROM CTE

As mentioned above, there should be a strong push to perform formative assessments to assess any accumulated ongoing damage from incident involving game play (or even during practice) that involve traumatic impact to their heads. From this, ongoing information can be collected regarding players' presumably increasingly worsening states of cognitive operations over their career from accumulated repeated traumatic impacts to the head. With this data, ideally this additional information can help inform novel and innovative treatments for both current and retired players. This will ideally allow them to live with a higher quality of life and hopefully prevent them from self-harm or hurting others as demonstrated in the cases of Mike Webster, Junior Seau, and Jovan Belcher discussed earlier. Additionally, it should also help in the future regarding lower profile athletes who also are at risk of suffering equally tragic deaths and challenging ends of life that have been presumably caused by the negative effects of CTE.

DISCOVER AND FUND NEW TYPES OF SPORTS EQUIPMENT TO MINIMIZE THE IMPACT OF REPEATED HEAD TRAUMAS

Given that repeated traumas to the head appear to foster the development of CTE, creating new types of sports equipment could presumably lower the risk of these harmful blows to the head. This would include new kinds of helmets, improved padding, or other innovative pieces of equipment to help deal with this issue.

For example, Dartmouth College's football coach Buddy Teevens teamed with the school's engineering department to create Mobile Virtual Player (MVP) (Grasinger, 2015; Mashable News, 2015). MVP is a remote controlled mobile tackling dummy that can participate on the field. By roaming the gridiron with a soft protective shell and being subject to hits by players, MVP allows team members to practice tackling and ideally reduce player-on-player hits during practice. In short, why tackle and potentially harm a fellow member of your squad when you can simply tackle MVP?

Modifying current equipment to disperse any deleterious impact on a player's head from direct contact could also help minimize the negative shock to their brain. For example, perhaps new helmets could have additional padding or become connected in some way to the rest of the body to absorb some of the impact that is exclusively absorbed by helmets, heads, and brains.

INCREASE MINIMUM AGE REQUIREMENTS FOR TACKLE FOOTBALL AT EARLIER LEVELS OF ORGANIZED AMATEUR FOOTBALL

Unfortunately, children can play tackle football at very young ages when their tender brains are still developing. As a result, the onset of head trauma from tackling can occur at incredibly young ages, even through inadvertent or unintentional contact (e.g., due to inexperience, young people can accidentally knock heads with one another when they do not need to). This would include Pop Warner leagues for children and youth where they first learn the skills involved in organized football. By pushing tackling to later years and instead playing touch football, ideally youth will continue to develop brain growth without additional trauma. Later on, when they are older, as they become teenagers or adults with fully mature brains and sufficient cognitive development, they will become better equipped to cope with any possible brain trauma caused through contact.

PROMOTE SAFER WAYS OF TACKLING THAT MINIMIZE REPEATED HIGH IMPACT HEAD TRAUMAS

Youth often imitate adults, both their good behavior and unfortunately also the bad. This form of imitation occurs in sports as well. Young people tend to look up to their athletic heroes for inspiration within their sport of interest. As such, children have an unfortunate tendency to follow the examples of explosive, no holds barred, head-on-head tackling they see on television, such as those broadcast on NFL games throughout the season.

These young people should instead be taught safer ways to tackle that do not involve direct head-on-head contact. For example, this would include learning to tackle opposing players using their shoulders and arms exclusively. Similarly, learning to tackle opposing players at a lower level of the body, instead of head-to-head, should be taught at all levels of football. Although this does hold promise, there are potential problems of causing impacts to vulnerable knees that could injure players in other ways (Lauletta, 2017). In short, it will be difficult to come to a fully agreed upon solution.

LIMIT FORMAL TACKLING TO GAMES OR MINIMALLY AT PRACTICE

On a similar note, the NFL began to modify practice schedules and rules through its most recent collective bargaining agreement; this includes forbidding two-a-day practices during training camp as well as the number of full contact padded practices to 14 per year with 11 of these during the first 11 weeks of the season (Brooks, 2011). Colleges, high schools, and Pop Warner leagues should similarly reduce the exposure of young people to contact during practice. Instead, they could spend time working on other skills like improving conditioning, learning formations, weight training, reviewing video of themselves playing, etc.

REVISIT ON-FIELD AND OFF-FIELD CONCUSSION PROTOCOLS TO ENSURE THE SAFETY OF PLAYERS BY REMOVING THEM FROM COMPETITION IF THEY ARE SUFFERING HARM

Football players at all levels can suffer concussive and subconcussive injuries depending on the severity of impact on their heads from regular gameplay. From raised awareness of this issue, the NFL became involved in passing laws across all 50 states and the District of Columbia that protect children from suffering concussions while playing sports (Associated Press, 2015). Unfortunately, an analysis of these laws found that less than half of them consist of the key principles found in a 2009 bill passed in Washington state (Associated Press, 2015). The original bill required a concussion information form be signed by players and their parents, removing children from games if there is the suspicion of a head injury, and mandated education for any coaches regarding concussion symptoms (Associated Press, 2015).

Related to this, ensuring that coaches, athletic trainers, referees, etc. who are involved in football are fully informed about concussion protocols will help minimize any undue risk to players. Due to the distinct possibility of additional long-term brain injury from repeated trauma to an already concussed brain, removal from competition and practice should be quick and decisive until all possible on-field and off-field concussion protocols have been met.

INCREASE THE SEVERITY OF ON-FIELD PENALTIES AND OFF-FIELD SUSPENSIONS FOR UNSPORTSMANLIKE TACKLING THAT INVOLVES CONTACT WITH THE HEAD TO DISINCENTIVIZE THIS BEHAVIOR

As above, bad behavior on the NFL field can be replicated among youth who want to imitate the playing style of their heroes. Stiff penalties at all levels of the game for dangerous head-to-head contact, from amateur to professional, can ideally help disincentive this unnecessary unsportsmanlike behavior, improve player safety, and minimize the risk of harm.

REDUCE YOUTH GAME SCHEDULES

The NFL is a lucrative business based on 16-week-long regular seasons as well as the playoffs. Division I football is similar big business as implied by Miami coach Nick Saban's $11.25 million contract (Moriarty, 2017). However, reducing high school football seasons or even revising rules to shorten the length of games at all levels of the sport will ideally contribute to a reduced exposure of athletes to injury and harm.

CREATE A SUSTAINABLE FINANCIAL FUND TO TREAT CURRENT AND FORMER PLAYERS SUFFERING FROM CTE

Medical treatment for acute brain trauma is very expensive. Given the current difficulty in accurately diagnosing the incidence rate of CTE in current and former players given the longitudinal and cumulative aspects of this disease, there should be provisions to allow the expansion of these types of funds to support current and former players with this level of uncertainty in possible future medical and legal costs borne by the NFL. For example, the co-lead lawyers who represented the class of retired NFL players who sued the league over concussion related damages filed a memorandum of law claiming they deserved $112.5 million for their legal work alone (Heitner, 2017). As such, it there is a spike in the number of current or former players who need medical help or are awarded expensive settlements, there will be sufficient funding to help them receive the high quality medical care they need.

CREATE TRANSPARENT PUBLIC RELATIONS CAMPAIGNS WITH PLAYERS AND FANS SO THEY KNOW THE RISKS OF PLAYING AMATEUR AND PROFESSIONAL FOOTBALL

Full knowledge that is current and constantly supported by additional information is a powerful resource. The NFL and other football leagues at all levels should inform their athletes and other stakeholders of the risks involved in playing. This is especially essential for more opaque, long-term dangers like brain trauma that are extremely difficult to assess from non-specialized coaches and athletic trainers. This will help create a more knowledgeable population and ideally increase public trust in the league and its stewards.

FUTURE RESEARCH DIRECTIONS

As further research emerges, ideally the National Football League (NFL), the league head office, the players association, and its players will continue to use additional scientific research to help deal with the ravages of chronic traumatic encephalopathy (CTE). Ideally, this will help them make informed choices to protect all current and former players with respect to their health, wellbeing, and any other related issues. With this in mind, future research should take into account the following issues among others when deciding its focus.

ALLOCATE MORE FINANCIAL RESOURCES TO THE STUDY OF CHRONIC TRAUMATIC ENCEPHALOPATHY (CTE)

Conducting research on CTE is necessarily costly due to the highly educated scientific and medical professionals who are involved in this type of work as well as the complicated analyses they must perform on an organ as delicate and complex as the brain. Also, carefully removing brains from players to preserve their integrity and transporting them in a medically appropriate manner is also clearly complex and expensive. As a result, any funding should be broadly focused on the longitudinal and cumulative aspects of CTE as well as their relation to the NFL and similar contact sports to help better understand this disease.

RESEARCH A WAY TO DIAGNOSE LIVING PLAYERS WHO ARE AFFLICTED WITH THE BEGINNING STAGES OF CTE

Any ability to collect and constantly analyze ongoing data regarding brain trauma on living players should help develop a more holistic view of any possible brain damage and its later presumed relationship to CTE. This will provide more current information to help researchers refine their work and provide ameliorative care for those who are suffering from CTE's onset at its earliest stages. Although collecting data on deceased players is useful and has contributed greatly to our current understanding of CTE, figuring out ways to gather additional medical information on them throughout the longer trajectory of their careers will also be useful for gaining a more comprehensive and accurate view of this challenging disease.

RESEARCH NEW TREATMENTS FOR CURRENT AND PAST PLAYERS WHO ARE SUFFERING FROM CTE

Providing advanced assistance to current and former NFL players that takes into account the knowledge gained by researchers should help those suffering from CTE at any stage of its occurrence. This will ideally provide them and their loved ones with a higher quality of life as well as a more effective way to cope with any negative behavior caused by CTE. Again, the highest quality and most current knowledge possible can only help.

RESEARCH AND FUND NEW TYPES OF SPORTS GEAR TO MINIMIZE REPEATED HEAD TRAUMAS

As mentioned earlier, Dartmouth College's Mobile Virtual Player (MVP) is an exciting development for helping current players learn the tackling skills they need to play football absent some of the attendant risk of one-on-one contact between colliding players (Grasinger, 2015; Mashable News, 2015). By taking one player out of the equation, it lessens this risk drastically. Unfortunately, the MVP technology currently costs approximately $3,500 per dummy (Grasinger, 2015; Mashable News, 2015). As a result, figuring out a way to minimize the cost of MVP or similar tackling technology would be useful in making it more effectively dispersed in an increasingly equitable way among the widest possible base of football teams. In addition, less capital intensive initiatives like new helmets that disperse the negative effects of direct impact, improved padding that could absorb greater amounts of impact, and new types of equipment, among other developments, could help protect players who are on youth teams that cannot afford more expensive technology like MVP.

CONCLUSION

And it sort of reminds me of the tobacco companies pre-1990's when they kept saying no, there is no link between smoking and damage to your health or ill health effects. And they were forced to admit that that was incorrect through a spate of litigation in the 1990's.

Representative Linda Sánchez (D-California) (Legal Issues Relating to Football Head Injuries, 2009 & 2010)

Chronic traumatic encephalopathy (CTE) research has been a standalone field of study for only a short period of time. For example, within the NFL, it has only been conducted for less than a decade (Omalu, Hamilton, Kamboh, DeKosky, & Bailes, 2010). Luckily, this scientific and medical work continues to be ongoing. The findings appear to be growing as more studies have been conducted. From this, the tragic deaths of a number of popular players have led to ever increasing mass media coverage of this issue and growing awareness among stakeholders in the NFL, its players, and their fans. The rules of professional football and the form of gameplay they encourage by their underlying logic make it a contact sport. As football has evolved over time and matured, it has involved increasingly bigger, stronger, and faster players that necessitate collision between their bodies on a finite playing space. As a result, there is an ever-present risk of injuries. By continuing research on CTE, improving tackling at the earliest levels, developing safer football equipment, making concussion protocols more proactive and rigorous, and providing treatment at the earliest stages of the onset of CTE, the NFL can continue to financially thrive with healthier players, retirees with a higher quality of life, more satisfied fans, as well as remain ethically, financially, and legally viable long into the future.

REFERENCES

Armstrong, K., Chinese, V., & Brown, S. R. (2012, December 3). Jovan Belcher leaves grisly car evidence of mayhem that preceded his shocking suicide. *New York Daily News*. Retrieved from http://www.nydailynews.com/news/national/jovan-belcher-death-car-article-1.1212182

Associated Press. (2009, November 18). Survey: Concussions inevitable. *Associated Press*. Retrieved from http://sports.espn.go.com/nfl/news/story?id=4668106

Associated Press. (2015, January 28). Youth concussion laws lack bite. *Associated Press*. Retrieved from http://www.espn.com/nfl/story/_/id/12242612/youth-concussion-laws-pushed-nfl-lack-bite-according-associated-press-analysis

Badenhausen, K. (2015, October 11). The NFL players who make the most from endorsements. *Forbes*. Retrieved from https://www.forbes.com/sites/kurtbadenhausen/2015/10/11/the-nfl-players-who-make-the-most-from-endorsements/#7f98a2f26277

Badenhausen, K. (2016, September 14). The NFL's highest-paid players 2016. *Forbes*. Retrieved from https://www.forbes.com/sites/kurtbadenhausen/2016/09/14/the-nfls-highest-paid-players-2016/#4fad780a3642

Battaglio, S., & James, M. (2017, February 6). Super Bowl's TV ratings slip for the second straight year. *Los Angeles Times*. Retrieved from http://www.latimes.com/business/hollywood/la-fi-ct-super-bowl-ratings-20170206-story.html

Berr, J. (2016, September 8). Are you ready to make some moola? NFL remains a financial powerhouse. *Moneywatch*. Retrieved from https://www.cbsnews.com/news/the-nfls-financial-juggernaut-is-decades-in-the-making/

Berr, J. (2017). Sliding NFL ratings could throw networks for a loss. *Moneywatch*. Rctrieved from https://www.cbsnews.com/news/sliding-nfl-ratings-could-throw-networks-for-a-loss/

Bloomberg News. (2015). Nike makes the most of its NFL gear with sales to fans. *Bloomberg News*. Retrieved from http://www.oregonlive.com/playbooks-profits/index.ssf/2015/12/post_87.html

Boston University CTE Center. (2017). *VA-BU-CLF Brain Bank: Case studies*. Retrieved from https://www.bu.edu/cte/our-research/brain-bank/

Boyd, J. (2017, January 17). Who are the highest paid NFL head coaches & what are their salaries. *BoydsBets.com*. Retrieved from https://www.boydsbets.com/highest-paid-coaches-nfl/

Breslow, J. M. (2013, October 6). The autopsy that changed football. *PBS.org*. Retrieved from http://www.pbs.org/wgbh/frontline/article/the-autopsy-that-changed-football/

Brooks, B. (2011, August 10). How practice changes could negatively impact NFL games. *NFL.com*. Retrieved from http://www.nfl.com/trainingcamp/story/09000d5d8215c8ab/article/how-practice-changes-could-negatively-impact-nfl-games

Carpenter, L. (2007, June 20). Compromise reigns at summit on concussions. *Washington Post*. Retrieved from http://www.washingtonpost.com/wp-dyn/content/article/2007/06/19/AR2007061902157.html

NFL Collective Bargaining Agreement. (2006). *NFL Collective Bargaining Agreement*. Article XLVIII-D 88 Benefit.

Concussion Legacy Foundation. (2015, September 3). Sports Legacy Institute announces rebrand to Concussion Legacy Foundation. *Concussion Legacy Foundation*. Retrieved from https://concussionfoundation.org/about/media/press-releases/sports-legacy-institute-announces-rebrand-concussion-legacy-foundation

Dailey, R. A. (2006, January 30). Steel Curtain seeks heavenly help. *Pittsburgh Post-Gazette*. Retrieved from http://www.post-gazette.com/ruth-ann-dailey/2006/01/30/Steel-Curtain-seeks-heavenly-help/stories/200601300146

Delsohn, S. (2014, September 30). OTL: Belcher's brain had CTE signs. *ESPN.com*. Retrieved from http://www.espn.com/espn/otl/story/_/id/11612386/jovan-belcher-brain-showed-signs-cte-doctor-says-report

Drenon, T. (2013, October 8). Mike Webster autopsy 'one of the most significant moments in the history of sports.' *Behind the Steel Curtain*. Retrieved from https://www.behindthesteelcurtain.com/2013/10/8/4814434/concussion-suit-mike-webster-thing

Engber, D. (2012, May 9). The concussion panic. Why are we so convinced that football head injuries lead to suicide? *Slate*. Retrieved from http://www.slate.com/articles/health_and_science/science/2012/05/junior_seau_s_suicide_are_concussions_responsible_.html

ESPN.com News Services. (2007, January 19). Pathologist says Waters' brain tissue had deteriorated. *ESPN.com*. Retrieved from http://www.espn.com/nfl/news/story?id=2734941

ESPN.com news services (2012, May 3). Junior Seau dies at 43. *ESPN.com*. Retrieved from http://www.espn.com/nfl/story/_/id/7882750/junior-seau-former-san-diego-charger-found-dead-cops-probe-suicide

Ezell, L. (2013, October 8). Timeline: The NFL's concussion crisis. *Frontline*. Retrieved from http://www.pbs.org/wgbh/pages/frontline/sports/league-of-denial/timeline-the-nfls-concussion-crisis/

Fainaru, S., & Fainaru-Wada, M. (2013, January 11, 2013). In brawl for Seau brain, a proxy war over concussion science. *PBS*. Retrieved from http://www.pbs.org/wgbh/frontline/article/in-brawl-for-seau-brain-a-proxy-war-over-concussion-science/

Fainaru-Wada, M., Avila, J., & Steve Fainaru, S. (2013, January 11). Doctors: Junior Seau's brain had CTE. *ESPN*. Retrieved from http://www.espn.com/espn/otl/story/_/id/8830344/study-junior-seau-brain-shows-chronic-brain-damage-found-other-nfl-football-players

Florio, M. (2017, March 6). NFL will reach $14 billion in 2017 revenue. *Pro Football Talk*. Retrieved from http://profootballtalk.nbcsports.com/2017/03/06/nfl-will-reach-14-billion-in-2017-revenue/

Forbes. (n.d.). Tom Brady: Profile. *Forbes*. Retrieved from https://www.forbes.com/profile/tom-brady/

Frontier Torts Project. (2013). NFL concussions: The current situation and policy implications. *Frontier Torts Project, Harvard Law School*. Retrieved from http://learning.law.harvard.edu/frontiertorts/wp-content/uploads/2013/04/NFL-Concussions-White-Paper-2.pdf

Gardner, A., Iverson, G. L., & McCrory, P. (2014). Chronic traumatic encephalopathy in sport: A systematic review. *British Journal of Sports Medicine*, *48*(2), 84–90. doi:10.1136/bjsports-2013-092646 PMID:23803602

Gavett, B. E., Stern, R. A., & McKee, A. C. (2011). Chronic traumatic encephalopathy: A potential late effect of sport-related concussive and subconcussive head trauma. *Clinics in Sports Medicine*, *30*(1), 179–xi. doi:10.1016/j.csm.2010.09.007 PMID:21074091

Gordon, M. (2003). Before 'Concussion': An inside glimpse of NFL player Mike Webster's utterly tragic final days. *Reader's Digest*. Retrieved from https://www.rd.com/health/conditions/mike-webster-brain-injury/

Grasinger, C. (2015, August 27). Meet the Mobile Virtual Player, a robotic practice dummy created to make football safer. *Mashable*. Retrieved from http://mashable.com/2015/08/27/football-mobile-virtual-player/?utm_cid=mash-com-yt-desc-link#RA1tIihUSGqg

Greene, D. [Host], & Trotter, J. [Guest] (2015, December 22). Seau's suicide helped to make concussions in football a national issue. *NPR Morning Edition* [Radio podcast]. Retrieved from http://www.npr.org/2015/12/22/460656805/junior-seaus-suicide-helped-to-make-concussions-in-football-a-national-issue

Hanna, J. M. (2012, October). Concussions may prove to be a major headache for the NFL. *New York State Bar Association (NYSBA) Journal*. Retrieved from http://www.goldbergsegalla.com/sites/default/files/uploads/JMH_ConcussionsNYSBAJournal_Oct2012.pdf

Heitner, D. (2017). This week in sports law: NFL concussion lawyers ask $112M, Under Armour sued, Darrelle Revis robbery. *Forbes*. Retrieved from https://www.forbes.com/sites/darrenheitner/2017/02/19/this-week-in-sports-law-nfl-concussion-lawyers-want-112m-under-armour-sued-dykstras-firm-demand/#5b55837758c7

Kaplan, D. (2017). Payouts from NFL concussion deal approved; League settles with insurance companies *SportsBusiness Daily*. Retrieved from https://www.sportsbusinessdaily.com/Daily/Issues/2017/08/07/Leagues-and-Governing-Bodies/NFL-CTE-Settlement.aspx

Kirk, M., Gilmore, J., & Wiser, M. [Producers], Kirk, M., [Director], Jim Gilmore, J., Fainaru, S., & Fainaru-Wada, M. [Reporters]. (2013, October 8). League of denial: The NFL's concussion crisis. *PBS Frontline* [Television series]. Retrieved from http://www.pbs.org/wgbh/frontline/film/league-of-denial/

Korngold, C., Farrell, H. M., & Fozdar, M. (2013). The National Football League and chronic traumatic encephalopathy: Legal implications. *The Journal of the American Academy of Psychiatry and the Law*, *41*, 430–436. PMID:24051597

Kounang, N., & Smith, S. (2014, September 30). Doctor: NFL player who killed girlfriend, self likely had CTE. *CNN*. Retrieved from http://www.cnn.com/2014/09/29/health/jovan-belcher-cte/index.html

Lauletta, T. (2017, September 20). Another NFL receiver is publicly asking defenders to stop hitting so low. *Business Insider*. Retrieved from http://www.businessinsider.com/terrelle-pryor-dont-hit-his-knees-2017-9

Legal Issues Relating to Football Head Injuries (Part I & II). Hearings before the House Judiciary Committee, Senate, 111th Cong. 111–82 (2009 & 2010).

Litsky, F. (September 25, 2002). Mike Webster, 50, dies; Troubled football Hall of Famer. *The New York Times*. Retrieved from https://www.nytimes.com/2002/09/25/sports/mike-webster-50-dies-troubled-football-hall-of-famer.html

Mannix, R., Iverson, G. L., Maxwell, B., Atkins, J. E., Zafonte, R., & Berkner, P. D. (2014). Multiple prior concussions are associated with symptoms in high school athletes. *Annals of Clinical and Translational Neurology*, *1*(6), 433–438. doi:10.1002/acn3.70 PMID:25356413

Martland, H. S. (1928). Punch drunk. *Journal of the American Medical Association*, *91*(15), 1103–1107. doi:10.1001/jama.1928.02700150029009

Mashable News. (2015, August 27). Meet the Mobile Virtual Player, a robotic practice dummy. *Mashable News*. Retrieved from https://www.youtube.com/watch?v=Cy4Xtfe3s14

McIntyre, D. A. (2017, February 6). Brady's endorsements of Under Armour and UGGs big Super Bowl winners. *24/7 Wall St*. Retrieved from http://247wallst.com/media/2017/02/06/bradys-endorsements-of-under-armour-and-uggs-big-super-bowl-winners/

Mellinger, S. (2014, September 29). Jovan Belcher's brain showed signs of CTE, according to post-mortem exam. *The Kansas City Star*. Retrieved from http://www.kansascity.com/sports/nfl/kansas-city-chiefs/article2296030.html

Moriarty, M. (2017, May 2). At $11M, Nick Saban might be America's highest-paid sports coach in 2017. *SB Nation*. Retrieved from https://www.sbnation.com/college-football/2017/5/2/15515544/nick-saban-11-million-salary-highest-paid-sports-coach-2017

Nathan, A. (2017, May 19). Tom Brady signs Aston Martin endorsement deal. *Bleacher Report*. Retrieved from http://bleacherreport.com/articles/2710577-tom-brady-signs-aston-martin-endorsement-deal

National Football Players' Concussion Injury Litigation. (2012). Plaintiff's Master Admin. Long-Form Complaint at 65, In re Nat'l Football Players' Concussion Injury Litig., No. 2:12-md-02323-AB (E.D. Pa. June 7, 2012).

NFL Collective Bargaining Agreement. (2006). *NFL Collective Bargaining Agreement*. Appendix C, § 9 at 251.

Niemcyzk v. Burleson, 538 S.W.2d 737, 740 (Mo. Ct. App. 1976).

North American Soccer League v. NFL, 670 F.2d 1249, 1252 (2d Cir. 1982).

Novy-Williams, E. (2015, July 20). NFL teams split $7.3 billion in revenue, Packers numbers revealed. *Bloomberg*. Retrieved from https://www.bloomberg.com/news/articles/2015-07-20/nfl-teams-split-7-3-billion-in-revenue-packers-numbers-reveal

Omalu, B. I., Bailes, J., Hammers, J. L., & Fitzsimmons, R. P. (2010). Chronic traumatic encephalopathy, suicides and parasuicides in professional American athletes: The role of the forensic pathologist. *The American Journal of Forensic Medicine and Pathology*, *31*(2), 130–132. doi:10.1097/PAF.0b013e3181ca7f35 PMID:20032774

Omalu, B. I., Hamilton, R. L., Kamboh, M. I., DeKosky, S. T., & Bailes, J. (2010). Chronic traumatic encephalopathy (CTE) in a National Football League Player: Case report and emerging medicolegal practice questions. *Journal of Forensic Nursing*, *6*(1), 40–46. doi:10.1111/j.1939-3938.2009.01064.x PMID:20201914

Ozanian, M. (2016, September 14). The NFL's most valuable teams 2016. *Forbes*. Retrieved from https://www.forbes.com/sites/mikeozanian/2016/09/14/the-nfls-most-valuable-teams-2016/#115df7363068

Parlour, R. R., & Jones, L. R. (1980). Theories of psychiatric defense in workmen's compensation cases. *The Bulletin of the American Academy of Psychiatry and the Law*, *8*, 445–455. PMID:6456785

Pro Football Reference. (2017). Junior Seau profile. *Pro Football Reference*. Retrieved from https://www.pro-football-reference.com/players/S/SeauJu00.htm

Prosser, W. L. (1964). *Law of torts* (3rd ed.). St. Paul, MN: West Group.

Rabadi, M. H., & Jordan, B. D. (2001). The cumulative effect of repetitive concussion in sports. *Clinical Journal of Sport Medicine*, *11*(3), 194–198. doi:10.1097/00042752-200107000-00011 PMID:11495325

Restatement, Second, Torts: Negligence. (1965). Restatement (Second) of Torts § 314 (1965). *American Law Institute*. Retrieved from https://www.ali.org/publications/show/torts/

Restatement, Third, Torts: Liability for Physical and Emotional Harm. (2002). Restatement (Third) of Torts § 26 (2002). *American Law Institute*. Retrieved from https://www.ali.org/publications/show/torts-liability-physical-and-emotional-harm/

Rothstein, M. (2017, August 29). Lions QB Matthew Stafford to become highest-paid NFL player. *ESPN*. Retrieved from http://www.espn.com/nfl/story/_/id/20491086/matthew-stafford-detroit-lions-agree-historic-5-year-deal

Satriano, D. (2012, December 18). Chiefs' Belcher texted secret girlfriend with Perkins threat: Report. *New York Post*. Retrieved from http://nypost.com/2012/12/18/chiefs-belcher-texted-secret-girlfriend-with-perkins-threat-report/

Schatz, P., Moser, R. S., Covassin, T., & Karpf, R. (2011). Early indicators of enduring symptoms in high school athletes with multiple previous concussions. *Neurosurgery*, *68*(6), 1562–1567. doi:10.1227/NEU.0b013e31820e382e PMID:21258259

Schiavenza, M. (2015, August 9). The tragic legacy of Junior Seau. *The Atlantic*. Retrieved from https://www.theatlantic.com/entertainment/archive/2015/08/the tragic-legacy-of-junior-seau/400856/

Schrotenboer, B. (2016, April 30). Ex-NFL doctor accused of gross negligence in treatment of Junior Seau. *USA Today Sports*. Retrieved from https://www.usatoday.com/story/sports/nfl/2016/04/30/chargers-doctor-david-chao-accused-gros-engligence-treatment-junior-seau/83777186/

Schuck, P. H. (1994). Rethinking informed consent. *Faculty Scholarship Series*. Paper 2765. Retrieved from http://digitalcommons.law.yale.edu/fss_papers/2765

Scott, R., Facio, G., Wolthoff, D., Shuman, L., & Cantillon, E. [Producers] & Landesman, P. [Director]. (2015). *Concussion* [Motion picture]. Retrieved from http://www.sonypictures.com/movies/concussion/

Shapiro, L., & Maske, M. (2005, April 19). 'Monday Night Football' changes the channel after 35 years on ABC. *Washington Post*. Retrieved from http://www.washingtonpost.com/wp-dyn/articles/A63538-2005Apr18.html

Silver, J. D. (2014, October 17). A life off-center: Mike Webster's battles. *Pittsburgh Post-Gazette*. Retrieved from http://www.post-gazette.com/ae/movies/2014/10/17/A-life-off-center-Mike-Webster-s-battles/stories/201410090319

Smith, C. (2015, September 14). The NFL's richest owners. *Forbes*. Retrieved from https://www.forbes.com/sites/chrissmith/2015/09/14/the-nfls-richest-owners/#7ef5079d94ba

Statista. (2017). *Average playing career length in the National Football League (in years)*. Retrieved from https://www.statista.com/statistics/240102/average-player-career-length-in-the-national-football-league/

Tanier, M. (2016, November 15). Growth of gambling across US is helping to pull NFL wagering out of the whadows. *Bleacher Report*. Retrieved from http://bleacherreport.com/articles/2664047-growth-of-gambling-across-us-is-helping-pull-nfl-wagering-out-of-the-shadows

USA Today sports. (2012, December 4). Belcher's girlfriend shot in chest, neck, abdomen, according to audio. *USA Today*. Retrieved from https://www.usatoday.com/story/sports/nfl/2012/12/04/jovan-belcher-audio-first-responders/1746603/

Vendel, C. (2012, December 4). Exclusive: Police reports detail Belcher, Perkins' last hours. *The Kansas City Star*. Retrieved from http://www.kansascity.com/news/local/article311755.html

Wilson, R. (2015, April 22). Judge approves concussion settlement, could cost NFL $1 billion. *CBS Sports*. Retrieved from https://www.cbssports.com/nfl/news/judge-approves-concussion-settlement-could-cost-nfl-1-billion/

Zucker, J. (2017, August 7). NFL settles with 6 insurance companies over concussion lawsuit expenses. *Bleacher Report*. Retrieved from http://bleacherreport.com/articles/2726106-nfl-settles-with-6-insurance-companies-over-concussion-lawsuit-expenses

Chapter 4
International Sport Business and Global Sport Governance

Efthalia Chatzigianni
University of Peloponnese, Greece

ABSTRACT

The purpose of this chapter is to introduce some fundamental concepts and principles that are associated with modern sport business in the framework of international organization and global governance. In the opening section, a discussion on terms related to the international organization and governance of sport and sport business will be presented along with relevant issues that have emerged in the modern international sport context. Then, an overview of sport business activity in the field of global sport will take place, followed by a brief presentation of several aspects of contemporary sport business in order to demonstrate the diversity and importance of international sport business stakeholders to contemporary global sport. Topics include corporate sponsorship, media and social media, and information and communication technology. The chapter will conclude with a discussion about the impact of modern sport business on global sport governance as the main goal of this chapter is to convey the message and highlight aspects of the significant impact of international sport business activity on the global governance of sport.

INTERNATIONAL SPORT BUSINESS AND GLOBAL SPORT GOVERNANCE

Fundamental Topics and Principles

There are continuing debates about how various concepts are defined and concepts within the sport world are no different. Even the term 'sport' has various definitions (Trenberth & Collins, 1999, p. 13), with the most prominent one given by the Council of Europe's European Sports Charter (1992) where:

DOI: 10.4018/978-1-5225-5387-8.ch004

sport means all forms of physical activity which, through casual or organized participation, aims at improving physical fitness and mental well-being, forming social relationships, or obtaining results in competitions at all levels.

Given that sport as an organized activity appears in the late nineteenth century, this definition of sport in the present chapter is viewed within the spectrum of the complex interaction of economic, social, legal, technological, and cultural factors (Wolfe, Meenaghan, & O' Sullivan, 2002).

Sport business must be studied in relation to globalization and global governance. For the purpose of the present chapter, globalization will be defined as:

a process through which space and time are compressed by technology, information flows, and trade and power relations, allowing distant actions to have increased significance at the local level. (Miller, Lawrence, McKay, & Rowe, 2001, p. 131)

Several forces from all spheres of human activity have been attributed to the increasing globalization in general and to the globalization of sport in particular (Andrews & Grainger, 2007; Thibault, 2009; Chatzigianni, 2017, 2018). That said, it can be argued that features of globalization such as technological development, economic liberalization, the breakdown of economic frontiers, and the availability of large amounts of venture capital allow, among other, unprecedented, and in many aspects, equal access to information technology and training techniques and programs, the expansion of domestic leagues and sport events, the capitalization of sport programs through exports and imports, the multiplication and diversification of sport stakeholders and the overall tendency for conducting business in the sport industry (Westerbeek, 2011). In this framework, Thibault (2012) provides a number of examples related to the forces that contribute to the increasing globalization of sport such as: economic forces which are responsible for the significant amount of money invested on professional and amateur sport as the hosting of sport events and sport competitions and related sport infrastructures around the world require the creation of a large number of jobs; social forces refer to the development of underprivileged regions worldwide through programs such as the International Platform for Development and Peace, and the Right to Play; technological forces that through the development of media; and communication technologies have made sport competitions accessible to people around the world and political forces which are related to the governance of sport at various levels.

The definition of a multinational (MNC) or transnational corporation (TNC) has also been a topic of debate among scholars (Judge, 1978; Archer, 2001). Regardless of whether they could be defined as international organizations, the present chapter agrees with Wells' argument that multinational companies *are clearly important international actors* (Wells, 1971, p. 113). Moreover, in this framework, Archer (2001) considers the creation and activity of multi-national companies as an indispensable part of the post-war international non-governmental organization as they are important international actors; he further notes that, in some cases, multinational companies make a fourth category of Transnational Organizations that consist of the business inter-national non-governmental organizations (BINGOs), also called multinational enterprises or corporations (MNEs or MNCs). As Archer (2001, p. 27) also points out that:

...The creation of a near-global economy in the post-war years has gone hand-in-hand with the extension of another form of non-governmental activity across frontiers – the multinational or transnational corporation. Such firms have been partly responsible for scientific and technical achievements and the internationalization of economic factors, but they have also been encouraged by the more general trend in this direction....

The participation and impact of the MNCs on global governance in the framework of globalization whether as a subject to the regulatory impact of international organizations, their participation on agenda-setting in terms of global regulation or their characteristics as a factor of global governance, have also been a topic of research among scholars (May, 2015). The term *governance* has various definitions in modern literature and its current significance to contemporary society results from a multidimensional interplay of the same factors as society, economy, culture, law, and technology pave the way to modern governance. Some authors use 'governance' as a synonymous to 'government' (Weiss, 2000, p. 795) when others, academics and international practitioners, use it in order, *to connote a complex set of structures and processes, both public and private* (Weiss, 2000, p. 795). While it has also been argued that academics are equally responsible for the confusion in the meaning of the term because its use in their writings varies (Dingwerth & Pattberg, 2006, p. 188), the definition of governance as a notion that encompasses self-regulation mechanisms of civil society, the authoritative power (regulation) of governments, and the co-regulation of public and private actors (Scholte, 2004) seems to be the most adequate in the current global governance context.

According to the Commission on Global Governance (Report, 1995, p. 1);

Governance is the sum of the many ways individuals and institutions, public and private, manage their common affairs. It is a continuing process through which conflicting or diverse interests may be accommodated and cooperative action may be taken. It includes formal institutions and regimes empowered to enforce compliance, as well as informal arrangements that people and institutions either have agreed to or perceive to be in their interest... At the global level, governance has been viewed primarily as inter- governmental relationships, but it must now be understood as also involving non-governmental organizations (NGOs), citizens' movements, multinational corporations, and the global capital market. Interacting with these entities are global mass media of dramatically enlarged influence.

In accordance with the above definitions, this text will adopt the following definitions of global sport governance which distinguish between traditional and modern global sport governance as a result of the effects of globalization and contemporary international organization on sport governance at a global level (Chatzigianni, 2017; 2018):

Traditional sport governance is defined as the process that is established on the structures and activity of the global sport governing bodies while modern sport governance is defined as the plethora of actors that participate in the international sport related policy-making and implementation system as a result of globalization.

The actors that participate in modern global sport governance have as follows (Chatzigianni, 2017; 2018):

- Traditional global sport governing bodies and their respective networks, such as the International Olympic Committee (IOC), the Fédération Internationale de Football (FIFA), etc.;
- International Intergovernmental Organizations, such as the United Nations, the European Union, the Council of Europe, and Regional Intergovernmental Organizations;
- Transnational Corporations;
- Media Corporations and Organizations;
- The modern regulators of sport, that is the Court for Arbitration for Sport (CAS) and the World Anti-Doping Agency (WADA) and;
- Civil Society Associations and Experts.

As one may see from the above classification, sport related business is directly represented in two of the categories, the transnational corporations and media corporations and organizations, even though they undoubtedly play a significant role in the other categories too, mainly as sponsors or in the framework of corporate social responsibility (CSR) activities.

In the following sections of this book chapter, some aspects of the impact of sport business activity at a global level will be discussed so as to demonstrate the evolving diversity and developing influence of contemporary business interests in the field of sport and its significance to global sport governance as a system which is responsible for the management of global sport activity in the framework of international organization.

SPORT BUSINESS IN THE GLOBAL CONTEXT

The process of globalization has had a great impact on sport activity (Chatzigianni, 2014; 2017; 2018; Thibault, 2009, 2012, Slack, 2003, Westerbeek, 2011). The rapid commercialization as well as technology and media development have influenced sport to the degree that nowadays, there is a well-established inseparable connection between sport and business. This connection is evident undoubtedly, in various sectors of sport business such as in sport sponsorship, in the development of sport industry, in amateur sport commercialization, in the relationship and interdependence between media and sport, and in the interaction between the public sector, and a significant number of sport organizations (Slack, 2003).

Contemporary sport is an important social activity that encompasses a great number of sport related activities that range from mass, amateur and sport for all sport, to elite, high level and professional sport. Sport is influenced by all the developments which characterize our society and derive from globalization. Consequently, modern sport has many functions: while as a physical activity it may serve as a cultural, educational, health, humanistic even political tool, it is also a multi-millionaire business and sophisticated industry. Modern sport is not just a game; it is a serious economic construction that extends well beyond the line of merchandising sales and season ticket sales for the various sport events.

Statistics prove the argument that, sport is a dynamic, developing industry around the globe. The global sports market which generated revenue of $46.5 billion in 2005 is expected to reach by the end of 2017 the amount of $90.9 billion (Statista, 2017). In the European Union, sport industry accounts for 1.76% of the EU Gross Value Added (173.86 billion euros) and 2.12% of the labour market (EU4Sports, 2014), when in North America, the sports market, which had a worth of $60.5 billion in 2014, is expected to reach $73.5 billion by 2019 (Heitner, 2015).

In relation to the definition of sport as a business activity, one may refer to the European Commission Statistical Classification of Products by Activity (CPA) (European Commission, 2008), to define sport as:

the sum of sporting services as defined in the system of national accounts (statistical definition) plus all products and services which are necessary as inputs for (doing) sport ("to produce sport as an output"- narrow definition) and all products and services which have a (direct or indirect) relation to any sport activity but without being necessary to do sport ("which draw upon sport as an input" – broad definition).

Pitts, Fielding and Miller (1991) define sport industry as the market in which, *the products offered to its buyers are fitness, sport, recreation, and leisure related. These products include goods, services, people, places, and ideas.* In this framework, sport industry products may include goods and services, for example, from the fitness and health sectors, the recreation and leisure sectors, the tourism sector, professional sport, etc.

The sport industry is comprised of a number of segments. A sport industry segment is a combination of a sport product variety (or varieties) and a group of consumers who buy this product. In general, according to Porter (1985, p. 233), sport industry consists of the following segments (Pitts, Fielding & Miller, 1994):

1. **Sport Performance Segment:** It refers to both kinds of buyers of sport performance, participants and fans. It includes amateur and professional sport, private and public funded sport, not-for-profit organizations, fitness and health firms, and sport education.
2. **Sport Production Segment:** It comprises products required or, even, desired to the production or influence of sport performance (including fitness performance). These products are or may be used by sport governing bodies and officials, sport medical specialists, fitness trainers, or sport facility management.
3. **Sport Promotion Segment:** It includes products that are used to promote sport industry products. This segment refers to sponsorship, sport media complex, sport endorsement and promotional merchandising products such as t-shirts, caps, jackets etc.

Given the above it is evident that the sport industry covers all aspects of sport activity, whether professional or amateur. Furthermore, one of the most significant components of the global sport system is the development of transnational sports industries such as Nike Inc, Adidas, and Reebok which produce a variety of sports products including clothing, equipment, and footwear (Maguire, 1999). Their products are consumed by a vast number of people around the world, whilst their activity has direct or indirect effects to the rural and urban landscapes of the countries as well as to national and international sport governance (Chatzigianni, 2017; 2018). Additionally, nowadays, famous athletes, such as David Beckham (football – retired in 2013), James LeBron (basketball – NBA), Tiger Woods[1] (golf) and Kobe Bryant[2] (basketball, NBA – retired in 2016), are also important business people with significant commercial, social and cultural influence and value at global level.

In many aspects, the globalization of sport is linked to the globalization of sport industry and the opposite. A good example is given by the activity of Nike. As its general manager said in 1994 (cited in Katz, 1995, p. 191): *The globalization of Nike will certainly continue in part because Global has become a Nike state of mind....*

As previously noted, two of the basic actors in the global sport governance scheme are transnational corporations and media corporations and organizations. Both of these categories reflect significant sport business interests. The following sport business sectors are selected to be presented in brief within the scope of the present chapter as evidence of the diversification and evolving multiplication of business interests in the field of global sport governance: corporate sponsorship, media and social media, and information and communication technology.

Sport and Corporate Sponsorship

Corporate sponsorship has been defined as the support which is provided to several events with the purpose of achieving particular objectives (Shuman, 1986; Garner & Shuman, 1988). The particular objectives underlying the sponsorship are related, mainly, to the creation, maintenance, or reposition of the corporate image, the generation of sales revenue, the provision of community support or the recognition of corporate responsibility (Kuzma & Shanklin, 1994) as well as the gain of direct media access, the targeting of a specific segment of the population, the entertainment of corporate clients, the satisfaction of the personal interests of a business executive and the construction of political links with politicians and other business leaders (Slack & Annis, 2004).

The first modern Olympic Games held in Athens in 1896 had the support of a small number of sponsors, such as Kodak. The 1984 Los Angeles Games marked a new era for Olympic and, in general, sport sponsorship. Cousens and Slack (2005) note that in the 1980's, sport organizations and corporations started to look to establish more stable and enduring relationships between them, and in many cases form strategic alliances, as means to strengthen their image, to further develop their relationships with consumers and benefit from each other's strategic objectives. A few examples include, the multi-million dollar partnership between Manchester United and US Aon Corporation, a risk adviser and human capital consultant, which runs until 2021 (Joy, 2013); the strategic alliance between The Sport Network (TSN) and Contec Innovations, a mobile media company that provides live news, sports finance and entertainment, to work together in order to produce real-time mobile value-added services for properties including the English Premier League to the National Basketball Association (NBA), Major League Baseball (MLB), National Football League (NFL), and National Hockey League (NHL) (Entertainment Newsweekly,

2008) in emerging markets starting with China and Southeast Asia; and the Reebok International (RBK) and NFL strategic alliance for licensed apparel (Hecox, 2007).

Today, a significant number of sport competitions have the names of their sponsors included in their titles such as Barclay's Premier League - Football, Heineken Cup - Rugby Union and many stadia have sponsored names such as Emirate's Stadium - Arsenal, Etihad Stadium - City of Manchester, and RICOH Arena – Coventry.

Sport sponsorship has both, positive and negative impact to sport business. On the positive side, through sponsorship, sport organizations can improve not only their media exposure and publicity but also their revenues. On the other hand, given the – frequently - major commercial investments of sponsors on sport, sponsors acquire significant control of major sport events as well as of sport organizations' governance, especially in the case of elite sport. As a result, the gap between voluntary sport and professional sport increases as well as the gap between minor and major sports. This contributes to a further commercialization of modern sport as one of the most significant characteristics of international modern sport organization.

Sport and the Media

Media is defined as:

the forms of communication that are designed to inform and educate the public about issues of relevance and importance to society, and also to entertain them.

Even though the broadcasting sector is part of the media it is also different from it and can be defined as, *the transmission of information and entertainment, via television, radio or internet, which is deemed to be of interest or relevance to society* (Byers, Slack, & Parent, 2012: p. 98).

For the past few years, sport media and sport broadcasting have had a remarkable impact on sport activity. Their effects are evident on every aspect of sport management and governance as well as the representation and perception of sport as a social phenomenon. The development of sport into the powerful commercial product that it is today is attributed to the revenue streams that are created by the interest of broadcasters in sport as a product of mass production (Byers, Slack, & Parent, 2012). Szymanski notes that the opposite is also valid: broadcasting has influenced sport but broadcasting has also been influenced by the 'potential of sports' (2006, p. 428). Similarly, Rowe (2009) also agrees with the significant role of media to the rapid sport commercialization but argues that *a reform of the media on grounds of sporting and social equity* is deemed necessary.

The inclusion of media in the category of powerful sport stakeholders in global sport governance is also examined by Wolfe et al. (2002). Using the network theory, the researchers discuss the power relationships between national governing bodies, corporate sponsors and the media and their implications on the management of commercialization, as a result of broadcaster stakeholders' activity, by sport organizations.

Even though the adoption of a number of codes of conducts by a number of international and national sport governing bodies, such as the International Olympic Committee (the IOC Code of Ethics), the United Nations Educational, Scientific and Cultural Organization (UNESCO Code of Sport Ethics), the National Basketball Association (NBA Fan Code of Conduct), and the Fédération Internationale de Football (FIFA Code of Ethics) has taken place as a response to the increase of unethical actions within the sport world, it seems that media and around the clock coverage of sport events and competitions play an equally important role to the disrepute of unethical actions in sport (Lumpkin, 2017).

It must be noted that, the greater exposure a sport, sport club or sport competition has through the media, the more powerful its governing body is at a national and global level. For example, the most popular football clubs in the Premier League enjoy for some time now wealth as well as political superiority in the field of sport in the UK (Stead, 2008) while the Premier League is considered to be the most powerful league in the world as a result of its media exposure, global audience and sponsorship appeal (lPilger, 2014).

The Use of Social Media

The use of social media in sport has had a significant impact on sport organizations. Even though the Internet is a major asset to sport organizations, it may also pose serious threats. Especially in relation to sport governance, the Internet makes connections with stakeholders much easier and transparent, and the operation of the sport organization accessible to the majority of key stakeholders; at the same time, though, it may create issues related, among other, to the management of organizational image, uncontrolled dissemination of information, personal exposure and violation of individual privacy, and ethical discrepancies. In this framework, as Layden notes (2003), a constant monitoring of the Internet and social media by the sport organizations themselves, in general, is required.

Furthermore, the last two decades have witnessed a significant change in the landscape of sport sponsorship as the appearance of social media has contributed to the increase of social consciousness among sport consumers (Cousens & Bradish, 2012). Consequently, sport provides the most evident arena for the promotion of social causes through partnership programs and corporate social responsibility programs in the area of a number of sport initiatives such as the 'Right to Play' (formerly known as Olympic Aid) which operates under the umbrella of 'Sport for Development and Peace' and aims to use sport as a tool for the development of the less advantaged associations and communities, the program of the National Basketball Association's 'NBA Cares', which promotes global cooperation for key social issues and the 'Football for Hope', an initiative established by FIFA which aims to contribute to social development globally.

Information and Communication Technology and Sport eBusiness

Information and communication technology have become an indispensable part of current sport business reality. Given that the Internet, as *a cooperative community of networks* (O' Beirne, 2012, p. 343) represents the most significant business instrument of our times, its use in the sport sector either as a communication tool by sport organizations or as a medium for successful eBusiness along with the use of management information systems and information technology has rendered eBusiness as one of the most important stakeholders of modern global sport governance. Furthermore, as globalization advances, the impact of technology on sport also advances. Interactive TV, ePublishing, electronic paper and mobile commerce are a few of the issues that are expected to have a major impact on sport and the way sport permeate daily life at a global level (O' Beirne, 2012).

Ebusiness is defined as *every type of business transaction or interaction in which the participants prepare or conduct business electronically* (Talha & Subramaniam, 2003). O' Beirne (2012) has identified the following three categories as the major categories in the field of sport eBusiness:

- Delivery of content of eMarketing sport and commercial sport by profit oriented sport organizations;
- Applications within sport organizations that aim to contribute to the education, training and coaching of athletes. These applications may include tools for observing and managing team performance, and;
- Delivery of contents and services to stakeholders and members of not – for – profit sport organizations.

Additionally, sport organizations may use the Internet as means to promote their community relations, and often to promote their organization's good works. For example, the NFL's New York Giants have established a fan registry on their website that the team and its fans use a means for social networking (Migala, 2000). Furthermore, Nike (www.nike.com), which has faced brand image issues in the past as a result of its labour corporate practices, features a section in its website with the title 'Nike Responsibility' in order to demonstrate to the global community its initiatives in the areas of sustainable and environmental practices and community investment social programs, as part of its corporate responsibility program.

THE IMPACT OF SPORT BUSINESS ACTIVITY ON GLOBAL SPORT GOVERNANCE

It is evident from the above that, as a result of globalization and technological development, sport business activity is multi-faceted and has a significant impact on most aspects of human life at a global level. Consequently, a plethora of modern business interests have emerged as significant players in the field of global sport. Furthermore, sport related MNCs have become part of the global sport culture and they function as a key stakeholder of global sport governance where responsibility in sport governance issues is shared among the traditional sport governing bodies and the mixture of institutions which participate in the modern global sport governance scheme. Whether evident or not, their activity has a direct or indirect impact on global sport governance.

First, they have a significant influence in the field of sport international organization and the decision-making processes within international organizations that are active in the field of sport, including sport governing bodies. As major sponsors of the majority of sport related activities, sport business represents a major economic opportunity for investors and broadcasters on the one hand, but they also can have a significant impact on less privileged communities as part of their not-for-profit programs.

Furthermore, in the case of the European Union, sport business is active in a number of policy areas that are related to sport. Given the huge economic and social impact of sport in the European Union and the significance of European sport to global sport, sport business' representatives try to influence intensely European sport related policy making and implementation. Whether in relation to the economic, social or cultural impact of sport on European people, sport business direct and/or indirect lobbying activity, of low or high level, is evident in all stages of European policy-making and implementation processes as the consultation process for the Commission White Paper for Sport (2007) has shown (Chatzigianni, 2010; 2014). The diversification of sport interests and their impact on European policy-making is also evident in the following two examples: first, in the lobbying activity exerted in the framework of EU – China trade negotiations by sport-related interests such as the European Sporting Goods Industry (FESI, created in the 1960s). FESI represents the interests of import-dependent footwear firms in the EU and participates in lobbying activities so as to promote the interests of its members (Eckhardt, 2015). Its members include a number of big European sport shoe producers such as Adidas, Fila, Asics, Diadora, Reebok and Puma. Another example is related to the current exit negotiations of Great Britain from the EU. Given the major impact that the upcoming Brexit will have on sport; sport – related interests exert significant lobbying activity in the framework of European and British institutions[3]. It is worth noting here, that among the most prominent represented interests in this process are the ones that are associated with the Premier League as the League is expected to be significantly influenced by the Brexit (Schofield & Criddle, 2015).

Second, sport business has a significant impact on the 'globalization' of the governance of traditional sport governing bodies, through their increasing demands on the issues of transparency and accountability within sport organizations (Chatzigianni, 2017; 2018). It must be noted that the notion of 'good governance' has also been introduced with the new millennium in the governance debate in relation to sport. Bevir notes that with the term 'good governance' one may refer either to the view of the World Bank that considers good governance as a strategy for development or the definition provided by the United Nations Development Program (UNDP) which focuses on socio-political issues and includes the following items: equality of participation in decision-making, responsiveness to stakeholders, attempts to secure a broad consensus, accountability to stakeholders, transparency in decision-making, the rule of law, the productive use of resources, and guaranteed rights (2009, p. 93). The current discussion associated with good governance in global sport, derives from the second definition as the following two significant examples demonstrate:

1. In the end of the previous millennium, IOC officials were accused of bribery during the 2002 bidding process who voted in favor of Salt Lake City to win the rights to host the 2002 Winter Olympic Games; what is known since then as the '2002 Salt Lake City bid scandal.' Developments that have taken place since the scandal have required an intense action from the IOC in terms, among other, of democratization, accountability, equal representation in decision making processes, and response to stakeholders. It is important to note that a significant number of MNCs which were also Olympic sponsors, were among those who asked for investigation on the scandal or else they would withdraw their support (Dichter & Kidd, 2012).
2. Fraud accusations against FIFA officials in the period 2014-2015 have led to the following:
    a. **To Legal Intervention:** From state authorities from at least two countries (USA, Switzerland) in FIFA operational procedures. In this case, charges against fourteen FIFA officials were pressed, including seven arrests;

b. **To Sponsorship Intervention:** In FIFA presidential elections following a period of corruption and bribery allegations against FIFA. In this case, the previous FIFA President, Sepp Blatter, even though re-elected for the fifth time in May 2015, was forced to quit. Blatter was further suspended from football related activities for a period of six years (The Guardian, 2015).
c. **To Sponsorship Pressure:** Exerted, among other, by *World Cup sponsors*, to the Congress of the football global sport governing body to tackle the corruption allegations. It is worth noting that World Cup sponsors include Budweiser, BP, Visa, Sony, Adidas and Coca Cola (The Guardian, 2014).

Consequently, one may assume that in the framework of globalization, the application of 'good governance' principles in the operation of sport governing bodies are nowadays a prerequisite for the MNCs to invest through sponsorships and strategic alliances in their activity. Even more so, it is apparent that the management of contemporary sport stakeholders and their expectations require a flexible and transparent management framework of international sporting events.

Additional challenges that contemporary sport world has to meet are related to the respect and promotion of ethical human values. Given the central role that sport plays in society, the ethical significances of these challenges have a major value to a significant portion of humanity. Whether amateur or professional, sport can serve both, positive and negative social functions, depending on the occasions and circumstances. Similarly, business interests that are associated with sport may promote or undermine ethical human values depending on the features and the requirements of their activity at a given moment and time. Plus, it is evident that MNCs have a major power to further promote positive human values around the world with the adoption of specifically targeted corporate sport related sponsorship programs.

To conclude, sport business consists an indispensable part of contemporary sport reality. First, sport business provides the means to promote cooperation and partnership through sport around the world; second, it facilitates the communication process between traditional sport governing bodies such as the IOC and sport stakeholders at a global level, including sport fans and spectators; and, third, it can further promote transparency and enhance good governance in the field of global sport organization.

Additionally, the present chapter suggests that contemporary sport business has assumed a central role not only in the exploitation of the sport product, the practice and performance of athletes, and the organization of sport events but also in the redistribution of influence and power among sport stakeholders at a global level.

REFERENCES

Andrews, D. L., & Grainger, A. D. (2007). Sport and globalization. In G. Ritzer (Ed.), *The Blackwell companion to globalization* (pp. 478–497). Malden, MA: Blackwell Publishing.

Archer, C. (2001). *International Organizations* (3rd ed.). London: Routledge. doi:10.4324/9780203192276

Bevir, M. (2009). *Key Concepts in Governance*. London: SAGE Publications Ltd.

Byers, T., Slack, T., & Parent, M. (2012). *Key Concepts in Sport Management*. Thousand Oaks, CA: SAGE Publications. doi:10.4135/9781473914599

Chatzigianni, E. (2014). Pluralism and Corporatism in Sport Interest Representation. *International Journal of Sport Policy and Politics*, *6*(1), 19–36. doi:10.1080/19406940.2012.694114

Chatzigianni, E. (2017). Global Sport Governance: Globalizing the Globalized. *Sport in Society*, 1–29. doi:10.1080/17430437.2017.1390566

Chatzigianni, E. (2018). *Sport Governance. Globalization, International Organization, Politics*. Athens: Sideris. (in Greek)

Commission on Global Governance (Report). (1995). *Our Global Neighborhood. Report on Global Governance*. Retrieved 10 January, 2018 from http://www.gdrc.org/u-gov/global-neighbourhood/chap1.htm

Cousens, L., & Bradish, C. (2012). Sport and Sponsorship. In L. Trenberth & D. Hassan (Eds.), *Managing Sport Business: An Introduction* (pp. 264–284). London: Routledge.

Cousens, L., & Slack, T. (2005). Field-level change: The case of North American major league professional sport. *Journal of Sport Management*, *19*(1), 13–42. doi:10.1123/jsm.19.1.13

Dichter, H., & Kidd, B. (Eds.). (2012). *Olympic Reform Ten Years Later*. London: Routledge.

Dingwerth, K. & Pattberg, P. (2006). Global Governance as a Perspective on World Politics. *Global Governance: A Review of Multilateralism and International Organizations*, *12*(2), 185-203.

EU4Sports Cluster Alliance. (2014). *Guide on EU funding for sports industry*. Retrieved November 15, 2017 from https://www.clustercollaboration.eu/sites/default/files/profile-article/guide_on_eu_funding_for_sports_industry_2014_-2020_.pdf

Eckhardt, J. (2015). *Business Lobbying and Trade Governance, The Case of EU - China Relations*. Houndmills, UK: Palgrave MacMillan. doi:10.1057/9781137325440

Entertainment Newsweekly (2008). *The Sports Network extends global reach in alliance with Contec Innovations, 18, 11 August*. Author.

European Commission. (2008). *Definition of Sport (Vilnius Definition 2.0 – Version 2) according to CPA 2008*. Retrieved December 2, 2017 from http://ec.europa.eu/eurostat/documents/6921402/0/Vilnius+Definition+Sport+CPA2008+official+2013_09_19.pdf/30838d11-01ea-431f-8112-50786e187c1c

Garner, M. P., & Shuman, P. J. (1988). Sponsorships and small businesses: Conceptual, strategic, and tactical issues. *Journal of Small Business Management*, *26*(4), 44–52.

Hecox, M. G. (2007). Strategic Alliances in the Sport Industry: A Case Review of Reebok International and the NFL. In B. G. Pitts (Ed.), *Sport Marketing in the New Millennium: Selected Papers from the Third Annual Conference of the Sport Marketing Association*. Morgantown, WV: Fitness Information Technology.

Heitner, D. (2015). *Sports Industry to reach $73.5 billion by 2019*. Retrieved November 30, 2017 from https://www.forbes.com/sites/darrenheitner/2015/10/19/sports-industry-to-reach-73-5-billion-by-2019/#33823291b4b9

Joy, O. (2013). Manchester United pen new multi-million dollar deal. *CNN Sport*. Retrieved July 30, 2017 from http://edition.cnn.com/2013/04/08/business/manchester-united-aon-deal/index.html

Judge, A. J. N. (1978). International Institutions: Diversity, Borderline Case, Functional Substitutes and Possible Alternatives. In P. Taylor & A. J. Groom (Eds.), *International Organization* (pp. 28–83). London: Frances Pinter.

Katz, D. R. (1995). *Just Do It. The Nike Spirit in the Corporate World*. Adams Media Corporation - Random House, Inc.

Kuzma, J., & Shanklin, W. (1994). Corporate Sponsorship: A framework for Analysis. In P. J. Graham (Ed.), *Sport Business: Operational and Theoretical Aspects*. Madison, WI: Brown and Benchmark.

Layden, T. (2003). Caught in the net. *Sports Illustrated*, *98*, 46–50.

Lumpkin, A. (2017). *Modern Sport Ethics: A Reference Handbook* (2nd ed.). Santa Barbara, CA: ABC-CLIO.

Maguire, J. A. (1999). *Global sport: Identities, societies, civilizations*. Cambridge, UK: Polity Press.

May, C. (2015). Who's in charge? Corporations as Institutions of Global Governance. *Palgrave Communications, 1*.

Migala, D. (2000). Remember these 5 Cs to make your content shine. *Sport Business Daily Global Journal*. Retrieved January 9, 2018 from http://www.sportsbusinessdaily.com/Journal/Issues/2000/07/20000717/No-Topic-Name/Remember-These-5-C146s-To-Make-Your-Content-Shine.aspx

Miller, T., Lawrence, G., McKay, J., & Rowe, D. (2001). *Globalization and Sport: Playing the World*. London: SAGE.

O' Beirne, C. (2012). Information and Communications Technology and its Use in Sport Business. In L. Trenberth & D. Hassan (Eds.), *Managing Sport Business: An Introduction* (pp. 338–349). London: Routledge.

Pilger, S. (2014). Why the Premier League is the most powerful league in the World. *Bleacher Report Football*. Retrieved March 2, 2018 from http://bleacherreport.com/articles/1948434-why-the-premier-league-is-the-most-powerful-league-in-the-world

Pitts, B. G., Fielding, L. W., & Miller, L. K. (1991, June). *Sport Product-markets: A Conceptual Model*. Paper presented at the Conference of the North American Society for Sport Management, Ottawa, Canada.

Pitts, B. G., Fielding, L. W., & Miller, L. K. (1994). Industry Segmentation Theory and the Sport Industry: Developing a Sport Industry Segment Model. *Sport Marketing Quarterly, 3*(1), 15–24.

Porter, M. E. (1985). *Competitive Advantage: Creating and Sustaining Superior Performance*. New York, NY: The Free Press.

Rowe, D. (2009). Media and Sport: The Cultural Dynamics of Global Games. *Sociology Compass, 3*(4), 543–558. doi:10.1111/j.1751-9020.2009.00225.x

Schofield, D., & Criddle, C. (2015, 24 June). Brexit wins: How will British sport be affected? *The Telegraph*. Retrieved on March,2 from https://www.telegraph.co.uk/sport/.../how-would-british-sport-be-affected-by-a-brexit/

Scholte, J. A. (2004). Civil Society and Democratically Accountable Global Governance. *Government and Opposition, 39*(2), 211–233. doi:10.1111/j.1477-7053.2004.00121.x

Shuman, P. J. (1986). *The Power of Perceptual Marketing: An Analysis of Sponsorships*. New York: Burson-Marsteller.

Slack, T. (Ed.). (2003). *The Globalization of Sport*. London: Frank Cass.

Slack, T., & Annis, J. (2004). Money for Nothing and your Cheques for Free? In T. Slack (Ed.), *The Commercialization of Sport*. New York, NY: Routledge.

Statista. (2017). *Global Sports Market - Total Revenue from 2005 to 2017 (in billion U.S. dollars)*. Retrieved December 3, 2017, from https://www.statista.com/statistics/370560/worldwide-sports-market-revenue/

Stead, D. (2008). Sport and the Media. In B. Houlihan (Ed.), *Sport and Society* (pp. 328–347). London: Sage Publications.

Szymanski, S. (2006). The Economic Evolution of Sport and Broadcasting. *The Australian Economic Review*, *39*(4), 428–434. doi:10.1111/j.1467-8462.2006.00432.x

Talha, M., & Subramaniam, M. (2003). Role of e-Commerce in Economic Growth. *Journal of Internet Marketing*, *4*(1), 1–7.

The Guardian. (2014). *Sepp Baltter Bemoans a Storm against FIFA over Qatar World Cup*. Retrieved January 7, 2018 from https://www.theguardian.com/football/2014/jun/09/sepp-blatter-storm-fifa-qatar

The Guardian. (2015). *Sepp Blatter re-elected as FIFA President for the fifth time*. Retrieved on January 8, 2018 from https://www.theguardian.com/football/2015/may/29/sepp-blatter-reelected-fifa-president-fifth-term

Thibault, J. (2009). Globalization of Sport: An Inconvenient Truth. *Journal of Sport Management*, *23*(1), 1–20. doi:10.1123/jsm.23.1.1

Thibault, L. (2012). Delivering Sport in the Global Context. In L. Trenberth & D. Hassan (Eds.), *Managing Sport Business* (pp. 231–257). London: Routledge.

Weiss, T. G. (2000). Governance, Good Governance and Global Governance. *Third World Quarterly*, *21*(5), 795–814. doi:10.1080/713701075

Wells, L. J. (1971). The Multinational Business Enterprise: What Kind of International Organization? In R. O. Keohane & J. S. Nye (Eds.), *Transnational Relations and World Politics* (pp. 97–114). Cambridge, MA: Harvard University Press. doi:10.1017/S0020818300026254

Westerbeek, H. (Ed.). (2011). *Global Sport Business: Community Impacts of Commercial Sport*. London: Routledge.

Wolfe, R., Meenaghan, T., & O' Sullivan, P. (2002). The Sports Network: Insights into the Shifting Balance of Power. *Journal of Business Research*, *55*(7), 611–622. doi:10.1016/S0148-2963(00)00191-0

ENDNOTES

1 According to Forbes (December, 23, 2016), Tiger Woods' net worth in 2016 was $740 million. Retrieved on March 1, 2018 from http://forbes.com

2 Kobe Bryant even won an Oscar in 2018 at the 90th Academy Awards for *Dear Basketball* in the category for the Best Animated Short film. Retrieved on March 5, 2018 from www.oscar.go.com

3 See for example, *Brexit Analysis Bulletin Sports* (2016), Shepherd and Wedderburn LLP. Retrieved March 2, 2018 from https://shepwedd.com/sites/default/files/Brexit_Analysis_Bulletin_Sports.pdf

Chapter 5
The Legal Validity of E-Sports as a Sport

Reyhan Mir
Independent Researcher, Spain

ABSTRACT

The chapter aims to investigate the e-sports phenomenon and analyze its legal relevance and validity with the traditional sports world. The chapter looks to provide the current framework of the e-sports field and its potential to be a sport, followed by the legal challenges it faces towards being possibly recognized as one. The second segment of this chapter additionally looks into the regulations currently in place as well as analyzes the minimum changes required in order to ensure the growth of this field. The chapter eventually concludes by analyzing the possible future for the field and suggestions to help facilitate its development.

INTRODUCTION

In general, it takes an activity about 50 years to be recognized as a sport by society, taking note that professional gaming tournaments began in the 1970's, the professional gaming industry is near achieving that 50 year milestone (Taylor, 2012). Considering its rapid growth and development over the past few years as well as the ever increasing reliance of society on technology, it is evident that the question of whether esports can be considered as a sport is a major topic for present as well as future discussion.

The traditional perspective of sport is that it would be an activity involving a form of physical exertion while also involving a social element. The development and advancement of technology and consequently esports has lead this conventional concept to be challenged. Over the past few years, there have been numerous articles

DOI: 10.4018/978-1-5225-5387-8.ch005

and perspectives put forward proclaiming esports as the sport of the new generation (Stubbs, 2017; Young, 2016). Such arguments have naturally caused controversy and debate as to whether esports can legitimately be termed as a sport. The numbers for the industry have been astronomical and have displayed an unprecedented growth rate with major endemic and non-endemic brands entering the field to provide sponsorships as well as major investors from traditional sports investing in various aspects of the industry.

The following chapter aims to investigate this phenomenon and analyse its legal relevance and validity with the traditional sports world. The chapter looks to provide the current framework of the esports field and its potential to be a sport, followed by the legal challenges it faces towards being possibly recognised as one. The second segment of this chapter would additionally look into the regulations currently in place as well as analyse the minimum changes required in order to ensure the growth of this field. Eventually the chapter would conclude with the possible future for the field and suggestions to help facilitate its development.

BRIEF INTRODUCTION INTO THE ESPORTS INDUSTRY

Esports (Darcy, 2017) is the term given to a select group of competitive videogames which are selected on the basis of their popularity and ability to incorporate multiplayer game play. Among others, the conventionally popular games have included League of Legends (LoL), StarCraft 2, Counter-Strike: Global Offensive (CS:GO) and the comparatively recent Overwatch.

Each of these games are governed by their respective developers such as Riot for LoL or Valve for CS:GO. Due to this setup, there are no universal regulations for all esports and it is usually dependent on the game publisher or particular tournament organiser to establish their preferred regulations. Therefore, it would be useful to provide a basic framework of the industry to provide clarity further into the chapter.

The monopoly of the industry resides with the game publishers and secondarily with the tournament organisers. Unlike other sports such as the International Tennis Federation for tennis, there is no overarching governing body for all esports which has lead to a lack of standardisation in governing the esports system with each esports title having its own set of rules and regulations. The game publishers such as Activision Blizzard, Riot and Valve can organise tournaments featuring their own games. In contrast, tournament organisers such as the Electronic Sports League (ESL), DreamHack and Gfinity would have to obtain licenses from the publishers to host tournaments featuring these games.

In May 2016, due to the evident lack of player and team influence, the ESL alongside various other esports teams formed another organisation called the World Electronic Sports Association (WESA) with the aim of providing player representation, standardising regulations and revenue sharing between teams. The effectiveness of this initiative has however been limited as the teams are mainly based in CS:GO and do not have sufficient influence in other games. Within the same context, Riot games themselves plan to introduce a players representation group to allow players to have more influence in the developments of the LoL (Conditt, 2017). An additional organisation to take note of is the International Electronic Sports Federation (IeSF) as they have attained some commendable accomplishments which have been helpful in recognising esports as a sport.

The Relevance and Potential of the Industry

The videogame industry is currently estimated to be worth USD 108.9 billion with a predicted 7.8 percent year on year growth (McDonald, 2017). The revenues for video games in fact are now comparable even to long established entertainment fields such as music and film. Naturally with the rise in interest for gaming there has been a rise in popularity of competitions which have increased at an exponential rate. For example, a report showed that esports tournaments held per year increased from 8809 in 2011 to 47,509 in 2014 (Lien, 2014).

A rising part of the growth in the video gaming industry can be attributed to esports. For example, from the most popular games sold in 2017 on Steam, a digital distribution platform, at least 5 of the 12 games were esports titles as compared to the non competitive games. Clearly, having a game become an esport would be an ideal long term target for any publisher as it would ensure continued relevance and popularity as well as revenues from the same title. This rapid increase in viewership has led to esports often being mentioned as 'the fastest growing spectator sport' (Paivinen, 2015) in the world.

As a caveat, although this may be true with such an unprecedented pace there are few statistics which need to be ascertained with caution. For instance, taking a statistic such as an esports tournament having a viewership comparable to that of the Super Bowl is a misleading claim and quite certainly exaggerated. The industry does have a huge viewership but requires to be evaluated in terms of its still growing phase. The Super Bowl, which has consistently had average viewership numbers of over 110 million, has been compared with the complete cumulative esports numbers which is a wrong interpretation of the data (The Next Level, 2017). The industry additionally has to be assessed as per where it currently stands and not against bodies which have been established decades earlier.

However having noted this, the following are a few noteworthy achievements which considering the industry's current nascent nature are truly incredible. For instance, the prize money for the recent LoL International Championship which was largely crowd funded with a value worth USD 20 Million is considered as one of the highest in any sport. Moreover, the fact it is still a growing industry with a majority of the viewership yet to be monetized means it would be a massive entity to consider in the future.

Furthermore, taking into consideration that society has a major influence on the law of countries, it would be particularly useful to observe the impact of esports on the current as well as future generations. The dynamic nature of the field naturally means that esports can adapt to the growing interests of a new audience while continuing to develop and implement new ideas and rules which is not possible in traditional sports. In effect, having this digital software which is completely under their control has allowed publishers to constantly update and improve the platforms and has ensured the games remain engaging and relevant presently as well as adaptable for the future. In addition, as with traditional sports, the culture of being brought up watching a certain form of sport would be carried on as children of the current generation would follow esports in a manner similar to the way watching traditional sports was a familial pastime during previous decades.

The unique quality within the field is it is not restricted to solely one game but is the practice of a variety of them. This effectively promotes not just a First Person shooter or FPS but also possibly a strategy game, enveloping a larger audience towards esports. Viewership numbers within field are increasing at an unprecedented rate as well with no signs showing it to be solely a trend but in fact a new field of interest for society. For 2017, reports have estimated the global viewership for esports to rise upto 385 million (Warman, 2017). However, the growth rate is such that any facts and figures published have to constantly be updated every few months to show the latest estimates as the progress of the industry growth come to the fore.

As to the source of the reports, at present two main market intelligence groups, Newzoo and Superdata have been specifically providing statistics on esports and but have had differing results in their reports on the current estimates for esports growth. Despite few differing statistics, both organisations concur in showing that esports has an exceptional growth rate and have sufficient substance and credibility within their reports to support this claim. In addition to Deloitte the announcement of Nielsen allocating a new market intelligence research group specifically for esports would provide a viewpoint from a traditional research intelligence organisation as well which would be helpful in providing another perspective to the exact growth rate (Nielsen, 2017).

In either regard, the massive popularity in combination with the potential viewership and revenue numbers has brought in numerous traditional and well known brands into the field. This has included the entry of numerous sponsors into the field such as Coca-Cola, BMW or even various football teams (The Next Level, 2016). Recent investments also include Amazon's acquisition of Twitch for USD 970 Million which is notable as the purchase was made within three years of Twitch's creation. YouTube has a specific section, YouTube Gaming, which has become a significant part of its platform. As a display of confidence shown towards gaming popularity, YouTube signed an exclusive agreement with FACEIT, a tournament platform which showcases CS:GO tournaments. Riot Games quite prominently as well have signed a streaming agreement with BAMTech in a groundbreaking deal for the industry with an estimated value of USD 300 Million for providing licensing media rights for solely 3 years.

While the above are the successes of the industry, its drawbacks at present should be looked into as well to provide a balanced perspective. Due to its relatively new existence, the return on investment for brands is still uncertain and can be complicated. As the content is geared towards a millennial audience, the general users have shown an aversion to traditional advertising methods such as sponsor related ads during streaming. Additionally, as the esports audience has not developed via television as with traditional sports but instead through the internet or via mobile platforms and apps, they can simply block any advertisements from sponsors. In effect, esports audiences have more control over the content they watch and the interactions with esports streamers for example via Twitch has proven to be one of the popular reasons for the growth of this field (ESports Heaven, n.d.). The new platforms also has generally been freely accessible as compared to the traditional broadcasting or pay-per-view model which has been generally used for sport. It can also be tricky to involve audiences older than the gaming generation such as the parents who have generally been the paying audience and who would not understand the interest in the phenomenon. If, however, sponsors do not find value on their investment it may hamper any future investment and consequently the overall growth of the industry.

Notwithstanding the fact uncertainty may still exist within the field, it is clear that there is much room to grow and develop as the audience is yet to be monetized and if a long term solution can be achieved it would be worthwhile prospect for all involved.

A part of this would also be dependent upon the recognition provided to the field and if it would be categorised as a sport or not. It is clear that being categorised a sport provides a variety of advantages for esports organisations which differ from country to country but would include tax reductions, lesser immigration issues as well as possible non profit status.

ESPORTS AS A SPORT

Having considered the above, the main part of the Chapter and following segment looks to assess the current legal criteria which are met by esports while purveying the current regulations which despite the necessity clearly display a lack of provisions specific to the current field.

Arguments in Favour

The subject of esports being considered as a sport has been controversial as there are differing philosophies and viewpoints of what would constitute a sport. The discussion of these may be endless and therefore the focus within this chapter would be on the current legal validity as a sport, and while hypothetical or subjective perspectives would be considered; more value would be provided to the tangible legal arguments which give credence to esports as a sport.

Taking the universality of the field of sport into consideration, it needs to be analysed as to what are the legal criteria required to establish a practice as a sport. Furthermore, is there one particular legal definition which separates those activities designated as 'sports' from others that are not.

Previous works on this subject have each had differing definitions. In this case, it would be most appropriate to allocate this responsibility to the organization whose function has been in recognizing activities as sports. As can be witnessed with it being the organisation with the most number of sporting bodies i.e. the GAISF formerly known as Sports Accord. Traditionally, when sports have been recognised by society they have followed the route of first being recognized by the GAISF which is followed by gaining entry into the IOC. It is rare for an organisation not a part of the GAISF to be an IOC member.

The IeSF, an organisation formed with the objective of legitimising esports as a sport, has applied to both the IOC and the GAISF for this recognition. It has notably adopted the CAS as its body of appeal for disputes which is a requisite for GAISF membership according to article 39, par. 1 of the GAISF Statutes. Furthermore we must judge that if the CAS were to be the body of appeal as in this case, it brings into consideration as to how an institution dealing with solely sports related disputes can be authorised to handle the disputes of an activity which is not a sport. Although the situation is yet to arise regarding appealing to the CAS it is unlikely to be denied due to CAS having asserted their criteria to accept cases as long as the clause would be 'related to sport' as well as having an arbitration clause for disputes in the statutes explicitly stating the CAS (Mavromati & Reeb, 2015). The main reason that the issue has not yet arisen at CAS would be due to the costs involved for the parties which due to the disproportionate nature of finances in the industry do not make it a viable option. In addition to the CAS, the IeSF has also incorporated the WADA code into its statutes for doping which is another mandatory requirement for sports institutions.

For entry into the GAISF a summer sport requires 40 national member federations from three different continents according to article 7A, par. 8 of the GAISF Statutes. At present the IeSF has 47 members out of which 22 have been recognised by the respective countries while 27 are as yet awaiting approval. On another note, esports has also attained IOC membership as a second level sport by being admitted into the Korean Olympic Association through the Korea e-Sports Association. The Olympic Council of Asia also announced that esports would be an official event at the 2022 Asian Games (Graham, 2017a). In addition, it has affiliated with the IAAF as well as is a recognised member of The Association of International Sport for All (TAFISA). Akin to a traditional athlete, an elite gamer trains extensively and can spend up to 12 to 14 hours practicing skill moves, strategising with coaches as well as making decisions in the space of milliseconds for himself and his team in games wherein the outcome is worth millions.

In terms of mental requirements esports can be compared with the elite level of sport. Utmost concentration is mandatory throughout as a minor lapse from an individual player can result in a loss for his entire team. Studies have found esports athletes to have the same mental attributes as traditional athletes. Additionally, StarCraft 2 which has been shown to be an excellent indicator of cognitive development, found regular gamers to have high levels of coordination, mental agility and reflexes when compared with the general population (Glass, Maddox & Love, 2013). For instance, elite gamers have been found to have an APM (Actions per minute) rate of 400 actions per minute.

These are characteristics which would quite definitely be reserved for people with exceptional ability. Moreover, with the increase in competition and prize money, teams have spent more time with mental preparation, bringing in sports psychologists to help enhance their performance as well. Reviewing all the above, it would be fair to say that esports satisfy the mental requirements of a sport. As an acknowledgment of this growth and recognition, this has even recently led to the Olympic Committee releasing a statement displaying its appreciation and mentioning possibly considering esports to be included in the 2024 Olympic Games to be held in Los Angeles (Graham, 2017b).

As to the physical requirements, it is undisputed that there is no display of physical fitness in esports which would contradict the conventional idea of the term 'sport'. However, it may be noted there are few studies which have found esports athletes to display a 'perceived' exertion similar to physical athletes during games (Kane & Bradley, 2017).

Moreover, a common expectation is that an esports athlete would be unhealthy, which would not be true for quite a few of the top professionals. In fact due to the long hours of sitting, gamers require a decent level of fitness in order to maintain focus, mental stamina and reaction times late into games.

Even if this may not be sufficient, we need to consider that there is no explicit legal requirement for a sport to be defined by a physical element. Examples of these can be provided with the games of Bridge and Chess which were both adopted by the IOC as sports in 1999. Albeit, with a subsidiary classification as 'mind sports'. The IOC has taken the initiative to give importance to mind sports as well as seen with their plans to reintroduce the World Mind Sports Games, a newer branch of Olympic competition similar to the Summer and Winter Olympics. This may be another alternative for the Olympics to introduce esports as a part of these games as well.

A few other points to take note of are that the IOC as well can take time to include organisations as members rather than providing instant memberships. For example, the American football federation formed in 1998 was recognised only in 2013 approximately 15 years later. In comparison, the IeSF was formed only in August 2008 and can still be said to be taking a normal amount of time to be considered a sport.

On another note, there is also a question of if becoming an IOC member truly recognises a sport. For example, the World Rugby Federation established in 1886, which is the international representative federation of the sport of rugby union, was recognised as a member of the IOC only in 1995. If the interpretation taken is, only a sport if federation is an IOC member, it would mean it took rugby union 124 years to be recognised as a 'sport' which would be a completely false assertion.

In terms of legal recognition from national bodies, in 2013, the US government provided an esports professional with a P1 Visa. The P1 visa has solely been reserved for athletes, which logically entails esports (or one of its disciplines) can be considered as sports within the USA for the purposes of immigration for players. Esports is also a recognised sport in Korea wherein professional gamers are treated in a similar fashion as athletes of traditional sports. Considering all the above, it is recognised as a sport in at least 22 nations including Italy, Russia as well as China (Donchenko, 2016) while also under process to be recognised by Germany (Anastasopoulos, 2018). There are a variety of challenges that have arisen as a result of not just the enormous growth rate but also its differing technological development which have not been considered and require to be addressed.

Legal Challenges Yet to Overcome

The legal issues in esports have involved a multitude of fields ranging from IP law and contractual disputes to sports specific disputes such as doping and more prominently gambling.

Despite all the above however, the most prominent issue currently facing the industry would be its lack of standardization for all esports stakeholders. In simple terms, while the sport of football may have FIFA as its governing body, esports has a Blizzard for Overwatch, Valve for Counter-Strike or Riot for LoL. Each publisher drafts the rules for their own games and due to it being the intellectual property of the publisher, they have complete control over the games and every participant has to accept all the rules stated to participate in both competitive and non-competitive play. By doing this, every participant effectively acquiesces a major part of their rights which would be inequitable in case of a dispute against the publisher.

The disparity is made all the more disproportionate as unlike a traditional sport, in this field the entire software for the game is owned by the publisher which can make it impossible for players to not just compete but also play the game if banned. Taking the example of football and its governing body FIFA, it would be possible for a player or team if banned to still play the game of football on any football pitch as long as it is not a competition under the jurisdiction of FIFA. This may not be possible with esports due to the digital software which acts as the field in this instance being unavailable to the player anymore. Such bans may also last effectively endlessly if the publisher so chooses.

Due to a lack of an external body to independently adjudicate decisions, it is quite possible for publishers to issue decisions without any inhibitions. A contentious example of such an issue is of the case wherein Riot banned Mykles, the owner of the Team Renegades, among others for not conforming to Riot standards of team structure, player welfare and for being guilty of collusion. Although the investigation and consequent sanction was conducted by Riot, they did not publish much evidence to support their decision besides stating they found the sanctioned parties to be guilty of these infringements and have been sanctioned in response (Rozelle, 2016). Consequently, Mykles (2016) released a response via YouTube with attachments denying any wrongdoing as well as debating the unfairness of the sanction. It is evident from this case, that while a sanction may be acceptable, the fact that there was not enough substantial evidence disclosed in their decision means there is a noticeable lack of transparency in the current system. While Mykles may have been resolute in his response, many players do not have any financial resources nor much knowledge or ability to dispute against a given sanction. Regardless of the outcome of this case, it is evident that Riot or any other publisher for that matter have the possibility of issuing sanctions which can be unfair in nature and it can be uncontested due to the weaker positioning of all participating parties within the games.

In general, disputes are settled via negotiations as the sanctioned party (team or player) would prefer negotiating for a compromised sanction rather than resorting to any legal measures due to the costs and time involved in these processes. As the career spans are short and extremely competitive for players, with the average player retiring by the age of 24 or the fact that the money earned for a large majority of the field is not stable (Glass, Maddox & Love, 2013); bringing disputes to a court of appeal is extremely rare. The lack of uniformity is also apparent with tournament hosts having differing bodies to handle disputes. For example, while the IeSF has the Court of Arbitration for Sport (CAS) as its body of appeal, WESA created an arbitration court solely for esports. Publishers on the other hand have their own system of sanctions, which may or may not include a body for dispute resolution. In effect, there are a variety of jurisdictions including state courts making outcomes of decisions uncertain and unforeseeable.

The segments with the weakest amount of influence in the industry are the teams followed by the players. While teams and organisers may have disputes with the publishers, the players as well may have disputes with the teams. Contractual breaches for example are commonplace and there is no system in place for the protection of players a prominent segment of whom are minors. Just as in any other sport for the millions that play the games, there are only few who turn professional. Although efforts have been made to change the situation, there has been a lack of standardisation of contracts between teams and players which detail the rights of players. This can lead to a large degree of exploitation by teams ranging from overworking the players to underpaying them. The fact that many are minors and relatively young while not having the appropriate knowledge to represent themselves makes it essential for a standardised protection for players from teams competing in tournaments.

Examples of forms wherein players can be exploited vary, for example, due to the long hours and rapid wrist movements, overuse injuries in the wrists or tennis elbow are common among professional gamers. In the case of Flash, the player required extensive surgery across his arm due to nerve damage (Brautigam, 2016). and while the team in this case was supportive of the player it may not apply for many others. Due to the extremely competitive nature of the field the players can find themselves being replaced and may end up injured and without any career prospects.

It is also essential to keep the players fit due to the sedentary nature and effects of sitting for long periods of time. Players require health benefits as well as mental and strategy coaches (Patridge, 2014). These facilities are available mostly for top level teams making it difficult for smaller teams to be successful. The IAAF has entered into a partnership with the IeSF in order to promote a health program and the advantages of physical training for esports players. Their tasks would include advocating for all clubs and tournaments organisers to have standard provisions within contracts which should include prevent exploitation of players. The nature of the field is such however that as there are differing organisers, teams have to select the competitions they play in and if they do not qualify, the tournaments may not have jurisdiction to sanction these teams. Although players are invited to file complaints with the publishers or tournament organisers, many may not know their rights.

The extreme levels of competition may also incite players to cheat or resort to hacking software to win games, examples of these include auto aim modifications or slowing down the opponents module among other alternatives. While most organisers have the ability to monitor for cheating not all of them can ensure it and hacking software is still a common occurrence in competitions (Smith, 2016).

Abuse of performance enhancing drugs has also been a part of the competitive culture of esports. A likely loophole for players to exploit is that they can use these drugs for the training period before a tournament, making them mentally agile and quicker during practice thus having an unfair advantage over their competition. However, facing no sanctions for it as tests are only made during the tournament phase wherein the drugs may have waned away from their system.

There is a lack of data and knowledge as well in implementing doping regulations. For tournament organisers, to implement testing along the lines of the WADA code would be unfeasible as the costs would be far too high to administer testing on all players. This would apply even in the qualification rounds of big tournaments as there are thousands of participants. Additionally, organisers may not be able to instil the same standards of doping control as other leagues. As the prize monies in esports tournaments are high and there are no concrete regulations in place teams can easily be incited to cheat. An example which can be provided is in the admission of Kory Friesen admitting his entire team was on Adderall during competition and that it was also a common practice among players. The ESL being an industry leader have adapted to conducting regular checks change post the Friesen admission. If the sport is to have a level playing field, it is quite evident that stringent measures need to put in place in order to contend with the doping and drug abuse. Not solely during the times of tournaments but to ensure prevention during training phases as well (Lumb, 2015).

These issues may however be a result of the still relatively nascent nature of the industry as compared to other traditional sports competitions. The gravity of issues may also vary from differing esports titles to differing tournaments, some such as ESL have been long established while others struggle with organisational issues and consistency (Auxent, 2016).

As to the current regulations from a national perspective, there have been differing methods which have been implemented to regulate esports. While esports may be deemed a sport in a few countries currently such as in Korea or Russia; they are not considered sports in other countries such as France.

Although the Korean system has been the first to recognise esports as a sport, and has been the longest established even having its own Ministry allocated specifically for esports. Due to the fairly recent match fixing investigations involving the Korean system (Liqipedia, n.d.) and to prevent such issues it would be better to have a look at other systems adopted by national bodies for recognising and regulating esports. The France model which although comparatively newly implemented, has been fairly successful and may be perceived as a guideline to regulate esports for other countries. However, it must also be taken into account that implementing regulations would differ from country to country, as the regulatory system in France may not be applicable to those of Spain or the UK.

Having one uniform body for all can prove to be difficult as well as each publisher would prefer their game to be subjected to the laws of the jurisdiction of their own domicile rather than to one of another region. For example, if Valve is headquartered in the US, it would be extremely difficult to convince the company to relinquish its rights to another body. Unlike in traditional sports, wherein the task may be difficult on its own, the publishers would not be willing to acquiesce the rights to their property to another organization and furthermore one from another country which would have different laws either.

At present besides the individual countries, the EU as well has yet to implement any changes to incorporate esports into EU law. A good example of the treatment that can be expected would be in analysing the recent judgment of the Bridge case wherein the Supreme Court found Bridge to not qualify as a sport. Although Bridge is a separate activity, the recent judgement made by the CJEU on whether Bridge would qualify as a sport can be taken as an indication as to the problems that may be faced by the esports industry if it is proposed to be adopted as a sport. While the English Bridge union case may have its differences, the outcome of the case has in fact made it more complicated for esports to be considered as a sport due to the similar characteristic of a lack of physical exertion during games. Despite its difference from esports, the lack of physical exertion did prove to be a crucial factor in the decision of the Court.

However, during the same judgement, the opinion of the Advocate General to the Court must also be noted wherein he did consider Bridge to have sufficient attributes to be considered a sport. His reasoning includes stating the fact that the IOC recognizes mind sports in addition to the then Sports Accord should be taken into consideration as both are the recognized organizing bodies of sport. He notes that there is no specific requirement for a physical element for an activity to be considered a sport as well as seen with the inclusion of Chess. The Advocate

General concluded that a mental element a mental element would be sufficient for an activity to be considered as a sport (Szpunar, 2017).

In either regard, in the event a case involving an esports discipline does arise in a similar manner, the outcome may be different. The issue rather than being one of involving an element of physical exertion may instead be mainly due to not having a requirement to be defined by previous EU regulations as was the case with the English Bridge Union. This may consequently render a more positive outcome for esports.

Another issue wherein esports may differ from traditional sports includes that while traditional sports started with the focus on the sporting aspect followed by becoming commercial businesses. Esports on the other hand, have taken another route as they have been initially based off commercial products which have further displayed the ability to act as a sporting platform. One of the main differentiating factors, include that esports titles are owned by a single entity and are effectively the intellectual property of these entities. The dispute of 2013 between the Korean Esports Association (KeSPA) and Blizzard over the broadcasting rights for StarCraft in Korea is a prominent example displaying the clear authority the publishers have over other bodies. In this case, KeSPA and Blizzard had previously had an agreement over these rights however when Blizzard decided to sell the rights to another organisation, KeSPA disputed this while implying they had the licensing rights to the games however due to the intellectual property being owned by Blizzard, KeSPA were ultimately not successful in their claim (Burk, 2013).

Naturally with all the above structural issues, it has been possible for the industry to be exploited. Despite all the above challenges the main problem at present for the industry is in the unregulated gambling, match fixing and betting markets. Prominent examples of these gambling issues range from that of the 2016 CS:GO skin betting controversy to the use of loot boxes being declared as gambling (Longley, 2017). The gravity of this situation is quite concerning has been quite concerning.

The regulated esports gambling market for the year 2016 was estimated to be USD 250 million, while the projected growth for 2020 was estimated to rise to USD 23 billion. In turn, the unregulated gambling market within esports, for the year of 2016 was estimated to be worth USD 8 billion, a majority of it, a 7.4 billion amount was solely from a form of betting specific to esports called skin betting. The most prominent game involved in this was CS:GO which surged to become the biggest esport by the end of 2016; part of this success could be attributed to its ease of access to skin betting.

A skin refers to a virtual commodity bought in game which can then be exchanged in return for virtual money. CS:GO was followed by rapid growth of websites which allowed the exchange of this virtual currency making it tangible real world gambling. Third party sites while not related to Valve could easily obtain access to the CS:GO

Steam engine. Steam was setup in a manner which did not deny access to these betting sites and consequently blamed to be responsible for inducing match fixing.

The Valve engine made it very easy for this market to function, and various betting sites wherein skins could be exchanged for money developed. In fact, the CS:GO Lounge, one of the primary betting sites became one of the 700 most popular websites on the web due to this, however, went by largely unnoticed due to the lack of knowledge or attention being paid to this area. The article published by Bloomberg which displayed the on goings of CS:GO skin betting led to widespread criticism of the lack of regulation in the Valve engine (Brustein & Novy – Williams, 2016). Despite heavy criticism regarding the format which promotes unregulated betting, Valve did not make many changes to the system and denied promoting skin betting despite it being quite evident that no efforts were being made to stop it.

As there is no governing body in place to enforce publishers from preventing such issues and unfortunately, considering the quickly developing field including the varying range of models and innovations in place, it can be difficult for national jurisdictions to draft in a regulation which would be universal in nature. YouTube stars who were stakeholders from one of the skin betting sites were shown to be playing and won an amount from it as well which displayed a clear conflict of interest (Pearson, 2016).

Yet judicial authorities have on previous occasions declined to find these companies at fault as the money lost was as per them of a virtual amount and not real money. This is however a dangerous precedent to set as there is a clear link between the virtual and real currency which could be exploited.

It must also be considered that a large part of the demographic would include minors as well which would make this a criminal action in many jurisdictions. Due to the lack of knowledge from the traditional public and its rapid rise in popularity however it has been possible for bodies to exploit the industry in such a manner. Regardless of the opinion of whether esports may be classified as sports, due to the undeveloped structure it is easy for unethical or even criminal organisations to enter the field. Regulations are therefore a mandatory requirement. While these issues are being considered in Europe now as well a concrete solution is yet to be universally decided.

ASSESSMENT OF SOLUTIONS FOR THE FIELD

It is clear that the rapid rise in popularity of esports has overtaken the structural placements of its governing bodies. There are a variety of esports bodies with differing regulations on how they regulate infringements. Players can be banned from one tournament yet compete in others even for serious offences such as match fixing or doping. Further examples include there being a lack of standardised regulations regarding ownership which can easily lead to competition law violations such as teams owned by one entity competing in a league owned by the same entity. Gambling websites can work of their own accord as well due to an organisational lack of jurisdiction or regulations. Flouting of doping rules likewise is also possible as no authorities are in place to prevent doping universally. Although the field is still comparatively in a stage of infancy, the reasons for a variety of issues are primarily due to a disjointed structure which entails a mandatory requirement for an overarching regulatory body.

There is no single solution for the current issue, there are varying viewpoints as to how it should be regulated, including considering it as a sport or even creating regulations specifically for esports. Due to a lack of standardization and the various stakeholders being fragmented in their views, there has not been much progress with regards to developing an appropriate solution. Moreover, each developer would insist their own game be considered a separate esport rather than one of its own.

As seen previously, due to the heavy influence of the game developers it can be difficult to implement external regulations on these games. To elucidate further, as they are published by these privately owned companies, they have all the authority to modify the games as per their preferences. Moreover, there is also the issue of the method of governance which differ between US based sports against European based sports. US based sports due to the difference in regulations or preference to deal with their disputes internally do not have the same regulatory authority as European bodies. Taking the example of basketball, the most popular league in basketball is the NBA, however the sport of basketball is recognised and played in the Olympics due to FIBA. The NBA does not this applies for almost all the traditional American sports wherein the most popular form of the sport, would not fall under the scope of the IOC as they prefer working and solving their disputes internally within a US specific system.

Riot, Valve, Psyonix, Blizzard, EA are all American based developers, and have generally been based in using the American system of arbitration and dispute resolution. Besides a fair few such as the cheerleading and the surfing federation, American formed sports organisations prefer to have their own system of regulations. Taken this into consideration as well as the fact that most of the publishers are based in the USA it is unlikely to have the control ceded to an European or Swiss based organisation. For esports to be considered as a sport with the IOC however there is the IeSF whose efforts have been aimed towards esports being considered a sport. Due to this monopoly it is inevitable that the system to be followed would be dependent upon the publishers.

Whether a conjoined system may work would be difficult to do as well with some of the issues arising being arranging a Players union or a promotion and relegation system against a single entity franchise model among differences.

In some instances, it is possible for both systems to work in a parallel manner, similar to the NBA and FIBA. However, more often than not both systems may clash and conflict each other. A clear display of such a situation can be seen with FIFA and the main US soccer body, Major League Soccer (MLS). The MLS is a body incorporated under the regulations of the US based franchise model. Any disputes that may arise have been acceded to the internal MLS system and FIFA refuse jurisdiction for any MLS related disputes. This is most logical alternative as under FIFA rules the single entity model which the MLS uses would be contravening FIFA regulations. However, there are instances wherein such a system may be problematic. Such as this would cause issues with making transfers for players from Europe or another association under FIFA jurisdiction to the MLS. While this system has been capable so far, it is not very well defined as players or teams have sufficient standing to challenge the system for lack of a well-defined regulations and impartiality. Miami FC, a team playing in the North American Soccer League (NASL) which was second division league in the US and under FIFA jurisdiction, brought a claim against the MLS to the CAS stating they were eligible for entry into the MLS following their achievements in the NASL. The primary fact is that MLS does not have a promotion and relegation system which is common in European models. The outcome however has not been defined as the MLS is not under the jurisdiction of FIFA and consequently the CAS. Moreover, the NASL have also recently been denied second division status due to not fulfilling the required criteria to be the second division league for US soccer which further complicates the issue for the Miami FC claim. For such a system to work therefore there would need to be a collaboration between the US and European governing bodies which would clearly define the rules in case of any disputes. For such an initiative to take place it would require a highly concerted cooperative effort which is highly unlikely as the governing bodies have been content using the current system.

The lack of standardization and the lack of an overall governing or regulatory body makes esports susceptible to corruption, match fixing and illegal betting. As a considerable demographic consist of minors it is a concerning issue which needs to be addressed immediately. Various players were found to have been found part of a match fixing scandal which consequently led to Valve banning over 20 CS:GO players (Te, 2016). There have been steps taken by taken by public authorities to clamp down on the betting and match fixing in esports prominently in the US, UK and France. The CS:GO scandals prompted the Washington State Gambling Commission to issue a letter against Valve requesting its legal validity under Washington law under the threat of criminal charges being imposed upon Valve.

Valve however strongly denied the allegation of them promoting gambling. Efforts made by the betting operators to prevent match fixing include Unikrn (an eSports specific company and betting provider), introducing an integrity certification which leagues/companies can participate in and achieve a reputation as per their performance. France has recently recognized the problem and has been taking steps to mitigate the issue. This has included appointing the French eSports commission assigned with the responsibility of evaluating the economic and social impact of eSports in France. The UK Gambling Commission has also charged two men with video game gambling under the Gambling Act 2005. The commission has also published a paper explaining the methods to clamp down on virtual betting which is quite comprehensive and can be adopted by European authorities.

The most effective in combating skin betting however was via the publisher, Valve. Following the continuous lawsuits and warnings, besides issuing a few technical changes to hamper in game betting, Valve issued cease and desist letters to over 23 skin betting sites, which proved to be quite effective. As seen with many closing down and prominently CS:GO lounge who have stopped skin betting and introduced a new form of betting in terms of virtual coins which comparatively is not as grave. Although there are still a few websites utilising skin betting, Valve has reduced their prominence drastically. Its effect has been so radical the projected amount for skin betting reduced from near $20 billion to less than $1 billion for 2020.

Such issues of match fixing and gambling have not been limited to solely one esport either as the 2015 StarCraft 2 scandal displayed a similar match fixing controversy to the CS:GO players as well (Bray, 2016). Methods that may be implemented include that of France which does not consider esports as sports but has created regulations specifically for the field. This may be adopted in countries which have differing views on the field.

Establishing an esports body however cannot be possible without support from the publishers. Therefore, if the publishers do choose the organisation with the most authority would be an American esports non-profit organization. It would also be highly important that the organisation be independent of any of the bodies which are already a part of the esports ecosystem. The esports regulations drafted by the French government wherein it supported its own new French esports federation to govern and supervise the growth and development of the activity in the field, would be a useful asset until the field would be capable to be regulated on its own, in which case the government may relinquish its control.

At present, the body with the most capability to combat illegal match-fixing, betting and doping universally is the Esports Integrity Coalition (ESIC). ESIC was created with the responsibility of regulating doping within matches as well as the gambling market. The mission of the coalition is to monitor the rapidly evolving developments within the field and providing an analysis of the scope and nature of the betting put in place. The ESIC uses a fraud detection service system with the help of betting operators which would serve to provide analysis on betting patterns. It has been difficult to implement its regulations on an overall basis due to differing cultures, standards and jurisdictions. Thus far, the ESIC has major tournaments such as the ESL and DreamHack as well as the cooperation of numerous betting operators. Nonetheless, considering the influence of publishers in the industry it would be of primordial importance that ESIC be supported by the publishers as well. While this may not solve the problem of whether esports can be regarded as a sport, it would serve to mitigate the more important issue of preventing the exploitation of the industry and its participants.

An option for publishers to consider for adapting an external body could be via establishing an initial trial tournament. For instance, Riot may use the ESIC as its body against match fixing, doping and gambling for a temporary period or tournament to ensure there is a degree of uniformity. If successful, which is quite possible, the publishers may choose to elect the ESIC as the body responsible to universally adjudicate the match fixing, betting and gambling areas of the industry. This would effectively cover the entire industry due to the monopoly of the publishers over the games. Moreover in case, there are other publishers which do not accept ESIC it would not still be sufficient having one, as esports is not solely the practice of one game but a practice or group of a variety of others. In effect, if Valve accept ESIC, CS:GO and all other Valve games would qualify under the IOC requirements and may be termed as a 'sport' not needing any further publishers which would leave out other games.

The inclusion of the games into the Asian Olympic Games can be influential however the IOC have a differing set of rules to adopt activities as sports. Although IOC have mentioned they could consider esports for the Olympics. An issue raised by the IOC is regarding the fact that a few esports games such as shooters which are inherently violent in nature do not correspond to the values of the Olympics.

Although there have been fears among traditional bodies of the mental effects of violence on people which can lead to more aggressive behaviour; this has not proven conclusive and is by appearance a fear at most. The outcome of studies made on this particular topic has in fact proven inconclusive and with no substantial proof that directly correlates video game violence with real life violence. In fact, the argument that it makes people aggressive may actually be an argument in support of esports being a sport. Watching esports matches similar to sports games incites competitiveness and passion, whether this be anger or disappointment in losing or extreme happiness upon a final minute win. These are traits of sport and not due to any violent content of the games (American Psychological Association, 2011). The fact that the players are more involved and invested with the game rather than watching it makes them enjoy this experience even further as compared to while watching a team. Moreover, initiatives by publishers such as Riot have been strong against any aggressive behaviour displayed by competitors regardless of it being during or out of competition.

FUTURE AND CONCLUSION

The as yet nascent nature would mean that consideration as a sport would still take a few more years and/or a combined effort from all stakeholders to bring esports into the same sports umbrella. The rapid growth rate and progress may definitely influence countries to change and adapt their regulations for the field in the future.

However, as minors are the community most affected by the lack of regulations and it would be the responsibility of game publishers, national government bodies as well as tournament organisers to ensure there are rules in place to prevent exploitation of minors (Hattenstone, 2017). There stands a real possibility of addiction to gaming as well. As seen with South Korea, wherein esports is one of the most popular activities among the youth, issues related to gaming addiction became a serious issue in the country. Failure to do so would be a failure on the parts of all involved in protecting the interests of future generations. As the growth and development of technology is inevitable, it is logical to state that future generations would follow upon the games that they were brought up on which for this generation would be esports.

Having considered the above, the requirement to establish a basic set of protections is far more important than to state the esports is a sport. Esports at present do not fit the criteria for GAISF to consider it as a sport, this may change either if the IOC changes its criteria or the publishers relinquish their control which is extremely unlikely.

While esports have qualified to become medal sports within the Asian games in 2022, without the acceptance of a minimum of 40 national federations from wherein all these national bodies are consider esports as a sport. As of the time of writing, the IeSF has 46 member federations, albeit with only 22 recognised which leaves far too many federations requiring acceptance prior to the whole field being adapted by the GAISF. At present due to the lack of structuring and a lack of support from publishers, the field is susceptible to being exploited as a market in match fixing, gambling and exploitation of participants. A collaboration with ESIC therefore could be a helpful step in reducing the overall uncertainty and discrepancy in the field. The other alternative of creating new forms of regulations specifically for esports would be a useful and most appropriate solution as well but would mean countries would have to implement new regulations which they may not yet be inclined to do.

Looking into the future, there are now newer forms of gaming being introduced as well with mobile gaming becoming one of the most lucrative forms of gaming in the industry. Tournaments for mobile based games have also been on the rise and it's quite possible for a mobile esport to emerge in this regard. The incredible success of Pokémon Go, an augmented reality based game may prove to be an indication of where the field may go next. Augmented reality platforms would require a multitude of differing regulations to be put in place as well and adapting to the current digital nature of the games would be a useful step to helping adapt to such platforms later in the future. Games involving virtual reality have also been released as well however have not had the widespread popularity as was initially expected. If either of augmented or virtual reality gaming increases in popularity which can be likely, the requirement of physical exertion may be fulfilled as well. In either regard, due to its ability to adapt to the demands of society it is logical to state that the field is set to have a permanent place in society and the sooner we adapt to accommodate it, the better we would be able to protect and regulate its participants.

REFERENCES

American Psychological Association. (2011, August 29). *Playing highly competitive video games may lead to aggressive behavior*. Retrieved March 1, 2018 from www.sciencedaily.com/releases/2011/08/110829114714.htm

Anastasopoulos, A. (2018, February 5). *German Coalition Parties to Recognize Esports as Sports*. Retrieved March 01, 2018, from https://esportsobserver.com/german-parties-recognize-esports/

Auxent, A. (2016, February 09). *Mega Gamer Brasil and other tournaments that fail to pay out prizes are dragging esports down*. Retrieved March 01, 2018, from https://esportsobserver.com/dragging-esports-down/

Brautigam, T. (2016, November 11). *Esports needs to face its injury problem*. Retrieved March 01, 2018, from http://esportsobserver.com/esports-needs-face-injury-problem/

Bray, J. (2016, August 15). *ESports Is Getting Big, And Here's The Scandals To Prove It*. Retrieved March 01, 2018, from https://supernerdland.com/article/esports-getting-big-heres-scandals-prove/

Brustein, J., & Novy-Williams, E. (2016). *Virtual weapons are turning teen gamers into serious gamblers*. Retrieved March 01, 2018, from https://www.bloomberg.com/features/2016-virtual-guns-counterstrike-gambling/

Burk, D. L. (2013). Owning E-sports: Proprietary Rights in Professional Computer Gaming. *University of Pennsylvania Law Review*, *161*, 1535–1578.

Conditt, J. (2017, July 6). *How League of Legends can shape the future of esports*. Retrieved March 01, 2018, from https://www.engadget.com/2017/07/04/league-legends-esports-lcs-changes-dignitas-liquid-immortals/

Darcy, K. (2017, July 6). *Why the Associated Press Stylebook went with esports, not eSports*. Retrieved March 01, 2018, from http://www.espn.com/esports/story/_/id/19860473/why-associated-press-stylebook-went-esports-not-esports

Donchenko, Y. (2016, December 14). *Which countries have just recognized eSports list*. Retrieved March 01, 2018, from https://cybbet.com/news/2973-Which-countries-have-just-recognized-eSports-List

ESports Heaven. (n.d.). *Twitch, AdBlock, and the Tragedy of the Commons*. Retrieved March 01, 2018, from http://www.esportsheaven.com/articles/view/5207/twitch-adblock-and-the-tragedy-of-the-commons

Glass, B. D., Maddox, W. T., & Love, B. C. (2013). Real-Time Strategy Game Training: Emergence of a Cognitive Flexibility Trait. *PLoS One*, *8*(8), e70350. doi:10.1371/journal.pone.0070350 PMID:23950921

Graham, B. A. (2017a, April 18). *ESports to be a medal event at 2022 Asian Games*. Retrieved March 01, 2018, from https://www.theguardian.com/sport/2017/apr/18/esports-to-be-medal-sport-at-2022-asian-games

Graham, B. A. (2017b, August 9). *ESports could be medal event at 2024 Olympics, Paris bid team says*. Retrieved March 01, 2018, from https://www.theguardian.com/sport/2017/aug/09/esports-2024-olympics-medal-event-paris-bid-committee

Hattenstone, S. (2017, June 16). *The rise of eSports: are addiction and corruption the price of its success?* Retrieved March 01, 2018, from https://www.theguardian.com/sport/2017/jun/16/top-addiction-young-people-gaming-esports

Kane, D., & Spradley, B. (2017). Recognizing ESports as a Sport. *The Sport Journal*, 19.

Lien, T. (2014, July 31). *Number of eSports tournaments in North America set to boom this year*. Retrieved March 01, 2018, from https://www.polygon.com/2014/7/31/5953611/esports-tournaments-2014-numbers

Liquipedia. (n.d.). *2015 Match-Fixing Scandal*. Retrieved March 01, 2018, from http://liquipedia.net/starcraft2/2015_Match-Fixing_Scandal

Longley, S. (2017, November 20). *Loot Boxes Are The New Skin Betting Battlefront In Esports*. Retrieved March 01, 2018, from https://www.esportsbettingreport.com/loot-boxes-new-skins-battlefront-esports/

Lumb, D. (2015, July 31). *Anti-Doping Regulations Come To Esports: A Q&A With Electronic Sports League's Michal Blicharz*. Retrieved March 01, 2018, from https://www.fastcompany.com/3049041/anti-doping-regulations-come-to-esports-a-qa-with-electronic-sports-leagues-michal-blicha

Mavromati, D., & Reeb, M. (2015). *The Code of the Court of Arbitration for Sport: Commentary, Cases and Materials*. Alphen aan den Rijn: Kluwer Law International.

McDonald, E. (2017, April 20). *The Global Games Market Will Reach $108.9 Billion in 2017 With Mobile Taking 42%*. Retrieved March 01, 2018, from https://newzoo.com/insights/articles/the-global-games-market-will-reach-108-9-billion-in-2017-with-mobile-taking-42/

Mykles, C. (2016, July 28). *Riot's Renegades Investigation*. Retrieved March 01, 2018, from https://www.youtube.com/watch?v=HXIcwyTutno

Nielsen. (2017, August 17). *Nielsen Launches New Esports Business to Help Define and Quantify Value for the Competitive Gaming Market*. Retrieved March 01, 2018, from http://www.nielsen.com/eu/en/press-room/2017/nielsen-launches-new-esports-business-to-help-define-and-quantify-competitive-gaming.html

Opinion of Advocate General Szpunar, C-90/16 The English Bridge Union Limited v Commissioners for Her Majesty's Revenue & Customs.

Paivinen, T. (2015, April 4). *The Fastest Growing Spectator Sport You're Not Watching*. Retrieved March 01, 2018, from https://medium.com/the-oddshot-loop/the-fastest-growing-spectator-sport-you-re-not-watching-e3fdae27b6bd

Patridge, J. (2014, June 18). *Mind game: How eSports psychology can help you win*. Retrieved March 01, 2018, from http://www.redbull.com/en/esports/stories/1331659424363/mind-game-how-esports-psychology-can-help-you-win

Pearson, D. (2016, July 6). *Prominent YouTubers revealed as owners of controversial CS:GO gambling site*. Retrieved March 01, 2018, from https://www.gamesindustry.biz/articles/2016-07-04-cs-go-gambling-scandal-deepens-as-prominent-youtubers-revealed-as-site-owners

Rozelle, W. M. (2016, May 9). *Competitive Ruling: Renegades and TDK*. Retrieved March 01, 2018, from https://www.lolesports.com/en_US/articles/competitive-ruling-renegades-and-tdk

Smith, I. (2016, April). *ESIC Threat Assessment*. Retrieved March 01, 2018, from http://www.esportsintegrity.com/wpcontent/uploads/2016/04/ESIC_Threat-Assessment_Apr-2016.pdf

Stubbs, M. (2017, December 2). *Are Esports A Real Sport? Riot Games Wades Into The Debate With 'League Of Legends' Video*. Retrieved March 01, 2018, from https://www.forbes.com/sites/mikestubbs/2017/12/02/are-esports-a-real-sport-riot-games-wades-into-the-debate-with-league-of-legends-video/#4b7b69552486

Taylor, T. L. (2012). *Raising the Stakes: E-Sports and the Professionalization of Computer Gaming*. Cambridge, MA: MIT Press.

Te, Z. (2016, January 5). *Valve Issues Life Bans to CS: GO Players Who Participated in Match-Fixing*. Retrieved March 01, 2018, from https://www.gamespot.com/articles/valve-issues-life-bans-to-cs-go-players-who-partic/1100-6433549/

The Next Level. (2016, November 23). *France Is On All In On eSports*. Retrieved March 01, 2018, from http://tnl.media/esportsproteams/2016/11/21/france-is-on-all-in-on-esports

The Next Level. (2017, March 9). *Time To Kill The "eSports Beats Sports Viewers" Stat*. Retrieved March 01, 2018, from http://tnl.media/esportsnews/2017/3/8/time-to-kill-the-esports-beats-sports-viewers-stat

Warman, P. (2017, February 14). *Esports revenues will reach $696M in 2017 and $1.5Bn by 2020*. Retrieved March 01, 2018, from https://newzoo.com/insights/articles/esports-revenues-will-reach-696-million-in-2017/

Young, H. (2016, May 31). *ESports: Is pro video gaming a sport?* Retrieved March 01, 2018, from https://edition.cnn.com/2016/05/31/sport/esports-is-professional-gaming-a-sport/index.html

Chapter 6
E-Sports at the Olympic Games:
From Physicality to Virtuality

Renata E. Ntelia
Institute of Digital Games, Malta

ABSTRACT

The chapter follows a comparison between e-sports and physical sports in terms of their formal properties as games. Through this approach, it is argued that e-sports differ essentially from physical games due to their spatiality. Specifically, it addresses how the virtual space of e-sports undergoes a different process of production from that of physical space in the sense that it does not adhere to social rules and the power of the hegemony, but rather to the code of the machine. This results to a negation of the physical body of the player, which is in dialectical antithesis to the spirit of the Olympic Games unlike any physical game.

INTRODUCTION

In 2016 the South Korea-based International eSports Federation, IESF, along with the British government-backed International eGames Committee, IEGC, submitted a request to the International Olympic Committee, IOC, to obtain information on how to gain inclusion for eSports in the Olympic programme as a medal event in the Paris summer games of 2024 (Graham, 2017). Since then a controversy has (re) sparked whether eSports should be included as part of the Olympic Games or not. The Olympic Council of Asia, OCA, made its position clear when it announced that eSports will be introduced as a demonstration sport at the 2022 Asian Games

DOI: 10.4018/978-1-5225-5387-8.ch006

in China, the world's second largest multi-sport event recognised by the IOC after the Olympic Games (Brautigam, 2017). OCA promotes eSports as official medal sport on the basis of their popularity among the youth. With a global audience of 292 million and global revenue of $463 million in 2016 eSports are indeed popular (Graham, 2017). Actually, there are already many events, in which eSports competitions take place, like the World Electronic Sports Games or the eGames of Rio 2016 (Foxx, 2016).

Purportedly, the inclusion of eSports in the Olympics will increase its millennial viewership, something which will in turn boost the value of Olympic programming (Tran, 2017). At the same time, it will help the institutionalization of eSports into a mainstream and acceptable sport (ibid). Apparently, eSports lack in credibility. They are considered by some to not even be real sports, since they miss the physicality that traditional sports feature (Johnson, 2015). Notwithstanding a study showing that people playing eSports are exposed to strains similar to those of conventional athletes, with the difference lying in that for the latter the exertion is caused by bodily action, while for the former due to mental processes, (Moosa, 2017; Schütz, 2016), eSports have not yet managed to acquire the status of athleticism that would land them effortlessly a spot among the Olympic Games. Indeed, the president of IOC, Thomas Bach, has refused for now their entry with the justification that eSports are contrary to Olympic Games' rules and values (Moosa, 2017).

The aim of this chapter is to address this issue. It is not an argument against or in favour of the inclusion of eSports in Olympic Games, since for that decision many factors will eventually be taken into account, not the least of which of a financial nature. Instead, the focus is given on the properties of eSports as games and how these are juxtaposed to those of the conventional Olympic Games. Specifically, the author argues that there are three major discrepancies between eSports and traditional sports, distinct but very closely interconnected: the production of space, the application of rules, and the treatment of the human body. These disparities do not make eSports and Olympic Games non-compatible by default, yet they are intrinsic characteristics that must be taken into consideration and examined thoroughly for the better understanding of how these, for now, separate fields can potentially converge.

GAME DEFINITION

It is not easy to define what a game is. Games encompass so versatile human experiences that to form a single definition is rather impossible. On one hand, if the definition is so generic as to engulf all the games, it will be impractical in the sense that it will accommodate non-games as well. On the other hand, if the definition is too specific, it is bound to exclude many activities that are games. Literature remains inconclusive. Indeed, it was only in the late 1930s that Johan Huizinga was the first academic to treat the subject. Huizinga (1949) talked about *Homo Ludens*, the playing man, examining play as a cultural phenomenon, whose formal characteristics he summed up as a free activity outside ordinary life connected with no material interest and profit, taking place in a secluded time and space zone according to fixed rules (p. 13).

Roger Caillois (1961) followed on Huizinga's thought and expanded on it by demarcating the different categories of games. According to him, Huizinga succeeded in formalizing the fundamental characteristics of play and demonstrating its cultural role. However, he points out that Huizinga deliberately omitted the categorization of play into distinct areas, since to Huizinga *they all respond to the same needs and reflect, without qualification, the same psychological attitude* (p. 4). But for Caillois play has more than one facet and so as to rightly define it, these facets must be examined and explained. Nevertheless, he adopts most of Huizinga's characteristics of play as an activity essentially free, as in not obligatory, separated by specific limits of space and time defined and fixed in advance, with uncertain course, creating no wealth nor goods, governed by rules that suspend ordinary laws, and finally make-believe; *accompanied by a special awareness of a second reality or of a free unreality, as against real life* (pp. 9-10).

Caillois added the element of uncertainty and make-believe to Huizinga's definition. Especially for the latter he analyzed it by suggesting that there are some forms of play that do not need rules, but rather improvisation and this feeling of playing a role, as for example when children play 'school', a game in which one of them is the teacher and the other player or players are the pupils. Caillois stresses the fact that make-believe games create a fictional situation in which *the sentiment of as if replaces and performs the same function as do rules* (p. 8, emphasis in original). Indeed, for Caillois rules and make believe are mutually exclusive, a game can either be ruled or make believe but never both. That is because rules already create their own fictions. When someone plays chess or polo *by the very fact of complying with their respective rules, is separated from real life where there is no activity that literally corresponds to any of these games* (ibid).

He goes on to categorize make believe games in a separate and distinct category from other types of games. As a matter of fact, he proposes:

a division into four main rubrics, depending upon whether, in the games under consideration, the role of competition, chance, simulation, or vertigo is dominant. I call these agon, alea, mimicry, and ilinx, respectively. (p. 12)

Agon is a game in which two or more opponents compete so as to determine who the best is in a single trait, for example in swimming, fencing or in basketball.

Usually, agon is a physical game and in this case it can be equalized with sports (p. 14), but it can be of a mental quality as well, such as chess. *Alea* describes games of chance, in which the player has little to no influence on the outcome and *winning is the result of fate rather than triumphing over an adversary* (p. 17). Alea games are most often betting and gambling games. *Mimicry* is the game of make-believe, of taking on an illusory (in ludo, in playing) identity that dictates how the player will behave. The aim of the game is itself the success and retention of this make believe by the player herself or by others as in theatrical performances. Finally, *illinx* is the kind of play that through physical activity one aims to create a sensation of vertigo: *to momentarily destroy the stability of perception and inflict a kind of voluptuous panic upon an otherwise lucid mind* (p. 23). Illinx includes dancing, swinging, and roller coaster rides in amusement parks.

Caillois is very particular in examining how the different categories of games can entwine with one another. In that he proposes a further demarcation of play, which he calls *paidia* and *ludus* (p. 27). The paidia is the play which is infused in improvisation and joy with total absence of rules. Once this free-spirited play is institutionalized with rules, which gradually become more intricate, sophisticated, and complex, is transformed into ludus, a form of play that is completely rule-based. Caillois' paidia and ludus are positioned in the opposite sides of a spectrum, they constitute play in its absolute, and the different types of games can oscillate from one end to the other. As Caillois points out *the first manifestations of paidia have no name* (p. 29), since they are free, improvised ad hoc play,

But as soon as conventions, techniques, and utensils emerge, the first games as such arise with them: e.g. leapfrog, hide and seek, kite-flying, teetotum, sliding, blindman's buff, and doll-play. At this point the contradictory roads of agon, alea, mimicry, and ilinx begin to bifurcate. (ibid)

Nevertheless, according to Caillois, there are some games that combine elements of more than one category. There are many games that share characteristics of both agon and alea, such as backgammon or most card games, and almost all of agon games, because are based on competition among equals so as to make the result as unknown as possible, random even, can become the object of alea games, which is essentially what betting is. At the same time, some forms of play are mutually exclusive. Caillois emphasizes how agon and mimicry can be combined but only when it comes to the spectators and not the participants. The participants of agon must not pretend: *it is a spectacle, which, to be valid, excludes simulation* (p. 22). The spectators, on the other hand, simulate the game by identifying themselves with the players in the same way that they could identify with the protagonists of a novel they are reading or the film stars of a movie they are watching. Sports many a time invoke features of an intrinsic rite: *with costumes, solemn overture, appropriate liturgy, and regulated procedures. [...] The nature of these spectacles remains that of an agon, but their outward aspect is that of an exhibition* (ibid).

Even from a superfluous reading of the theory of play it becomes apparent that sports and eSports do not belong to the same category. ESports are digital games and as such they constitute simulations, which Caillois segregates from agon games, to which sports belong. However, this discrepancy cannot be taken at face value, especially because Caillois' taxonomy did not accommodate for digital games and as a result his use of the term simulation does not encompass the application of the word in computerized systems. For that, both physical sports and eSports need to be examined further so as one to reach a safe conclusion regarding their affinity or lack thereof. Here the approach taken is that of an analysis of their characteristics in terms of their most basic and essential properties, which are closely interlinked, namely their spatiality, implementation of rules, and employment of the body.

GAME SPACE

Caillois' theory remains still the prime philosophy of play that has influenced a number of academic fields (see for example Armstrong, 2000; Milam, 2000). It continues to be the point of reference of most contemporary takes on play (like in Rowe, 1992; Sutton-Smith, 1997; Motte, 2009). Indeed, in an analysis that encompasses eSports it is particularly essential, since it has been employed by theorists of digital games as well (Juul 2003; Salen & Zimmerman 2004). Arguably not all digital games are applicable to eSports competitions, at least as those have been formed until now since most of the times eSports include games that demand high dexterity and eye-hand coordination. For example, in the 2017 Asian Indoor and Martial Arts Games in Turkmenistan, players competed in Fifa 2017, and MOBA, Multiplayer Online Battle Arena, and RTA, Real Time Attack, gaming genres (Graham, 2017).

Nonetheless, Caillois' theory is not without its faults. Its most problematic point is that it segregates games and play from real life in terms of space and time. In that Caillois follows Huizinga's claim of the magic circle. Huizinga's proposition is that play has a certain locality and temporality, which separates it from ordinary life and where the rules of play reign. For Huizinga this segmentation of space for play has no essential difference from the demarcation of sacred places or places for all kinds of rituals, which include practices of art, law, commerce, and science. 'The turf,' he writes, *the tennis-court, the chessboard and pavement-hopscotch cannot formally be distinguished from the temple or the magic circle* (p. 20). Even though Caillois disagrees with Huizinga in equating the sacred with play, he takes for granted that play and games are separated from the real or ordinary life in terms of time and space.

The trouble with the magic circle is that it creates bubbles of practices that are isolated from everyday life. One bubble of space and time is play, another is the religious ritual, another is work etc. But if that is true, then what does it remain for the everyday life to consist of? As many critics against both Huizinga's and Caillois' view have argued (Ehrmann, 1968; Motte, 2009; Calleja, 2012), play does not work like that. When a game is played, this activity is part of the everyday life by means of both time and space. Games are not something separated from life, but a part of it. In turn, they formulate life's consistency, since reality is not something stable but morphed by its various practices, one of which is games. Indeed, games belong to the repertoire of human experiences and activities and they cannot be segregated from real life. The reason for that are players themselves, who are neither spatially nor timely segregated from real life but experience their existence in continuum.

Rather as Thomas Henricks (2010) points out, even though he finds this criticism against Caillois and Huizinga unfair, the *players decide how seriously they will take the game* (p. 164). By that he means that by agreeing to play, the players give their consent to follow the rules while the game lasts and at the same time they promise that they will not let the outcome of the game influence their behavior afterward, for example by getting angry in case they lose. Hence, it is this ludic attitude, this 'sportsmanship' as he calls it (ibid), that creates players and games and not the other way around. This is a very important distinction to show that games are not already conceived spaces that the moment a person enters or encounters is transformed into a player. On the contrary, it is the intention of the person that allows games and play to form. Since their origin is the intention of one person and this person can have more intentions than one, and most of the times at once, then games cannot be separated in terms of space and time. They can surely dictate or superimpose other intentions of said person so as to define her actions and attitude, but they never have spatial and timely boundaries of their own.

This can be easily understood by how strongly games' influence follows them even after they finish. Michael Tiberius (1996) informs us that in ancient Greece people used to demolish their city's walls upon the return of their Olympic champion in a symbolic gesture of respect; if they had citizens of such calibre then they did not need walls for protection. Or the champions would smash a certain part of the wall themselves by passing through it with their chariots so as to create a new entryway; because they were considered demigods they could not use the same gates as common men. Later, in Roman years, emperors and generals continued this tradition and would enter a city through arches and gates specifically designed for this purpose. The arch of Handrian in Athens, Greece is a construction of this type as it is the Arc de triomphe in Paris, France. In the same context lies Olympic Truce, a treaty signed in 9th century BCE so as 'the athletes, artists and their families, as well as ordinary pilgrims, could travel in total safety to participate in or attend the Olympic Games and return afterwards to their respective countries' (Olympic Truce). Actually, the Olympic Games are a circumstance in the history of games, in which the stadium and the temple coincide. They took place exclusively in Olympia, Greece, a site dedicated to the worshipping of Zeus and Hera, king and queen of the Olympian Gods (History).

In contemporary times, the Olympic Games have retained elements of the old rituals only as means of a continuation of the ancient traditions and linkage with the past. Instead, most games and sports have turned into full time and lucrative professions. Huizinga denied the status of games to activities that entail profit, but Caillois was not so antithetical to the notion. Even though he also defined games as unproductive, he did not see much of a difference when the player is paid, because she returns to reality once the game finishes. In this aspect, Caillois could not be farther from the truth. It is without a doubt that the reality of professional athletes is completely different to the reality of common people and this is absolutely due to their status as professional athletes. Actually, the top athletes are part of the international jet set, earn fortunes, and celebrate a modus vivendi of a star quality. At the same time, while they are playing, they are not only players but corporate commodities serving other functions as well; most importantly that of advertising various merchandise. Their influence is so prevalent that it continues even after their professional retirement. They become public figures and their opinion and example shapes the minds of millions of fans.

For Caillois it is understandable that this deification, basically, of athletes is innocuous, a *harmless compensation to the masses, who are resigned and have neither hope nor opportunity of attaining the luxury and glory by which they are dazzled* (p. 125), since for him it is confined in the space and time of the game. However, this is not the case, because this idolization shapes the conscience of the many and influences their life as a whole. Actually, Caillois himself shows how play is not unique in that by saying that this identification with the athletes can happen also with movie stars, singers, even characters from a book. Therefore, this is a universal tendency people have; it affects their whole life. As games are one of the many applications of this tendency, they must by default be part of this whole, thus part of life.

This is further exemplified if we look at games through the lens of the philosophy of space, particularly the theory of production of space by Henri Lefebvre. In his homonymous book, Lefebvre (1991) argues that space is at the same time conceived, perceived, and lived. A working interpretation of these concepts could equate conceived space with the space of mathematical figures, the perceived space with the space of physical movement, and the lived space with the subjective space of people's sense-making (Zhang, 2006). For example, a playground is designed on paper and then constructed by engineers in its physical form. Its space is first conceived and then perceived. But when it opens its gates to the people of the city it is experienced. This interaction of the space of the playground with the inhabitants transforms it to something lived and therefore prone to change. The designed on paper playground bears little resemblance to the physical playground after it has been lived in. This new playground creates new experiences of its space and thus new perceptions and new conceptions of what space is and how it should be approached. In other words, people do not simply act in space, but experience it and think about it. It is a dynamic, interactive process that never ceases; a production that shapes space and the people. This is why space cannot be regarded in a vacuum or as a static object. Space is an experience and at the same time its experience is what creates it. Game space, in particular, is produced by the players in every gaming session; it does not exist before, after or without them like the being of the player cannot be without the space that accommodates it.

Let us examine an example of this production in a physical game. A football field is a designated space for playing football. Its space is conceived, designed, with the specific purpose of hosting football matches. Very schematically, a football field has green grass, goal posts, and white lines. In this spatial conception people, players that is, perceive its space, act upon it, with the intention of playing football. At the same time, the players experience the football field, meaning they create its mental image in their mind, according to how they live it, namely by playing football. To this production of the football field one should add the historical and cultural production of football fields, which result to this specific football field. Furthermore, this specific football field contributes to the spatial production of all football fields and the space of humans in general.

It is important to note that one should not equate space with topographical coordinates, constructions and/or physical boundaries. Instead, space is its production. A football game is space not because it takes place in a stadium, even though the stadium is part of its space, but because the players produce its space. The football space is the field and the stadium, yet it is also the bodies of the players, their perception of the game, their actual gameplay, and also the rules of the game which dictate their spatial practice. At the same time, the football space coexists with other spaces. A stadium conventionally has administrative offices, locker rooms, a nursery, and bleachers, where the audience sits, watches the game, and cheers or jeers the players. Just like the voice of the audience, space cannot be confined nor secluded.

With that being said, the production of space is a matter of convention. People are indoctrinated into producing space in a certain way, which is in direct contact with their bodies and in a second, yet no lesser, degree with their society and culture. This is why for Lefebvre the production of space is essentially political, concentrated to the hands of the agents that exercise power, namely society, knowledge, and institutions (Elden, 2004). For Lefebvre, the production of space is power possession and exercise by the hegemony; an establishment of the norms of how other people, the ones who do not possess power, should treat space. A playground is conceived by the state with the intention of people playing in it. On the contrary, a hospital ward is not. How spatial conventions come into place and how specific spatial conceptions match spatial practices is a whole different subject. The crucial thing to keep here is that even though the production of space is arbitrary, adhering to natural laws, it is infused furthermore with social rules, which transform it to social space, the space of social interaction or of communication, as Lefebvre calls it (p. 19).

Since social space is a product of communication between the people that produce it, it is understandable that it is not stable and pre-ordered. On the contrary, it is in a state of flux. At the same time, some spaces are more institutionalized than others, meaning that for various reasons their conception, perception, and experience are so systematized that have become a norm or tradition. This does not mean that they are spatially segregated, because even in those cases the social rules that hold them together can still break or accommodate other meanings. In an Olympic stadium, for example, an athlete participates in 200 meters sprint. The space allocated for this sport is regulated to detail. The runners start behind a common line and the first to reach the finish point wins. The winner perceives this game space to win this game. Yet simultaneously she may break a World or Olympic record, hence transforming the same space to a different game space without negating the first.

Of course, there is a scale that regulates the appropriateness of each spatial practice according to their distance from the designated purpose of a space and the social conventions. Playing football on a dangerous minefield has lower acceptance from playing football on a deserted alley, which in turn has lower acceptance from playing football on a designated football field. This system of relations and acceptability, what Lefebvre calls 'spatial economy' (p.56), is a complex construction fashioned by many variegated factors that depend, in turn, on how space is produced. The institutions of power regard the spatial practices of the public and in case of divergence enforce the return to the supposed production with an infliction varying in severity according to the acceptance scale. At the 1968 Summer Olympic Games in Mexico City American sprinters Tommie Smith and John Carlos stood atop the medal podium and raised black-gloved fists during the playing of the national anthem in a symbolic gesture of black power (Cosgrove, 2014). In that case, the Olympic space became synchronously a game space and a political space. At the time, their behavior was considered atrocious and it resulted in their suspension from the U.S. track team and death threats (Davis, 2008). Nowadays, people see them as pioneers of the Black Lives Matter movement (Brown, 2017).

So, in the context of social space the obedience to the game rules has something of a sacrifice in it. In Olympic Games these rules are extended to the general conduct of an athlete. The Olympic Games, and their space, are not superimposed on people.

Rather people comply with arbitrary and conventional rules, in order to participate in the games, both as competitors and as spectators, and thus produce them. In this sense, games are indeed a presupposition of culture as Huizinga wanted them (p.1). People conform to rules that have no outside meaning than the one assigned to them by people themselves so as to be able to organize the chaos of their existence to sustainable order. When these rules become institutionalized they form the Law. Playing, therefore, is an unconscious study to social being, interaction, and order. People come together and agree to a catholic consensus, which demands a part of their freedom in return for the guarantee of coexistence with the sole purpose of the success of this coexistence. The more institutionalized a game, the more strict and rigid those rules; sports being probably the most institutionalized of all with federations, international organizations, and a specialized branch of the Law engaging only with the implementation of the sports law with its own jurisprudence (see Court of Arbitration for Sport).

Things are different when it comes to eSports. Unlike physical sports, eSports are digital games so they constitute virtual spaces; they are coded simulations that are actualized by the player the moment she is playing by her input commands. The machine translates these commands according to the code of the game and outputs the results so as for the player to respond and so on. It is obvious that digital games differ from traditional games in terms of materiality. This affects their production as spaces in multiple ways, but what matters the most here is their being social spaces. While physical game spaces are the product of social interaction between people, virtual game spaces are de facto the product of interactivity between the human and the machine. Even in multiplayer games, the spatial communication between the players is always mediated by the machine through the code of the game.

This creates itself a distance between eSports and physical sports. Caillois, as it was shown previously, places sports under the category of agon as formal competitions of a physical nature. In agon the communication is between humans. One person strives to defeat others in a specific skill. A person cannot compete alone. As Henricks points out: *people want to be well regarded by others. They wish to interact and to be watched, and they understand themselves by comparing what they do to the achievements of others* (p. 170). Even when an agon game is played alone, it is done with a competitive attitude. According to Caillois, this is what differentiates agon from ludus, in which *the conflict is with the obstacle, not with one or several competitors* (p. 29). This holds true particularly for the Olympic Games. In 2016 the Russian pole vaulter Yelena Isinbaeva, who had been banned from taking part to the Olympic Games in Rio due to a doping scandal regarding the Russian Federation, uploaded an Instagram video that showed her jumping over 5.06 meters, which is her world record, alone in her hometown of Volgograd (Kouroupaki, 2016). She then announced her retirement during a press conference saying that she congratulates the Greek gold medalist, Katerina Stefanidi who had jumped to 4.85 meters, though she did not exactly win the gold medal, because she competed without Isinbaeva there (ibid).

In eSports, on the other hand, the competition is first and foremost with the code and secondarily with the other person. The winner is the one who will beat the code better and first, so there is always a medium, an intermediary in the form of the machine. Arguably, physical games may also include solitariness, like puzzles. Yet in this case there is no social communication with a medium, but rather a handling of a tool, a toy. Instead, digital games are simulations and as simulations they are systems that communicate with the player and the player must in return communicate constantly with them (Frasca, 2003). They are spaces and not static objects. However, unlike physical sports they are produced on the basis of a code and not of social rules, a feature that influences their production as spaces in an essential manner.

GAME RULES

One discerning feature of games is that they are comprised by rules. These rules are conventional and meaningless, yet meaning inducing. They are there so as for the game to have a distinct structure and purpose. This is why they cannot be imposed; they have to be respected. In Caillois' words, play entails *rules that are respected for their own sake* (p. 157). It is telling that in most – if not all – sports there is at least one referee or judge so as to make sure that the rules of the game are followed. In basketball it is forbidden by the rules of the game for players to start kicking the ball with their feet. Yet the can do it, they have the physical ability, even though they do not do it, because they respect the rules of the game and they know they will get penalized in case they do not. Not only that, but if they start kicking the ball with their feet they will have formed an altogether different game. In digital games this respect of the rules is not consensual. The player can only perform those actions that are permitted by the code of the game. If the code does not allow a certain spatial practice, then the player cannot actualize it. If in digital basketball the kicking of the ball is prohibited, then the player simply cannot perform it. It is not any more about sportsmanship or consensus, but rather an ultimatum, a take it or leave it situation.

Unlike in physical games, where the rules are social conventions, in digital games the rules of the code are translated to natural laws. The participants of eSports do not consciously acquiesce to a certain number of rules so as to play a game. The rules of the digital game are hard-programmed in its code and unless one breaks that code she cannot overpass the code's rules. Even when it comes to glitches, one takes advantage of gaps in the code, in order to perform actions that are considered illogical in the context of the said game yet are still permitted by the code. The production of the virtual game space depends on its conception by the code, which dictates what this space allows and demands from the player regarding its perception, and how the player experiences it. In a digital rendering of Sudoku, the designers and programmers of the game code conceive its spatial production, which then the player actualizes the moment she decides to play the game. The code of the game dictates what the spatial practice of the player may be; filling the empty slots with numbers. Through her spatial practice, the player experiences Sudoku and its lived space completing thusly its production of space.

Furthermore, the code of the games is digital, meaning that it either allows or not allows something. They are no gray areas that are open to interpretation, but rather a continuous understanding of the machine. This holds true also for games that invoke affective or evolving bottom-up game design, namely games that adapt more to the player's feedback than just being rigid pre-established blocks of coding. Affective computing and quantum game design is still a work in progress so it is not as of now part of the eSports. However, even in that case it is the communication with the machine that is further developed, so the mediation of the code, albeit in a different structure, cannot be overpassed. The same applies when digital games are influenced by the physical space rules in the sense that the players adapt their ludic behavior according to social standards, in spite of them not being imposed by the digital game rules.

This happens often in online games. As Tristan Donovan (2010) mentions, when Ultima Online (Origin Systems, 1997) was first published, many players utilized the game system to turn against other less experienced players and rob them or kill them. Despite the moderators' efforts to control the phenomenon, their intervention was insufficient. As a result, players started to organize themselves in vigilante online groups that protected the community from in game attacks banning in reality the sly players from continuing the way they behaved inside the game; an action that in spatial terminology is translated to a prohibition of their spatial practice, and their enforced compliance with the spatial practice of the many. However, this spatial practice conformed to social rules that are exogenous to the game itself. Respectively, a similar situation can be seen when a group of friends are playing a multiplayer digital game and one of them pushes buttons at random ridiculing, in result, the game. This player will most probably face the wrath of the other players that will force her to behave or else stop her from playing. This ludicrous behavior is not constrained by the game code, but by the social rules that the other players impose.

As it was argued before, the digital game space, as space, is not confined to a certain locality. Naturally, it is influenced by the physical space, since it is played by players, who are physical beings. It is understandable, therefore, that the players bring along social spatial conventions which they have been conditioned to obey so as for games to be functional and meaningful. The difference lies in that this applicability in digital games is once removed, namely this physical fair play is imposed on digital games only because the players have learnt to treat physical game space in that manner. If they had not been exposed to the social rules of the physical space in the first place, then the digital space would not have elicited these responses from them because its production follows different principles. Even in this scenario, what the social rules can affect remains in what the code allows. If the code does not allow in game robbing, then the player cannot conform to not rob other players. In this, the social rules are an optional super-structure over the basis of the code rules. The player can still choose to ignore them or bypass them, yet she does not have the same choice with the rules of the code.

It has to be noted, nonetheless, that even in the most rule-based digital games players have the ability to dissociate themselves from what is expected from them. Yet, here the compliance with the rules is not a matter of goodwill or choice, because if the player does not perform the spatial practices that the code demands, then there is not a different production of space, as it would be the case in physical games, but the negation of production of space in total. In most games this negation is realized as the death of the player. Alternatively, it can mean that the production of space stops until the player complies with the intended spatial practice. As Olli Tapio Leino comments (2012) to play a digital game means that us, the players, *must find out what the designers wanted us to do in a game. If we fail to figure this out we are most likely to get stuck or find ourselves in front of a game over screen.* So instead of providing meaning to space, we have to discover the meaning that someone else, the designer, imposed on this space.

Since games are the 'residue of culture' (Caillois, 1961, p. 58), we are actually talking about a shift in culture. In a meaningless world where nothing is for certain we need the reassurance of directions, thus most physical spaces show their intended use, defined by the institution of power, through signs that we are culturally conditioned to interpret in the right way; because if we do not the counter effects can vary from absurdity and lack of communication with our space to social exclusion and correctional – or not – punishment. Digital games still punish us for not complying with the hegemony, but in their case the hegemony is the code and not the abstract power of society. In this sense, digital games do not involve the social dialogue of learning to play by the rules in order to exist in peace and harmony with one another. Instead, they train us to better understand how to operate a machine, how to acquire an individualistic trait that deems society obsolete.

Indeed, when it comes to eSports one does not even need a human opponent. The machine can take up this role. Actually, the human element in eSports as of now is rather subdued. Certainly the players do not need to share the same physical space, since they do not have to interact with each other. It is only in the game space that they compete. This applies to members of the same team as well. Their exclusive channel of communication is the headphones with the attached microphones. It becomes apparent that in order to win the game, the players have to be infused as much as they can in its virtual space, what in digital games is called immersion or incorporation (Calleja, 2011). This is why in eSports tournaments the focus is given on the screen, where the true action takes place.

Instead, the physical bodies of the players are more or less static. The players sit on chairs in front of said screens and, their mental processing notwithstanding, they do not show much physical motion apart from their hands and specifically their fingers. If their movements were to be extracted from their effect, they are nothing more than repeated pushing of buttons. Moreover, their physical activity does not have one to one equivalence with the activity performed on screen; they merely press different buttons for the various virtual spatial practices. Hence, theoretically, a champion in one digital game can easily become a champion in another digital game. This is why we talk about eSports in general and not about one specific digital game as it is the case with physical games, in which one person is a runner, another one is a wrestler etc.

Hence, if eSports become part of the Olympic Games, it will not be on the same condition as any other physical sport. It will not even be the same as chess or bridge for that matter. The discerning point is that unlike physical games and sports, the result of the action in eSports is moved from physical space to virtual space. This is not to say that eSports are not real sports. As it has been shown the virtual is not in dialectical antithesis with the real, but with the actual (Levy, 1998; Aarseth, 2007). Caillois himself did not differentiate between games that involve primarily mental or primarily physical skills. Yet in eSports it is not so much about physical or mental skills, but rather about physical and virtual space. In eSports the virtuality is not only introduced, it also takes central stage. In this it takes away emphasis both from the physical space and from the physical body.

THE BODY IN GAMES

Since ancient times the focus of Olympic Games has been the body itself. In most Olympic sports we celebrate the bodily idolization, the body reaching unachievable limits, breaking barriers that up to that point were considered impossible. As Eugen Fink (2016) writes, in competitive play the body is linked with health and beauty, and essentially with philosophy. It is a different essence from play as a 'technical occupation', which for him is the play when technology is implemented, like for example in Formula 1 races (p. 247). In eSports this difference is by default more prominent, because unlike other physical sports that entail technology but still take place in the physical world, in eSports the focus is moved from the body to the results of its extension to another materiality, the virtual space of the screen.

Indeed, eSports negate the physical body. This is self-evident if we compare the body image of an Olympic athlete to that of an eSports champion. ESports competitors train as many, if not more, hours as traditional athletes, yet their physical activity is inconsequential (Schütz, 2016). Even though it is due to the physical body that they are able to use and communicate with the machine, once that happens their physicality is reduced to a mechanical movement and it is instead the machine that comes alive. They, as bodies, are transformed into a new existence that participates in the production of the virtual space. In that respect, eSports share more elements with mimicry than with agon; the what-if of mimicry becomes systemized. Caillois informs us that:

In one way or another, one escapes the real world and creates another. One can also escape himself and become another. This is mimicry. (p. 19)

Henricks further analyzes this notion as:

Mimicry is connected [...] to the obsessive desire of humans to escape the boundaries and limitations of their own selfhood, to lose themselves in the patterns of the world. (p. 160)

This affects eSports both as a form of play and as a form of spectacle. In physical sports, the spectators do not participate per se in the game, yet they share the same physical space with the players and the game space. Since as it was aforementioned space is a production, the spectators may not actively participate in the game, however their presence still shapes its space. Many a time it has been emphasized by professional players and athletes how important the role of their fans is for them. Of course, this is also a matter of marketing and promotion of tickets, yet anyone that has ever played, albeit recreationally, a game or participated in a sports event can attest to that. The spectators influence the psychology of the player and thus the game itself.

In eSports the spectators do not regularly look at the players. They may shoot a glance at them, but naturally their attention is drawn where the action takes place, that is the computer screen. In that they do not share anymore the space of the game. Rather the game space is transformed for them into an environment, where a production of space is taking place but it does not communicate with them. They are part of the production of physical space, but not of the virtual space. They are excluded by default. Their body is limited to a pair of eyes. The players cannot even hear them. They wear headphones and are totally engrossed, immersed to another existence, the one taking part in the production of the virtual space, while their physical self has been limited to mechanic movements that have no referential or even abstract meaning in the world they share with their audience.

In that it could be argued that Huizinga's magic circle in this case functions awkwardly. It is not the game that is secluded from real life, because a game is not something static neither is real life. On the contrary, they are the spectators, the bodies not participating in the game, which are secluded from the spatial production of the game. As Lefebvre argues, experiencing space with the eyes only results in that *the bodies are transported out of themselves, transferred and emptied out, as it were, via the eyes* (p. 98), which in turn is responsible for *the decomposition of the body into localized functions and its abandonment as a totality* (p. 204). Therefore, eSports negate the physical body, both in spectators and players, in principle. This negation continues to exist, albeit not that acutely, also in digital games that implement the physical body as a whole, for example in Wii sports (Nintendo, 2006). The physical activity notwithstanding, the attention of the players is still on the screen, not as an object of their physical space but as an entry point to a virtual space. Hence, this negation of the physical is to be understood as a reduction of the human body to a set of referential movements that have no meaning and no effect on the physical space, but instead are part of the active production of the virtual space.

In this, eSports are proven to be indeed contradictory, if not antithetical, to the principles, values, and approach of the Olympic Games, whose aim has always been the apotheosis of the physical body. In physical sports the achievements of the athletes are tangible and continue to affect the physical space, life, and world even after the game finishes. A physical body that competes and wins is an accomplished body on its own. Instead, a body that wins in a virtual world does not carry these bodily effects on the physical world. That is not to say that eSports are secluded from physical life, because they are not. ESports champions enjoy privileges in the real world as much as other athletes. Also, they still have skills and trained abilities. The difference is that the emphasis in eSports is not given to the body as an object itself, but as a vehicle, a medium for the passage to another space, that is virtual, hence ideological in nature.

If in Olympic Games every time a winner 'steps on the rostrum to be crowned with an olive wrath', we revel in *the glorification of the body, the apotheosis of our sensuous existence [...] which conducts itself like the playing child of the Ephesian thinker* (Fink, 2016, p. 248), in eSports we are dealing with the division of physical and virtual of Aristoteles. This is not a priori negative neither does it render impossible for eSports to become part of the Olympic Games. Indeed, this negation of the physical body may result to an egalitarianism that is not possible with physical sports. For example, eSports teams can include players of all genders or of various disabilities for that matter. What it is argued, however, is that the inclusion of eSports in Olympic Games will indeed change the nature of Olympic Games unprecedentedly in a fashion that no other physical sport or game could ever do, to the point of altering the deep core of what Olympic Games are. This change, as all changes, will have both positive and negative effects, the degree and actualization of which is a matter of politics and economics and an important subject for further research.

CONCLUSION

In the current chapter the author compared physical and digital games in terms of their formal properties as games in the context of whether eSports can be part of the Olympic Games. Using the theory of play by Roger Caillois as orientation, the author argued that physical games and eSports differ in how they treat space, implement rules, and finally approach the body. Unlike physical games, eSports, being digital games, are virtual spaces, In that they employ a distinct materiality from physical games, which results in them being produced differently as spaces. Following on the philosophy of space by Henri Lefebvre, the author showed that eSports are produced according to the code of the game and not according to social rules and the power of the hegemony like physical sports. The consequence of this is a distancing in the function of play itself. While in physical sports one should respect the rules of the game for their own sake in an appropriation of how society and the law works, in digital games the rules take on the form of natural laws, since if the code does not permit a certain spatial practice, then the player cannot perform it.

In actuality, the focus is transferred from the physical space to virtual space. The physical spatial practices of the player are only a mechanically repeated movement. It is in the screen of the machine where the actual action takes place. In that, eSports negate the physical body and existence of the players in an original and intrinsic to the medium way that no other physical sport does. Hence, eSports are indeed antithetical to the Olympic Games, which since antiquity have always put the physical body as an object at the forefront. This concludes that the potential inclusion of eSports in Olympic Games will irrevocably affect their quality. The nature of this effect can be the subject of a further study through the prism of various paragons, arguing both the negative and the positive aftereffects.

REFERENCES

Aarseth, E. (2007). Doors and Perception: Fiction vs. Simulation in Games. *Intermédialités*, *9*, 35–44.

Brautigam, T. (2017). *Esports comes to the second largest multi-sports event in the world*. Retrieved 28 October, 2017 from https://dotesports.com/business/esports-asian-games-14151

Brown, D. L. (2017). *They didn't #TakeTheKnee: The Black Power protest salute that shook the world in 1968*. Retrieved 26 October, 2017 from www.washingtonpost.com/news/retropolis/wp/2017/09/24/they-didnt-takeaknee-the-black-power-protest-salute-that-shook-the-world-in-1968/?utm_term=.1cc199b070c6

Caillois, R. (1961). *Man, Play, and Games* (M. Barash, Trans.). Chicago, IL: University of Illinois Press.

Calleja, G. (2011). *In-game: From Immersion to Incorporation*. Cambridge, MA: The MIT Press.

Calleja, G. (2012). Erasing the Magic Circle. *Philosophy of Engineering and Technology*, *7*, 77–91. doi:10.1007/978-94-007-4249-9_6

Cosgrove, B. (2014). *The Black Power Salute That Rocked the 1968 Olympics*. Retrieved 28 October, 2017 from http://time.com/3880999/black-power-salute-tommie-smith-and-john-carlos-at-the-1968-olympics/

Davis, D. (2008). *Olympic Athletes Who Took a Stand*. Retrieved 27 October, 2017 from www.smithsonianmag.com/articles/olympic-athletes-who-took-a-stand-593920/

Donovan, T. (2010). *Replay: The History of Video Games*. East Sussex, UK: Yellow Ant.

Ehrmann, J., Lewis, C., & Lewis, P. (1968). Homo Ludens Revisited (C. Lewis & P. Lewis, Trans.). *Yale French Studies*, *41*(41), 31–57. doi:10.2307/2929664

Elden, S. (2004). *Understanding Henri Lefebvre: Theory and the Possible*. New York: Continuum.

Fink, E. (2016). *Play as Symbol of the World and Other Writings* (I. A. Moore & C. Turner, Trans.). Bloomington, IN: Indiana University Press.

Foxx, C. (2016). *Video game Olympics announced for Rio*. Retrieved 28 October, 2017 from www.bbc.com/news/technology-35987839

Frasca, G. (2003). Simulation vs. Narrative: Introduction to Ludology. In M. Wolf & B. Perron (Eds.), *The Video Game Theory Reader* (pp. 221–234). New York: Routledge.

Graham, B. A. (2017). *ESports to be a medal event at 2022 Asian Games*. Retrieved 24 October, 2017 from www.theguardian.com/sport/2017/apr/18/esports-to-be-medal-sport-at-2022-asian-games

Henricks, T. S. (2010). Caillois's Man, Play, and Games: An Appreciation and Evaluation. *American Journal of Play*, 157–185.

History. (n.d.). Retrieved 28 October, 2017 from www.olympic.org/ancient-olympic-games/history

Huizinga, J. (1949). *Homo Ludens: A Study of the Play-Element in Culture*. London: Routledge and Kegan Paul.

Johnson, E. (2015). *Video Games on ESPN? It's Time to Stop Pretending eSports Are 'Real' Sports.* Retrieved 28 October, 2017 from www.recode.net/2015/4/27/11561916/video-games-on-espn-its-time-to-stop-pretending-esports-are-real

Kouroupaki, G. (2016). *Yelena Isinbayeva: The last jump and rueful goodbye of the pole vault tsarina.* Retrieved 28 October, 2017 from www.cnn.gr/news/sports/story/43413/gelena-isinmpageva-teleytaio-alma-kai-pikro-antio-apo-tin-tsarina-ton-aitheron [in Greek].

Lefebvre, H. (1991). *The Production of Space* (D. Nicholson-Smith, Trans.). Oxford, UK: Blackwell.

Leino, O. T. (2012). Death Loop as a Feature. *Game Studies, 12*(2).

Lévy, P. (1998). *Becoming Virtual: Reality in the Digital Age* (R. Bononno, Trans.). New York: Plenum Trade.

Moosa, T. (2017). *Esports are real sports. It's time for the Olympic Video Games*. Retrieved 24 October, 2017 from www.theguardian.com/commentisfree/2017/aug/11/esports-olympic-video-games-ioc-gaming

Nintendo. (2006). *Olympic Truce*. Retrieved 28 October, 2017 from www.olympic.org/olympic-truce

Origin Systems. (1997). *Ultima Online*. Microsoft Windows.

Schütz, M. (2016). *Science shows that eSports professionals are real athletes.* Retrieved 23 October, 2017 from www.dw.com/en/science-shows-that-esports-professionals-are-real-athletes/a-19084993

Tiberius, M. (1996). *When they were demolishing the walls.* Retrieved 28 October, 2017 from www.tovima.gr/opinions/article/?aid=81574 (in Greek)

Tran, K. (2017). *Esports in consideration for 2024 Olympics.* Retrieved 28 October, 2017 from www.businessinsider.com/esports-in-consideration-for-2024-olympics-2017-8

Zhang, Z. (2006). What Is Lived Space? *Ephemera: Theory & Politics in Organization, 6*(2), 219-223.

ADDITIONAL READING

Armstrong, P. (2000). The politics of play: The social implications of Iser's aesthetic theory. *New Literary History, 31*(1), 211–223. doi:10.1353/nlh.2000.0001

Court of Arbitration for Sport. Retrieved 28 October, 2017 from www.tas-cas.org/en/index.html

Juul, J. (2003, November). *The Game, the Player, the World: Looking for a Heart of Gameness.* Keynote presented at the Level Up conference, Utrecht.

Milam, J. (2000). Playful constructions and Fragonard's swinging scenes. *Eighteenth-Century Studies, 33*(4), 543–559. doi:10.1353/ecs.2000.0042

Motte, W. (2009). Playing in earnest. *New Literary History, 40*(1), 25–42. doi:10.1353/nlh.0.0076

Rowe, M. W. (1992). The Definition of 'Game'. *Philosophy (London, England), 67*(262), 467–479. doi:10.1017/S0031819100040663

Salen, K., & Zimmerman, E. (2004). *Rules of Play: Game Design Fundamentals.* Cambridge, MA: The MIT Press.

Sutton-Smith, B. (1997). *The Ambiguity of Play.* Cambridge, MA: Harvard University Press.

Chapter 7
Physical Education and Religious Freedom:
The ECtHR Perspective

Konstantinos Margaritis
University of Crete, Greece

ABSTRACT

Freedom of religion has been constantly characterized as one of the foundations of a democratic society. On the other hand, the significance of physical education in the development of children's overall personality is beyond dispute. Thus, the question that arises is, What happens in a case of a conflict involving the above? The aim of this chapter is to provide an answer on the basis of the case law of the European Court of Human Rights. In particular, the fundamental cases of Dogru vs. France and Kervanci vs. France will be examined, as well as the recent case of Osmanoglu and Kocabas vs. Switzerland. Through the analysis of the cases, useful conclusions will be drawn on the possible impact of religious freedom on physical education.

INTRODUCTION

Beyond dispute, religion plays a significant role within a person's identity. Apart from the dogmatic approach, religion contains important cultural characteristics that essentially enhance multiculturalism. This being the case, religious diversity needs to be protected, especially in the era of globalization, where global connectivity is increased and fundamental rights, particularly those of minorities, face new challenges (Brysk, 2002).

DOI: 10.4018/978-1-5225-5387-8.ch007

On the other hand, physical education undoubtedly completes the concept of education. The Roman satirical poet Juvenal explicitly incites to pray for a healthy mind in a healthy body (mens sana in corpore sano) presenting it first in the list of what is desirable in life (Satire X) (Rudd, 1991). In the same spirit, the pre Socratic philosopher Thales answers the question "what man is happy?" by stating: *he who has a healthy body, a resourceful mind and a docile nature* (Diogenes Laertius (-Hicks), 1972). In modern terms, physical education has been included in both primary and secondary education curricula in a form of public policy sometimes described even as a constitutional demand.[1]

So, the main question is what happens if the two aforementioned principles collide? The aim of this chapter is to provide an answer on the basis of the case law of the European Court of Human Rights (hereinafter: ECtHR, the Court). In particular, the fundamental cases of Dogru vs. France and Kervanci vs. France will be examined, as well as the recent case of Osmanoglu and Kocabas vs. Switzerland. Through the analysis of the cases, useful conclusions will be drawn on the impact of religious freedom on physical education.

FREEDOM OF RELIGION IN THE EUROPEAN CONVENTION ON HUMAN RIGHTS

The protection of freedom of religion is guaranteed in the European Convention on Human Rights (hereinafter: ECHR, the Convention), since the Convention came into force in 1953. In particular, article 9 states:

1. **Everyone Has the Right to Freedom of Thought, Conscience and Religion**: This right includes freedom to change his religion or belief and freedom, either alone or in community with others and in public or private, to manifest his religion or belief, in worship, teaching, practice and observance.
2. **Freedom to Manifest One's Religion or Beliefs Shall be Subject Only to Such Limitations as are Prescribed by Law and are Necessary in a Democratic Society in the Interests of Public Safety**: For the protection of public order, health or morals, or for the protection of the rights and freedoms of others.

As can be easily observed, paragraph 1 refers to the right itself, including several aspects, such as the freedom to change religion and the freedom to manifest religion. The Court has emphatically underlined the importance of religious freedom stating that:

as enshrined in article 9, freedom of thought, conscience and religion is one of the foundations of a "democratic society" within the meaning of the Convention. It is, in its religious dimension, one of the most vital elements that go to make up the identity of believers and their conception of life, but it is also a precious asset for atheists, agnostics, sceptics and the unconcerned. The pluralism indissociable from a democratic society, which has been dearly won over the centuries, depends on it. (Kokkinakis vs. Greece)

Therefore, religious freedom is proved to be crucial not only to believers, but also to atheists, agnostics, skeptics and the unconcerned since they can seek protection for their own ideas based on the very same provision. In that sense, pluralism is preserved that constitutes a key element in a liberal, democratic society.

Religious freedom contains rights that can be exercised either individually or in a collective manner (Ahdar & Leigh, 2013). For that reason, religious communities enjoy a certain level of autonomy from State interference; the Court has identified this parameter by characterizing the autonomous existence of religious communities as *indispensable for pluralism* and *an issue at the very heart of the protection which article 9 affords*. This aspect is directly related to enjoyment of religious freedom by its active members since, as the Court observes, *were the organizational life of the community not protected by article 9 of the Convention, all other aspects of the individual's freedom of religion would become vulnerable* (Hasan & Claush vs. Bulgaria).

Nevertheless, restrictions to manifest religion may be imposed under the direction of paragraph 2. Under this provision, in order for the State to interfere with that particular right, three conditions must be met: the restriction must be prescribed by law, must pursue a legitimate aim and be necessary in a democratic society (Renucci, 2005). The first condition is somewhat self-evident; the restriction must be accompanied with the necessary formalities in order not to be arbitrary and therefore preserve the rule of law. The term "law" includes statutory provisions and administrative regulations, as well as case law. The second condition refers to aims of exceptional importance for society, which are explicitly mentioned in the provision itself; public safety, the protection of public order, health or morals, the protection of the rights and freedoms of others (Martinez-Torron, 2012). The third condition imposes that the restriction of religious freedom must be proportionate to the legitimate aim pursued. Indeed, the term "necessary" is quite complex and for that reason hard to be defined. That is the reason why the outcome is determined on a case by case basis under certain principles that have been developed through the Court's case law. In addition, what is considered to be necessary shall refer to democratic standards which all contracting parties to the Convention are bound by and not methods of absolutism (Sicilianos, 2017).

The application of the abovementioned principles in certain physical education activities has been examined before the Court in several cases the most important of which will be seen in the following chapters.

THE CASES BEFORE THE ECTHR

Dogru vs. France and Kervanci vs. France

Both cases refer to secondary school Muslim students who refused to remove their headscarf for the physical education classes, despite repeated requests by the respective teacher, since they could not participate actively otherwise. In both cases, the school disciplinary committee expelled the students for breaching the duty of assiduity, a decision that was later upheld by the courts in France. The applicants alleged a violation of article 9 ECHR, along with the right to education as guaranteed in article 2, Protocol 1 ECHR.

Initially, wearing a headscarf reflects manifestation of a religion, falling within the scope of article 9, par. 1 ECHR. Thus the prohibition in the particular cases, for the purpose of active participation in physical education classes and the subsequent expulsion of the students on the ground of refusing to remove the headscarf constitute interference on behalf of the state authority with the exercise of the right to religious freedom. What is left to be examined is whether a lawful limitation under article 9, par. 2 ECHR applies under the circumstances.

The Court found that, although not explicitly, the prohibition of wearing a headscarf during the physical education classes could be safely derived from factors that were prescribed by law, namely the duty to attend classes regularly, the requirements of safety and the necessity of dressing appropriately for sports practice (Dogru vs. France, par. 53-59; Kervanci vs. France, par. 53-59). Here, the Court confirmed its approach that the term "law" does not only refer to formal law, but may include lower ranked enactments, as well as case law (Dogru vs. France, par. 52; Kervanci vs. France, par. 52). Moreover, based on the facts of the cases, the Court acknowledged the existence of a legitimate aim in the State interference (Dogru vs. France, par. 60; Kervanci vs. France, par. 60).

The argumentation of the Court regarding the third condition (limitation necessary in a democratic society) is based on two main, interrelated factors. First, the general matter of church – state relations where France has adopted a secular model (Soper, den Dulk & Monsma, 2017). A principle of constitutional value,[2] secularism reveals a position of neutrality towards every religion, which is also reflected in the state school system. Indeed, the States enjoy a margin of appreciation regarding the church – state relations, since it belongs to the core of the social and historical development of a State. In that sense, religious freedom recognized and even restricted, under the requirements of secularism appears legitimate under values underpinning the ECHR (Dogru vs. France, par. 72; Kervanci vs. France, par. 72). Secondly, the rationale of the decision itself; the prohibition of headscarves during physical education classes was not imposed for any reason other than the health and safety of the students and the active participation in class. As far as the principle of proportionality is concerned, expulsion from the school was not the immediate reaction to the incident; several attempts to explain the abovementioned reasoning have been made by the state authorities before reaching that conclusion. In addition, the ban to wearing a headscarf was not general, but strictly limited to the physical education classes on the basis of specific reasons. For all the above, the Court found no violation of the right to religious freedom.

Osmanoglu and Kocabas vs. Switzerland

In this case, a couple, two Muslim parents, refused to send their minor daughters to compulsory swimming classes on the ground that their religious belief prohibited them from letting their children participate in mixed swimming lessons. Despite the efforts on behalf of the school principal, the applicants continued to refuse complying with the educational program. In the end, they were imposed a fine of 1.400 Swiss francs in total for failing to fulfill their parental responsibilities. The applicants claimed that the compulsory character of the mixed swimming classes was contrary to their right to manifest their religion as guaranteed in article 9 ECHR.

Similarly to the previously examined cases, the matter touches upon the right to manifest religion, hence the Court had to explore whether this limitation constitutes a lawful one in accordance with article 9, par. 2 ECHR.

Regarding the first condition, the Court emphasized on the quality of law and identified two prerequisites in order to have the restriction "prescribed by law" (Osmanoglu and Kocabas vs. Switzerland, par. 51-52). First, the piece of legislation or case law must be sufficiently accessible for the citizen and second the "law" shall be sufficiently precise in the sense that enables the citizen to understand what that law allows or prohibits. In that particular case, the compulsory swimming classes were referred in the study plan available online, as well as the possible fines imposed in case of violation; thus the disputed measure was prescribed by law (Osmanoglu and Kocabas vs. Switzerland, par. 53).

In addition, the insertion of compulsory swimming classes in the curriculum aims at assisting foreign children with a different cultural and religious background to integrate and generally promoting respect for compulsory schooling and gender equality (Osmanoglu and Kocabas vs. Switzerland, par. 64). In this context, all students could enjoy the very same form of education which limits the possibility of social exclusion, especially in the case of foreign students. The aim of the measures at stake was found to be legitimate for the purpose of article 9, par. 2 ECHR.

The matter of necessity in democratic society was then considered. Once again, the Court repeated the wide margin of appreciation that the States enjoy concerning the church – state relationship. All the more, although the States should refrain from adopting an educational system which embodies indoctrination, they are free to organize the relevant program in line with their traditions and needs (Osmanoglu and Kocabas vs. Switzerland, par. 95). Moreover, the aforementioned legitimate aim could not be otherwise achieved. Apart from the indisputable importance of sports activities to the development and health of children, most importantly, it is practiced in groups which allows students to develop their social skills. At the end, the approach adopted by the State ends to no student being exempted due to religious or philosophical beliefs of the parents (Osmanoglu and Kocabas vs. Switzerland, par. 98), whilst all necessary accommodation were provided. A last point of consideration was the gravity of the penalty from a proportionality perspective. Taking into account the objective pursued, namely the physical education as well as social integration of children, the Court found that the fine (1.400 Swiss francs in total) does not violate the principle of proportionality (Osmanoglu and Kocabas vs. Switzerland, par. 103). Therefore, article 9 ECHR was not infringed in the particular case.

STRENGTHENING THE ROLE OF PHYSICAL EDUCATION

After presenting the ECtHR cases, it could be argued that the common denominator is the upholding of the significance of physical education in the curriculum, even at the expense of a human right of utmost importance for a democratic society, such as the right to religious freedom. In balancing all parties' interests, the Court clearly identified that active participation in a form of teamwork enhances the children's social skills and promotes equality which valuably assist foreign students in better integrating within society.

One basic argument mainly derived from the cases of Dogru vs. France and Kervanci vs. France is the duty of assiduity with reference to physical education. Diachronically, physical education has been considered to be neglected within the school programme and its value for children in several dimensions is underrated (Smiles, 1838; Bremmer, 1974; Boorman, 1996). In the same line, the European Parliament (2007) encourages the member states to improve their physical education policies, principally to ensure that a balance is struck between physical and intellectual activities in schools, to invest in quality sports facilities and take appropriate measures to make sports premises and sports curricula at schools accessible to all students and invites all Member States to ensure the teaching of physical education at all levels, including primary school, by specialized physical education instructors.

By directly referring to the duty of assiduity, the Court essentially equalized physical education with all other classes and accepted specific standards for active participation which include the removal of headscarves and thus, noncompliance with those standards legally ends up in disciplinary measures. Although the position of France on the matter of wearing religious symbols at both elementary and high schools has raised a considerable amount of criticism (McGoldrick, 2009), the measures adopted in the examining cases are based on reasons of academic discipline and safety, necessary in order to achieve the aim of complete education.

Another substantial element that demonstrates the value of physical education can be obtained from the case of Osmanoglu and Kocabas vs. Switzerland. Once again, the right to manifest religion is not of such weight in order to justify an exemption this time from mixed swimming classes. In this regard, the Court found the opportunity to address the matters of integration of foreign students through physical education. As have been aptly observed (Wiborg, 2009), the different levels of comprehensiveness regarding school education (elementary and secondary) in different regions affect the degree of social integration. In fact, a unified educational system that involves all children, regardless of their cultural, ethical and religious background, in equal terms, assist minorities to be incorporated into the social structure of the host society. This particular case concerned precisely pupils of foreign origin which are considered to belong to a minority within the Swiss society (Knobel, 2013), a factor of considerable weight in the Court's decision.

Furthermore, the Court stressed the role of physical education in children's development and health. Since the aim of education is to prepare students for adulthood, they will learn to adopt a more active lifestyle in the future (Haywood, 1991). Physical education represents an umbrella term for a wide range of purposeful physical pursuits that enrich lives and improve the quality of living (Almond, 2000). Indeed, as has been indicated (Palmer, 2006; Kelso, n.d.), the problem of child obesity and the emergence of a sedentary lifestyle, stress the need for physical education programs. Hence, the introduction of physical education classes becomes essential for developing the mentality needed to effectively combat those problems.

Besides body exercise in the strict sense, the improvement of certain skills, the acquisition of self-discipline and the sense of enjoyment are additional significant benefits. Under the Laker's paradigm (2000), the content of an affective domain as it related to physical education contains the development of a moral attitude and an aesthetic attitude. The moral sub-domain includes autonomy, altruism and responsibility whist the aesthetic one refers to the appreciation of movement forms, the striving for gratefulness and playfulness. Through physical activities students learning dimension is broadened and certain values are embodied which are valuable for the overall development of their character. In that sense, the Court concluded that the applicants' daughters benefited greatly from the swimming classes. Not only exercise their bodies and mentally maturate but also strengthen their relationships with classmates, instead of being marginalized due to their parents' religious beliefs. Therefore, those benefits for the children outweighed their parents' right to manifest their religion.

THE RIGHT TO (PHYSICAL) EDUCATION

Regardless of the aforementioned benefits of physical education, the question remains: do parents enjoy the right to decide on whether their children will participate on those classes on the basis of their religious beliefs?

Relevant to this question is the provision of article 2, Protocol 1 ECHR which states: no person shall be denied the right to education. In the exercise of any functions which it assumes in relation to education and to teaching, the State shall respect the right of parents to ensure such education and teaching in conformity with their own religious and philosophical convictions (Fortin, 2009). The provision primarily guarantees the right of everyone to receive education within the State's educational system. Additionally, it creates and obligation for the State: to respect the right of parents, as legally responsible for the education of their children, to ensure such education in conformity with their religious and philosophical beliefs (Kjeldsen, Busk Madsen and Pedersen vs. Denmark). The second part of the provision aims at safeguarding pluralism in education which is essential in a democratic society.

The Court had the opportunity to further clarify the scope of this provision in the case of Folgero and Others vs. Norway. First of all, the power to formulate the educational programme lies with the State. Being in the core of State policy, the curriculum reflects the priorities in education which normally include the teaching of principles and values that ensure the continuation of the nation. In that sense, parents do not enjoy any right of interference in the formation of the curriculum.

Nevertheless, this State power is not unlimited; in fulfilling the functions in regard to education and teaching, the State must observe that information or knowledge included in the curriculum is conveyed in an objective, critical and pluralistic manner. In other words, the State is forbidden to pursue an aim of indoctrination that might be considered as not respecting parents' religious and philosophical convictions. The term "respect" is broadly interpreted meaning more than simply "acknowledge" or "take into account". Moreover, the State's obligation is not exhausted in religious classes, but is applied throughout the entire education program (Folgero and Others vs. Norway, par. 84).

Given the aforementioned, the solution to a possible clash could be revealed as a right of the parents to ask for exemption of their children for a particular course, the teaching of which does not comply with religious beliefs. However, could that possibly apply at will to all courses of the curriculum, physical education classes in particular? In order to answer that question one may take into account the content and teaching methodology of the course provided. The fundamental requirement that the Court imposed was that impartiality should be guaranteed throughout the educational program. By nature, the content of physical education course is neutral, not involving any religious dogmas or any philosophical thoughts. Therefore, no interference can be claimed with the thoughts, conscience or religion of the students in that particular incidence. Hence, demand for exemption from physical education courses on the ground of the right to education falls outside the scope of article 2 Protocol 1 ECHR. The opposite approach would inevitably lead to an education a la carte where parents could substantially differentiate their children's program at will which would lead to the deregulation of State education.

In physical education classes, several measures can still be adopted in order to reduce the impact of the children's attendance on their parents' religious convictions. For example in the Osmanoglu and Kocabas vs. Switzerland case, the authorities allowed the daughters of the applicants to wear a burkini in the swimming classes and undress without the presence of boys (par. 101). Those measures compromise the obligation to participate as directed by the State educational programme with the indisputably significant right to religious freedom and the right of parents to ensure education of their children in line with their beliefs.

CONCLUSION

By analyzing the case law of the ECtHR regarding possible violation of the freedom of religion arising from physical education classes, several conclusions may be drawn. First of all, the Court fully acknowledged the significance of physical education in the curriculum and its impact on the development of children's personality. This being the case, the Court found hard to prioritize the respected parents' right to manifest their religion over the benefits that children themselves will obtain by actively participating in physical education classes, especially in the case of students of foreign origin where a different treatment could possibly create problems with their integration procedure. Therefore the interference with the right to religious freedom was in conformity with article 9, par. 2 ECHR.

Essentially, the Court's decisions provide guidance for the interpretation of the right to education and the right of parents to ensure such education in conformity with their own religious beliefs. The Court applied its well established approach that the State retains the power to legislate on matters concerning the structure of the educational programme, having the obligation not to indoctrinate through education. At the same time, the parents enjoy no right of interference to that level of public policy, but only their religious or philosophical convictions to be respected. In that respect, physical education classes fall completely outside the scope of article 2 Protocol 1 ECHR.

REFERENCES

Ahdar, R., & Leigh, I. (2013). *Religious Freedom in the Liberal State* (2nd ed.). Oxford, UK: Oxford University Press.

Almond, L. (2000). Physical Education and Primary Schools. In R. Bailey & T. Macfadyen (Eds.), Teaching Physical Education 5-11 (pp. 3-13). London: Continuum.

Boorman, P. (1996). The Contributions of Physical Activity to Development in the Early Years. In G. M. Blenkin & A. V. Kelly (Eds.), *Early Childhood Education: A Developmental Curriculum* (2nd ed.; pp. 218–235). London: Paul Chapman Publishing Ltd.

Bremmer, R. H. (Ed.). (1974). Children & Youth in America: A Documentary History, Volume III: 1933-1973, Parts 5-7. Cambridge, MA: Harvard University Press.

Brysk, A. (2002). Introduction. In A. Brysk (Ed.), *Globalization and Human Rights* (pp. 1–16). Berkley, CA: University of California Press.

ECtHR Dogru vs. France, application no. 27058/05.

ECtHR Folgero and Others vs. Norway, application no. 15472/02.

ECtHR Hasan and Claush vs. Bulgaria, application no. 30985/96.

ECtHR Kervanci vs. France, application no. 31645/04. ECtHR Kjeldsen, Busk Madsen and Pedersen vs. Denmark, application no. 5095/71, 5920/72, 5926/72.

ECtHR Kokkinakis vs. Greece, application no. 14307/88.

ECtHR Osmanoglu and Kocabas vs. Switzerland, application no. 29086/12.

European Parliament. (2007). *Resolution of 13 November 2007 on the Role of Sports in Education*. Retrieved January 10, 2018, from http://www.europarl.europa.eu/sides/getDoc.do?type=TA&language=EN&reference=P6-TA-2007-503

Fortin, J. (2009). *Children's Rights and the Developing Law* (3rd ed.). Cambridge, UK: Cambridge University Press. doi:10.1017/CBO9781139168625

Haywood, K. M. (1991). The Role of Physical Education in the Development of Active Lifestyles. *Research Quarterly for Exercise and Sport*, *62*(2), 151–156. doi :10.1080/02701367.1991.10608705 PMID:1925038

Hicks, R. D. (Ed.). (1972). Diogenes Laertius. *Lives of Eminent Philosophers*. Retrieved January 2, 2018, from http://www.perseus.tufts.edu/hopper/text?doc=Perseus%3Atext%3A1999.01.0258%3Abook%3D1%3Achapter%3D1

Kelso, C. (n.d.). *The Importance of Physical Education*. Retrieved January 12, 2018, from http://www.veanea.org/home/1000.htm

Knobel, B. (2013). Switzerland and Religious Minorities: Legal, Political and Educational Responses. In D. M. Kirkham (Ed.), State Responses to Minority Religions (pp. 137-150). Farnham, UK: Ashgate Publishers.

Laker, A. (2000). *Beyond the Boundaries of Physical Education: Educating Young People for Citizenship and Social Responsibility*. Oxford, UK: Routledge.

Martinez-Torron, J. (2012). Freedom of Religion in the European Convention on Human Rights under the Influence of Different European Traditions. In H. Zacher & M. A. Glendon (Eds.), *Universal Rights in a World of Diversity: The Case of Religious Freedom* (pp. 329-355). Vatican City: Pontifical Academy of Social Sciences.

McGodrick, D. (2009). Muslim Veiling Controversies in Europe. In J. S. Nielsen (Ed.), *Yearbook of Muslims in Europe* (Vol. 1, pp. 427–474). Boston, MA: Brill. doi:10.1163/ej.9789004175051.i-562.60

Palmer, S. (2006). *Toxic Childhood: How the Modern World Is Damaging Our Children and What We Can Do About It*. London: Orion.

Renucci, J.-F. (2005). *Article 9 of the European Convention on Human Rights: Freedom of Thought, Conscience and Religion*. Strasbourg: Council of Europe Publishing.

Rudd, N. (1991). *Juvenal: The Satires*. Oxford, UK: Oxford University Press.

Sicilianos, L.-A. (Ed.). (2017). *European Convention on Human Rights: Commentary by Article* (2nd ed.). Athens: Nomiki Bibliothiki. (in Greek)

Smiles, S. (1838). Physical Education or the Nature and Management of Children Founded on the Study of their Nature and Constitution. Edinburgh, UK: Oliver & Boyd, Tweeddale Court and London: Simpkin, Marshall & Co.

Soper, J. C., den Dulk, K. R., & Monsma, S. V. (2017). *The Challenge of Pluralism: Church and State Relations in Six Democracies* (3rd ed.). London: Rowman & Littlefield.

Wiborg, S. (2009). *Education and Social Integration: Comprehensive Schooling in Europe*. New York, NY: Palgrave Macmillan. doi:10.1057/9780230622937

ENDNOTES

1 For example according to article 16, par. 2 of the Greek Constitution, education shall aim at the moral, intellectual, professional and physical training of the Greeks.

2 Article 1 of the French Constitution reads: "France shall be an indivisible, secular, democratic and social Republic."

Section 2
Case Studies

Chapter 8
"Body Culture":
A Spiritual Echo of Olympia and the Fragmented Nature of Physical Education in the Modern-Day School in Greece

Konstantina Gongaki
National and Kapodistrian University of Athens, Greece

ABSTRACT

"Body culture," a modern term in Western Europe, owes its philosophical content to ancient Greece and especially to Olympia. Altis turned out to be a creative place for presence and mixture of cultural elements of a set of people that through this exchange of ideas gradually conquered its first characteristics as a nation. Philosophically, the ideology that was cultivated formed the reflection of the deepest background position which the classical culture identified with coexistence of the opposites. The physical perfection of the Olympic model was reflected in art as the symmetry of Kouros, with a transcendent and spiritual dimension, idealizing the human body. The Olympic athlete reflects harmony and symmetry, the most complete form of the perfect citizen, the concept of moral beauty, as it is defined by Plato and Aristotle. But sport that is provided by the school in Greece today, instead of being an integral part of mainstream education, as it was in antiquity, represents a compressed and therefore inadequate education tool. Sport in Greek schools operates within an oppressive organization framework that is basically imposed because of competition. As a result, the final aim of sports "education" is to teach discipline and physical efficiency with the view to ultimately promoting an organized performance industry. But this obsession, about wanting to be first, in addition to being a source of personal stress, only achieves is to develop the student's personality with competition as the

DOI: 10.4018/978-1-5225-5387-8.ch008

prevailing principle. Moreover, this pursuit of personal affirmation through sports ranking depreciates personal value and the individual as a whole, whilst breeding insecurity and the need for personal recognition through unsafe means. What's more important, instead of being the best tool for bearing social life and reducing egocentric subjectivity, it inflates egocentrism and creates human beings susceptible to individualism. In this way, a type of "one-dimensional man" is cultivated, which Marcuse describes as the most dangerous of all because it destroys society's cohesion by deconstructing man's perception of coexistence.

INTRODUCTION

Body culture, a widely-used term in education and culture in modern Western Europe, owes its philosophical content to ancient Greece, and especially Olympia, as the Olympic athlete reflects *harmony* and *symmetry,* the most complete form of the perfect citizen, the concept of *moral beauty*, as defined by Plato and Aristotle.

Today, however, the state's fragmented treatment of physical education in school, especially in Greece, has isolated the physical aspect of the pupil, focusing on the intellectual aspect with rigid course curricula, and downgrading physical education to secondary or even tertiary importance. In doing so, the state deprives the pupil, and by extension the future athlete, from the harmony and symmetry that develops the wholeness of the psyche.

And when the state does put priority on physical education/sport, it does so with a view to competitive, or "championship" sport, with the objective of "producing" champions that will bring "glory" to the state that can be capitalized on, quite the opposite of the objective of the sporting competition in Ancient Greece, where the champion, or victor, brought a philosophical glory to the state.

"BODY CULTURE" AS A SPIRITUAL ECHO OF OLYMPIA

"Body culture", is a term of art in modern Western Europe. It owes its philosophical content, however, to ancient Greece and especially to Olympia. To appreciate its significance, one must appreciate the multidimensional role of the Olympic Games during the period of the establishment of the Games of Olympia as a social institution. Its development is strengthened mainly by two factors: the first factor is of an urban and political character as it coincides with the process of creation of the city-state; the second is of a religious and social character as it coincides with the completion of the Olympic pantheon (Finley & Pleket, 1976).

Olympia, an important Doric center of worship of the time, turned out to be a place for creative cooperation and synthesis, with its mixture of cultural elements and peoples that developed its first characteristics as a nation. In fact, ancient Olympia sent forth, on the occasion of the Olympic Games, the whole spiritual atmosphere that prevailed in Greece in antiquity, which was not a single state as it is to day but was comprised of several city-states. It was an atmosphere of energy and cultural fermentation. Philosophically, the ideology that was cultivated reflected the underlying concept with which the classical culture identified: coexistence and, indeed, the balanced coexistence of opposites.

The spiritual atmosphere of Olympia was in some respects contrary to modern day sports spectacles. It was imbued with works of art, poems, speeches, dramatic contests[1], and visual creations which during the period of competition were protected by the political institution of "ekecheiria", the sacred truce, conceived of as a "flower" that stemmed from the hardships of war (Finley & Pleket, 1976). The human being, the athlete, was at the centre of the piece; he competed in the nude as a proof of his purity and beauty and through his victory reached the sphere of the divine. The wreath of the Olympic victory was not a personal matter but rather a genealogical and urban achievement, Pindar claims, which brought honor to his race and hometown respectively. The athlete himself was happy because due to his inherent virtue and physical constitution, he was favored by the gods (Bowra, 1971; Goggaki, 2004).

Pindar gave form to the athletic ideal depicting and developing upon earlier beliefs, i.e. that the games were a (then) modern extension of an heroic past. The echo of the Homeric society where excellence is understood to contribute to the manifestation of virtue. The heroic spirit of former times was gradually substituted by a blending of strength and bodily beauty into an athletic ideal of human excellence. At the same time the change in the letters and arts was apparent (Pfeijffer, 1999). From the 5th c to the first half of the 4th c BC the main objective of physical education is to contribute to human perfection (Pleket, 1975; Vernant, 1991; Goggaki, 2002). The Olympic athletic participant, a representative of his culture, creates the model which was the focus of the city. The physical perfection of the Olympic model was reflected in art as the symmetry of Kouros, with a transcendent and spiritual dimension, idealizing the human body. The Olympic athlete reflects *harmony* and *symmetry,* the most complete form of the perfect citizen, the concept of *moral beauty*, as it is defined by Plato and Aristotle.

Plato gives priority to the soul, claiming that *physical exercise* (or 'gymnastics' in its original definition with its roots in the Greek 'Gymnastiki'or 'ekgymnasi', which means 'to exercise'. Thus, physical education in Greek schools is referred to as Gymnastiki) and *music* do service to soul. In the ideal *Politeia* (Plato's *Republic*) the 'gymnastiki' which is of interest to him is not the athletes who compete in the *stadion* and who aspire to athletic victory. Rather, the 'gymnastiki' who concern him is exclusively the rank of the guardians. Because they are entrusted with the task of protecting the city from its enemies, Plato calls them *athletes of the supreme contest* and *athletes of* war (Gardiner, 1930/1980; Morrow, 1960). Physical exercise aims at the stimulation of the spirit of nature (Fairs, 1968; Dombrowski, 1979; Russ, 1995).

Moreover, athletic specialization - where the focus is on specific limbs, for example, as opposed to overall physical conditioning - is rejected by Socrates. Excessive exercise is denounced by Hippocrates and Galen while, on the contrary, moderate exercise, ball exercises, playing, dancing, or a combination of the above, are recommended (Miller, 1991). To be one-sided in Gymnastiki (physical training) is criticized both by Plato and Aristotle, while overtraining is not only disadvantageous but also hazardous to physical health (Gongaki, 2003a). Those who exercise one-sidedly without cultivating music (with music representing, according to Plato, the so-called 'sciences' – mathematics, geometry, philosophy, in other words simultaneous cultivation of the intellect and soul, or *psyche)* become *fiercer than necessary*, more aggressive, whereas those who exclusively practice music become *softer than is necessary*. The above characteristics, *fiercer* and *softer*, are considered qualities of the intellect, and most importantly of the soul. Proper upbringing results in brave affective reactions and a calm and decent philosophical nature, otherwise man remained uneducated in the arts, without symmetry, 'wild' and crude or uncultivated.

Physical exercise, during that period, from the easiest and natural to the most difficult, was not an end in itself. Its purpose was not exclusively the improvement of the physique, aimed at the cultivation of the intellect and the soul (psyche) of the young people. The citizen is treated as a whole personality, the duality of which is equally valued and revered (Gardiner, 1930;1980; Sargent Robinson, 1955;1980; Miller, 1991). Furthermore, special attention is given to children's play. Children's play is allowed during the educational process, provided it is appropriate for free citizens (Chryssafis, 1930). Play and free time were considered equally important elements of well-being and the formation of an all-rounded individual as knowledge. According to Aristotle, most games children play imitate areas of the scientific knowledge that the young people will study later and, by extension, areas of their professional occupations. Consequently, play should, without being an end in itself, be faced as a recreation, and held during free time.

It should be noted here that what is referred to as the Olympic legacy is not associated with *aristeia* (excellence), but rather with harmony and moderation. Hence aristeia, as a term or value, refers only to a specific period of time, namely the Homeric, or Mycenaean, era, during which the social 'ideal' was the 'heroic' and the term 'athlete' was synonymous with the term 'hero'. This was due to the fact that the main characteristic of the society during that period was war, and the 'athlete' or 'hero' at the time belonged to the ranks of the aristocracy, not the general public.

In the Classical era, however, with which the comparisons are being drawn in this paper, democratic institutions were developed for the first time, and were inevitably reflected in the social ideals of that period. Thus, the social, or citizens', 'ideal', was the 'metron' (or measure), that formed the foundation of the Classical civilization.

'Body culture', as it evolved in tandem with humanity over the ages, assimilates and reflects the elements of the society's values at each given time. From the Homeric physical strength and the classical Olympic symmetry of the *stadion* and *gymnasion*, body culture was transformed in an era of Roman 'degeneration' and the ethos of the 'arena': the human body is pierced by gladiators; it is dismembered by wild animals; it is wounded shamelessly; and its bloody destruction becomes the supreme spectacle (Henderson, 1903; Pleket, 1975; Hardy, 1977; Wacke, 1977). This period was followed by the gradual redefinition of the body during the Early Christian period, the degradation of the body during the Medieval period, the deep belittlement of manual laborers, and the ensuing quest for a new role during the Renaissance. Afterwards, during the Enlightenment, the human body demanded recognition of its value as an equally important element as the mind, having grown tired of the previous rejections and degradations. Later, near the end of the 18th century, within the general European tendency of return to the principles of Classical antiquity, a trend emerged for the revival of Classical values.

EVOLUTION OF THE CONCEPT OF BODY CULTURE

The revival of the Olympic Games in the war-ravaged Athens in 1896 enhanced national pride in Greece which had been at a very low ebb. It also rekindled interest in introducing sport activities in schools and athletic associations. It was at this time that physical education was incorporated into the school curriculum. However, the teaching methods and the content of school physical education activities resembled the rigidity of a military education rather than sport and enjoyment. The ensuing concentration on the rigid Swedish physical education regimen, which was foreign to the more carefree Greek mentality towards sport and physical exercise as something to be enjoyed, acted as a deterrent to spurring interest among the youth for involvement in sport activities.

The people in Greece, with the state's assistance, have been conditioned to identifying sports, by contingent association, with some isolated instances of athletes taking part in competitions, and, consequently, with anything pertaining to "championship", or competitive, athletics and sports. Interest has focused on that category of sports which, comprising a specific sector of the athletic structure, enjoys the fragmented and piecemeal support of the official State, since it is through that category of sport that national projection is achieved, which in turn reflects back on the State. Conversely, anything to do with 'public' or 'popular' athletics, (sports for the masses, or 'sport for all') has not been the subject of serious interest and effort by the State, with the exception of a scattering of inept, uninspired and ineffectual actions, the result of which has four parameters: 1) school sport (physical education); 2) out-of-school (extra-curricular) sport, activities; 3) popular (mass) sport, and; 4) competitive (championship) sport.

THE FRAGMENTED NATURE OF PHYSICAL EDUCATION IN CONTEMPORARY GREEK SCHOOLING

This paper will restrict itself to the first aspect, or parameter (the other parameters will be examined in other papers, as all four require in-depth and lengthy analysis), namely school sport/physical education, and the negative effect on it resulting from its fragmented treatment by the state.

Contemporary state provision of physical education, instead of being an integral part of overall education as it was in antiquity, represents a separate, compressed and therefore inadequate educational medium. Physical education is an activity that is today practically devoid of educational content, unconnected to broader educational processes. The Greek State school system is a full time process with respect to hours, but not to substance. It literally absorbs the students' spare time, by implementing a static, monotonous and non-functional curriculum of courses. A look at the schools in Western Europe, for comparison purposes, shows how superior they are with respect to their vivacity, their action and as sources of creativity. Regarding sports in particular, the considerable time that is devoted in the curriculum in most European schools is further enhanced by apparatus, excellent facilities, fully-equipped gyms, swimming pools and courts, where students can exert their physical energy. Consequently, sport activities in most European schools are not dissociated from overall education but are an integral part of the students' daily routine. Learning to swim, for example is a required course of the school's curriculum.

In Greece, the enthusiasm and interest of boys and girls for sport, in junior and high schools, is declining, according to the results of a relevant statistical study (Gongaki, 2003b). Spontaneous mobility and innate competitiveness, failing to find an outlet in the school curricula, are ebbing as a result of harshly restricted movement and the school's lack of response to the children's need for play, activity and expression. Apart from the fact that there is no "sports education" or promotion of "lifelong physical activity" in Greek schools, we also witness a deprivation or obstruction of even the young people's natural inclination for motion, or physical action. Most school buildings do not meet requirements, and do not have even a simple gravel or sand pit. In addition to the lack of proper conditions for the harmonious integration of sports in school, pupils are frequently treated as old people.

The athletic system in Greek schools formulates a generally oppressive organizational framework that is basically imposed because of competition. Thus, the end goal of athletic "education" is to teach discipline and physical performance ultimately aimed at promoting the organized industry of performance, observes G. Berthaud (1972). A large number of physical education teachers, serving this purpose instead of fulfilling their role as 'educators', turn into talent hunters and exponents of order and authority. Students who do not follow this logic are frustrated and become marginalized, while the school sports system follows a one-way course to top performance sport. Students who have the physical attributes for developing into athletes (height, body mass, weight, strength, energy, etc.) are acknowledged and supported, while those lesser endowed are simply ignored. In this way, a kind of physical racism develops, as well as a kind of inequality and exclusion, based on physical attributes, in an area where the principles of equality should predominantly apply (Berthaud, Brohm, Gantheret, & Laguillaumie, 1972).

But why should a school student fervently seek to be first in sport? It is one thing to try to achieve the best one can, their own personal best, but quite another thing to strive, at all costs, to be the best of all. This obsession with wanting to be first, apart from being a source of personal stress, serves only to build the student's personality with competition as the prevailing principle. Moreover, this pursuit of personal affirmation through sports ranking, depreciates the individual's overall personal value, the person as a totality, while it also breeds insecurity and the need for personal recognition, and through unnatural and unsafe means (i.e. excessive specialization, doping, etc.).

More importantly, though, the collective physical activity at school (school team/s) should comprise the best tool for teaching social life and reducing egocentric subjectivity (Mauco, 1993) - by putting the emphasis on inter-action, inter-dependence and the principle of collective effort for attaining the common goal. Instead, it inflates egocentrism and molds human beings susceptible to individualism and unable of being interested in anything other than themselves (a 'Most Valuable Player' mentality, a tendency of wanting to be the dominant player in the team). Thus, a type of "one-dimensional man" is cultivated, which Marcuse describes as the most dangerous of all, because it destroys society's cohesion by deconstructing man's perception of coexistence (Marcuse, 1964).

School sport, frequently due to the insistence of the parents themselves, seeks to build "champions" rather than instilling the educational value of exercise that is compatible with the student's mentality (Carr, 1998). The playful nature of sports education has a bearing on the learning process and its psychological and emotional aspects, and in the modern-day demanding and lengthy school schedule it should provide the much-needed outlet for young people to release pent-up energy (Huizinga, 1950;1995). Games, being a reflection of life itself, of which today's students will be tomorrow's protagonists, lay down the corner-stone for the development of a spirit of cooperation and a collective conscience. Children base their games on ideas drawn from their own world, as an abstract of specific aspects of real life situations. At the same time, when playing, the youngsters develop new processes of learning and realization of principles and rules that will accompany them throughout their future life. Since the planning of our modern cities does not provide for streets, courtyards, gardens and squares where children can play, schools of all levels, and more so at primary level, need to revise their curricula so as to take this parameter into account, which is a cancer of "contemporary" life in the 'jungle' of the big city.

Elementary and secondary education comprise the decisive period during which children, both age-wise and fundamentally, not only develop intellectually but also seek and discover their 'physical' self. The heavy school curriculum, which burdens them with obligations and fragmented knowledge in order to prepare for an uncertain future, does not take into account, or respect, their need for physical activity and exertion. Nor does it draw on this valuable living resource for instilling principles and values, the lack of which will inevitably boomerang against society at some point in time like a boomerang. It is only through education that the present-day phenomena of violence, hooliganism, racism, doping, xenophobia and corruption that arise in sport can be analyzed, interpreted and curtailed, phenomena that are not restricted to the sector of sport but also extend to the social and political spheres. By failing to provide public sports education, the state reveals not only its absolute lack of attention and care, but perhaps its own irresponsibility as well.

Unless of course this attitude of the state is not the result of a lack of responsibility but is, rather, due to a conscious ideological choice of the ruling class which pursues other aims: by turning education into a strenuous and coercive process, students are drained of their time and can in fact be manipulated and disoriented towards other directions. In other words, what is sought through the educational system's acting as a sword of Damocles dangling over the youth's time, is the youth's ultimate integration into the system, so that the ruling class may advance its choices, unhindered. Instead of having the youth on the "opposite side", it essentially weakens, - through a coercive educational system and by putting forward the 'incentive of collecting skills and qualifications in view of the uncertain future ahead of them - the 'energy' and momentum of the youth that could turn against it. Thus, the youth are trained, or conditioned, to be passive receivers instead of dynamic and proactive individuals.

Regarding the downgrading of sports education in public schools, it would be useful to compare it to the situation in private schools. In private schools, sports activities are advertised as being comprehensive, with modern, state of the art facilities and equipment and sports events as part of the curriculum or as extracurricular activities and all material-technical resources for sports practice, thus presenting it as an important factor in choosing a private school. This picture of extensive playgrounds, tartan coated tracks, gym apparatus and courts, acts as a strong incentive for selecting one private school over another private school. Sport in this instance is used as a commercial lure, turning it into a product that can be sold or purchased. In projecting upgrade facilities - the school facilities in general, since the sport facilities are a 'package deal' with the overall building/school campus facilities - a subliminal message is given is that, if 'x' private school has such "high quality" (sport plus) facilities, it provides a better education compared to other private schools as well as public schools. In that context, sport activities literally become "client bait" because the setting with its beautiful facilities will naturally make parents feel that they are giving their child the best. These "perks" may not be linked, necessarily, to the quality of the general education that is provided to students, but they do attempt to give the impression that conditions are certainly much better than those found in gloomy neighborhood school buildings of grey concrete, without a single tree.

The general result is that a large number of parents and pupils are prompted to choose private education, which gives off a 'sense' of culture, resulting in a decline in preference for public education. The question that arises, then, is whether the Greek school could become for political parties and any given government, a national center for learning and propagating its cultural values? Has it yet to be realized, despite the enlightened voices heard since antiquity, `that a change in society's values has to go through education? That if it continues as it is today, perpetuating the present-day values of utilitarianism, nouveau riche, pseudo-culture and half-learning, what will be the visible future?

CONCLUSION

The absence of physical education, properly conceived, in public schools and in Greek society is provocative, unfair and counter-productive; but instead of improving, it appears to be becoming the rule of thumb. Very soon, children will be unable to climb stairs, figuratively speaking, or will be unmotivated to do anything that requires physical exertion and opt, rather, to sink into the armchair of immobility. They will be much happier sitting for hours in front of a computer screen and interact with friends electronically instead of meeting outdoors to kick a ball around or gather at a friend's house to laugh and play. Young people will have lost contact with nature, especially in the large urban centers, and their physical body and, lacking the ability to establish a connection between the two, will "forget" the usefulness and pleasure of motion, play and physical activity. The car will carry their heavy, flabby body, computers will replace playing, and the stifling concrete city environment will replace the playground. At home, at the office, machines will "replace" hands and feet. Leaving behind the physical activities of primitive communities, modern society and technological culture have substituted machines for physical activity, but also the use, or "exertion", of the mind as well.

Is there still hope of upgrading the overall role of education and providing a well-rounded general education to youth, thus influencing all the aspects that comprise it, such as thinking, judgment, communication, poetry, music, art and sport? Can this downward trend in physical exertion be stopped? The critical approach is the only approach that can constructively introduce change, react to entrenched, obsolete repetitions and set as its objective the realization of the vision. "Education" is, broader concept which, apart from the learning formally provided, is also received from other sources and mechanisms in the wider, social and cultural environment. If public education is governed by ethics and merit, then by extension, ethical values will be disseminated in a corresponding ideological context, since these concepts are inter-related and mutually complementary. So, what applies in other social sectors will also apply in sports: the perception of school sport is mutually influenced by the social environment and value system and vice versa.

REFERENCES

Berthaud, G., Brohm, J.-M., Gantheret, F., & Laguillaumie, P. (1972). *Sport, Sport, Culture et Répression*. Paris: Libraire François Maspero.

Bowra, C. M. (1971). *Pindar* (2nd ed.). Oxford, UK: Clarendon.

Carr, D. (1998). What Moral Educational Significance has Physical Education? A Question in need of Disambiguation. In M. J. McNamee & S. J. Parry (Eds.), Ethics & Sport. London: E & FN Spon.

Chryssafis, J. E. (1930). Aristotle on Physical Education. *The Journal of Health and Physical Education*, *7*, 3–19.

Dombrowski, D. A. (1979). Plato and Athletics. *Journal of the Philosophy of Sport*, *VI*(1), 29–38. doi:10.1080/00948705.1979.10654148

Fairs, J. R. (1968). The Influence of Plato and Platonism on the Development of Physical Education in Western Culture. *Quest*, *11*(1), 14–22. doi:10.1080/00336297.1968.10519652

Finley, M. I., & Pleket, H. W. (1976). *The Olympic Games. The First Thousand Years*. London: Dover Publications.

Gardiner, E. N. (1980). *Athletics of the Ancient World.* Chicago: Ares. (Original work published 1930)

Goggaki, K. (2002). The Wreath of Athletic Victory and Its moral Symbolism. *International Journal of Physical Education (Muzaffarnagar), 39*(4), 32–38.

Goggaki, K. (2004). The Athletic Victory as a Value in the Pindaric Odes. *Nikephoros, 17*, 123–134.

Gongaki, K. (2003a). *The Conceptions of Ancient Greeks concerning Athletics.* Athens: Typothito - G. Dardanos. (in Greek)

Gongaki, K. (2003b). Opportunities for, and sentiments associated with, physical education and sports activities among the primary and secondary pupils population in Attica Prefecture. University of Athens study. *Antitetradia tis Ekpaidefsis, 67*, 42-48. (in Greek)

Hardy, S. (1977). Politicians, Promoters and the Rise of Sport: The Case of Ancient Greece and Rome. *Canadian Journal of History of Sport and Physical Education, 8*(1), 1–15. doi:10.1123/cjhspe.8.1.1

Henderson, B. W. (1903). *The Life and Principate of the Emperor Nero.* London: Methuen.

Huizinga, J. (1995). The Nature of Play. In W. J. Morgan & K.V. Meier (Eds.), Philosophic Inquiry in Sport (2nd ed.). Champaign, IL: Human Kinetics Publishers. (Original work published 1950)

Mandell, R. (1984). *Sport. A Cultural History.* New York, NY: Columbia University Press.

Marcuse, H. (1964). *One-Dimensional Man: Studies in the Ideology of Advanced Industrial Society.* Boston, MA: Beacon.

Mauco, G. (1993). *Psychanalyse et Education.* Paris: Flammarion.

Miller, S. G. (1991). *Arete. Greek Sports from Ancient Sources* (2nd ed.). Berkeley, CA: University of California Press.

Morrow, G. (1960). *Plato's Cretan City. A Historical Interpretation of the Laws.* Princeton, NJ: Princeton University Press.

Pfeijffer, I. L. (1999). *Three Aeginetan Odes of Pindar. A Commentary on Nemean V, Nemean III, and Pythian VIII.* Leiden: Brill.

Pleket, H. W. (1975). Games, Prizes, Athletes and Ideology. Some Aspects of the History of Sport in the Greco-Roman World. *Stadion*, *1*, 49–89.

Russ, J. (1995). *L'Aventure de la Pensée Européenne. Une Histoire des Idées Occidentales*. Paris: Armand Colin éditeur.

Russell, B. (1973). *On Education Especially in Early Childhood*. London: George Allen and Unwin.

Sargent Robinson, R. (1980). *Sources for the History of Greek Athletics*. Chicago: Ares. (Original work published 1955)

Vernant, J.-P. (1991). *Mortals and Immortals*. Princeton, NJ: Princeton University Press.

Wacke, A. (1977). Unfälle bei Sport und Spiel nach römischem und geltendem Recht. *Stadion*, *3*, 4–43. PMID:11633297

ENDNOTES

1 There, in Olympia, drama performances were staged of major tragedians such as Eyripides, who, in fact, lost in the 91st Olympiad to his competitor Xenocles.

Chapter 9
Legal, Ethical, and Integrity Issues in Sports Industry:
The Russian Experience

Igor Ponkin
Kutafin Moscow State Law University, Russia & The Russian Presidential Academy of National Economy and Public Administration, Russia

Olga Shevchenko
Kutafin Moscow State Law University, Russia & International Association of Sports Law, Russia

Alena Redkina
Kutafin Moscow State Law University, Russia

ABSTRACT

This chapter focuses on the issues of the sports industry. Since sport, in addition to its other aspects, is a fast-growing industry, the chapter considers the importance of sports industry for the sector as a whole. The chapter shows the basic elements of sports industry structure, together with the peculiarities of Russian sports industry legal support in general and in some particular directions. The authors give definitions of "sports industry," "sports product," "sports entertainment product," "professional sports," "professional athlete," "sports ethics," and "sports integrity." Being a good basis for sports business development, the legislation of the Russian Federation in the sphere of legal services for business and commercial activities within the sports industry takes into account sports-specific features and its principal functions enabling professional sports sector to provide benefits to economy and society. However, there is still space for further development.

DOI: 10.4018/978-1-5225-5387-8.ch009

INTRODUCTION

Besides its other features, sport is a fast-growing industry. Professional sports sector is more similar to the show business industry than to the sports segment as it is, which implies the existence of particular business interests (Ponkin & Ponkina, 2014a). Nowadays, the specified professional sports industry is characterized by significant scales and their growth trend. At the same time, there is a process of convergence between sports industry and entertainment industry. To a large extent, it depends on the continuing commercialization and internationalization within the sports industry (Shevchenko & Ponkin, 2014).

The financial capacity of the sports industry is very high. According to some estimates, only in 2010 the income of the world's sports industry amounted to 121.4 billion U.S. dollars. This financial strength largely determines the existence, activity, and prosperity of the entire sports sector.

Besides public administration, the sports sector is supervised by self-government authorities, which include extra-legal regulatory norms lex sportiva, and by private commercial corporate governance (focused on those sports aspects which refer to sports entertaining show-business events and corresponding activity, sport product manufacturing and distribution, the functioning of sports infrastructure and entire industry), which includes lex mercatoria norms. The peculiarities of interaction between the two legislative policies are of considerable interest to sports law science and encourage interest in sports industry.

Government's responsibilities for sports industry legal services also include promotion of such corporate governance which would encourage efficient and steady development of sports industry in general. In addition, when exercising public administration within the sector, the government should firstly take into account the sports specific character which exists even in the conditions of growing commercial interests and still has a significant impact on the activity of sports individuals and their interference, Secondly, the government should consider its own interests and society's sports involvement. In this way, in spite of growing sports commercialization and professionalization, the sports sector performs certain social functions, and the government is obliged to maintain and support the fulfillment of these functions, minimize possible negative effects, and maximize positive effects of sports industry activity for the economy as a whole.

This work contains a broad description of sports regulatory and legal support in the Russian Federation and draws special attention to the legal support of certain fields of activities within the sports industry.

Definitions of Key Terms

- **Sports Industry (The Industry of Sport):** Social relations and business sector oriented to gain profit from the turnover of sports entertainment product by using individual and collective human interest in sports competitiveness in general and in entertainment and leisure activities (with uncertainty and aesthetics elements) in particular;
- **Sports Product:** An integral concept, including:
    - Sports entertainment product;
    - Sports product on the market of intellectual property items in sports sector, sports services (e.g., an opportunity to use sports facilities), sports goods (sports clothes and footwear, souvenir products, sports equipment);
    - Financial sports product;
    - Professional athletes' sports labor product;
- **Sports Entertainment Product:** Key product in the sports industry, as the entertainment, leisure, and culture recreation sector. The product combines its integrated character with the dominance of non-material values, whose attractor (drawing attention phenomenon) is expected and presumed uncertainty of sports events final results. Such uncertainty provokes (as motivation to consume the product and as its significant product features) interest in participating in sports events, given the expectation on their effects, on experiencing emotional outburst (excitement, stress, emotional tension) about an event and its results, on hope and anticipation of future sports results as well as foreseen and presumed staginess (appealing character, beauty and bright aesthetic qualities, technicality, and dramatic performance) of sports event;
- **Professional Sports:** A set of sports activities and corresponding public relations (including sports relations, sports labor, business relations as well as disciplinary and hierarchic work relations in sports organizations) concerning:
    - Organization and running of sports events (including sports entertainment events) by public authorities, sports organizations, and other entities to gain the profit and/or to develop a certain kind of sports activity according to regulatory norms of an organization and rules of holding such events;
    - Preparatory training and competitive-demonstrative participation in sports events of professional athletes who, on a regular basis, take part in the specified activity for remuneration in the form of material

(salary, compensation, award fee, and others) and/or (as a complement) non-material (reputation, gaining sports qualification of a certain level) benefits from hosts of venues, sports organizations, sponsors, etc., individually or as a member of a professional sports team for the purposes of achieving high sports results and/or championship;
  - Setting, fixation, and announcement of final results of sports events by professional referees, as well as providing the referees, following sports rules and other regulatory norms during sports events and results setting established within the sports sector (Ponkin & Ponkina, 2014b, p. 28);
- **Professional Athlete:** An individual who, entering into sports labor and hierarchic work relations with a sports organization (involved into organization and holding of sports events of a specific kind), takes part in sports events (within the sports norms), for a certain remuneration, as well as in qualification examinations and preparatory training sports events to maintain and improve personal skills for future achievement of the results;
- **Sports Ethics:** A set of moral and ethical principles, values, and rules regulating competition relations in the sports sector (observance of sports rules and fair play principles, dedication to ideas of Olympism and sports in general);
- **Sports Integrity:** A feature of the sports sector connected with the specific organization of the activity within the sector, taking into account its differentiation (i.e., the ability to be realized in a variety of forms with different relation structures). According to this feature, each of the parties of the sports organization system pursues its own interests considering public aims and concerns, including integrity and intersectionality of relations within competitive sports activity, sports as a form of leisure activity and culture, sports industry, sports ideology as well as interference between professional and amateur sports, high performance and mass sports including the ability of independent self-governance.

MAIN FOCUS OF THE CHAPTER

Sports Industry Structure

The key criterion for the activity to be referred to the sports industry is the commercial aspect, i.e. such activity should be profit-oriented (even if, in accordance with the institutional form, the majority of sports organizations do not have the right to allot profits among the owners).

The sports industry covers the following work areas:

1. Commercial activity concerning organization, support, and holding of mass sports entertainment events, including the ticketing of sports entertainment events (tickets issue and distribution), fundraising for events management and for the support of sports organization to participate in such events;
2. Commercial activity concerning the trade of licensed goods with logos, symbols, and emblems of a sports organization or a sports team, images of team players, other sportsmen, and concerning commercial exploitation of brands, trademarks, tradenames in the sports sector, and other legal objects of intellectual property including mechanisms of sports advertisement sponsorship;
3. Commercial activity concerning sports events broadcasting (i.e., presentation of sports entertainment product) on television and radio via earth, satellite, television, and radio stations, the Internet and intranet, mobile devices as well as concerning broadcasting rights and other release of sports entertainment product on media markets;
4. Commercial activity concerning functioning of sports schools, including training of sportsmen and their "sale" to sports clubs;
5. Commercial activity concerning provision of sports services (e.g., offering opportunities to use sports facilities, coaching support, fitness services, renting of sports facilities & equipment);
6. Commercial activity concerning manufacturing and trade of sports goods (i.e., sports clothes and footwear, souvenir products, sports facilities and equipment, sports ships and aircraft, cars and motor cycles, sports security systems and facilities);
7. Commercial activity concerning the production, issue, and distribution of print, radio, and Internet media in the sports sector;
8. Commercial activity concerning the exploitation of sports technical objects;
9. Commercial activity concerning the generation of sports fashion trends, their wide spreading, and support;
10. Activity concerning fundraising for sports development; and
11. Commercial activity concerning sports advertising.

Almost each of the mentioned areas within the sports industry has a reference in the Russian sports legislation in some way (directly or indirectly), and such activity significantly refers to professional sports.

Sports Industry Legal Regulation in Russia

The expansion of sports commercialization (not only in Russia, but also abroad) goes back to the end of the 19th century and the – beginning of the 20th century, when sports product manufacturers realized the demand for these products and organized appropriate marketing. In the USSR the sports industry was not a very significant sector; however, there are good grounds to confirm the existence of the sports industry at that time. After the Soviet breakup in the process of the establishment of the free market economy, the commercialization in Russia was increasing and, in some cases, it contradicted sports moral principles. Nowadays, the sports industry is going strong thanks to its great investment potential and attractiveness as well as to its prospective development into a comprehensive sector within the formal economy.

Besides a great deal of other different factors, the Russian sports industry is developing under the influence of important international sports events that were held (e.g., XXVII 2013 Summer Universiade in Kazan, 2013; World Combat Games in Saint Petersburg, XXII; Winter Olympics and XI Winter Paralympics in Sochi) and are being prepared (e.g., 2016 IIHF World Championship in Moscow and Saint Petersburg, 2017; FIFA Confederations Cup, and 2018 FIFA World Cup) in Russia out of necessity of correspondence between national legislation and standards for the organizations of such events.

At the moment, the sports legislation of the Russian Federation does not confirm the concept of sports industry, but it contains both general and specific provisions concerning commercial activity in the sports sector.

The Sports industry legal support in Russia is being intensively developed along with the sports industry itself. This is mentioned in the Strategy for Development of Physical Culture and Sports in the Russian Federation for the period up to 2020 approved by the RF Government Decree of August 7, 2009, No.1101-p. According to this document, current restrictions in the field of public-private partnership prevent the sports entertainment industry and the sports industry from developing intensively, including the availability of sports and health & fitness services. In view of this, the strategy is expected to facilitate measures to change this situation.

Among the basic laws and regulations within the sports industry in the Russian Federation, there are the following:

- Federal Law of December 4, 2007, No.329-FZ (as amended on November 3, 2015) "On Physical Culture and Sports in the Russian Federation";
- Civil Code of the Russian Federation (all parts);
- Tax Code of the Russian Federation (all parts);
- Code of Administrative Offences of the Russian Federation of December 30, 2011;
- Budget Code of the Russian Federation of July 31, 1998, No. 145-FZ (as amended on March 30, 2016);
- Federal Law from June 7, 2013, No. 108-FZ (as amended on June 8, 2015):

On Preparation and Holding in the Russian Federation of 2018 FIFA World Cup, 2017 FIFA Confederations Cup and on Amendments to Certain Legislative Acts of the Russian Federation.

- Federal Law of December 1, 2007, No. 310-FZ (as amended on June 28, 2014):

On Organization and Holding of XXII Winter Olympics and XI Paralympics in the year of 2014 in Sochi, Development of Sochi as a Mountain Climate Resort and on Amendments to Certain Legislative Acts of the Russian Federation.

- Federal Law of March 13, 2006, No. 38-FZ (as amended on March 8, 2015), *On Advertising*;
- Federal Law of December 28, 2009, No. 381-FZ (as amended on December 31, 2014): *On Basic Principles of State Regulation of Commercial Activity in the Russian Federation*;
- Federal Law of July 13, 2015, No. 224-FZ (as amended on December 29, 2015):

On Public-private Partnership, Municipal-private Partnership in the Russian Federation and on Amendments to Certain Legislative Acts of the Russian Federation.

- Federal Law of December 3, 2011, No. 380-FZ (as amended on July 23, 203), *On Economic Partnership*;
- Federal Law of December 29, 2014, No.473-FZ (as amended on July 13, 2015), *On the Territories of Progressive Social and Economic Development in the Russian Federation.*

The Russian legislation within this sector is rather fragmented, so it is hardly possible that integral and universal sports industry legal support will soon exist. Nevertheless, particular issues of the sports industry are regulated sufficiently.

The development of the sports industry can be carried out with indirect government support when it pursues other goals concerning the general development of sports.

For example, the objectives of the State Program of the Russian Federation *Development of Physical Culture and Sports*, that was approved by the RF Government Decree on April 15, 2014, No. 302 (as amended on September 16, 2015), include successful holding in the Russian Federation of the largest international sports competitions and the improvement of competitiveness of Russian sports on the international level.

In accordance with Section III of the Strategy for Development of Physical Culture and Sports in the Russian Federation for the period up to 2020, that was approved by the RF Government Decree of August 7, 2009, No.,1101-p, the objectives of the strategy include the development of the infrastructure within physical culture and the sports sector, the improvement of financial support of sports activities (Paragraph 6), as well as the creation of a sports security system at sports facilities and the organization of work with fans and their associations (Paragraph 7).

In accordance with Section VIII of the Concept of the Federal Target Program *Development of Physical Culture and Sports in the Russian Federation between 2016-2020*, that was approved by the RF Government Decree of January 2, 2014, No. 2-p, financial support for the implementation of this program is supposed to be provided by the funds of the federal budget, the budget of federal subjects of the Russian Federation, and extra-budgetary resources that will ensure the integrated efforts of public authorities, local authorities, commercial, and non-profit organizations.

The Strategy for Development of Physical Culture and Sports in the Russian Federation for the period up to 2020, that was approved by the RF Government Decree of August 7, 2009, No. 1101-p, provides solutions for the following problems (including the application of appropriate measures):

- Improvement of sports facilities providing them with the necessary sports equipment for physical culture and sports activities (Sub-paragraph 3, Paragraph 1, Section X);
- Modernization of the enterprises involved in the production of goods for physical culture and sports activities (Sub-paragraph 4, Paragraph 1 Section X);
- Development of a set of measures on small business and public private partnership development within physical culture and sports sector (Sub-paragraph 5, Paragraph 1, Section X);
- Creation of a national brand of sports clothing and equipment (Sub-paragraph 2, Paragraph 3, Section X);
- Development and implementation of investment programs within physical culture and sports sector in the conditions of modern market economy (Sub-paragraph 3, Paragraph 2, Section X), and;
- Development of leasing of sports equipment, inventory, and related materials (Sub-paragraph 7, Paragraph 2, Section X).

Further in the article, the authors consider the details of the legislation applied to specific areas of business within the sports sector.

Sports Events Ticketing

The Russian legislation does not contain specific provisions concerning legal regulations of sale of entrance tickets for mass entertainment events, including sports events. In view of this, the activity of sports events ticketing is primarily regulated by general principles of civil law related to deal making and additionally by a range of other norms.

Sports events ticketing is of great importance for the income of events organizers and for the segment share of the sports industry in Russia. Accordingly, legislators could not pass by the full-fledged legal segment of sports events ticketing.

The provisions of the Russian Federation addressing the issue of sports events ticketing and related matters can be classified as follows:

- General applicable legal provisions, regulating civil law relations;
- Some legal provisions on physical culture and sports;
- Legal provisions establishing the rights of sports events organizers for the issue and distribution of entrance tickets and for their price regulation;
- Antimonopoly legal provisions prohibiting unfair competition; and
- Applicable tax legislation.

As a rule, the specified legislation is applicable to ticketing for official sports events (sports events included in the unified schedule of interregional, national, and international physical culture and sports events, schedules of sports events and activities of constituent and municipal entities of the Russian Federation, in accordance with Paragraph 9, Article 2 of the Federal Law of December 4, 2007, No. 329-FZ as amended on November 3, 2015, *On Physical Culture and Sports in the Russian Federation* and to the protection of rights of sports events organizers.

Specific provisions related to sports events ticketing are contained in the relevant Federal Legislation on physical culture and sports.

In this way, Paragraph 2.1, Article 20 of the Federal Law of December 4, 2007, No. 329-FZ, *On Physical Culture and Sports in the Russian Federation* provides that organizers of official sports events and owners and users of sports facilities establish requirements connected with the ticketing of these events (except the requirement to sell entrance tickets against personal identification documents).

In general, such regulatory norms are oriented to assure ethical conduct of sports events visitors. Accordingly, the stated article also institutes obligatory personal identification at the entrance for official sports events supported by the Government of the Russian Federation.

The visitors' rights after the purchase of the tickets for sports events are illustrated in The Rules of Conduct of Spectators during the Official Sports Competitions, that were approved by the RF Government Decree of December 16, 2013 No. 1156. In particular, according to Sub-paragraph "g" of its Paragraph 3 spectators who have the entrance ticket or a substituting document during official sports competitions have the right to enter the venue of an official sports event to attend them.

The Federal Law of June 7, 2013, No. 108-FZ (as amended on June 7, 2015), *On Preparation and Holding of 2018 FIFA World Cup, 2017 FIFA Confederations Cup in the Russian Federation and on Amendments to Certain Legislative Acts of the Russian Federation*, contains a number of norms concerning sports events ticketing.

Thus, in accordance with Paragraph 1, Article 17 of this Federal Law states that: *FIFA owns the property rights related to the events organization including...the rights to sell the entrance tickets or other documents for the events.*

Article 21 of the specified Federal Law regulates the rules of the sale of entrance tickets and other documents, giving the right to attend the events. It establishes that the sale, replacement, and refunding of the tickets for sports events, as well as the criteria and rules connected with the distribution of seats among spectators, are regulated by the FIFA, by permission of this sports organization or in accordance with its rules.

In accordance with Article 9 of The Federal Law of December 1, 2007, No. 310-FZ (as amended on June 28, 2014), *On Organization and Holding of XXII Winter Olympics and XI Winter Paralympics in Sochi, Development of Sochi as a Mountain Resort and on Amendments to Certain Legislative Acts of the Russian Federation*, selling procedures for entrance tickets for sports events and ceremonies of Olympics and Paralympics were approved by the Government of the Russian Federation and the ticket price was approved according to the agreement with the International Olympic Committee and International Paralympic Committee, respectively.

In addition, the procedures of ticketing for these sports events were determined by the RF Government Decree of February 7, 2013, No. 98, *On the Approval of the Provision on Ticketing for Sports Events and Ceremonies of XXII Winter Olympics and XI Winter Paralympics in 2014 in Sochi.*

In reference to the application of antimonopoly legislation to the activity of sports events ticketing, Article 20 of the Federal Law of June 7, 2013, No. 108-FZ (as amended on June 8, 2015), *On Preparation and Holding of 2018 FIFA World Cup, 2017 FIFA Confederations Cup in the Russian Federation and on Amendments to Certain Legislative Acts of the Russian Federation* states that the breach of antimonopoly legislation of the Russian Federation and demonstration of unfair competition include:

- The use of entrance tickets or other documents as means to attend events for the purposes of advertising, competitions, games, and advertising campaigns;
- The use of entrance tickets in the range of offers for tourism, accommodation, and other services, without the official permission of FIFA; and
- The organization of advertising and marketing initiatives for the purposes of sponsorship and of activities aimed at a target audience including the owners of entrance tickets, without the permission of FIFA (according to Paragraphs 6 and 7 of the same article).

In accordance with Paragraph 13, Article 149 of the Text Code of the Russian Federation, the sale of entrance tickets and membership cards, the form of which is established on a settled basis as an accountable form by physical culture and sports organizations for sports entertainment events, is not subject to taxation (exempted from taxes).

Accordingly, the Russian tax treatment of organization of sports entertainment events (at least related to ticketing) is very favorable.

Within the legislation documents, the definition of "Ticket" is mentioned only in Paragraph 2 of The Rules of Conduct of Spectators during Official Sports Competitions, that were approved by the RF Government Decree of December 16, 2013, No. 1156, according to which the entrance ticket is a document having the form established by the organizers of the official sports event, confirming the right of an individual to attend the official sports event.

In addition, Annex 3 of the Order of the Ministry of Finance of the Russian Federation of February 25, 2005, No. 20n, *On the Approval of Accountable Forms*, contains the sample of a ticket for mass sports events.

In general, the Russian legislation regulating this kind of activity is rather superficial; however, this can hardly be considered as a disadvantage because of the absence of necessity for complete regulation of sports issues.

Commercial Activities Related to the Broadcasting of Sports Events

The activity related with the cession and enjoyment of the rights to broadcast sports events is one of the most important and developing segments of the sports industry.

The broadcasting of sports events brings substantial financial resources to their organizers in Russia. However, this segment of the sports industry is characterized by reduced profitability because of the lack of legal support in comparison with other countries. At the same time, this area continues to develop, and in this regard the analysis of the relevant legislation is particularly interesting.

The sale of rights to television, the Internet, and radio broadcasting of sports events ranks third in terms of sales within the world sports industry, and the rights to broadcasting are affected less by economic short-term tendencies because the majority of these rights are formalized in the contracts on a long-term basis (Kozmik, 2014, p. 4).

The constant development of the mass media sphere and the growing interest in professional sports have led to the formation of the market of rights to broadcast sports events. The appearance of the first sports programs on the radio and television coincided with the development of cooperation between sports events organizers and broadcast organizations (Kowalski, 2010, p. 4). The technological basis for the considered relations is growing rapidly.

As Zaitsev (2010) notes, sports events are developing more and more every year, and new technologies are used more and more, increasing rapidly the viewership of sports broadcasts.

The World Intellectual Property Organization (n.d.) indicates that for the majority of sports organizations selling rights to broadcast sports events is the largest source of income, which allows to receive the financial sources necessary to fund large-scale sports events, to finance sports infrastructure, and to carry out activities for the development and promotion of mass sports.

For this reason, and also due to the specific character of the broadcasting of sports events, the relations within the sector require the realization of certain relevant approaches to ensure their legal support.

In Alexander Shaub's opinion (2002, p. 4), the coverage of sports events on television (or on the radio) has the following specific features: 1) being the object of broadcasting, a sports event appears to be a hardly replaceable product because the viewer who expects to see it is unlikely to be satisfied with the broadcasting of any other sports event, and; 2) the concentration of rights to broadcast sports events belonging to sports federations significantly reduces the availability of such rights, as well as conclusion of contracts related to the implementation of the rights to long-term broadcasting or in respect of a large number of sports events which strengthens the market position of the largest broadcasters. Furthermore, according to this researcher, a sports event itself is in this case very "ephemeral" and a short-life product, and viewers tend to be more interested in live broadcasting than in its delayed version. The viewer is not very interested in watching the delayed broadcast of a sports event after a relatively long period of time from its ending.

The government is interested in providing more favorable and efficient legal regulation for the activities related to the broadcasting of sports events because the government aims to ensure social cohesion and to engage the majority of the population in sports activities, which can be realized with the help of sports programs.

Sports have a significant impact on social and cultural life, social cohesion, and solidarity by virtue of mass media. The largest sports events attract much more television viewers than any other TV program.

According to the World Intellectual Property Organization (n.d.), broadcasting organizations should have the right to:

- Ensure the protection of their expensive investment in television broadcasting of sports events;
- Recognition and rewarding of entrepreneurial efforts of broadcasters; and
- Recognition and promotion of their cultural contribution.

As to this issue, the Legislation of the Russian Federation contains separate provisions in different legal acts and in a number of intergovernmental agreements and decisions.

As a specialized federal regulatory act in this sphere, the Federal Law of December 4, 2007, No. 329-FZ, (as amended on November 3, 2015), *On Physical Culture and Sports in the Russian Federation*, does not contain the concept of broadcasting of sports events and poorly regulates the relations in the field of selling the rights to broadcasting.

Only Part 4, Article 20 of this Law specifies that the organizers of a sports event own the rights for its coverage, broadcasting visual and (or) sound information of the event by any methods and (or) using any kind of technology, including the recording of the above-noted broadcast and (or) shooting of the event.

Third parties can use these rights only upon written permission from the organizers of the events (Part 5, Article 20 of this Federal Law). In other words, this norm allows the organizer of a sports event to gain benefit from the implementation of these rights.

This issue is explained in detail in Paragraph 15, Article 2 of the Federal Law of June 7, 2013, No. 108-FZ (as amended on June 8, 2015), *On Preparation and Holding in the Russian Federation of 2018 FIFA World Cup, 2017 FIFA Confederations Cup and on Amendments to Certain Legislative Acts of the Russian Federation*. Indeed, the article defines the "FIFA broadcaster" as a legal entity that is authorized by FIFA, or another person acting on the basis of the agreement with FIFA, to provide the coverage of the events broadcasting, visual and (or) sound information by any means and (or) using any kind of technology, including the recording of the above-noted broadcast.

In accordance with Paragraph 23, Article 2 of this Federal Law, the producer of FIFA media information is a legal entity that is authorized by FIFA, or another person acting on the basis of the agreement with FIFA, to carry out:

- Creation and transfer of audio, video, audiovisual, text, and other materials connected with the event to FIFA or authorized individuals;
- Planning and organization of an international broadcast center, created in accordance with the requirements of FIFA, for events concerning the preparation and implementation of FIFA World Cup and FIFA Confederations Cup, by agreement for the development of sports competitions and by the Bid Book that are used for the purposes of television and radio broadcasting and for broadcasting using other types of technologies; and
- Provision of related services to FIFA broadcasters.

Part 2, Article 3.1 of the Federal Law of December 1, 2007, No. 310-FZ (as amended on June 28, 2014), *On Organization and Holding of XXII Winter Olympics and XI Paralympics in the year of 2014 in Sochi, Development of Sochi as a Mountain Climate Resort and on Amendments to Certain Legislative Acts of the Russian Federation*, identified the official broadcasting organizations, such as foreign organizations having received the exclusive rights to broadcast the Olympics and Paralympics within a certain country or on a certain territory (including the rights to broadcast on digital and other communication channels).

According to the above-named standards, together with the term "broadcasting", the term "translation" can be used.

In other respects, the activities of broadcasting organizations related to sports events broadcasting are regulated by the Civil Code of the Russian Federation, Article 1329, which contains the concept of organization of over-the-air or cable broadcasting. It refers to the legal entity that independently determines the content of radio and television programs (set of sounds and/or images or displaying images) and implements its broadcasting through the cable using its own resources or through third parties.

According to Paragraph 1, Article 1330 of the Civil Code of the Russian Federation, the organization of over-the-air or cable broadcasting owns the exclusive right to use the broadcast, either over-the-air, by the cable or by any means which do not violate the law (exclusive rights to radio and television broadcasting). At the same time, the organization of over-the-air or cable broadcasting may dispose of the exclusive right to broadcast radio and television programs.

Part 2, Article 1330 of the Civil Code of the Russian Federation provides the following ways to use a radio or television message:

- Message recording, i.e., its fixation in any material form, which allows it to be repeatedly perceived, reproduced, or communicated;
- Playback of a radio or television program, i.e., making of one or more copies of the message recording;

- Message distribution, sale, or any other disposing of the original or copies of the message recording;
- Retransmitting, that is the reception and simultaneous communication over the air (including by satellite) or by cable of a complete and unchanged radio or television program or its substantial part, reported in the air or cablecast by the broadcasting organization;
- Bringing a radio or television program to the public, so that anyone can access radio or television broadcasts from any place and at any time (availability to the public);
- Public performance, that is broadcasting of any radio or television program by technical means in places with entrance charged; and
- Hire of original or copies of a radio or television program.

The Federal Law provisions on advertising establishing certain requirements to advertising during broadcasting of sports events are also of great interest.

For example, in accordance with Paragraph 8, Article 14 of the Federal Law of March 13, 2006, No. 38-FZ (as amended on March 8, 2015), "On Advertising", live or recorded broadcasting of sports events (including sports games, fights, races) can be interrupted by advertising, including sponsorship advertising, only during the breaks within the sports competitions or during their stops.

In addition, Part 9, Article 14 of the Federal Law of March 13, 2006, No. 38-FZ (as amended on March 8, 2015), "On Advertising", establishes that live or recorded broadcasting of sports events, when the breaks or stops are not foreseen, may be interrupted by advertising if the broadcast interruption does not lead to the loss of essential information related to this sports event. The total duration of such advertising may not exceed twenty percent of the actual time of the sports event broadcasting.

It should be pointed out that, in accordance with Paragraph 2, Section III of the decision of Council of CIS State Leaders *On Strategy for Development of Physical Culture and Sports of State Parties of the Commonwealth of Independent States for the period up to 2020* of May 30, 2012, the cooperation of the State members of the CIS in the field of physical culture and sports is implemented, including the sector of the support of sports-oriented mass media.

In addition, Paragraph 3, Section III of the Decision of Council CIS State Leaders *On Strategy for Development of Physical Culture and Sports of State Parties of the Commonwealth of Independent States for the period up to 2020* of May 30, 2012, emphasizes that the effective implementation of the goals and objectives of this strategy will be promoted by the use of such forms of cooperation in the field of physical culture and sports as mass media coverage of the CIS sports events and the positive experience of State members of the CIS in the implementation of state policy in physical culture and sports sector.

Among the international documents, a mention should be also given to the European Convention on Transfrontier Television signed by the Russian Federation on May 5, 1989 (Council of Europe, 1989). In particular, its Article 10 stipulates that each broadcasting party should provide broadcasters of European programs with appropriate means, where it is possible, with the majority of TV time, except the time of news, sports events, games, advertising, teletext, and teleshopping. Part 2, Article 14 of the European Convention on Transfrontier Television of May 5, 1989, also adds that advertisement and teleshopping are placed in sports programs only during the breaks or gaps between the parts.

Such requirements for the positioning of advertising during sports events broadcasting is determined, primarily, by the specific character of sports entertainment products, and particularly by the fact that too long interruptions of live sports events can cause the consumers' discontent for the sports entertainment product because of its low quality.

The tax regime of the implementation of activities concerning the rights to broadcast sports events is also interesting. In some cases, a special tax regime for the most important sports events can be established.

According to Part 2, Article 143 of the Tax Code of the Russian Federation (Part 2) of August 5, 2000, No. 117-FZ (as amended on May 4, 2016), official broadcasting organizations do not pay added-value taxes in accordance with Article 3.1 of the Federal Law of December 1, 2007, No. 310-FZ, *On Organization and Holding of XXII Winter Olympics XI Winter Paralympics in 2014 in Sochi, Development of Sochi as a Mountain Climate Resort and on Amendments to Certain Legislative Acts of the Russian Federation*. Article 3.1 refers to the production and distribution of media products (i.e., official broadcasting, including digital and other communication channels), carried out in accordance with the agreement that was signed with the International Olympic Committee, or the authorized organization, and to the XXII Winter Olympics and XI Winter Paralympics in 2014 in Sochi. In accordance with Part 3 of the above-mentioned Article 143, being foreign organizations (in terms of the implementation of activities corresponding to the events approved by legislation) producers of media information for FIFA, they are not to pay taxes.

Business Activities Associated With Sports Attributes and Symbols

Business activity associated with sports attributes and symbols is another important and large segment within the sports industry.

The significance of legal protection of the right of intellectual property items referred to sports attributes and symbols is determined not only by the need for the protection of property interests of market participants lawfully having the right to exploit commercially sports attributes and symbols, but also by the necessity to avoid threats to sports ideals and common sports interests.

It is necessary to clarify the concept of sports symbols. The definition of the term is stipulated in the relevant federal legal act in the sector of physical culture and sports.

Paragraph 11.1, Article 23 of the Federal Law of December 4, 2007, No. 329-FZ (as amended on November 3, 2015), *On Physical Culture and Sports in the Russian Federation*, establishes that the symbols of sports events include the flag, the logo, the anthem, and the motto of sports events organizers; the official name of a sports event and symbols associated with the organizer formed on the basis of similar words, phrases, and names when referring to corresponding sports activities, registered as trademarks and protected as industrial patterns, and (or) copyright objects of the organizer talismans, posters, identity symbols, design items of these events, cups and medals of participants of sports competitions; literature and art treasures protected as copyright objects of the organizer, as well as objects of related rights of the organizer containing symbols identifying these activities; any other symbols and objects designed by the event organizer for the official use during such events.

It also follows that the exercise of the rights to sports symbols and these rights protection are regulated by the relevant provisions of Part 4 of the Civil Code of the Russian Federation. In particular, Chapter 76 of this legal act recognizes the rights to the means of personalization of legal entities, goods, work, services, and enterprises.

In accordance with Paragraph 2, Part 1, Article 16 of the Federal Law of December 4, 2007, No. 329-FZ (as amended on November 3, 2015), *On Physical Culture and Sports in the Russian Federation*, states that all-Russian sports federations have all the rights to use the symbols of sports teams of the Russian Federation referring to corresponding kinds of sports and the name "Russian Federation", with the exception of the RF state symbols.

Regional sport federations have the same rights (according to Paragraph 2, Part 1, Article 16.1 of the Federal Law).

In accordance with Part 2, Article 20 of the Federal Law of December 4, 2007, No. 329-FZ (as amended on March 11, 2015), *On Physical Culture and Sports in the Russian Federation*, the organizers of a sports event own the exclusive rights to use the name and symbols of this event.

The above-mentioned rules illustrate the relevant provisions of legal acts related to the implementation of significant large official international competitions in the territory of the Russian Federation.

At this rate, in accordance with Paragraph 1, Article 7 of the Federal Law of December 1, 2007, No. 310-FZ (as amended on June 28, 2014), *On Organization and Holding of XXII Winter Olympics and XI Paralympics in the year of 2014 in Sochi, Development of Sochi as a Mountain Climate Resort and on Amendments to Certain Legislative Acts of the Russian Federation*, Olympic and Paralympic symbols include fire, torch, flag, anthem, motto and emblem, symbols, and nominations related these sports events, as well as events that preceded or follow them. Furthermore, Olympic and Paralympic symbols include the names "Olympic", "Olympian", "Olympiad", "Sochi 2014", "Olympic", "Olympian", "Olympiad", "Olympic Winter Games", "Olympic Games", "Sochi 2014", "Paralympic", "Paralympics", "Paralympian", "Paralympiad", "Paralympic Winter Games", "Paralympic Game", as well as related words and phrases and other works of art that contain Olympic and Paralympic symbols.

Accordingly, the use of such symbols is carried out on the condition that appropriate agreements with the International Olympic Committee, and (or) the International Paralympic Committee, or their authorized organizations (with some exceptions), are signed.

The Federal Law of December 4, 2007, No. 329-FZ (as amended on March 11, 2015), *On Physical Culture and Sports in the Russian Federation*, determines that the Russian Olympic Committee, in accordance with the Olympic Charter of the International Olympic Committee, takes measures to protect the rights belonging to the International Olympic Committee referring to the use of the Olympic symbol, motto, flag, and anthem, names "Olympic Games", "Games of the Olympiad" in the Russian Federation. Russian Olympic Committee uses the Olympic symbol, motto, flag, and anthem, words "Olympic" and "Olympiad" for its own names and for the purposes of the development of the Olympic movement in accordance with the order established by the International Olympic Committee, and has exclusive rights to the Olympic emblem of the Russian Olympic Committee, motto, flag, and other Russian Olympic symbols (according to Article 11, Part 6).

These points are also confirmed by Article 1 of the Nairobi Treaty on the Protection of the Olympic Symbol of September 26, 1981 (World Intellectual Property Organization, 1981), by which any participating state shall deny registration or invalidate the registration as a mark and prohibit by appropriate measures to use as a mark for commercial purposes any sign, consisting of or containing the Olympic symbol as it is defined in the Charter of the International Olympic Committee, except the cases when it is authorized by the International Olympic Committee.

As Gorodov (2011) highlights, in general the need to establish a special legal protection of the Olympic symbol is explained by the fact that the volume of legal protection obtained under the trademark law could not properly ensure the protection of the exclusive right of a holder registered as a trade mark of the Olympic Symbol.

In accordance with Article 19, Paragraph 2 of the Federal Law of June 7, 2013, No. 108-FZ (as amended on August 6, 2015), *On Preparation and Holding in the Russian Federation of 2018 FIFA World Cup, 2017 FIFA Confederations Cup and on Amendments to Certain Legislative Acts of the Russian Federation*, the symbols of 2018 FIFA World Cup and 2017 FIFA Confederations Cup include the flag, logo, anthem, motto of FIFA, the official names and symbols of these activities in different languages formed on the basis of these words and phrases, and similar names containing the word "football" or in any other way associated with football as a kind of sport, other FIFA trademarks protected in the territory of the Russian Federation, including talismans of these sports events, logos, posters, identification symbols designed for the official use, as well as pieces of work containing the above symbol names.

These symbols refer to the items of intellectual property rights and FIFA holds the exclusive rights to it (in accordance with Part 1, Article 19 of the Federal Law).

According to Part 1, Article 17, FIFA owns the property rights associated with the organization of events, including the right to use the symbols of sports competitions. The use of these symbols is permitted only on the condition that the appropriate agreements with FIFA are signed (in accordance with Article 19 of the Federal Law).

The legal support of relations referred to the use of sports symbols is also expressed by the antimonopoly legislation of the Russian Federation.

Article 20.1 of the Federal Law of December 4, 2007, No. 329-FZ (as amended on March 3, 2015), *On Physical Culture and Sports in the Russian Federation*, is dedicated to ensuring fair competition in the organization and implementation of sports events and is aimed to protect the commercial rights of the organizers of these events. In particular, according to this article, unfair competition is recognized as follows:

- Illegal use of sports events symbols (or the use of similar means of individualization) for sale, exchange, or other introduction into merchandise turnover, execution of works, or provision of services (Paragraph 1);
- Implementation of any marketing activities (including activities aimed at the realization and (or) promotion of goods, pieces of work, services) which are to help the consumer to set the vision of the organizer of sports events using symbols of a sports event, or in any other way without the permission of the organizer of the event (Paragraph 2);
- False representation, concerning co-partnership between the organizers of sports events on the one side and the manufacturer of goods and (or) sponsor advertiser, partner, assistant, co-organizer, agent, licensee, supplier of goods and services on the other side, or in any other way (Paragraph 3);

- False representation, including false understanding of the approval, recommendation, certification by an organizer of a sports event of goods, works, and services, as well as any connection with goods, works, and services with sports activities (Paragraph 4);
- Development of events for commercial purposes, creating a false representation of their attitude towards sports events in particular as a sponsor as well as the financing of such events without formal permission of the organizer of sports events (Paragraph 5); and
- Organization or implementation of advertising, exhibition, or marketing activities to influence the spectators (including those who carry the tickets) during the sports event, without formal permission of the organizer (Paragraph 6).

In addition to the above, according to Paragraph 2, Article 8 of the Federal Law of December 1, 2007, No. 310-FZ (as amended on June 28, 2014), *On Organization and Holding of XXII Winter Olympics and XI Paralympics in the year of 2014 in Sochi, Development of Sochi as a Mountain Climate Resort and on Amendments to Certain Legislative Acts of the Russian Federation*, the following actions violate the antimonopoly legislation of the Russian Federation as they are considered to be examples of unfair competition:

- Introduction of goods using Olympic and (or) Paralympic symbols illegally;
- False representation concerning the involvement of the producer or advertiser in the Olympic Games and (or) the Paralympic Games, in particular as a sponsor.

In accordance with Article 20 of the Federal Law of July 6, 2013, No. 108-FZ (as amended on August 6, 2015), *On Preparation and Holding of the 2018 FIFA World Cup and 2017 FIFA Confederations Cup in the Russian Federation and on Amendments to Certain Legislative Acts of the Russian Federation*, the introduction of goods using the symbols of 2018 FIFA World Cup and 2017 FIFA Confederations Cup illegally and the implementation of marketing using these symbols without the formal permission of FIFA refer to unfair competition and violate antimonopoly legislation.

The responsibility for unfair competition is regulated by the Code of Administrative Offences of the Russian Federation. Article 14.33 of this Code foresees a penalty on public individuals, ranging from twelve thousand to twenty thousand rubles; for legal entities this sum ranges from one hundred thousand to five hundred thousand rubles. Besides, Article 14.33 establishes that unfair competition in the form of introduction of goods using the results of intellectual activity and means of individualization of goods, works, and services illegally invokes administrative penalty imposed on public individuals in the amount of twenty thousand rubles or disqualification for a period of three years; for legal entities the penalty ranges from one hundredth to fifteen hundredth of the income the violator has gained from selling goods, works, or services on the market where the violation has taken place, but not less than one hundred thousand rubles.

In addition, some related decisions of the Office of the Federal Antimonopoly Service of the Russian Federations should be considered.

Resolution of the Office of the Federal Antimonopoly Service in Moscow on the Imposition of Administrative Penalty in the Case of Administrative Offence No. 4-14.33-191/77-15 (2016). On the basis of the government contract Open Joint Stock Company "Sportloto" was involved into holding All-Russian state lotteries to support organization and holding of XXII Winter Olympics and XI Winter Paralympics in 2014 in Sochi. This organization has the right to use trademarks on the evidence in the process of production, advertising, and promotion of licensed goods/services referring to Class 41 of the International Classification of Goods and Services (organization of lotteries).

Closed Joint-Stock Company "Interlot" organizes and hold lotteries Russkaya Troika, Kozyrnaya Karta, and Zolotoj Kliuch in the territory of the Russian Federation, in accordance with the relevant permissions.

The Office of the Federal Antimonopoly Service in Moscow also determined that Closed Joint-Stock Company "Interlot" and Open Joint Stock Company "Sportloto" conduct their activity on the same market and appear to be competitors.

In order to hold a series of lotteries, Closed Joint-Stock Company "Interlot" manufactured and sold out lottery tickets decorated with naming units "Olimpijskij" and "Sochi 2014", even though Closed Joint-Stock Company "Interlot" is not considered to be a partner, sponsor, and licensee of the International Olympic Committee, International Paralympic Committee, and ANO Organizing Committee "Sochi 2014".

Thus, Closed Joint-Stock Company "Interlot" used Olympic symbols illegally (according to Paragraph 1, Article 7 of the Federal Law on Olympics) for these lotteries and gained groundless benefits as compared with its business competitors, particularly Open Joint Stock Company "Sportloto" which renders similar services without the use of Olympic symbols. Closed Joint-Stock Company "Interlot" violated the legislation of the Russian Federation.

The Office of the Federal Antimonopoly Service in Moscow stated that the direct benefit that Closed Joint-Stock Company "Interlot" gained by the usage of Olympic symbols consists in the reduction of costs for the acquisition of the rights to use these symbols (for example by signing a license contract); this gives a privilege in comparison with the entities that provide services (realization of goods) legally.

In its turn, Closed Joint-Stock Company "Interlot"'s actions can be considered as the reason for its direct competitors' losses, causing a decrease in consumers for the organizations providing goods (services) legally.

Consequently, Closed Joint-Stock Company "Interlot"'s actions were considered to be the breach of the legislation on fair competition, although, according to the arguments of this organization, it did not intend to gain benefits by using Olympic symbols and, in its turn, the usage itself did not result in positive growing dynamics of sales of decorated goods.

The decision of Moscow Arbitration Court with regard to the case No. A40-184735/2014 (2014). Open Joint Stock Company "AMF" applied to the arbitration court to challenge the resolution of the Office of the Federal Antimonopoly Service in Moscow region of October 28, 2014, with regard to the case on administrative offence No. 05-21/65-14. The stated claims were determined by the insignificance of the offences detected.

By the decision of July 3, 2014, within the case No. 05-15/25-14, the Committee of the Office of the Federal Antimonopoly Service in Moscow region established a violation in the activity of Open Joint Stock Company "AMF" in accordance with Paragraph 1, Part 1, Article 14 of the Federal Law *On Protection of Competition*, concerning the realization of goods using the result of intellectual activity illegally and using the means of identification of legal entities, means of identification of work and services expressed by the use of Olympic symbolic colors, alongside with words and expressions which contain naming units "Olimpiada", "Olimpijskie", and "Sochi 2014".

Thus, the antimonopoly authority found Open Joint Stock Company "AMF" guilty of administrative offence and the appellant admitted the fault.

The papers on the case contain the e-mail on February 3, 2014 from the e-mail address noreply@amf.ru to mailto.alenush@gmail.com, reporting the following:

Olympic bunches of flowers from AMF! We're cheering for Russia! XXII Winter Olympics in Sochi are opening on February 7. Congratulate the champions! We've been looking forward for this moment and finally it is time for it! 2014 Olympics in Sochi are opening! You can place the order for flowers on our site and congratulate all sports fans with this event...

These actions were taken by Open Joint Stock Company "AMF" without signing the agreement on the use of Olympic symbols with the International Olympics Committee and ANO Organizing Committee "Sochi 2014".

According to the Moscow Arbitration Court, the argument of Open Joint Stock Company “AMF” concerning the insignificance of the offence and the absence of significant threat to the relations under protection, providing grounds to be released from administrative responsibility in accordance with Article 2.9 of the Administrative Code of the Russian Federation, is to be rejected since in this case a significant threat is not in the absence of any material consequences of the offence, but in the negligence of the society to the performance of public legal obligations and to formal requirements of public law.

The decision of the Office of the Federal Antimonopoly Service in Novosibirsk region with regard to the case No. 06-01-02-14-15 towards Open Joint Stock Company “Stolica” (2015). The office of the Federal Antimonopoly Service established the violation of the antimonopoly legislation by Open Joint Stock Company “Stolica” using the Olympic symbols for the individualization of the autocentre “Olimpijskij”, which can be used only upon the agreements with the International Olympic Committee and (or) ANO Organizing Committee “Sochi 2014”. The symbols were used to attract interest in the services rendered taking into account the ongoing XXII Winter Olympics in 2014 in Sochi.

Above the entrance into the workshops of “Olimpijskij”, the images of symbols BMW, Audi, Mercedes, LEXUX, and Land Rover were put into five circles situated by analogy with the Olympic rings (Act of documented information). The circles into which the symbols were put looked similar to the recognized international Olympic symbol.

In this case, the intention to get benefits within the business activity violating antimonopoly legislation was demonstrated by Open Joint Stock Company “Stolica” by using Olympic symbols as means of individualization for the autocenter, which can be used only upon the agreements with the International Olympic Committee and (or) ANO Organizing Committee “Sochi 2014”, as well as creating false representation concerning the involvement of the company into the Olympics and Paralympics. The symbols were used to attract interest in the services that were rendered, considering the ongoing XXII Winter Olympics in 2014 in Sochi.

The organization was proved not to have signed the corresponding agreements and as a result Open Joint Stock Company “Stolica” had used the symbols illegally.

The office of the Federal Antimonopoly Service in Novosibirsk region concluded that the above-mentioned actions could attract consumers’ interest in the company’s services, taking into account the ongoing XXII Winter Olympics in 2014 in Sochi. In addition, the above-mentioned actions could cause losses to the company’s competitors as a result of the decrease in demand.

Business Activity Within the Sports Sector Related to Sponsorship and Advertising

Sponsorship within the sports sector turns up to be quite a significant segment within the sports industry in the Russian Federation.

As Alekseev (2011) has noted, a sponsor is one of the main subjects in the field of development of sports and advertising relations. It is involved in the financing of physical culture and sports projects holding different sports events within the fast growing sports movement and advertising industry.

Sports sponsorship differs (at least it is not identified) from non-profit sponsorship (whose forms and features are also regulated by the legislation of the Russian Federation), as sports sponsorship implies commercial purposes of a sponsor that expects to gain profit from the investments (Taymazov, 2012, p. 153).

However, in practice the difference between commercial and non-profit sponsorship is not obvious.

The key features of sports sponsorship can be specified as follows:

- Sports sponsorship is a system of interrelations and cooperation between interested parties;
- Sports sponsorship includes the provision of financial or non-monetary support to the sponsored entity (as a sponsored entity can appear sports organizations, sportsmen, sports teams, sports events, and sports brands); and
- Commercial organization playing a role of sponsor can pursue its own marketing purposes.

Nonetheless, despite the significance of sponsorship activity within the sports sector, the specific legislation on physical culture and sports does not clear up the issue to the full extent.

Thus, only Article 20.1 of the Federal Law of December 4, 2007, No.329-FZ (as amended on November 3, 2015), *On Physical Culture and Sports in Russian Federation*, mentions the phenomenon of sports sponsorship concerning the provision of fair competition referring to the organization and holding of sports events. The article establishes that unfair competition includes false representation referring to sports events or their organizers about the co-partnership between the organizers and producers and (or) advertiser as a sponsor (Paragraph 3 of this Article), as well as the holding for commercial purposes of events creating false representation about the relations of producers and advertisers to these sports events as a sponsor (Paragraph 5) and the use of sports events without formal permission of their organizers to implement advertising, exhibition, marketing, and sponsorship activity to influence spectators of sports events, including those who carry entrance tickets.

As a result, the sponsorship is implemented only with the formal permission of the organizer of the sports event.

The corresponding rights are also established by Article 20 of the Federal Law of June 7, 2013, No. 108-FZ (as amended on June 8, 2015), *On Preparation and Holding of 2018 FIFA World Cup, 2017 FIFA Confederations Cup in the Russian Federation and on Amendments to Certain Legislative Acts of the Russian Federation.* This Article prohibits the sponsorship of the corresponding sports events without the formal permission of FIFA.

In general, sponsorship activity is regulated by the Civil Code of the Russian Federation (which does not contain specific provisions on sponsorship), as well as by the Federal Law of March 13, 2016, No. 38-FZ (as amended on March 8, 2015) *On Advertising*, which does not put a special emphasis on the regulation of this activity either.

In accordance with Paragraph 9, Article 3 of the Federal Law of March 13, 2016, No. 38-FZ (as amended on March 8, 2015), *On Advertising*, a sponsor is an individual providing financial support to the organization and (or) for the holding of sports, culture, and any other event, creation and (or) broadcasting of radio and television program, and (or) for any use of other results of creative work.

In this case, sponsorship advertising is defined as advertising distributed upon the condition of obligatory mention of the name of the sponsor (according to Paragraph 10 of this Article).

Only an individual can act as a sponsor and this individual is to be defined as a sponsor in advertising. The advertiser can define himself as a sponsor in any form to define the participation in the sponsoring event. However, an advertising indicating that a commodity or trademark acts as a sponsoris not referred to sponsorship advertising. Sponsorship advertising has a number of preferences. Thus, for example, the break of television and radio programs by sponsorship advertising can be carried out without preliminary message about the next advertising broadcast (Badalov, Vasilenkova, Kartashov, Kotov, & Nikitina, 2011).

In terms of advertising within the sports sector, it is necessary to mention that the rights to the positioning of advertisements of goods, works, and services at venues of sports events belong only to the organizers of this event (according to Part 2, Article 20 of the Federal Law of December 4, 2007, No. 329-FZ (as amended on November 3, 2015: *On Physical Culture and Sports in Russian Federation*). In this case, as established by this Article, the profits gained by the organizers of sports event exercising a right to position advertisements of beer and beer-based beverages at the places of the venue, as well as the right to position the specified advertisements during television and radio broadcasting of sports events, are spent in accordance with the rules approved by the federal executive authority within the sector of physical culture and sports.

As established by Part 1, Article 17 of the Federal Law of June 7, 2013, No. 108-FZ (as amended on June 8, 2015), *On Preparation and Holding of 2018 FIFA World Cup, 2017 FIFA Confederations Cup in the Russian Federation and on Amendments to Certain Legislative Acts of the Russian Federation*, FIFA owns property rights concerning the holding of these events, including the rights to the positioning of advertising.

In addition, according to Paragraph 1, Article 3 of the Federal Law of March 13, 2006, No.38-FZ (as amended on March 8, 2015), "On advertising", advertising is information spread by any means, in any forms and using any sources addressed to a specific audience and aimed to attract attention to the advertised item, form, and support the interest in its promotion within the market. In this case, in accordance with Paragraph 2 of this Article, a sports event can also appear as an advertised item.

The legislation of the Russian Federation does not almost contain specific requirements to advertising in the sports sector, particularly to advertising during sports events.

Although the Federal Law of June 7, 2013, No.108-FZ (as amended from June 8, 2015), *On Preparation and Holding of 2018 FIFA World Cup, 2017 FIFA Confederations Cup in the Russian Federation and on Amendments to Certain Legislative Acts of the Russian Federation*, contains some detailed requirements related to advertising during the specified events.

Thus, in accordance with Part 1, Article 18 of this Federal Law, during the specified period of time within the competitions, the positioning of advertisements at the venue of such events and in a radius of less than 2000 meters from their borders can be performed only upon the corresponding agreement with FIFA or by formal written permission from this organization or the authorized one. The same rules are applied to the positioning of advertisements on sports outfit, equipment, and facilities used during the competitions.

In accordance with Part 3 of the specified Article, the advertising is considered to be unfaithful if it contains unfaithful information concerning the involvement of the advertiser into the events, FIFA, and (or) Organizing Committee "Russia-2018", in particular as a sponsor, partner, broadcaster, assistant, co-organizer, agent, licensee, official supplier of goods, works, and services, or in any other way, as well as information concerning recommendations, approval of FIFA and (or) Organizing Committee "Russia-2018" of the advertised object.

In general, the above-mentioned provisions define the principles on the use of advertising during sports events which are included in the other legal laws and regulations.

Paragraph 11, Article 2 of the Federal Law of December 4, 2007, No. 329-FZ (as amended on November 3, 2015), *On Physical Culture and Sports in the Russian Federation*, includes the concept of professional sports, according to which sportsmen are to receive remuneration or nonmonetary benefits for the preparation and participation in sports competitions providing that sports is the main kind of activity for such sportsmen.

In accordance with Part 2, Article 20 of the Federal Law of December 4, 2007, No. 329-FZ (as amended on November 3, 2015), *On Physical Culture and Sports in Russian Federation*, the organizers of sports events own exclusive rights to:

- Use the name of the event and its symbols;
- Position advertising of goods, works, and services at the venues of sports events;
- Define the producers of sports outfit, equipment, and facilities used during the sports event.

In this case, the funds gained by the organizers of sports events, exercising the right to position advertisements of beer and beer-based beverages at the places of venue of such events as well as the right to position the specified advertisements during television and radio broadcasting of sports events, are expended in accordance with the rules approved by the Ministry of Sports of the Russian Federation.

Chapter 8 of the Federal Law of June 7, 2013, No. 108-FZ (as amended on June 8, 2015), *On Preparation and Holding of 2018 FIFA World Cup, 2017 FIFA Confederations Cup in the Russian Federation and on Amendments to Certain Legislative Acts of the Russian Federation*, is related to the peculiarities of protection and implementation of property rights of FIFA concerning the development of events. In particular, according to Part 1, Article 17, FIFA owns property rights related to the organization of events, including the rights to use the symbols of these sports events, the control of the access to the venues of sports events; the distribution of entrance tickets and other substituting documents; the choice of FIFA's commercial partners and contractors; the position of advertising; the selling and distribution of goods, works, and services at the venues of the events; the choice of the producers of sports outfit, equipment, and facilities used during the events; the coverage of the events broadcasting visual and (or) sound materials by any means and (or) with any technologies; the dissemination of the events in public places using audio-, video recordings and (or) photo content.

Additionally, this chapter contains provisions on:

- Requirements to advertising, peculiarities of positioning, spreading of advertising and trading activities during the events (Article 18);
- Use of symbols of 2018 FIFA World Cup and 2017 FIFA Confederations Cup (Article 19);

- Fair competition within the organization of sports events (Article 20);
- Distribution of entrance tickets and other substituting documents (Article 21);
- Peculiarities of the distribution of goods, works, and services by FIFA, FIFA's commercial partners, FIFA's suppliers of goods and services (Paragraph 22).

Sports Ethics and Sports Integrity Within the Sports Industry

Although the activity within the sports industry related to the organization and implementation of sports events is mainly of commercial nature, it should be regulated by ethical rules, some of which are mentioned in the legislative norms and regulations. Professional sports, which are considerably commercialized and often referred to as a business activity, continue to contribute to the implementation of some social functions.

The issue of ethics in sports is quite extensive and can cover different kinds of activities in sports and different aspects of sports, such as relations among sportsmen, relations between sportsmen and sports organizations within which they work or carry out specific kind of activity, relations among sports organizations (both horizontal and vertical ones), and relations between sports industry subjects and the consumers of sports entertainment products.

As the topic of this section is dedicated mainly to the peculiarities of legal regulation of the sports industry in the Russian Federation, it would be reasonable to describe the issue connected with the observance of ethical norms by sports organizations during the implementation of their activity within the Russian sports industry and the peculiarities of the Russian legislation concerning the regulation of ethical norms.

The following directions of ethical norms provision within the sports sector (issues which should be taken into account by sports organizations) can be specified:

- Provision of sportsmen with their rights protection, dignity, safety, life, and healthcare;
- Prevention of and fight against discrimination within the sports sector;
- Fight against dope application and turnover within the sport sector;
- Observance of main sports principles, such as fair play; and
- Prevention of illegal influence on the results of sports competitions.

In the following, some specific provisions of the Russian legislation concerning the issue of ethics in sports are illustrated.

The specialized Federal Law in the sector of physical culture and sports mentions the necessity of observance of sports ethics only in one article.

In accordance with Paragraph 3, Part 2, Article 24 of the Federal Law of December 4, 2007, No. 329-FZ (as amended from November 3, 2015), *On Physical Culture and Sports*, sportsmen shall observe ethical norms within the sports sector.

There are also some other provisions of the Federal Act defining obligations of the subjects of physical culture and sports to observe ethical norms.

Thus, Article 3 of the Federal Law of December 4, 2007, No. 329-FZ (as amended from November 3, 2015), *On Physical Culture and Sports in the Russian Federation*, contains the main principles of the Russian legislation concerning physical culture and sports. They include prohibition on discrimination and violence in the sports sector, on illegal influence on the results of the official sports competitions (Paragraph 5 of the Article), as well as safety protection of life and health of individuals involved in sports activities, including participants and spectators of sports events (Paragraph 6).

The organizers of sports events are to take measures to prevent dope application and turnover within the sports sector, in accordance with Part 11, Article 26 of the Federal Law of December 12, 2007, No. 329-FZ (as amended on November 3, 2015), *On Physical Culture and Sports in the Russian Federation.*

The provisions of Article 26.2 of the Federal Law of December 12, 2007, No. 329-FZ (as amended on November 3, 2015), *On Physical Culture and Sports in the Russian Federation*, are aimed to prevent illegal influence on the results of official sports competitions and to fight against the actions related to that.

In this case, illegal influence on the results of sports competitions in Russia implies criminal responsibility. Article 184 of the Criminal Code of the Russian Federation imposes sanctions in the form of money penalty, imprisonment, community service, as well as deprivation of the right to hold certain positions or carry out certain activities. These sanctions are imposed in case of bribing sportsmen, referees, coaches, sports team managers, and other participants or organizers of the official sports competition (including employees), as well as jury members, participants, or organizers of entertainment commercial competition for the purposes of influencing the results of such events or competitions, inducing others to this influencing or previous concert with them.

The Russian legislation determines the responsibility for the breach of the requirements to prevent dope application and turnover within the sports sector. Article 6.18 of the Code of Administrative Offences of the Russian Federation imposes sanctions in the form of disqualification of a coach, sports medicine specialist, or any other employee in the sector of physical culture and sports for the breach of requirements to prevent dope application and turnover consisting in the use of prohibited substance and (or) prohibited method towards a sportsman, regardless of his consent if these actions do not contain any penal offence.

Within the sports system, the activity is divided into several directions, such as professional and amateur sports, high performance and mass sports. Although the final goals of all these directions can be different, the sports system has its common integrity goals, the achievement of which is implemented integrally.

Thus, the commercial activity within the sports sector cannot be implemented separately from the system. Professional sports can also contribute to the development of amateur and mass sports as well as high-performance sports with the help of specific techniques.

Article 10 of the Federal Law of December 4, 2007, No. 329-FZ (as amended on November 3, 2015), *On Physical Culture and Sports in the Russian Federation*, describes the basics of the activity of physical culture and sports organizations, and provides that such organizations can be both commercial and non-profit, regardless of their organization legal form. In accordance with Part 2 of this article, such organizations participate in the development of physical culture and sports among different social groups, provide conditions for safety and health promotion of sportsmen and other individuals participating in sports competitions and training events, provide sportsmen and coaches with the conditions for training, and facilitate the achievement of high results.

The Russian Federation appears to be a state member of the Council of Europe. Then, there is a necessity to mention ethical principles within the sports sector in the Recommendation No. R (92) 14 REV of the Committee of Ministers to Member States *On the Revised Code of Sports Ethics* (2001). The specified Code of Sports ethics in particular establishes that the principle of fair play is to be observed by the following parties:

- Government;
- Sports organizations including sports federations, physical culture educational establishments, and others; and
- Individuals (including spectators of sports events).

In general, the main functions on the provision of ethics norms in the sports sector are carried out by Russian sports organizations which, in view of the principle of sports autonomy established by Paragraph 3, Article 3 of the Federal Law of December 4, 2007, No. 329-FZ (as amended on November 3, 2015), *On Physical Culture and Sports in the Russian Federation*, (in the form of the principle of combination of state regulation of relations in physical culture and sports sector, with the self-regulation of these relations by the subjects of physical culture and sports) have a certain level of autonomy related to establishing their own internal rules.

Such organizations often determine ethical norms or codes of ethics in their regulation standards.

In particular, the Regulations of the Russian Football Union on Ethics (2012) can be referred to as an example.

CONCLUSION

Being an efficient basis for the development of sports business activity, the legislation of the Russian Federation within the legal support of business and commercial activity in the sports sector also takes into consideration the specific character of sports and its functions, which allows professional sports to provide benefits to economy and society. However, there is still space for further development.

Sport is considered to be a well-balanced, integral, complex system, although it is constantly influenced by a number of external factors related to sports globalization and economic activity. Within this system, all parts of sports, including professional and amateur sports, high-performance and mass sports, are closely interacting and influencing one another, particularly when considering the influence of professional sports on the development of mass sports in terms of the population's motivation to be engaged in sports activities.

REFERENCES

Alekseev, S. (2002). Legal regulation of sports sponsorship. *Sports: Economics, Law, Management, 4*.

Badalov, D., Vasilenkova, I., Kartashov, N., Kotov, S., & Nikitina, I. (2011). *Commentaries to the Federal Law of 13.03.2006 number 38-FZ "On Advertising"*. Retrieved April 29, 2016, from http://fas.gov.ru/documents/documentdetails.html?id=998

Committee of Ministers of the Council of Europe. (2001). *Recommendation Nº R (92) 14 REV of the Committee of Ministers to member states on the revised Code of sports ethics (adopted by the Committee of Ministers on 24 September 1992 at the 480th meeting of the Ministers' Deputies and revised at their 752nd meeting on 16 May 2001)*. Retrieved April 29, 2016, from https://search.coe.int/cm/Pages/result_details.aspx?ObjectID=09000016804cf400

Council of Europe. (1989). *European Convention on Transfrontier Television, Strasbourg, 05.V.1989*. Retrieved April 29, 2016, from http://www.coe.int/ru/web/conventions/full-list/-/conventions/rms/090000168007b0d8, https://rm.coe.int/CoERMPublicCommonSearchServices/DisplayDCTMContent?documentId=090000168007b0fa

Gorodov, O. (2011). On legal protection of Olympic symbols. *Competition Law, 2.*

Kowalski, K. (2015). *The rights to TV broadcast of sport events* (Master Thesis). University of Lapland, Rovaniemi, Finland. Retrieved April 29, 2016, from https://lauda.ulapland.fi/bitstream/handle/10024/62155/Kowalski.%20Karol.pdf?sequence=2

Kozmik, V. (2014). Recent marketing trends of sport in the world and in Russia. The rise of the sports industry in Russia - a consequence of the major sporting events or growth economic environment? *Naukovedenie, 4.*

Moscow Arbitration Court. (2014). *Decision on the case number A40-184735.* Retrieved April 29, 2016, from http://solutions.fas.gov.ru/to/moskovskoe-oblastnoe-ufas-rossii/05-21-65-14

Office of the Federal Antimonopoly Service in Moscow. (2016). *Resolution on administrative punishment in the case of administrative violation Nº 4-14.33-191 / 77-15.* Retrieved April 29, 2016, from http://solutions.fas.gov.ru/to/moskovskoe-ufas-rossii / 4-14-33-191-77-15

Ponkin, I., & Ponkina, A. (2014a). Limits of State Intervention and Non-Intervention inthe Sports Field. *Kutafin University Law Review, 1*, 92–105.

Ponkin, I., & Ponkina, A. (2014b). To a question about the content of the concept of "professional sport". *Laws of Russia: Experience, Analysis, and Practice, 9*, 24–28.

Russia Novosibirsk, O. F. A. S. (2015). *Decision of the Commission on the case number 06-01-02-14-15 against "Stolica".* Retrieved April 29, 2016, from http://solutions.fas.gov.ru/to/novosibirskoe-ufas-rossii/bn-2c53b7c6- c887-41b8-b217-1042605f249c

Russian Football Union. (2012). *Regulation of the Russian Football Union on Ethics.* Retrieved April 29, 2016, from http://www.rfs.ru/rfs/documents/strategies/

Schaub, A. (2002). Sports and Competition: Broadcasting Rights of Sports Events. *Jornada dìa de la competencia.* Retrieved April 29, 2016, from http://ec.europa.eu/competition/speeches/text/sp2002_008_en.pdf

Shevchenko, O., & Ponkin, I. (2014). On development of legal doctrine in the field of sport. *Teoriya i Praktika Fizicheskoy Kultury, 6*, 32–34.

Taymazov, E. (2012). Evaluating the effectiveness of public-private partnerships in the sports sponsorship. *Proceedings of the St. Petersburg University of Economics and Finance, 6*, 153-157.

World Intellectual Property Organization. (1981). *Nairobi Treaty on the Protection of the Olympic Symbol / Adopted in Nairobi 26.09.1981.* Retrieved April 29, 2016, from http://www.rupto.ru/docs/interdocs/nayrobi?starblind=100

World Intellectual Property Organization. (n.d.). *Broadcasting & Media Rights in Sport*. Retrieved April 29, 2016, from http://www.wipo.int/ip-sport/en/broadcasting.html

Zaitsev, Y. (2010). The right to coverage of sporting events in the Russian Federation. *Sports: Economics, Law, Management, 4*.

Chapter 10
Problems of the Fight Against Doping in Professional Sports:
On the Example of Russian and World Experience

Anatoly Peskov
Russian International Olympic University, Russia

ABSTRACT

Doping became, as many experts note, not only more diverse, highly specialized, and efficient, but also dangerous for the health of athletes. One of the main factors that allows athletes to escape responsibility is corruption. The author pays particular attention to research and new technologies in the field of sports medicine, including generating new kinds of doping. The chapter also examines the practice of international standard on granting exceptions on therapeutic use of drugs. The author suggests reconstructing the existing system of criminal and administrative law to develop new enforcement mechanisms in the fight against doping to impose a ban on the testing of new drugs on professional athletes.

INTRODUCTION

Doping is not only a result of fraudulent actions of athletes, their desire to win at any cost and break the rules of fair play in order to get cash bonuses and undeserved rewards. Doping is also the result of the actions of politicians who want to win political opponents, to show the world the superiority of their countries and nations through the victories of their athletes. Doping is also a consequence of competition

DOI: 10.4018/978-1-5225-5387-8.ch010

doping and Anti-Doping technologies that producing in the laboratories of the most developed and advanced countries. We have only one way to solve the problem of doping. It is necessary to unite all international community against this evil. All countries should strengthen administrative and criminal liability for violations of Anti-Doping laws, to join efforts to combat international organized crime, illegally distributing prohibited substances. It is necessary to introduce access on an equal basis to athletes of all countries to modern technologies of sports medicine, to ban testing on athletes for new pharmacological agents. Drug manufacturers should be required to indicate in the specifications possibility to use medical drugs in professional sports. The main purpose of this chapter to familiarize a reader with doping practices, causes and conditions of its distribution, to identify ways to combat this negative phenomenon.

BACKGROUND

Recently the doping scandals shuddered professional sports. In December 2014 ARD - the German TV channel - broadcast Hajo Seppelt's documentary film *The Doping Secret: How Russia Creates Champions* where Russia was accused of athletes' doping support at the country level (Kabanov, 2014).

According to the film, it is easy in Russia to buy doping on the Internet and the Russian athletes tried to eliminate revealed positive doping tests for bribes, and there a large-scale falsification of doping tests took place in the Russian Anti-Doping laboratory. Sports doctors quasi helped athletes to use the new prohibited performance enhancing drugs and to remove them from athletes' body in due time. Therefore, the concrete facts and surnames of officials were specified in this film.

Following the broadcast film there was a big scandal in the sports world, WADA initiated investigation of the facts mentioned in the film, and in November 2015, it published a report following the results of this investigation. *WADA's Independent Commission confirmed these facts and declared that Grigoriy Rodchenkov, the head of the Moscow Anti-Doping laboratory, in spite of requirements of the World Anti-Doping Code had destroyed 1417 doping tests in his laboratory. Valentin Balakhnichev*, the former head of the Russian Athletics Federation, as well as Grigoriy Rodchenkov was also accused for falsification of doping tests and bribery (*WADA: Two Moscow Laboratories Eliminated Doping Tests).*

Rodchenkov's illegal actions caused the situation when achievements of our many athletes at the previous Olympic Games and International Championship raised doubts about it. Following the results of investigation WADA came to the following conclusion: *The culture of cheating has taken roots deeply in Russia.*

According to the investigation the consent with cheating at all levels is widespread and it exists for a long time. Then WADA recommended to disqualify all Russian athletes from any international competitions and to disqualify five coaches and five athletes for life. International Association of Athletics Federations (IAAF) supported these recommendations and suspended Russia's membership in this organization for an indefinite period. (*Russia May be Disqualified from Athletics Competitions)*.

So how did Russia react to this scandal? There were many emotions, talks on slander and lie, double standards, that there was no such problems in the Russian sport and that it is gross lie of the West, etc. The official reaction was different. The Ministry of Sport made an official statement on November 10, 2015 that it respected WADA's independent investigation and it would fight doping rigidly in association with international sports organizations (Ministry of Sport of Russia Made Statement to WADA's Accusations, 2015).

The Russian President Vladimir Putin also responded to these events. He demanded to perform the domestic investigation in coordination with the international organizations and to protect health of our athletes (*Putin Against Doping Scandal has Invoked to Protect Athletes from Administration of the Forbidden Drugs,* 2015*)*. The work of the Moscow Anti-Doping laboratory was suspended. Mr. Rodchenkov, director of this laboratory, was dismissed. The Administration of RUSADA gave up its power; the business of this organization was suspended. After these tragic events in February 2016, the chairman of executive council and the executive director of RUSADA died due to illness (Petrov, 2016).

However, Hajo Seppelt continued the revelations and in March 2016, he presented the third film "Russia's Red Herrings" where he stated that the death of RUSADA's Executive Director could be deliberate, as he had been going to provide to the West the confidential information on doping in Russia. Moreover, he had accused Russia's government of failure to take drastic measures for improvement of the doping case *(ARD Broadcaster Informed About New Doping Violations in the Russian Sport*, 2016).

The doping scandal had also the contrary consequences. For example, it took only one day for Professor Timofei Sobolevskii, the deputy chief of Moscow Anti-Doping laboratory, to get a job in Anti-Doping laboratory in Los Angeles (USA). The former chief of laboratory where according to WADA many FSB undercover employees worked got it with success (Ganeev, 2015).

By the way, this case with Mr. Rodchenkov, the chief of the Moscow Anti-Doping laboratory, is not the first case. On the eve of Sochi Olympic Games (2014), one of the Russian athletics medalists of London Olympic Games informed WADA on falsification of positive doping tests for money in this laboratory. Even at that time, these facts had been confirmed. Moreover, the chief of laboratory Mr. Rodchenkov and his relative had been detained by FSB of the Russian Federation in Moscow on suspicion of doping distribution (Kelnerand Harrisand, & Stewart, 2013). Disciplinary Committee of WADA on the eve of the Olympic Games recommended withdrawing accreditation of the Moscow Anti-Doping Center due to "inadequate reliability". Many efforts was made to cancel this decision. However, WADA obliged the Moscow Anti-Doping Laboratory to employ international independent experts, to develop a new program for control of sampling quality and allowed laboratory to work at Winter Olympic Games in Sochi. The Government of Russia allocated 27 million EUR for Anti-Doping arrangements, reconstruction and equipment of two laboratories in Moscow and Sochi (*Russia Spent 27 Mln EUR for Two Laboratories*, 2013).

There were other scandals in 2015. Due to the mass doping in the Olympic training center for race walking (Saransk, Mordovia, Russia) in 2015 V. M. Chegin, a famous coach and order bearer, was forced to leave elite sport (the Center was even named after this coach). Mr. Chegin prepared more than 50 Masters of Sport of International Class. His pupils became winners of World Championships and Olympic Games. However, for some reason they were constantly pursued by doping scandals. Before the Olympic Games 2008 (Beijing, the People's Republic of China), five of his racewalkers were disqualified from competitions due to presence of EPO. Before the World Championship 2013, the doping was found in blood of four of his racewalkers, and they refused participation in competitions. In July 2014 Elena Lashmanova, also his pupil, was disqualified, a deadly doping was found in her blood. At last, in 2015 Chegin's pupils: Kirdiapkin, Borchin, Kaniskina and Kanaikin were disqualified based on Biological Passport Index (Chegin, & Mikhailovich, 2016).

The doping was also actively used in other Russian sports previously. In 2012 - 2013, the multiple World and Europe champion swimmer Iuliia Efimova and the six-time javelin champion of Russia Lada Chernova were caught in doping. In particular, Iuliia Efimova was disqualified by the International Swimming Federation for 16 months. The sportswoman admitted that she periodically administered bioactive additives and one of them had a prohibited drug, and it was specified on a label (Efimova, 2014).

Winter Olympic Games in Sochi (Russia, 2014) were not devoid of doping scandals. A week prior to the Games EPO was found in blood tests of our biathlonists Ekaterina Iurieva and Irina Starykh. The Russian weightlifter, the world and Europe champion - A. Lovchev and three other Russian weightlifters were recently accused of doping at Weightlifting World Championship in Houston (USA, 2015) (*Lovchev's Dope: Politics or Shame?,* 2015).

All these doping scandals in Russia in 2015-2016 have created public opinion in the world that the Russian sport cannot exist without doping and all sporting wins are a result of illegal manipulations with athletes' health. However, is it true? Are the western professional sportsmen so faultless?

DOPING IN PROFESSIONAL SPORTS

Of course, not. Doping is an international problem and it concerns all countries in the world. During the Games in Sochi (Russia, 2014) the German biathlonist, the five-time Olympic champion and the six-time world champion Evi Sachenbacher-Stehle, the skier of the Ukrainian Olympic Team Marina Lisogor, the hockey player of the Latvian National Team Vitalii Pavlov, the Italian bobsledder William Frullani, the Swedish hockey player Nicholas Backstrom were accused of doping. Moreover, the German police sought through Evi Sachenbacher-Stehle's house for presence of the prohibited drugs and biological additives as doping was a penal act in Germany.

After Winter Olympic Games in Sochi (Russia, 2014) the doping was found in blood test of the Austrian skier Johannes Dürr and the Polish bobsledder Daniel Zalewski. The Disciplinary commission of the International Olympic Committee (hereinafter referred to as IOC) immediately annulled all their sporting achievements in Sochi. Moreover, it is not necessarily mean that there will be no any new revelations among the athletes participating in the Sochi Olympic Games since samples have been taken at 45% of participants of these Games and according new rules the result will be stored within ten years.

In particular, the unexpected information was provided in May 2013 by a "watchdog" of the World Anti-Doping Agency (hereinafter referred to as WADA) about the fact that representatives of sports official delegations from seven countries had brought a large number of intravascular infusion lines to Winter Olympic Games in Sochi (Russia, 2014). Besides there were found utilized needles and syringes near the residence of some national Olympic teams. In addition, this is, as we know, already a violation of Anti-Doping rules. Among sources of this information, there were such reputable services as Federal security service and Federal Customs Service of the Russian Federation (*Seven National Teams Were Suspected of Doping in Sochi Games,* 2014).

History of the World Doping

However, no facts surprise. The doping problem in professional sport is as old as the sea. Even in the ancient Olympic Games, athletes used sesame seeds and some species of psychotropic mushrooms (amanita extract, etc.). Some of them drank wine with a lot of lamb meat and garlic, ate sheep testicles before the competition, which were a dope source under the name of testosterone.

The beginning of modern professional sport development in the nineteenth century was connected with use of such stimulators as caffeine, cocaine, codeine and strychnine. At that time, some athletes usually used caffeine or wine enriched with cocaine as a doping. The doping was actively distributed in the modern

Olympic Games. For example, at the Olympic Games in St. Louis (the USA, 1904) marathon runner doctors rescued Thomas Hicks after he had drunk a significant dose of brandy with strychnine.

However, at that time it was not considered violation of rules of morality and right. The first and only "Olympic" violator of Anti-Doping rules was revealed at Summer Olympic Games in Mexico City (Mexico, 1968) when the drug test really appeared. This violator was the Swedish athlete Hans Gunnar Liljenwall who had the excess amount of alcohol in blood (Steinbach, 2008). However, at the Olympic Games in Munich (Germany, 1972) it was found out that already seven athletes had used doping. Henceforth the Olympic Games always had a large number of doping scandals. For example, on the eve of the Olympic Games in Salt Lake City (USA, 2002) almost all Finnish ski national team members were disqualified, then the American bobsledder was disqualified. The prohibited drug was also found in the Russian skiers Natalia Baranova, Olga Danilina and Larisa Lazutina. The last of these had earlier been granted title of Hero of the Russian Federation for outstanding sporting achievements.

Moreover, if at the beginning of the XX century athletes often used drugs and alcohol which could numb pain and fatigue, then later the improved types of doping were used, including anabolic steroids – substances influencing the person at the hormonal level. Anabolic steroids were especially widely adopted in the American sport – bodybuilding and weightlifting in the late 1950s and early in the 1960s. It is interesting that it was legal in the USA, It was promoted by means of the large advertising campaign, medical recommendations and prescription of doctors. Anabolic steroids gained the greatest popularity in 1970-1980s as a drug for stimulation of athletes' energy supply systems and revival after great training and competitive stress (*Pharmacological Products and Other Substances Prohibited in Sport,* 2012).

Due to doping the high sporting achievements began to be registered everywhere in the world. Historians describe this "doping era" as follows:

Artificially calmed shooters began to shoot better and quickly excited runners began to show the best start speed. Tireless players provided higher rate on fields what increased the staginess of matches. In addition, the weight began to rise on the weightlifting platform! It is unbelievable. The audience was delighted. People watched Games with ecstasy. (Kurinoi, 2010)

Further, there appeared new substances: *erythropoietin* (increases endurance and force), diuretic (removes liquid, increases flexibility and masks doping, etc.). Then people learned to transfuse blood of athletes, to oxygenate it with special substances, to carry out other manipulations with blood.

As many experts noted the doping became more various, targeted and effective, as well as hazardous to health of athletes. For many international organizations and countries, the doping was not an everyday occurrence any more, it was considered as a serious violation and in some countries as a crime.

The death of the cyclist from Denmark Knud Jensen at the Olympic Games in Rome (Italy, 1960) became a landmark in modern history of fight against doping. At first, the officials declared that he died of heart attack caused by sunstroke. However, the autopsy showed a significant concentration of amphetamine in athlete's organism. Therefore, the doping version of death became official (Steinbach, 2008).

This incident entailed a chain of other important historical events connected with development of fight against doping:

- **1963:** The Council of Europe created a special committee on fight against doping. In that year, France became the first country, which had adopted the Anti-Doping legislation;
- **1966:** The International Federations of Cycling and Football (FIFA) officially implemented the doping control at the World Championships;
- **1967:** The IOC assigned a special medical commission for doping control;
- **1999:** WADA was founded;
- **2003:** The World Anti-Doping Code was adopted;
- **2005:** UNESCO approved the International convention on fight against doping in sport. As a result, the network of the international and national authorities on fight against doping was founded. Now in the world there are over 30 Anti-Doping laboratories accredited by IOC where samples of ca. 120 thousand athletes are tested annually *(Role of the World Anti-Doping Agency in Control of Doping in Sport, 2014).*

However, Anti-Doping organizations continue their development. Due to the doping scandals in Russia in 2014-2016, the International Olympic Committee made decision on creation of independent Anti-Doping body at the international Court of Arbitration for Sports (CAS). This division (CAS Anti-Doping Division) shall perform and make decisions on the doping facts instead of the Disciplinary commission at Summer Olympic Games in 2016 in Rio de Janeiro (Brazil) *(IOC Makes Doping Results Management and Sanctioning Independent,* 2016).

The Concept of Doping

What is a doping in general? The word "doping" according to one of the versions means the African stimulating drink from a grape peel made by Zulu warriors; according to another version, it is a mix of tobacco and datura. There is also an assumption that the English verb "to dope" with meaning "to hurry a horse on race" is the cornerstone of doping. Indeed previously, the doping was widely used in horse races (Mkrchian, 2012). However, we care not about the philological meaning of this word, but the interpretation of the word "doping" from the legal point of view, in particular, of the international sports law. According to the article, one of the World Anti-Doping Code the doping is defined as commitment of one or several violations of the Anti-Doping rules provided by this code.

First, it is presence of a prohibited substance, its metabolites (intermediates and products of metabolism) or marker (character) in sample of athletes. Default of athlete in providing the biological sample is also a violation.

Besides, intravenous infusion of "improved" blood, physical and chemical blood manipulations, in particular, boosting the number of red blood cells in the bloodstream (blood doping), use of genetic cells to improve athletic performance (gene doping) are forbidden. An attempt to use these prohibited substances and methods is also a violation.

According to the so-called "rule of strict liability", the athlete will be punished even if he or she confirms that he or she took biological additives with a label without a list of corresponding ingredients. For example, he/she proves that the prohibited substances were prescribed by the personal doctor or the coach beyond his/her will. On the other hand, he/she confirms that he/she didn't know about presence of the prohibited substances in food or drinks and his/her personnel suppressed this fact. Anyway, the athlete will be guilty.

Article 2.1.1 of the World Anti-Doping Code states the following:

It is athlete's personal duty to ensure that no prohibited substance enters his or her body... Accordingly, it is not necessary that intent, fault, negligence or knowing Use on the Athlete's part be demonstrated in order to establish an Anti-Doping violation... (World Anti-Doping Code, 2015)

In fact, athlete's guilt is only significant for estimation of degree of punishment. However, the athlete will be always guilty if any banned substance is found in his or her body. In fact, the principle of strict liability prevails in the World Anti-Doping Code, which was used by Stalin during mass repressions in the USSR. In those days, a person was convicted upon a statement of his neighbor or workfellow, and ascertainment of guilt was not obligatory.

Whether it is for good or for bad when an innocent athlete is punished - this is a subject of another research. Nevertheless, to our opinion there is a positive moment in modern rules of WADA. Each athlete has to realize the responsibility to ensure that no prohibited substance enters his or her body and no prohibited method is used; and to understand that no defensive arguments can help him or her avoiding real punishment.

WADA annually updates the international standard, which contains the list of prohibited substances and prohibited methods. Professional excellent athletes should know this list, in particular the substances and methods which should not use under any circumstances and which should not use only during the contest season. For example, it is at any time prohibited to use anabolic steroids, peptide hormones, beta-2 agonist, hormones and metabolic modulators, diuretics and other drugs, which conceal doping. Performance-enhancing drugs (amphetamine, bromantane, etc.), glucocorticosteroids and cannabinoids (cannabis, hashish, etc.) are prohibited during the contest season. It is also prohibited to use so-called beta-blockers, which cause decrease in arterial pressure and decrease in heartbeat (Atenololum, Carvediolum, etc.).

Narcotics and Alcohol

As for recreational drugs, recently discussion about expediency of such prohibition was conducted in sporting world. In May 2013 WADA's executive committee made a sensational decision at the meeting in Montreal (Canada) to increase threshold value of marijuana content in athlete's body by 10 times (up to 150 nanograms for 1 urine milliliter). In practice, it means that the athlete can smoke some "pot" 2-3 days prior to competitions *(Executive Committee and Board of Founders of WADA are Going to Present the Final Version of Code,* 2015).

In our opinion, this is rather controversial decision, which will promote "recreational" drugs not only in the sports environment, but also in the whole world. In addition, this decision appears to be unfair in relation to the athletes who have been ignominiously punished before for marijuana. In this regard, we would like to remind that football players R. Apcharch (1983), R. Dent (1987), boxer T. Witherspoon (1985), basketball player E. Griffin (1988) and many other athletes were disqualified for this default.

At the same time, the other drug - cocaine - is still being considered as a doping. For example, recently the Belgian judoka Charline Van Snick, who had won bronze in the Olympic Games in London (Great Britain, 2012) was caught in use of cocaine at World Championship in Rio de Janeiro 2013. Moreover, the Belgian judoka is not the only one. Many worldwide famous athletes, in particular, the Cuban high jumper, multiple world record-holder Javier Sotomayor, the Romanian football player Andrian Mutu, the Swiss tennis-player Martina Hingins, the English football player Paul Gascoigne, the world heavyweight champion Mike Tyson and many others were into cocaine. For example, Paul Gascoigne confessedly could use cocaine with nine more portions of brandy before a football match (*Top-5 Athletes, Who Ruined Career with Drugs*, 2014).

Diego Armando Maradona, the best football player in the history according to The Times was perhaps a cocaine user number one and the fan of other types of doping in the history of professional sport. Maradona was arrested many times, convicted for storage of cocaine and persistent violations, disqualified for use of doping. There was even a special sentence about his obligatory doping control after each football match.

However, it must take into account that cocaine can get to athletes' body beyond the will. For example, the facts of detection of cocaine in Colombian football players who drank tea with coca leaves, which was a national tradition at local restaurants, are widely known.

Alcohol for some sports during contest season is also a doping. In particular, excess of alcohol threshold value above 0,10 g/l can lead to disqualification in motorsport, aeronautics, motor boating, motorsports and archery. For example, some archers would not mind to drink alcohol from a flask with a secret straw to get rid of shiver in hands and to relax.

Food Supplements

However, it is necessary to admit that the drug and alcohol is not a topical issue for professional sport now. Nowadays athletes are interested in another thing - they use the best pharmaceutical drugs and the latest technologies provided by sports medicine. In particular, all athletes without any problems can get so-called food supplement (hereinafter referred to as food supplement). Food supplements do not belong to drugs and therefore do not pass strict clinical studies, often they are produced without exact description of the ingredients used at production, and they are sold on the Internet freely and without supervision. Owing to this fact, they became "favorite treat" of enormous number of athletes.

Lately the food supplements with *methylhexaneamine*, which was earlier produced, of a geranium for treatment of nasal stuffiness became popular. This WADA prohibited substance suddenly increases performance of athletes. Now it is actively used under various names in food supplements. Without knowledge of this, many athletes use these food supplements and involuntarily become violators of Anti-Doping rules.

Therefore it isn't recommended to athletes to buy unknown food supplements, especially which contain words "muscles", "force", "explosion", "energy" and even no formula information at all. However, this situation concerns many food supplements. According to the Medical commission of the IOC, which investigated 600 most popular food supplements, almost every fifth supplement contains a substance prohibited by WADA, which was not specified on the label by the producer (Vdovin, & Vdovin, 2014).

The same goes for common medicines. The list of the *medicines* prohibited by medical commission of the IOC exceeds 10 thousand units. In fact, according to experts anything can improve performance: various tranquilizers, vaccines, vitamins and even drugs that regulate menstrual period and Viagra. As a result, some athletes cease using common drugs necessary for recovery and health promotion due to fear of negligent doping.

The funny thing is that athletes began to be afraid of taking not only medicine, but also usual food. For example, 196 Chinese athletes before the Olympic Games in London (Great Britain, 2012) refused to eat pork, beef and mutton due to previous cases of addition of substances, prohibited by WADA, to meat products by the Chinese producers (*Olympic Favorites Starve for Medals).* Unfortunately, this fear has reasonable ground to believe in it. There are some cases in the history when chicken with increased concentration of testosterone was given to athletes, or when Coca-Cola with caffeine over prescribed limit by several times was given at the Olympic Games. Moreover, it is quite possible that that was done on purpose.

However, the prohibited substances and methods do not cover the list of Anti-Doping violations. For example, what to do if an unknown substance is found in athlete's body and nobody knows whether it is a new pharmaceutical invention or it has other unknown origin? The answer is simple. According to WADA's international standard all the pharmacological substances prohibited by government authorities as therapeutic agent, which are found in biological samples of athletes, are a doping with all that it entails. These substances include medicines, which are under preclinical or clinical examination. It follows that they never should be tested on athletes.

The Violations of Anti-Doping Rules

Falsification or attempt of falsification of any doping control procedure is also a violation of Anti-Doping rules. For example, falsification of doping control may include fraud of athlete who undergoes test with urine of other person by means of a micro-container and catheter implanted into the body. Deliberate deterioration of urine with aroma compounds, change of identification numbers of biological samples, allegedly accidental vessel breaking the vessels with these samples, etc. will aggravate athlete's guilt.

The fact of illicit possession of prohibited substance by athlete or service members in the rooms, which are under their control, is equal to the use of doping as well. The anabolic steroids found, for example, in the car of the athlete is a violation of Anti-Doping rules if the athlete doesn't prove that someone else used the car and the found drugs belong to this person. However, it is not simple to prove it in practice. Even the fact of purchase of doping by the athlete in Internet or in a different way is unambiguously considered by WADA as possession of prohibited substance, even if the purchase is made for a friend or relative.

The violations of Anti-Doping rules also cover non-informing WADA on the location by the athletes entering a testing pool.

The thing is that these athletes according to the international rules have to inform WADA about their daily location and possibility of testing by means of a special electronic Anti-Doping Administration and Management System – ADAMS. In addition, if they provide insufficient information on their location (for example, somewhere in the woods near the settlement), it will be considered as skipped test. For example, if the athlete is not available for test in time and the place specified by him, then his absence is considered as violation. Moreover, if he commits three violations within 12 months, then he may be disqualified for violation of Anti-Doping rules, and deprived of all sports awards, points and prizes.

A marvel even such severe and rigorous control measures that can be carried out by the international and national Anti-Doping authorities at any time and in every location in the world do not stop some representatives of professional sport using prohibited substances and methods.

For example, in 2012 the Russian Anti-Doping agency took over 22 thousand samples of the Russian athletes in Russia and five countries of the world. In addition, it was revealed only 124 cases of violation of Anti-Doping rules and 187 so-called atypical results, i.e. analyses demanding additional research (overall share of the specified indices makes only 1, 9% of total number of samples). In general, adverse dynamics of doping in 2012 was noted in the Russian Weightlifting, Powerlifting, Swimming, Cycling Federations and Federation for sport of persons with spinal cord injury, as well as in the Russian football union (*Report on RUSADA Business, 2012)*. At the same time, it must be taken into account that many violations of Anti-Doping rules are not revealed among the athletes especially who are out of the sphere of the international and national doping control.

Revealing of Anti-Doping violations in high performance sport is very difficult as some scientific sports and medical centers, sports doctors, coaches and athletes take the systematic and rather qualified actions for concealment of use of doping traces:

If the doping course is estimated properly, the Vdovins says, and all its traces are removed from the body in due time, then chances to catch the athlete are almost zero: pharmacologists are always at least on a half-step ahead of laboratories of the International Olympic Committee. (Vdovin, & Vdovin, 2014)

Some athletes try to stimulate the organism all by themselves and to hide traces of the prohibited substances and methods used by them. They do a lot of things: they eat enormous quantity of lemons, drink red dry wine in large volumes, administer antibiotics and diuretics, stick testosterone plasters on the body, eat epysterone in large volume (for maintenance of normal level of testosterone), etc (*How to Hide Administration of Steroids and Prohibited Preparations).*

Some athletes even perform autohaemotherapy, i.e. before competition, they intramuscularly insert with the syringe their own blood, which has been extracted earlier from the vein in order to stimulate the organism.

International Standard on Granting Exceptions on Therapeutic Use of Drugs

However, there is a way to use doping quite legally. According to the World Anti-Doping code (Article 4.4) and *the International standard on granting exceptions on therapeutic use of drugs,* each athlete can use the prohibited substance or method if he or she has the corresponding documentary medical grounds and official permits. For example, many "asthmatic athletes" rather often use such permits. That enables them to use doping legally, in particular, to use various inhalers with Beta-2 agonist which significantly increase endurance and physical activity.

All experts note that proportion of "asthmatic athletes" in national teams of the certain countries is by three and more times more than proportion of asthmatics in the population of these countries. So, at the Summer Olympic Games in Sydney (Australia, 2000) 600 of more than 10 000 thousand athletes had asthma. At the Winter Olympic Games in Salt Lake City (USA, 2002) practically all Norwegian skiers and biathlonists also needed therapeutic treatment due to this disease (Pilipenko, 2007).

For some reason, the athletes of the Olympic team of the USA have asthma very often. "Asthmatic athletes" won significant number of all Olympic medals for the USA. In particular, among famous "asthmatics" from the USA are nine-time Olympic swimming gold medalist Mark Spitz; six-time Olympic swimming gold medalist Amy Van Dyken; Olympic swimming champion Nancy Hogshead; multiple Olympic champion and World champion - track and field athlete Jackie Joyner-Kersee and many others (*Asthma and Sport. Out Speak About Sport).*

It is strange but neither the IOC, nor WADA do not give an assessment to these facts for many years and, in particular, answer questions: whether "legal" doping creates advantage to "ill" athletes in comparison with "healthy" athletes? Moreover, whether issuance of such therapeutic permits is always lawful? Nevertheless, we will hope that soon the corresponding explanations and decisions at the international level from the IOC and WADA will be provided.

Statistics of Doping in Russia

In 2012 ca. 268 ths. various biological samples were taken in the world in total and only 1,8% ths. was positive or had atypical result. However, absolute values are rather high. According to official statistics in 2012, there were revealed ca. 3 ths. athletes in the world, mainly of the international level, who achieved good and outstanding results in professional sport only owing to prohibited substances and methods. And as well as in the Russian Federation in the whole world positive tests were connected with use of anabolic agents (50,6%), stimulators (15, 5%) and also cannabinoids (9%), glucocorticosteroids (8,1%) and other prohibited substances (*WADA Anti-Doping Testing Figures Report*, 2012).

It should be mentioned that there is a problem of doping by young athletes including athletes in children and youth sports schools. Unfortunately, now the Russian Law does not regulate age when children can go in for sports. Age limit for a concrete sport, as a rule, is defined only by regulations of the correspondent Sport Federation. Candidates for professional sport are selected paradoxically at the age of three for figure skating and at the age of four for rhythmic-sportive gymnastics, etc.

They try to make professional athletes out of perspective children, expose children now and then to unreasonable physical and psychological stress, not compatible to the age, providing children's body with special food and supplements and sometimes a doping. 15-35% newcoming athletes in Russia use reportedly anabolic steroids regularly *(Role of the World Anti-Doping Agency in Control of Doping in Sport).* In practice, it is possible to state that in some cases children are used for mercenary purposes of professional sport that is forbidden by the European Code of Sports Ethics adopted by the Council of Europe (1992).

In this regard, we would like to remind some coaches that according to the specified international legal document it is forbidden to place expectations surpassing opportunities of children behave to them as "little adults", disregard their physiological and biological changes and features. Moreover, it is immoral and illegal to offer prohibited substances and substances with unknown effect.

Unfortunately, these recommendations are not always executed and there is a bit different educational practice in Russia. At the age of 14-15 years some "skilled" coaches focus their pupils on victory "at any sacrifice", including the use of the prohibited substances and methods. It is for a reason that surveys show that a significant number of young Russian athletes (80%) is ready to use prohibited drugs and methods for high performance even if they know that inevitable disability is payback (*Olympic Review. All Gender Scandals in Sports World).*

We are very concerned about it. Therefore, for example, even short-term use of anabolic steroids by athletes in the prepubertal or pubertal age can lead to the arrest of development or degenerative disk disease (Epifanov, 2006). This problem became topical issue, so that in November 2013, the Russian Olympic Committee conducted the scientific and practical conference devoted to problems of fight against doping in sport for children and youth.

Health of Athletes and Doping

So why is doping so dangerous for athletes? The doping allows improving performance of athletes, creates conditions for unfair victories, contradicts "spirit of sport", brings a public shame and disgrace, stressful and tragic changes in life and represents actual risk for health not only of young people, but also of athletes of all age groups.

For example, stimulators cause insomnia, trembling, dystaxia, anxiety, combativeness, and heart attacks. So, growth hormones will disorder liver, thyroid body, heart, joints and compromise vision, they can also change human face, increase the forehead, super ciliary arches, skull and jaws. The "favorite" erythropoietin makes blood thick and sticky, can cause high pressure, palpitation, as well as apoplectic attack.

Drugs suppress immune and respiratory systems, motion coordination, slow down pulse, cause psychological and physical dependence, as we know. For example, even above-mentioned recreational drug as marijuana worsens memory, causes bronchitis and laryngeal cancer, and reduces endurance and accuracy of movements. Besides, it can be present in body for a long time.

The anabolic steroids have a very adverse impact on health of athletes. Acneiform rash, strong body odor, hair loss, hepatic disorders and cardiovascular diseases are features of use of anabolic steroids. Anabolic steroids lead to uncertainty of temper of athletes, aggression and even emergence of propensity to suicide. Use of these prohibited drugs for a long time can cause biliary disorder, hepatitis, hepatic and renal carcinoma. After use of these anabolic steroids, young athletes can become impotent with small testicles, which are not capable to produce sperm normally for men or to get female breast for women.

Vice-versa young sportswomen can become men with a gruff voice, a bristle and moustaches on a face. At the same time, their body will have irreversible changes: breasts will decrease, the menstrual period will be disturbed, the clitoris will increase, the uterus will atrophy, female sex hormones will not be produced, etc.

In front of many sport fans at the end of the last century female athletes, including famous Soviet sportswomen, turned into men more and more:

Anabolic steroids have provided an explosion of results several decades ago. Women with a bristle, broad shoulders and voice as a bass part in good men chorus, I.I. Kurinoi says, began to throw track and field objects to the longest distance, to paddle with great strength, to run tirelessly. Heaven was in triumph. Ratings shot upward. (Kurinoi, 2010)

For example, there was much talk about gender of the famous Soviet sportswomen Irina and Tamara Press. It is known that the following athletes failed the gender identity test: athlete from India Santhi Soundarajan, from the Republic of South Africa Caster Semenya, from Poland Ewa Kłobukowska and many other sportswomen. It may be no accident that in 1968 the IOC introduced the gender control in order to exclude persons with hermaphroditism features from female competitions. Now women - participants of the Olympic Games, world and national championships, are allowed to compete upon availability of certificate on this control.

Moreover, oddly enough but sometimes it is difficult to establish gender identity. Genetic methods are often used, and the gender is established on quantity of so-called chromatin in epithelial cells (women 20-70%, men only up to 5%).

Some sportswomen even began to change the gender. In this context, the prime example is German champion of Europe, shot putter Heidi Krieger. It is known that she was systematically doped with anabolic steroids in the national team of GDR. In fact, Krieger turned into a man. Then she underwent gender reassignment surgery and became a transman. In addition, she married to the former swimmer Ute Krause. The German champion of Europe in pole vaulting Yvonne Buschbaum followed her example *(Olympic Review. Modern Doping Drugs).* Some men also changed the gender, including change under influence of various hormonal drugs, in particular, the football player from Australia Martin Delaney, the kickboxer from Thailand Nong Toom, a golf champion in game from the USA Lana Lawless became a woman too (the former police officer by the name of Dick), etc.

These cases became widespread so that the IOC was forced in 2004 to allow athletes who had changed the gender after surgical intervention to participate in the Olympic Games in two years after the correspondent legal decisions. Most recently the IOC (January 2016) allowed transgender athletes to participate in the Olympic Games without gender reassignment surgery. They only should show now that their level of testosterone is below the stated level, at least, one year prior to the first official competition (*Transgender Athletes Will be Allowed to Participate in OG Without Gender Reassignment Surgery,* 2016).

The use of doping causes not only chronic diseases, but also increase of mortality among athletes. Experts note that in general the average duration of life of the professional athlete is 10-15% below the value of a common person (Skvortsov, 2006). Chronic diseases are found in nearly a half of the examined athletes. Frequency of sudden death of athletes is much higher than of common people. For example, ca.

115 sudden deaths of athletes are registered in the USA annually. For the period (from 1994 to 2006), 1290 athletes died suddenly at competitions or during the out of competition period in this country (Gavrilova, 2011). The situation in Russia and other countries is no better. However the corresponding statistics is not conducted in Russia, and we learn about these cases only from mass media.

Researches show that among the reasons causing the increased mortality among athletes, doping plays a special part. Moreover, doping indirectly influences the increased mortality quite often. For example, use of anabolic steroids can be the trigger of development of dangerous rhythm disturbance and of emergence of life-threatening thromboembolic episodes, pulmonary infarct, myocardial infarct and apoplectic attack. For example, this effect as noted belongs to erythropoietin, which causes blood viscosity and cerebral thromboembolism by athletes. No wonder why in 1987 erythropoietin was recognized as a cause of death of 20 European bicycle racers (Gavrilova, 2011).

World Statistics

However, the doping is not only the lot of professional athletes, as many people think. Representatives of extreme professions are fond of doping too. These are, first, military men, police officers and firefighters. Workers of penal system are also convicted of consumption and distribution of doping in many countries. In total, according to the famous researcher of doping problems Alessandro Donati at least 15, 5 million people in the modern world use doping and anabolic steroids. Athletes make only 35-37%, military men 38-40%, police officers 4-6%, representatives of show business 1-2%. About 700 tons of anabolic steroids, 70 tons of testosterone, 34 million tons of erythropoietin ampoules are produced every year (Donati 2007). Some experts estimate the volume of world illegal doping at about 50 billion USD that is comparable to illegal realization of drugs (Zubareva, 2012).

What are the reasons of widespread distribution of doping in professional sport? There is no definite and simple answer. It is difficult to answer this question as to answer the following question: why do people commit crime or become alcoholics? Distribution of doping is promoted by a complex of economic, social and psychological reasons: commercialization of sport and deformation of professional conscience of athletes; policy of pharmaceutical companies; participation of organized crime in distribution of doping; imperfection of legal base and low efficiency of controlling, supervising, law enforcement bodies in fight against doping.

REASONS AND CONDITIONS OF DOPING PROPAGATION

Many athletes try to gain material welfare and don't think of consequences of excessive physical activities during sports competitions and combats, of harmful effect of drugs and methods prohibited by the World Anti-Doping Agency (hereinafter WADA). At the same time, these athletes not only use the prohibited drugs and methods and violate the principles of "fair play", but later they also get involved in an asocial way of life. They begin to use also drugs and alcohol systematically, commit crime for purchase of them, etc.

Unfortunately, distribution of doping is also promoted by other objective circumstances including intrusion of doping to athletes by sports officials, chiefs of sports clubs, coaches and doctors. Under influence of such "sports management" some athletes even began to believe that serious sporting achievements aren't possible without doping at all and that every self-respecting professional athlete has not to be "greedy" and just be able to use them in order not to be the caught by Anti-Doping international and national agencies.

Public Confessions of Athletes

Many famous athletes use doping systematically and with impunity. In particular, recently excellent eminent athletes stated in public that they had used doping with impunity during their sports career. For example, the two-time Olympic biathlon champion, the three-time world champion in cross-country skiing Anfisa Reztsova declared publicly that "fair sport" had never existed: and she personally was "acupunctured" and this helped her to achieve high performance.

Believe me, she declared, each athlete deliberately goes for it. The chief, the doctor, the coach and the athlete meet and decide all together: whether you want to do it or not. And the doctor plans the program to everyone. In her opinion, everyone use doping, but those who have the "bad" doctor, the weak coach, the stupid chief or don't follow the recommendation of doctors about timely removal of drugs are caught on doping. At the same time, the famous sportswoman makes a conclusion: *In modern sport it is impossible without doping. Indeed! That's the modern life* (Reztsova, 2009).

The same outspoken statements are made by many other famous and eminent western athletes. For example, the French road racing cyclist, the champion of the Olympic Games Philippe Gaumont wrote a book "Prisoner of doping" in which he explained that during competitions he liked to use doping, especially drug cocktail "pot belge" - a mix of cocaine, heroin, caffeine and amphetamines. Other famous American road racing cyclist, the seven-time winner of "Tour de France" Lance

Armstrong also declared publicly that during all his sports life he used doping, mainly erythropoietin. Moreover, without doping, he would never become the seven-time winner of these races. Moreover, L. Armstrong as it turned out afterwards was the chief organizer of the criminal scheme of distribution of doping among members of the team. As known, in 2012 he was disqualified for doping for life and deprived of all sports titles since 1998 (*Lance or Cheater. Sports Hero of America Was a Doping King,* 2012).

However, how it is possible if all world-renowned athletes are checked for doping at any time and any place in the world both during the contest season and out of contest season? The answer is banal and simple. Corruption is one of the main factors, which allow athletes avoiding liability for doping. The facts when in Anti-Doping divisions corrupt practices take place, in particular, when positive samples disappear or doping tests are falsified, etc., become known more often. L. Armstrong admitted that he gave money to officials of the International Cycling Union many times for concealment of positive doping samples.

Unfortunately, not only mentioned circumstances are behind doping scandals. Political interests of some countries and profit of large pharmaceutical companies underlie distribution of doping in professional sport. The largest pharmaceutical companies "Organon", "Schering" and "Ciba" financed medical-biological researches on creation of the cheap injectable synthetic testosterone by scientists in 1935, which afterwards became the most widespread doping in the world.

Doping and Totalitarian Regimes of Power

Some countries especially with totalitarian regime were an overriding concern in "doping" researches. It is their medical-biological secret laboratories where the so-called "legal doping", first, for military purposes was created. Fascist Germany, for example, has created a doping under the brand name *Pervitin*. Spies, pilots and tankmen used it extensively. Well, Hitler liked to get injections of pervitin as well (*Methamphetamine,* 2015). Fascists constantly improved this drug, made experiments on prisoners, forced them to go around in a circle after use up to 90 km with 20 kg backpacks loaded with stones. Prisoners cheerily marched with songs within a day, and then many of them fell and died.

"Temmel", the German company, produced 29 million tablets of this drug to fascist troops for the purpose of creation of an ideal soldier – a "live" robot. Soldiers of the Third Reich amazed with endurance and intelligence indeed. In the last years of World War II fascists created even more perfect doping – "Energiepille" – mix of pervitin, cocaine and morphine which now are a part of famous and banned in many countries psychostimulant "extasy" (*Pervitin is a Weapon of the Third Reich,* 2008).

According to some experts, fantastic sporting achievements of fascist Germany at the Olympic Games in 1936 were connected with use of this doping (Bombela).

During Cold War, the leading countries of the world began to establish special pharmacological laboratories, which created new drugs being destructive to athletes' health. Unfortunately, politicians of the different countries of the world were only one-step removed from Nazi philosophy concerning the Olympic victories as *military victories in peace time*, and began to use sport as a tool of political prestige, an indicator of the superiority over opponents, other political systems and the regimes of power. For achievement of these purposes and receipt of prestigious Olympic gold medals, they sacrificed life and health of athletes and forget about development of mass sport and its main tasks connected with improvement of spiritual and physical entity of a person, formation of healthy lifestyle of population.

For example, according to unclassified data of GDR secret services ca. 10 thousand world-class athletes of this country were participants of a doping special program. In 2007, 167 former athletes of GDR received compensation from the German government for the compelled use of doping during their sports career (*German Athletes Will be Paid for Use of Doping,* 2006). For this reason, the German swimmer Christiane Knacke-Sommer decided to abandon the gold medal won at the Olympic Games in Moscow in 1980. However, it is not clear whether it was a nobility or politics (Borisova, & Morozov, 2011).

Mass media also reported about encouragement of use by government bodies of some countries of a so-called "sex doping". In particular, allegedly in some Olympic teams of east countries sexual contacts of young sportswomen with men during competitions, artificial termination of pregnancy on the eve of competitions, etc. were encouraged as all this had doping value, influenced muscles and blood circulation of female body well. So, according to some information active sexual life of young sportswomen from the national teams of GDR was "supported" by the whole staff of coaches, doctors and masseurs. Therefore, "sex doping" turned young girls of age 14–16 into super champions (Pilipenko, 2007).

Political Competition Determines the Development of Doping and Anti-Doping Technology

Athletes of the western countries, for example, Germany, were the same; they used steroids, testosterone, estrogen, and erythropoietin and above mentioned Pervitin under pressure of sports politicians. In 1955 physiologist, John Ziegler developed the modified molecule of synthetic testosterone with increased anabolic properties (*Dianabol*) for the national weightlifting team of the USA. The salad bowls filled with Dianabol (also known commonly as methandrostenolone), named also "Champion's breakfast" were eaten by athletes in unlimited quantity. Then the American weight lifters, athletes and team sport athletes began to show unprecedented results at the international competitions *(Brief Doping History in Sport).*

Some countries tried to exert influence on results of Anti-Doping analyses. According to some researchers the USA, for example, was purposely provided to WADA the methods of determination of doping used by athletes of the socialist countries. At the same time the American scientists produced doping, which was very effective in the past - Stanozolol, an anabolic steroid that was impossible to be found in body. Thus, the USA controlled the international Anti-Doping policy and defined who could be caught on doping and who could be unpunished (Bombela).

However, nothing is secret that shall not be made manifest. For example, the world famous Canadian athlete Ben Johnson had been using Stenazolol with impunity for many years. Nevertheless, he was exposed at the Olympic Games in Seoul (South Korea, 1988) where he showed fantastic performance. However new techniques allowed to reveal Stenazolol in his sample. However, Moscow experts exposed Ben Johnson. As it later became clear, in 1986, they found the traces of this doping in his sample on Goodwill Games in Moscow, but they did not disclose this fact for political reasons (Dzhusoyti).

Moreover, this history proceeds in modern days. At the beginning of 2016, the most famous Russian tennis-player M. Sharapova and many other famous Russian athletes were caught in use of Mildronate (Meldonium). That was another scandal when the Government of Russia and the Russian Ministry of Foreign Affairs made the corresponding inquiries to WADA. Many representatives of the Russian sports society began to suggest that this substance has been entered to WADA banned list by representatives of the USA in order to compromise the Russian athletes who earlier "were fond" of this drug in large quantities *(Mildronate Became Doping Upon an Initiative of the Americans).* The history will show whether these judgments are correct.

Competition among countries generated competitive fight also between doping and Anti-Doping technologies. As a rule, in the beginning there are new substances and methods invented in special medical-biological laboratories, which facilitate setting up unprecedented sports records. Then it turns out that they result in unacceptable health risks to athletes. Then there are created new lists of banned substances and methods, as well as new technologies for identification and recording of these banned substances and methods. It becomes more difficult to reveal new types of the banned substances and methods.

As mentioned before it is not for nothing that the new edition of the World Anti-Doping Code 2015 provides a 10-year period of prescription (earlier 8-year period) for doping violations. It will help to find doping by means of modern technologies, which, for example, ten years ago was "successfully" removed before competitions from athletes' body by consummate "experts of sports medicine" in full confidence of impunity of their actions.

New Kinds of Doping

Doping is revealed eventually, despite use of modern doping scientific technologies. Recently, for example, there was created the *gene doping*. The gene doping is officially determined by WADA and included to the banned list. At first, this doping was impossible to reveal. Meanwhile it is very dangerous both for health of athletes and for other people as it can cause dangerous genetic mutations in body of future human generation.

However, most recently scientists wrote about the "progressive" direction in science – "sports genetics", which was capable to provide "selection" of athletes at gene level. It is known that such countries as the USA, the Great Britain, the Netherlands and Canada succeeded a lot in confidential research on sports genetics. For example, by means of genetic engineering scientists learned to build up the muscle mass of the athlete with little effort or to "improve" vessels for intense oxygen transportation, or to suppress athlete's pain thresholds.

Time went by. Now the international sports society thinks of how to secure sport against genetic engineering. Especially that it is rather difficult to reveal artificial changes at the gene level, as according to experts the genes, which are artificially entered into the body, are almost indistinguishable from real genes. Now WADA spends about 1 million dollars a year for development of Anti-Doping technologies in the sphere to sports genetics (*Role of the World Anti-Doping Agency in Control of Doping in Sport).*

Most recently "*Blood doping*" had the same situation, some experts also considered fight against this doping as impossible or ineffective. However, as we know, the biological passport of the athlete was created for prevention of frauds with athletes' blood. Now it is improved and includes *hematologic* (for definition of blood values), *steroid* (definitions of steroid hormones) and *endocrine* passports in Russia. The opportunities of fight against a so-called "blood doping" increased significantly (Malinovskaya, 2012).

We cannot shut out emergence in years ahead of any essentially new types of doping, for example, with *use of nanotechnologies and biotechnologies*, in particular, bionic prostheses, implantation in bodies of athletes of any devices, which enhance locomotor system with provision of additional force, speed, flexibility, etc. Moreover, perhaps, there will be doubts in efficiency of fight against new types of doping in the sphere of nanotechnologies and biotechnologies. It will also be necessary to look for new Anti-Doping methods of identification of "improvement of body" and to define new standards of behavior of athletes and procedures of doping control. Apparently, this fight between doping and Anti-Doping technologies will exist until professional sport exists, as battle between good and evil. Defeats and victories will interchange each other forever and every time on a new round of development of science and opportunities of human body.

In addition, we cannot shut out *legalization of some types of doping* as it has happened to marijuana. Maybe biotechnological modifications of human body, such as, for example, "Cheetah Flex-Feet" of the Paralympic champion Oscar Pistorius will become an everyday occurrence in professional sport:

In the context of biotechnical modifications it is quite logical to doubt expediency of WADA, Mia Andy and Beatriz Garcia says, we live in the era when not only athletes change themselves by means of various technologies. Whether will the fact that the athlete takes drugs for improvement of the performance concern anyone if the same is done by all other members of society? (Mia, & Garcia, 2013)

Doping and Sports Medicine

It should be noted that now high-performance sport could not exist without new technologies and achievements of sports medicine, without use of results of modern medical-biological researches and new effective drugs of pharmaceutical industry any more. More and more victories of athletes are a result of collective work of coaches and sports doctors, so-called "biomedical support" of sports activity, but not a result of an athlete.

Medical-biological researches for the benefit of high performance sport are conducted in all developed countries, including Great Britain, the USA, Germany, Australia, Canada, China and Korea (the English Sport Institute, the Federal Institute of Sports Sciences in Bonn, the Australian Sport Institute, etc.). Russia is not an exception. Now "athlete-star" of modern Russia is surrounded by the whole group of people in white coats: a team doctor, clinical pharmacologist, biomechanic, physiotherapist, massage therapist, dietitian, reflexologist, medical psychologist, etc. For high performance sport the electronic medical cards are created, there are also created special cross-disciplinary laboratories, pools with underwater athletic track, climatic rooms, rooms for video analysis, psychological testing, manual influences and so forth (Kotenko, 2013).

Athletes from *high performance sport* are literally *stuffed* with various modern biological additives and pharmaceutical drugs on the eve of big sports events. The so-called expensive *vitamin and mineral complexes* for athletes are often made of exotic types of raw materials (for example, biomass of larvae or internals of the

African catfish, etc.), and delivered to athletes on an individual basis taking into account their genetic and biological analysis (*Report of the Chief of FMBA of Russia V. V. Uiba on Enlarged Session of Board of FMBA as of July 23, 2013).*

However, it can be noted that some modern pharmaceutical preparations and medical technologies used are near to doping. Moreover, maybe someday they will be included to WADA's banned list. In particular, according to the World Anti-Doping Code (Art. 4.3 of the Code) for this purpose it is necessary that methods or substances correspond to two of three criteria: 1.) improved performance; 2.) represented real or potential risk for health of the athlete, and; 3.) contradicted to "spirit of sport".

It can be stated with full confidence that all medical methods are directed to achievement of high performance in sport therefore, they already correspond to one of criteria of WADA. In addition, there is a probability that in future WADA will be able to find in modern medical methods other criteria, in particular connected with potential risks for health of athletes or contradiction to "spirit of sport".

For example, it is always possible to raise doubts about observance of "spirit of sport", the principle of "equal opportunities" and "fair game" at the Olympic Games when athletes of "poor" and "rich" countries are placed in a position of inequality. Some athletes are under careful attention of well-qualified medical personnel in expensive stationary and mobile medical complexes. They are "fed" in large quantity with "authorized" biological additives, special food and drugs, placed in pressure chambers for oxygen-helium therapy, etc. Other athletes from the "poor" countries are deprived of such opportunities at the Olympic Games and other great international sports competitions.

There are also doubts in assessment of legitimacy of some drugs and methods used by doctors for improvement of performance. For example, according to the banned list 2016 WADA excluded all forms of procedure with blood or its components, including physical or chemical methods. However sports medicine use regularly the methods of low intensity laser therapy which allow "raising high-speed and power components of muscles" and blood transport functions, stimulating hemostasis, metabolism, etc. The experts should answer a question whether laser radiation is one of types of such "procedures" with blood.

There is another example. Some countries widely use pressure chambers with pure oxygen, which can increase transfer of oxygen to athlete's cells by 10-15 times. Meanwhile, as we know, many substances and methods have been prohibited by WADA due to *accelerated oxygen supply*. Now many experts do not know, for example, how to qualify the use of pressure chambers in sports medicine (Mia, & Garcia, 2013). In Norway, use of pressure chambers by athletes is even prohibited by the law, in Italy the athletes can be placed under criminal jurisdiction for use of pressure chamber and so-called *hypoxic centers* (Pilipenko, 2007). Also, legitimacy of use of so-called "oxygen" cocktails (inhalation of xenon) by the Russian athletes during the international competitions raised doubts as according to international experts these cocktails stimulated production of erythropoietin in athletes' body. It is not for nothing that in May 2014 WADA equated inhalations of xenon and argon to the use of doping. Now the use of these gases will lead to immediate punishment of all athletes (*Substances, Which the Russian Athletes Used in Sochi are Stated as Doping,* 2014).

One must not exclude that now some pharmacists in some countries continue to search for the substances, which can be removed from athletes' body as fast as possible so that the athletes could be "good" ahead of doping control. New types of doping are also produced. For example, according to the Chief of MFBA V. Uibu the new *psychological doping* has been used in a number of the Asian countries when by means of special psychotechnics from olden times the athletes turn to "zombies". In his opinion, the destiny of these athletes can be sad if their consciousness is blocked for whatever reason (Merkacheva, 2013).

Therefore, it would seem that all countries in the nearest time have to combine efforts in order to decide finally, what modern achievements in sports medicine are doping and what are not. In addition, WADA should find the actual border between modern technologies of sports medicine and the prohibited substances and methods. All should put into operation the international standards of the sports law and standards in the sphere of sports medicine, obligatory for all countries, in this regard.

Besides, it would seem that the International Olympic Committee, WADA and other international sports and medical organizations have to define system of measures for equalizing of rights and opportunities of athletes of "rich" and "poor" countries, in particular, affordability of advanced technologies of sports medicine to all athletes, especially during the Olympic Games and great international sports competitions.

In our opinion development of uniform sports complexes for the period of the Olympic Games and other international sports competitions available to all athletes of "rich" and "poor" countries would ensure the principles of "fair game" and equal opportunities in sport, sports ethics and rules of the international sports law. We'd really appreciate if in this regard all politicians and sports officials remember that the main thing in sport, as baron de Coubertin, the father of the modern Olympic Games, repeatedly emphasized, is a noble and fair victory and that according to rules of the Olympism the competition is executed among the athletes, but not among the countries.

Organized Crime and Doping

Distribution of doping in professional sport is supported also by forces with which government authorities of various countries of the world fight an irreconcilable war. In particular, the international organized crime plays a negative role in distribution of doping in sports world.

The history of the international organized crime in the doping market originates from the beginning of the 1970s when a "brilliant" idea of distribution of anabolic steroids came to the management of the Italy-American mafia, which was engaged in transportation, and sale of drugs. In order to promote use of anabolic steroids the Italy-American mafia financed the movie "Pumping Iron", 1977, devoted to bodybuilding where Arnold Schwarzenegger had had the leading part. Later he admitted that he had used anabolic steroids (Donati, 2007). The movie developed by mafia made commercial success and a grotesque character of Schwarzenegger with his enormous muscles became a factor of distribution of anabolic steroids around the world. Mafia actively distributed anabolic steroids not only in sporting world, but also among show business stars, famous movie, theater and ballet actors who sometimes had strong physical overworks in their professional life.

However, the Italy-American crime was overpowered by "the Russian mafia", which in the middle of 1990s offered tons of cheap and rather high quality anabolic steroids, as well as animal growth hormones to the international market. According to the western experts, doping from Russia was made based on the former Soviet medical-biological laboratories, which were known for high scientific technologies (Donati, 2007).

However, the competition exists also in the criminal underworld. In addition, today the victory is won by the "Asian mafia", which has massive opportunities for production and supply of cheaper doping. The general scheme of production and sale of doping is the following. The prohibited substances are made generally at the small enterprises in China, India and Thailand where the low labor is situated and the pharmaceutical industry is developed. Sometimes also, the large pharmaceutical companies are engaged in this illegal business. Profitability of this criminal business is unbelievable. The income surpasses expenses in hundreds times.

The main international doping traffic has tended from Thailand, China and India to Europe and the USA now. Every year about 30 million doses of various prohibited substances for the sphere of professional sport and extreme physical activity are produced in India (Donati, 2007).

According to the statement of WADA, 99 percentage materials for production of doping are supplied by the organized criminal communities from the People's Republic of China. China reacted to this statement rather painfully and began the total check upon this charge (*China was Accused of Production of Doping,* 2013). Indeed the Chinese preparations prevail in the doping market now.

In the world of globalization and Internet, it is easy and legal to buy doping on a mass basis for sports clubs, using Internet technologies. Therefore, for example, recently it was found out that the Spanish football club "Real Sociedad" officially spent about 300 thousand EUR a year for purchase of the prohibited drugs for the players (*President LFP Knew About Purchase of Doping,* 2013).

There is the same situation in Russia. Everyone can make sure of it after requesting many WADA banned substances in any search system in Internet. The courier could bring them to you without asking any recipes from doctors. The revenue of only one doping online store was estimated by experts at 40 million dollars a year (Zubareva, 2012).

However, it is rather difficult to reveal this trading system on the Internet as it is often integrated into the general system of medicine trade. It is also easy to sell doping at fitness-centers to so-called "gym rats" and body builders (persons who are engaged in bodybuilding). The doping in these centers is being sold illegally by coaches, in sport bars, etc. *to the maximum.*

Some so-called "black" sports doctors also go in for doping sales who sell expensive banned drugs or drugs under testing to elite athletes, as well as give them the *deep scientific consultations* on methods of concealment of use of banned substances. The income of these black doctors who work in the sphere of professional sport is estimated at 30 thousand dollars a year for one elite athlete (Zubareva, 2012).

LEGAL PRACTICE OF FIGHT AGAINST DOPING IN RPOFESSIONAL SPORT OF THE RUSSIAN FEDERATION AND OTHER COUNTRIES

It is impossible to agree with statements that doping in Russia is promoted at the country level. Charitably speaking, such statements are false. Moreover, recently many laws regarding fight against doping were adopted in Russia. In 2008, a new chapter was included to the Labour code of the Russian Federation, (Shevchenko, 2015) which was devoted to key elements of regulation of work between athletes and coaches. The labor duties of athletes and coaches include observance of Anti-Doping rules; the authority of employer is also defined there. In particular, the duty of the employer is to acquaint the athlete with the Anti-Doping rules against signature, the employer also has right to dismiss the athlete for a single violation of Anti-Doping rules (Art. 348.11 of the Labor Code of the Russian Federation). At the same time, the employer must receive from him/her the corresponding monetary compensation for non-performance of the employment contract (Art. 348.12 and 192 of the Labor Code of the Russian Federation).

In 2010, the essential changes were made to the Law on physical training and sports in the Russian Federation in order to fight against doping. Responsibility of the Russian sports organizations, organizers of sports events and sport educational institutions was strengthened in that respect. The authority of the Russian Anti-Doping organization was defined as well. The Ministry of Sport of the Russian Federation adopted a number of the departmental regulations in order to settle the fight against doping. In particular, there was developed an Anti-Doping strategy and the doping control procedure (2009), as well as Anti-Doping support of national teams of Russia (2010). The Russian Anti-Doping rules (2015) were also approved.

Legal Problems of the Fight Against Doping in Russia

However, the Russian criminal legislation does not contain any special rules intended directly to fight against illicit doping trafficking, in particular, it does not establish in this regard special rules of responsibility for athletes, personnel of the athletes, sports managers and persons involved in organized crime. The current standards on trafficking of drugs, psychotropic, strong and toxic agents in the sphere of sport are almost not applied.

Elite sport in Russia always was and is a "sacred cow" which was protected by the country from any troubles and risks. Athletes in the USSR and Russia were always national pride, and the country cherished and protected them from any troubles. Due to this fact, the Russian law enforcement agencies were never engaged in sport affairs without special need. However, times change. The latest juicy doping scandals let the Russian government and society look at a role of sport in a new way. In addition, at all levels of the Russian society people started talking about need of strengthening of responsibility of athletes for their offending behavior.

In our opinion, we need the rules for establishment and strengthening of special criminal liability for persons involved in doping illegal trafficking. Criminal liability has to be established, first, for those persons who induce athletes to perform these illegal actions, provide them with illegal supply of doping and doping services. Apparently it is necessary to establish the criminal liability of experts in sports medicine, personnel of the athlete and all officials in the sphere of physical training and sport for illicit production, processing, purchase, storage, transportation and transfer for sale, distribution of the substances and methods prohibited by WADA and RUSADA. The same criminal liability has to be established for assistance in these illegal actions (promotion of doping, recommendations for use and concealment of traces, etc.). This idea is actively supported by a number of experts (Melnik, 2012).

It is seemingly required to establish even stronger criminal sanctions for the persons who distribute or render assistance in distribution of the banned substances and methods among minor athletes. In our opinion, special criminal liability has to be also established for members of the organized criminal networks, which specialize in illegal supply of doping and rendering doping services.

Using of Anti-Doping Legislation in the Different Countries

These suggestions are based on the analysis of the international practice of fight against doping. So, criminal liability for illicit trafficking and use of doping already takes place in Austria, Greece, Italy, Ukraine, China, Poland, the USA, Switzerland, France, Finland and a number of other countries.

In Austria, for example, in 2009-2011 the following persons were sentenced to jail for different periods for distribution of doping: cyclist K. Kerschbaum, cross-country skiing and biathlon coach V. Mayer, sports agent S. Matshiner and other persons connected with professional sport.

In Greece, the persons who dope the athlete with prohibited natural, chemical, biotechnological materials or use the illegal methods in relation to the athlete for improvement of sports results can be imprisoned for a period of up to 5 years or penalized with up to 50 thousand EUR. Moreover, if this is performed in relation to minor athlete, the punishment can be 25 years of imprisonment. Athletes are also punished for doping in Greece. In particular, criminal proceedings of these offenses were taken against the gold medalist of the Olympic Games in Athens (Greece, 2004) - hurdler F. Halkia, sprinters D. Regas, T. Gulsis, K. Kenteris, K. Tanu, the weight lifter L. Sampanis.

Italy Criminal Law also provides strong sanctions for doping. Many famous Italian athletes have been punished for illicit trafficking and doping in criminal order. At the Olympic Games in Turin (Italy, 2006) the famous Russian biathlonist Olga Medvedtseva (Pyleva) who had won a silver medal in 15 km race at these Games was charged with a one-year suspended sentence in this country for use of doping Carphedon (analog of fenotropil (Pilipenko, 2007).

Illicit trafficking of doping in Switzerland can lead to imprisonment for a period of max 3 years and under aggravating circumstances of max 5 years. At the same time the aggravating circumstance in the Swiss Law is participation in organized criminal network, receipt of large profit, danger for life and health of athletes due to doping, prescription for use or supply of doping to minors (Soloviev, Ponkin, & Ponkina, 2013).

In the USA in 2004, the problem of doping was widely discussed in the Congress. In addition, from that time Anti-Doping agency of the USA began to pursue violators of doping rules. In particular, in 2008 the famous runner M. Jones who had won three gold and two bronze Olympic medals was convicted for perjury on doping scandal and spent some time in prison (Chapple, 2012).

In France obstruction to court officers and agents, officials of the Ministry of Sport and French agency on fight against doping can turn into criminal penalty in form of imprisonment for 6 months and a penalty in the amount of 7 500 EUR. Illegal trafficking of doping, falsification of doping control procedures, provision of doping to athletes in this country can lead to max 5 years of imprisonment and a penalty in the amount of 75 thousand EUR. If "doping" crimes are committed by an organized group of persons, or in relation to a minor or by the person *who has power of authority in relation to one or several athletes*, then the punishment will be a period of 7 years of imprisonment, as well as the penalty in the amount of 150 thousand EUR (Soloviev, 2011).

It is true that that now the French legislation is one of the best legislations of the world regulating the sphere of professional sport, including fight against doping. In addition, the French police actively apply this legislation, in particular, the standards of the Sports code. Here it is possible to get to prison if, for example, the prohibited substances are found in the athlete's pocket. In particular, storage of doping without due medical need is punished in form of one year of prison or a penalty in the amount of 3 750 EUR. The French police acted effectively upon suppression of doping among cyclists on Tour de France when many participants of this well-known race were arrested and convicted.

In our opinion, the Russian administrative legislation connected with illicit trafficking and use of doping requires improvements. It is expedient to Russia to establish a legal liability of legal entities and individuals (sports federations, clubs, and their chiefs) on example of other countries in case of large-scale and ongoing violations of Anti-Doping rules in these organizations. Besides such sports, organizations seemingly have to lose the financial support. Moreover, the relevant standards seemingly should take place in the Code of the Russian Federation about administrative offenses and the Federal Law on physical training and sport.

Such international experience already exists. In Brazil, for example, the Sports Justice Code is in force and the legal entities - sports organizations can be fined up to 500 thousand Reals for violation of the Anti-Doping legislation (Soloviev, 2010). Similar administrative practice is also in force in France. In particular, the sports organization can be fined by court in amount of up to 150 thousand EUR for violation of the Anti-Doping legislation (Papanicolau, 2011).

However, it is not enough to have good laws. The most important is following these laws and operation of corresponding law-enforcement mechanisms. The principle of inevitability of punishment for the offenses connected with violation of the Anti-Doping legislation should be maintained. For example, the Code of the

Russian Federation about administrative offenses included Art. 6.18. *Violation of requirements of doping prevention in sport and fight against it established by the law on physical training and sport* under Federal Law as of 06.12.2011 No. 413-FZ. Under this article *coach, sports medicine expert or other expert in the field of physical training and sport* can be punished and disqualified for violation of Anti-Doping rules for the period of 2-3 years depending on circumstances of commission of doping violation. However practically nobody has ever been punished for these violations.

The Concept of the Intelligence-Based Testing

One of the reasons of such situation is that police officers do not know how to reveal and register such offenses. It is difficult to perform this work because many athletes and their *mentors from the sphere of sports medicine* have learned to remove banned substances effectively by means of the most modern technologies. Therefore, the role of evidences on use of substances banned by WADA by athletes and processes with use of special investigative methods and different ways of obtaining information increases. Some experts speak about it as a new trend in fight against doping. There appeared such a concept as intelligence-based testing. It means that the target doping testing is conducted according to operational information of law enforcement agencies and security services. For example, the Australian Anti-Doping Agency uses operational information of Boarder Guard Service and Customs Service, Anti-Doping Agency of Great Britain (UKAD) of Organized Crime Control Bureaus, which regulate the drug control, etc. In some countries there is special software allowing comparing operational data of law enforcement agencies and secret services with the international Anti-Doping information system ADAMS (Anti-Doping Administration and Management System) *(Derevoidov,* 2012). In this regard, the experience of integration of anonymous hot lines for athletes, coaches and members of sports delegations for reporting about violations of Anti-Doping rules deserves our attention.

Problems of the Illicit Trafficking of Doping

One more unresolved legal problem deserves close attention – illicit trafficking of doping by means of distance sales, including Internet. As previously reported, it is not a problem to get doping on Internet in Russia.

However, the question now arises of whether such distribution and purchase of the prohibited substances is lawful. The answer is it is illegal. According Goods Distance Sales Regulations (cl. 5) the distance sales of goods (including Internet) which are banned or limited by the legislation of the Russian Federation is prohibited.

The doping belongs to goods the realization of which is limited not only by the Russian, but also by international legislation. In Russia, for example, dispensing is possible if the seller has the corresponding license, in particular, anabolic drugs can be sold only upon presentation of medical recipes.

Import of medicines from other countries is possible only if they are included in the State Register of Medicinal Remedies, have manufacturer's certificate of origin, and in certain cases they should have permission of authorized Federal Executive Authority (Art. 47 of Federal Law as of 12.04.2010 No. 61-FZ "On drug circulation").

However, who does provide control of drug circulation in the Russian Federation? This organization is called Federal Service for Supervision in the Sphere of Health Care (Roszdravnadzor). Fight against illegal distribution of doping and anabolic steroids should be also performed by Authorities of the Ministry of Sports of Russia, the Ministry of Health and Social Development of the Russian Federation, Rospotrebnadzor, Federal service for fight against drug trafficking, Federal Customs Service (FCS), the Ministry of Internal Affairs, FSB and Rospatent. However, a rule of thumb states that there is no due coordination of work among various departments in the sphere of fight against doping. In addition, perhaps it is time to create the special state commission for coordination of this work.

Of course, there are also required the certain changes in the Russian and international legislation regulating circulation of drugs with substances prohibited by WADA. First, it is seemingly necessary to demand that drugs manufacturers should specify on mandatory basis the presence of substances prohibited by WADA, as well as risks and contraindications for the sporting persons in Instruction for use of drugs. These duties should be established for all drugs manufacturers.

In this regard, it would make sense if formulators were obliged upon application of drug for state registration to provide the corresponding information on presence of substances prohibited by WADA and possibility of use of a concrete drug in professional sport.

Above-mentioned measure would help athletes define what is a doping and what is not. In addition, it would allow avoiding the "doping" risks connected with the use of common drugs by athletes during illness. In addition, it is desirable that these rules would be established by the international legislation.

It is also seemingly necessary to increase legal and pharmacological awareness of athletes about doping and its consequences, as well as about licensed drugs. In this regard, the experience of France where doctors conduct open and anonymous consultations for athletes in the special medical centers for the prevention of use of doping deserves attention. In France these centers are a general part of public health system, they are founded with support of different socially oriented government authorities. Every athlete can get advice and examined anonymously there. And it is very important as athletes have an opportunity to be convinced themselves of legitimacy of the drugs prescribed by doctors, to learn about presence of banned substances in food supplements and quality of the food cooked for them.

Preclinical and Clinical Tests in Professional Sports

One more problem deserves close attention. It is a problem of illicit trafficking of substances under preclinical and clinical tests in professionally sport. According to WADA, banned list as it was already mentioned any pharmacological substances prohibited for use as therapeutic agent by the correspondent government bodies, for example, drugs under preclinical and clinical tests are considered as a doping.

However, in practice it is very difficult to do. Especially, when the developed states officially encourage carrying out medical-biological researches for the benefit of the elite sport. That is why it is very important to settle all issues connected with use of drugs in the developmental stage at the legislative level.

How then are conducted clinical studies and tests of new drugs in the Russian Federation? According to Article 43 of Federal Law as of 12.04.2010 No. 61-FZ "On drugs circulation" participation in clinical studies of drugs for medical use is voluntary. The voluntary consent of patient for participation in clinical studies should be confirmed by his signature on a special information leaflet.

According to this Article 43 implementation of clinical studies of drugs for medical use with participation of orphan children, pregnant and lactating women, military personnel (except for drugs developed for military operations), law enforcement officers, persons who serve sentence in custody and also persons who are in custody in pretrial detention centers is forbidden.

However, there is no legal ban on implementation of clinical tests of new drugs for such category of examinees as professional athletes. Meanwhile, exactly this category of persons is attractive to the various researches connected with effect of innovative drugs and methods at extreme physical activities. This category of persons should not be object of such studies what follows from the international obligations of the Russian Federation, in particular, from provisions of the World Anti-Doping Code and the International Standard, which specifies the list of methods and substances, prohibited for athletes. In our opinion, the tests of new drugs on professional athletes have to be definitely banned. Moreover, these bans should be imposed in other countries of the world.

CONCLUSION

Sport belongs all world and humanity. Sport is always a fair sports victory; it is a tool of improvement of physical and moral qualities of the person. If sport is deprived of these ideals and unsophisticated and high-minded ideas, sport will not be sport and will lose its attractiveness.

Politicians of all countries of the world have to realize finally that sport is not a tool of victory of one country over another; it is not an indicator of the political superiority. It is a way of association of humanity based on the fair competition and the atmosphere of friendship. Moreover, they have to do everything in order to bring sport out of the sphere of politics, to combine efforts in fight against doping and to create equal conditions to athletes of all countries for fair victories.

REFERENCES

ARD Broadcaster informed about new doping violations in the Russian sport. (n.d.). Retrieved March 21, 2016, from http://www.newsru.com/sport/07

Asthma and Sport. Out speak about sport. (n.d.). Retrieved December 20, 2013, from http://stop-asthma.ru/astma-i-sport

Bombela, I. (2008). *Anabolic steroids: elimination of illiteracy 2*. Retrieved February 21, 2012 from http://steroid.su/anabolicheskie-steroidy-likvidaciya-negramotnosti-2

Borisova, T., & Morozov, G. (2011). *Unfair Games*. Retrieved November 12, 2014, from http://rormistr2011.foxibiz.com

Brief doping history in sport. (n.d.). Retrieved March 2, 2014, from http://zmix.ru/food/chemistry/articles-doping/item

Brusnikina, O., & Peskov A., (2014). The practice of doping. *National interests priorities and safety, 31.*

Brusnikina, O., & Peskov A., (2014). Legal problems of the fight against doping in professional sports. *Law and the State: Theory and Practice, 9*(117).

Brusnikina, O., & Peskov A. (2014). The causes and conditions that facilitate the spread of doping in professional sports. *Law and the State: Theory and Practice, 10*(118).

Chapple, J. (2012). *International Olympic Committee and Olympic system. Management of world sport*. Moscow: Publishing House Rid Media.

Derevoidov, A. (2012). Fight against doping: innovative approaches to testing planning. *Bulletin of RMOU, 2.*

Donati, A. (2007). *World Traffic in Doping Substances.* Montreal: WADA.

Dzhusoyti, A. (2001). *Oh, sport, you are the syringe. The informal Doping World Cup continues.* Retrieved May 8, 2012, from http://www.compromat.ru/page_24442.htm

Efimova, I. (2014). *Preparation with dope is my mistake.* Retrieved from May 20, 2014, from http://summer.sport-express.ru/aquatics/reviewrs/44482

Epifanov, V. (Ed.). (2006). *Sports medicine: study guide.* Moscow: TEOTAR-Media.

Executive Committee and Board of Founders of WADA are going to present the final version of Code 2015. (n.d.). Retrieved January 1, 2016, from http://www.rusada.ru/print/5269

Ganeev, T. (2015, December). The defendant in doping case got the same job in the USA. *Izvestia*, 28.

Gavrilova, E. (2011). *Sudden death in sport.* Moscow: Soviet Sport.

German athletes will be paid for use of doping. (*2006*). Retrieved November 7, 2012, from http://lenta.ru/news/2006/12/13/doping

How to hide administration of steroids and prohibited preparations. (n.d.). Retrieved November 7, 2012, from http://sportswiki.ru

International Olympic Committee. (2016). *IOC makes doping results management and sanctioning independent.* Press Release IOC. 01 March 2016.

IOC makes doping results management and sanctioning independent. (2016, March 1). Press Release IOC.

Kabanov A., (2014, April 12). Doping is supported in Russia at the state level. *Commersant.*

Kelnerand, M., Harrisand, N., & Stewart, W. (2013, November 16). Victory in our fight for Russian doping justice: Drugs, bribery and cheating no more investigation triggers official probe. *The Mail on Sunday.*

Kotenko, V. (2013). High performance medicine and sport. *Who is who in medicine, 5.*

Kurinoi, I. (2010). Games acceptable before Heaven. Astrel, AST.

Lance or cheater. Sports hero of America was a doping king. (2012). *Lenta.ru.* Retrieved January 5, 2013, from: http://lenta.ru/articles/2012/10/16/armstrong

Lovchev's dope: politics or shame? (n.d.). Retrieved January 25, 2016, from http:www.sport-express.ru

Malinovskaya, E. (2012). *The Biological Passport of Athlete – Results and Prospects*. Collection of materials of II Russian scientific and practical conference "Doping in sport: risks, counteraction, and prevention". Moscow: RUSADA.

Melnik, T. (2012). *Legal liability and modern approaches to fight against doping* Collection of materials of II Russian scientific and practical conference "Doping in sport: risks, counteraction, and prevention". Moscow: RUSADA.

Merkacheva, E. (2013, December 10). Victory gene. MK has found out what scientific developments are used by athletes at the Olympic Games in Sochi. *Moscow Komsomol.*

Mia, E., & Garcia, B. (2013). *Fundamentals of Olympism*. Moscow: Rid Media.

Mildronate became doping upon an initiative of the Americans. (n.d.). Retrieved December 14, 2016, from http://www.ntv.ru/novosti/1612376/

Ministry of Sport of Russia made statement to WADA's accusations. (in press). *Sport-Express.*

Mkrtchian, V. (2012). *Doping: history and facts*. Retrieved January 29, 2014, from http://www.yerkramas.org/2012/07/05/doping-istoriya-i-fakty

NEWSru.com. (2016). *ARD Broadcaster informed about new doping violations in the Russian sport*. Retrieved March 21, 2016, from http://www.newsru.com/sport/07

NTV.ru. (2016). *Mildronate became doping upon an initiative of the Americans.* Retrieved December 14, 2016, from http://www.ntv.ru/novosti/1612376/

Olympic favorites starve for medals. (n.d.). Retrieved March 7, 2012, from http://sport.rbc.ru/news/5755320b9a7947102987b73d

Olympic review. All gender scandals in sports world. (n.d.). Retrieved December 2, 2015, from: http://olimpiadalife.ru/interesnye-fakty/vse-gendernye-skandaly-iz-mira-sporta.html

Olympic review. Modern doping drugs. (n.d.). Retrieved December 2, 2015, from http://olimpiadalife.ru/doping/sovremennye-dopingovye-preparaty.html

Papanicolau D. (2011). Fight against doping in France. *Sport: economy, law, management, 4.*

Pervitin is a weapon of the Third Reich. (n.d.). Retrieved December 18, 2013, from http://ynik.info/2008/07/30/pervitin

Petrov, A. (in press). The former chief of RUSADA Nikita Kamaev died. *Commersant*.

Pharmacological products and other substances prohibited in sport. (n.d.). Retrieved April 21, 2012, from http://sportswiki.ru

Pilipenko, D. (2007). *Crime in sport*. Moscow: Geleos.

President LFP knew about purchase of doping. (n.d.). Retrieved November 15, 2014, from http://rsport.ru/football/20130205/643454533.html

Putin against doping scandal has invoked to protect athletes from administration of the forbidden drugs. (n.d.). Retrieved January 17, 2016, from http://www.newsru.com/russia/11nov2015/putinolimp.html

RBK Daily. (2013). *China was accused of production of doping*. Author.

Report of the chief of FMBA of Russia V. V. Uiba on enlarged session of board of FMBA as of July 23, 2013. (n.d.). Retrieved November 19, 2014, from http://www.gcgie.ru/Kollegia-FMBA2013/Doklad-Kol.pdf

Report on RUSADA business in 2012. (n.d.). Retrieved November 19, 2014, from http://www.rusada.ru/about/annual_reports

Reztsova, A. (2009). *In modern sport, it is impossible without doping. That is the modern life*. Retrieved from http://www.skisport.ru/news/index.php?news=8539

Role of the World Anti-Doping Agency in control of doping in sport. (n.d.). Retrieved May 17, 2014, from http://sportswiki.ru

Rusada. (2015). *Executive Committee and Board of Founders of WADA are going to present the final version of Code 2015*. Retrieved January 1, 2016, from http://www.rusada.ru/print/5269

Russia may be disqualified from athletics competitions. (n.d.). Retrieved from http://www.newsru.com/sport/09nov2015/wada.html

Russia spent 27 mln EUR for two laboratories. (in press). *Sport-Express*.

Seven national teams were suspected of doping in Sochi Games. (n.d.). Retrieved February 2016, from http://www.newsru.com/sport/14may2014/wada .html

Shevchenko, O. (2015). *The legal doctrine of regulation of work in the sphere of professional sport and ways of realization in Russia*. Moscow: Prospect.

Skvortsov, A. (2006). *Infliction of harm of life and health in sport. Problems of criminal and legal qualification*. Wolters Kluwer.

Soloviev, A. (2010). *Brazilian Sports Codes//Actual problems of the sports law. Version 4*. Moscow: Commission of the Sports Law of Association of Lawyers of Russia.

Soloviev, A. (2011). *Doping liability according to the Sports code of France*. Moscow: Commission of the Sports Law of Association of Lawyers of Russia.

Soloviev, A., & Ponkin, I. V. I., (2010). Sports code of France. Reglamentarny part – Decrees. Books I and II.//Actual problems of the sports law. Version 5. Moscow: Commission of the Sports Law of Association of Lawyers of Russia.

Soloviev, A. I. V., Ponkin, I., & Ponkina, A. (2013). *Legal regulation of sport in Switzerland//Actual problems of the sports law. Version 18*. Moscow: Commission of the Sports Law of Association of Lawyers of Russia.

Sport-Express. (2015). *Lovchev's dope: politics or shame?* Retrieved January 25, 2016, from http:www.sport-express.ru

Sport-Express. (2015, November). Ministry of Sport of Russia made statement to WADA's accusations. *Sport-Express*, 10.

SportWiki. (2015). *How to hide administration of steroids and prohibited preparations.* Retrieved November 7, 2012, from http://sportswiki.ru

Steinbach, V. (2008). *Reverse of the medal*. Moscow: Chelovek.

Stop-astma.ru. (2013). *Asthma and Sport. Out speak about sport*. Retrieved December 20, 2013, from http://stop-asthma.ru/astma-i-sport

Substances, which the Russian athletes used in Sochi are stated as doping. (n.d.). Retrieved June 15, 2014, from http://www.newsru.com/sport/20may2014/xenon.html

Top-5 athletes, who ruined career with drugs. (2014). *Bigmirnet*. Retrieved February 21, 2014, from http://sport.bigmir.net/football/other/1558149-TOP-5-sportsmenov--pogubivshih-kar-eru-narkotikami

Transgender athletes will be allowed to participate in OG without gender reassignment surgery. (n.d.). Retrieved February 15, 2016, from http://lenta.ru/comments/news/2016/01/25/transgenderathletes/

Vdovin, A., & Vdovin, D. (2014). *Everyone take doping. Only poor are caught.* Retrieved May 14, 2014, L: http://www.shooting-ua.com/books/book_18.3.htm

WADA Anti-Doping Testing Figures Report. (2012). Retrieved February 2, 2014, from http://www.wada-ama.org/en

WADA: two Moscow laboratories eliminated doping tests. (n.d.). Retrieved May 19, 2016, from http://ria.ru/sport/20151109/1317524622.html

Wikipedia. (2006). *Methamphetamine.* Retrieved December 7, 2015, from http://ru.wikipedia.org/wiki

Wikipedia. (2015). *Chegin, Viktor Mikhailovich.* Retrieved February 2, 2016 from https://ru.wikipedia.org

World Anti-Doping Code 2015. (2016). Moscow: RUSADA.

ZMIX.RU. (2008). *Brief doping history in sport.* Retrieved March 2, 2014, from http://zmix.ru/food/chemistry/articles-doping/item

Zubareva, A., (2012). Sporting wheels. *RBK (Business Magazine),* 9.

Chapter 11
The Emergence of Sports Law in Kenya

Asha Mikinyango
Mount Kenya University, Kenya

ABSTRACT

Sports law is a relatively new topic in Kenya. Once played for recreational purposes and entertainment, sports have become professionalized and commercialized. This evolution led to government intervention to prevent a conflict of interest. The government in Kenya created and regulated the infrastructure supporting these sports, as well as provided dispute resolution mechanisms for arising issues. This infrastructure included both the legal and structural frameworks of the industry. The government intervention ran through the legislature and the judiciary. Through the legislature, the government created laws to regulate the sports industry. The judiciary adjudicated issues demanding judicial treatment. Sports have grown into a highly competitive industry with global pervasiveness. This chapter will discuss regulative and structural frameworks within the sports industry by highlighting the legislation primarily providing sports law. The chapter then highlights contemporary issues as well as make recommendations on the same.

INTRODUCTION

This chapter will track sports law in Kenya by studying the country's emergence from pre-colonial colonization to its postcolonial position. This chapter will summarize Kenya's historical background, which will lead to the current government's legal interventions. After defining sports law in Kenya, it will examine both the administrative and legal frameworks under the Sports Act 2013. Then, the chapter

DOI: 10.4018/978-1-5225-5387-8.ch011

will focus on contemporary issues in sports. The author's main argument is that Kenya's current sports law does not exhaust all challenges. Therefore, it needs to be amended to regulate sports.

BACKGROUND

Several definitions exist for the term *sport*. According to Elias (1971, p. 88-115), *sport* can refer to *nonwork-related forms of physical activity with or without an element of competition*. In terms of this abstract usage, sport is a socio-cultural universal phenomenon. However, the term can also be used more concretely to refer to a group of competitive physical activities, which are modern in key respects. A sport has physical activity, side-by-side competition, self-motivation, and a scoring system. The difference of purpose is what characterizes sport, as well as the notion of individual skill or prowess.

According to Kenya's Sports Act 2013, *sport* includes all forms of physical or mental activity to express or improve physical and mental well-being, form social relationships, or obtain result in competition at all levels. This is achieved through casual participation, organized participation, or training activities. Therefore, sports can be for leisure or professional competition.

For this study, the Sports Act's definition was adopted. This chapter is concerned with how the law and sports interact in Kenya. Sport, which is now modernized, was a social recreational activity. Following its definition, sport can be recreational, social, or competitive. It ranges from informal participation to serious organized club sport with complete commitment in pursuit of the highest levels of excellence at Olympic and world levels.

Kenya, a country in East Africa, borders states like Uganda and Tanzania. Its surface area is 582,646 square kilometres; its population is 47,251,000 (Kenya National Bureau of Statistics, 2011).

The development of sports law in Kenya is categorized into three periods: (1) pre-colonial; (2) colonial, and; (3) postcolonial. Pre-colonial Kenya traces to a period when Kenya was an unclaimed territory. During this time, groups of individuals first claimed the territory. Reportedly, 2,000 ethnic groups from across Africa settled its vast area, which was later called Kenya by the colonizers (Ndege, 2009).

During this period, the inhabitants engaged in games and activities, including wrestling, racing, stick fights, hunting, board games, bull fights, dances, and rustling (Kamenju, Ritaungu, & Mwangi, 2016). These games, however, were not known as sports. In fact, they developed from daily activities. For example, without trains or cars, people walked or ran long distances to communicate or trade. Spear throwing was necessary for hunting; learning to swim was essential for fishing (Rintaugu,

Mwisukha, & Munayi, 2011). The skills gained from such activities were for recreational purposes and cultural integration. There were neither codified laws nor regulation of sports under customary laws. This was because sports activities were not commercial in nature and were generally used to promote cultural identity, as well as enhance social and physical skills (Aketch, n.d.). This position changed during the colonization period.

Colonization of Kenya by the British led to a restriction of indigenous sport. Sports deriving from European cultures took centre stage as the colonial settlers introduced activities and professionalized events, sports clubs, and competitions restricted to the British (Nteere, n.d.).

The position changed as several events, including active resistance to colonial rule, led to the decolonization of Kenya (Nteere, n.d.) In 1963, the British handed over power to the first Kenyan government. After independence, Kenya adopted and integrated European sports into Kenyan sports culture. Several sports promote culture, enhance social cohesion, and promote physical health. Professional sports led to training and competitions in local and international events. Sports in Kenya include rugby, basketball, football, golf, cricket, motor sports, swimming, handball, tennis, and martial arts.

After gaining independence, the control and administration of sports in Kenya were regulated by private associations independent of the government because the government used a noninterventionist model of sports regulation (Nteere, n.d.). Although people participated in sports, it was generally regarded as a pastime activity or interest of children (Rintaugu, Mwisukha, & Munayi, 2011). Sporting activities outside of the school were run by the local authorities or voluntary sporting clubs and organizations. These groups facilitated the participation of a few of Kenya's sportsmen and women in major international sporting events, including the Olympic Games, All-Africa Games, and Commonwealth Games.

The increased interest in competitive sports led the government to establish the Kenya National Sports Council as an umbrella for the sports federations (Rintaugu, Mwisukha, & Munayi, 2011). The council was tasked with overseeing and coordinating the activities of the federations. A department of sports was also created to formulate and implement the national policy on sports. The sports industry was still self-regulatory at this point. However, there was a growing need for direct government intervention.

The sports industry grew from a mere entrainment avenue to a powerful economic industry. Significant revenue is generated through local and international sports activities. International wins have drawn many fans to explore Kenya. Kenya has also hosted several international and regional competitions, which contributed to the country's economic development through sales of sporting goods, promotion of tourism, and convergence of the sports and business industry though sponsorships, merchandising, and endorsements (Mwisukha, Njororai, & Onywera, 2003). These activities overwhelmed the free-from-regulation state with conflicts of interest and financial interests. This led the government to pass an act to regulate and restructure sports in Kenya. This intervention led to the sports law currently regulating the sports industry.

Modernity caused sports to evolve into a profession. This, in turn, led to the commercialization of sports. According to Mukul (2011), an evolution that causes a convergence of sports and commerce leads to subsequent increases in financial stakes in sports. This causes several issues requiring legislative intervention. Kenya's sports industry is actively engaging in profit-making businesses through sponsorships, endorsements, and merchandising deals (Mikinyango, 2017). According to PricewaterhouseCoopers Limited (2013), in their report on Kenyan entertainment and media outlook, revenue in the sports industry is generated through gate revenues, exploitation of media rights, sponsorships, endorsements, merchandising, and sports betting, which produces a projected estimated revenue of approximately US$150.4 million in 2017. The commercialization of sports, as well as the financial interests involved, has made it necessary for the government to regulate the industry and adjudicate disputes. This led to the laws governing sports in Kenya.

The Kenyan government's role is to create and regulate the infrastructure supporting sports in Kenya, as well as provide dispute resolution mechanisms. This infrastructure includes the legal and structural framework of the sports industry. The government intervenes through legislature and the judiciary. Through the legislature, the government creates laws to regulate the sports industry; the judiciary adjudicates issues that demand judicial treatment in sports.

The main objective of sports law is to control all sports-related issues and provide fair solutions. This chapter considers whether contemporary issues (i.e., gender equality, image rights, and sports contracts) are efficiently covered by the current sports law in Kenya.

LEGAL AND INSTITUTIONAL FRAMEWORK

Sports started off as a social recreational activity. It has become politicized because of the professionalization and commercialization of sports in Kenya. This evolution led to legislative interventions by the government through the Sports Act.Under the Act, regulation of sport occurs on five levels (Aketch, n.d.):

1. Formulation of the rules of sports;
2. Application of immediate sanctions during sports should a breach of the rules occur;

3. Disciplinary proceedings performed by administrative bodies who punish those who contravene the rules and provide an opportunity for review of decisions;
4. State intervention when a participant's behavior infringes criminal law or a civil action is brought and international interaction through international institutions.

This section establishes legislation governing sports in Kenya, as well as institutions involved in its governance.

SPORTS LEGISLATION IN KENYA

The Constitution of Kenya (2010)

Kenya's government's long-term support for sports involves the building of a just and cohesive society that enjoys social development in a clean and secure environment, as established in KenyaVision 2030 (Korir, 2015). This requires legislation that protects the interests of sports persons and maintains public policies. The Constitution of Kenya provides for the national government and county governmentswith separation of powers between legislative, executive, and legislative arms of government. It further provides for the distribution of functions and powers between the two levels of government. The national government is tasked with the promotion of sports and sports education in Kenya through enacted laws and policies (Kenya Law Reports, 2010).

In Kenya, sports incorporate and reinforce society's existing values. It can be a useful political tool to promote culture, social values, and peace (Aketch, n.d.). The sports industry also contributes to the country's economy. However, its success depends on its legislative and economic support. For social-economic development of the sports industry, the government must ensure that Kenya's sports industry receives the necessary infrastructure and financial support.The overall objective is to develop sports in Kenya (Korir, 2015).

The Sports Act (2013)

The first legislation regulating sports in Kenya was the Sports Act. This law was enforced on January14, 2013. It was deemed necessary to assist the government to harness sports for development, encourage and promote drug-free sports and recreation, provide for the establishment of sports infrastructure, and manage governance in sports.

There was no act regulating sports in Kenya prior to 2013. This is because the Kenyan government took a noninterventionist approach to sports (Aketch, n.d.). However, industry issues resulting from the professionalization and commercialization of sports led to sports law. In 2013, the Act was promulgated. As it formalized the industry, it replaced all policies and practice rules in sports. Existing sports organizations were required to register under the Act. The Act is silent on several the issues, including but not limited to sports contracts, corporate governance, employment issues, and commercial rights (i.e., image rights, sports licensing, and merchandising). These contemporary issues will be discussed later in the chapter.

Anti-Doping Act (2016)

As mentioned, the Sports Act was silent on issues prevailing in the sports industry. A major issue was doping. Wekesa (2010) raised and discussed this issue under integrity and ethics of sports. Doping is a challenge to ethics in sports. If the issue went uncontrolled, it put Kenya at risk of being banned from international competitions.

The government created the Anti-Doping Act of 2016 (KE) as a tool to give effect to the World Antidoping Code and the United Nations Educational Scientific and Cultural Organization Convention against Doping in Sport. Under this Anti-Doping Act, the government ensured that sports activities were free from doping by establishing mechanisms to deter doping, punish offenders, and prevent use of banned substances in sports.

The Anti-Doping Act is administered by the Anti-Doping Agency of Kenya (ADAK), a body cooperating with the mandate to fight doping in sports by establishing anti-doping values and providing informative campaigns. The agency carries out doping tests among Kenyan athletes to identify those abusing prohibited substances and uphold the integrity of sport through intelligence gathering, investigations, and results management of anti-doping rules violations under the Anti-Doping Act of 2016 (KE) S. 7.

The Anti-Doping Act is an indication that the Kenyan government supports clean sport by fighting corruption because doping is cheating. The Anti-Doping Act 2016 S. 2 defines doping as the use of prohibited substances and methods in any sporting activity (competitive or recreational) to artificially enhance performance. It is fundamentally contrary to the spirit of sport, endangers the health of athletes and of those who emulate and aspire to become athletes, and undermines the otherwise positive impact of sport in society. Accordingly, Kenyan government considers the elimination of doping in sport as an important public policy objective.

A lot of work remains to be done with regards to doping. This includes establishing infrastructures under the act and policies, creating awareness among sports persons and the public, and rolling out mechanisms for prevention of doping in Kenya. Although it will not be an instant achievement, it will be a progressive challenge (Chebet, 2014).

Institutional Organization

The industry has been restructured in compliance with the Sports Act 2013 to facilitate high-level performance within the sports industry in Kenya. Institutional organization of the sports industry can be categorized based on roles. Institutions fall under three categories. First, regulatory institutions are involved in the creation and application of legislation governing the sports industry. The Ministry of Sports, Culture, and the Arts, the Sports Disputes Tribunal, and the Registrar of Sports Organizations make up the regulative institutions. Second, supervisory institutions oversee the implementation of law created by regulatory institutions. Sports Kenya, National Sports Fund Board of Trustees, and Kenya Academy of Sports are such institutions. They oversee implementation of sports policies by co-coordinating their respective area at the national and county levels. Third, administrative institutions organize and conduct sports events. Sports organizations fall under this category.

This section discusses their roles in the sports industry.

The Ministry of Sports, Culture, and the Arts

The sports industry falls under the Ministry of Sports, Culture, and the Arts. The ministry is tasked with the development of sports and arts as industries for the creation of wealth and employment. It is also a tool for national cohesion and the de-ethnicization of the Kenyan society (Rintaugu, Mwisukha, & Munayi, 2011). The ministry governs through the cabinet secretary in charge of sports. The ministry is mandated to develop and coordinate sports by promoting and creating facilities, as well as spearheading the expansion of the sports industry.

The cabinet secretary is the ministry's principal secretary responsible for sports and the registrar for sports appointed under section 46 of the Act. The cabinet secretary oversees sports industry. Duties include approval of industry regulation fees and practice rules, appointment of trustees and committee members, and intervention of sports organizations when the Act is contravened (Sports Act 2013, s. 55).

The ministry formulates and articulates sports policies to enable an environment for all stakeholders (Korir, 2015). By creating and passing laws, it regulates sports, which includes a dispute resolution mechanism.

The Sports Disputes Tribunal

The Sports Disputes Tribunal, which is established under the Sports Act 2013, s. 56(1), arbitrates sports disputes in Kenya. The Tribunal's role is to provide a dispute resolution mechanism relating to sports (Sports Act, 2013). It falls under the judicatory obligation of the government in settling sports disputes. It has jurisdiction to determine appeals by national or umbrella sports organizations whose rules allow for appeals to be made to the Tribunal. Issues include appeals against disciplinary decisions, appeals against not being selected for a Kenyan team or squad, appeals from decisions of The Kenya's Registrar of Sports Organizations, and other sports-related disputes.

The Kenya's Registrar of Sports Organizations

The Office of the Sports Registrar is a public service office established under the Sports Act 2013, s. 46. Appointed by the public service commission, the Registrar is responsible for registration and regulation of sports organizations and multisport bodies. These include sports organizations at the national level, licensing of professional sports and professional sports persons, arbitration of registration disputes between sports organizations, and maintenance of a register of registered sports organizations. The Registrar plays a role in registration and protection of sports image rights as mandated by law due to the regulatory position accorded to the office.

Sports Kenya

Sports Kenya is established under the Sports Act 2013, s. 3 as a corporate body with perpetual succession and common seal. It replaces Kenya's sports stadia management board (SSMB).With its supervisory role, it promotes, coordinates, and implements grassroots, national, and international sports programs in Kenya. It is mandated to establish, manage, and maintain Kenya sports facilities.

Sports Kenya has several other functions under the Act, including oversight of the identification and development of sporting talent, provision of sports equipment and facilities, and technical training with county governments, learning institutions, and stakeholders. It also facilitates the preparation and participation of Kenyan teams in international events and host-country events. Sports Kenya controls the clearance of foreign sports persons and technical personnel prior to engagements by national sports organizations and other sporting bodies in Kenya. The board of Sports Kenya has the power to appoint a director general to run the organization as directed by the Sports Act 2013, s.8.

National Sports Fund Board of Trustees

The Sports Act 2013, s. 13 established the National Sports Fund. The fund holds proceeds of allocations by parliament, gifts, grants, donations, investment proceeds, sports lottery, and other payments required by this Act to be paid into the fund. Its goal is to develop sports in Kenya by financially supporting sports persons and sports organizations. The chief executive officer of the board is appointed by the president. Board members, referred to as trustees, are appointed by the cabinet secretary upon nomination. This falls under the state's mandate to financially support the sports industry as the government recognizes that the promotion and development of sports benefits the public and state. Its bodies naturally play a major role in the funding of sports in Kenya (Korir, 2015).

The board's main objective is to manage, control, and administer the assets of the fund to promote the purpose for which the fund is established. The fund is made up of financial allocation by the government, gifts, grants, donations, or endowments, sports lotteries, and investments.

Kenya Academy of Sports

The Kenya Academy of Sports is established under the Sports Act 2013, s. Sp33(1). This is a corporate body with perpetual succession and a common seal. Its primary objective is to oversee and manage sports training in Kenya. This is achieved by establishing and managing training academies to promote sports courses for technical and administrative personnel. It also promotes research and development of talent in sports in collaboration with institutions of higher learning, national sports organizations, and other stakeholders.

This chapter's author believes that sports can be used as a tool of social change because they build personality, group cohesion, loyalty, and social values. To maintain these positive influences, sports should be integrated into all levels of education. It is also important to endorse uniformity and ethics in sports competition. Therefore, the government must intervene to ensure that sports adhere to societal values and principles by treating sports as a part of education.

The Academy of Sports becomes the central guide in sports training and uniformity. It maintains and disseminates tangible and intangible historical sports material to the public, sports organizations, researchers, and institutions of learning in a bid to promote sports. Its management is vested in a council; the Academy is run by a chief executive officer appointed by the council (Sports Act2013, s. 31).

Sports Organizations

Sports organizations include associations, businesses, and social institutions that contribute to the promotion and development of physical and sports activities. The highest-level organizations are national sports associations. These are by county associations, sports federations, and sports clubs. Sports persons are at the bottom of the hierarchy. The provisions of the Sports Act 2013 seek to establish a link between the government and sports industry by allowing the industry to have an independent governance structure. This is because the government regulates legal relationships and ensures adherence to law and ethics. Kenyan sports must grow to meet international standards. This requires cooperation between public authorities and private entities to achieve its goals in promoting and developing physical and sports activities.

Government regulatory institutions create legislation and rules to govern sports. The sports governance bodies act as supervisory bodies to oversee the creation of private infrastructures to implement the law. Under the same governance structure, administrative bodies are created to apply the law. This forms the governed population. This accountability and transparency translates to order.

In Kenya, a body can only operate as a sports organization if it is registered as a sports club, county sports association, or national sports organization under the Sports Act 2014, s. 47(1). Registration applications are submitted to the sports registrar. According to Noll (2003), a sports organization is an entity that sponsors, organizes, schedules, or conducts a competitive game in which one or more professional athletes participate. Obonyo (2013, p. 1161) describes such organizations as administrative in nature as their main objective is to organize and schedule sports events locally or internationally, following regulation and infrastructure already established by the state.

National sports organizations are at the top of the organizational hierarchy. They include national umbrella bodies responsible for Olympic, non-Olympic, Paralympics (www.paralympic.org), or Deaflympic sports. These national bodies are responsible for all sports disciplines or recreational bodies or body responsible for a sport nationally. For example, National Olympic Committee Kenya, an organization that dates back to January of 1955 created as a national representative of the International Olympic Committee created under the Olympic Charter (The National Olympic Committee Kenya, 2017). In Kenya, NOCK is the only body with authority to select where and how Olympic Games can be organized in Kenya. Further, no Kenyan sports person can be allowed to participate in Olympic Games if not authorized by NOCK. This means that NOCK has the final say in selection of Kenyan representatives at the Olympics. It is therefore the body that represents Kenya internationally in all matters related to Olympic games.

National sports organizations registered under the Act are open to the public in their leadership, activities, and membership. This ensures transparency and the upholding of sports ethics in governance. There can only be one national sports organization for a particular discipline. On the other hand, county sports associations operate at the county level and can liaise with other county and national sports organizations. Such associations can promote sports at the county level and come in after the national organizations.

Sports federations, the next level in the hierarchy, are central to the organization of sports in Kenya. They act as relays between the world of sports and Olympic sports. They also interact with public authorities. They generally organize the practice of one or more sports disciplines.

Sports federations are associations affiliated as professional clubs, individuals, and organizations. These groups, which focus on gain and profit, include health and recreational clubs, specifically in the practice of one or more disciplines (for example, Football Kenya Federation (FKF), Kenya Basketball Federation (KBF), and Kenya Rugby Union (KRU)). These federations are organized in a decentralized manner. For the most part, this is in the form of leagues, committees, sections, or clubs representing the federation at the local levels. They organize events and allow sports persons in various disciplines to compete professionally. They also issue technical rules on discipline and rules on the organization of events open to their licensed athletes. The federations are made up of clubs to which individual sports persons belong.

Professional sports persons sit at the bottom of the organization. These persons are registered in various disciplines or compete individually. They are subject to the Sports Act, as well as the federation's rules and regulations (including sports clubs). The main objective of sports clubs is to satisfy a community's motivation to practice physical activity and socialization by designing and offering activities at a recreational or competitive level. Examples of sports clubs include school sports clubs (i.e., colleges, universities, or secondary school sports clubs), public social clubs, and professional clubs (i.e., football, basketball, and other sports clubs in Kenya).

Professional clubs are restricted to professional sports persons. However, other clubs are open to the public through a membership set by the club's constitution. Sports organizations and individual sports persons engage in commercial transactions for financial support through merchandising, endorsements, and sponsorship deals. These structures create order in sports. However, sports law is new in terms of full application and ability to meet current issues in Kenyan sports. The following are prevailing issues in sports law.

ISSUES IN KENYAN SPORTS LAW

This chapter's author sought out current developments in the law and practice of sports law. In addition, the author looked for insight into future directions of the law by giving an overview on the current and emerging problems of sports law in Kenya.

Employment Issues

Sport is a cultural and entertainment aspect of the Kenyan society. However, the professionalization and commercialization of sports have made it subject to several existing laws. These include the law of contract and employment laws.

The law of contract plays an essential role in the commercialization of the sports industry in Kenya. All commercial agreements in Kenya are formulated and performed as contracts. Most obligations within Kenya's sports industry are contractual in nature. Kenya's law of contract is derived from the English common law, as well as some statutes applying to specific types of contracts. This position is established by the law of contract (Law of Contract Act, Chapter 21).

Ultimately, the law of contract framework enables a sports person to be employed individually. In addition, this person can form associations recognized under the Sports Act 2013. These relationships, which are created through contracts, provide the regulative bodies an avenue to set rules according to sports in Kenya. As a result, no commercial transaction involving sports, sports persons, or professional sport can take place without a contract.

Although employment contracts are governed by general employment laws, employment relationships in Kenya are formed through contracts and, therefore, must meet the essential provisions of contract law. There are many labor-related statutes in Kenya. However, the Employment Act 2007 provides the basic terms applicable to all employment contracts. It defines the fundamental rights of employees, provides basic conditions of employment, regulates employment of children, and sets the principle rules of employment. Section 2 of the Employment Act, 2007 defines *employee* as a person employed for wages or a salary, including an apprentice and indentured learner. According to this law, an employer is any person, public body, firm, corporation, or company who or which has entered into a contract of service to employ any individual. This includes the agent, foreman, manager or factor of such person, public body, firm, corporation, or company.

The Act's definition of an employee, according to the author, does not fully apply to all contractual relationships in sports. For instance, the relationship between sports person and agent, promoter, or manager may look like an employment contract, but the context of the relationship is not within the ordinary job description for sports managers or agents for instance. There is need to develop policies specifically regulating sports employment contracts as well as remuneration. Lack of a remuneration order to guide the sports industry is adding to employment woes.

This position is based on the fact that current employment laws in Kenya apply to contracts of service rather than contracts for services. It can be difficult to know the nature of sports when parties are hired for seasonal service without intent for retention. With a lack of intent to create a contractual relationship, the parties cannot claim rights under the employment act.

This implies that sports persons will face many issues if they do not scrutinize their contracts or seek legal advice before signing contracts. These issues include wrongful termination, wrongful conduct during employment, allowances, and terms of termination. This was also observed by Majani (2013), a Kenyan sports lawyer who noted arising issues from contractual sports relations in Kenya.

Another issue troubling sports employment contracts is the dispute resolution mechanism. Under the Sports Act 2013, s 55(1), the Sports Disputes Tribunal was created to arbitrate sports disputes when the parties agree to subject themselves to its jurisdiction. There is also an option of appealing to the Court of Arbitration for Sports (CAS) if there is an agreement between the parties.

Further, the Labour Institutions Act 2007provides for the creation and management of institutions dealing with labour. This includes the industrial court, which deals with labour-related disputes. In both situations, a specialized approach of sports law and nature of sports is needed to develop the jurisprudence of sports employment contracts. It paves the way for clearer terms and standard contract conditions to avoid conflict.

To avoid future disputes, sports persons should seek legal representation in the negotiating and drafting of contracts. Individuals may avoid lawyers until there is a dispute. However, this is problematic. Specialized legal knowledge is most important from the commencement of a legal relationship.

Gender Inequality

Gender inequality is another prevailing issue in sports law. Kenya's African cultures have entrenched patriarchy in mindsets and cultural laws. There has been a default belief that some things are preserved for men. According to Kanyi (2017), this belief lingers in Kenya. From childhood, boys are more entitled to education, sports, and inheritance of property. Girls, however, are expected to take care of household chores. This unfair distribution of resources and opportunities follows the girl to adulthood through limited job opportunities, lower wages, and other forms of sexism.

Onsongo (2009) reported that the Kenyan government is attempting to do away with gender inequality. When fighting gender inequality, the first government employed affirmative action policies and laws to increase female participation and representation at all levels. Currently, the Constitution of Kenya (Kenya Law Reports, 2010) guarantees equality and protection from all forms of discrimination. This includes gender under article 27(1), which provides that every person is equal before the law and has the right to equal protection and equal benefit of the law. Article 27(3) states that women and men have the right to equal treatment, including the right to equal opportunities in political, economic, cultural, and social spheres. By enshrining this right in the constitution, its seriousness and priority is established. Yet, the law is useless unless there are means to implement it.

Regardless of these efforts, disparity between the sexes remains an issue in Kenya, especially in sports. According to research, sport is an area where gender inequality is manifested. (Mwisukha & Ritonga, 2013; Wamaitha, 2015). A current challenge surrounding gender equality in sports is that men and women are treated differently. To some extent, men are still considered the better sex. Gender inequality is seen in sports, leadership, and financing.

There is a need to address this form of discrimination in sports. This can be done through specific affirmative action policies or employment equity. The intervention of policy makers is needed because inequality creates an unfair competitive environment in sports. This, in turn, is contrary to sports ethics. The importance of gender equality in sports has been supported by the United Nations (2007) in their published report *Women 2000 and Beyond.* Luckily, the government of Kenya shares similar sentiments (Government of the Republic of Kenya, 2013). The government has been working to counter customary forms of discrimination against women through laws, policies, and education.

Sports Image Rights

Image rights are the rights of an individual to command the business-related use of his/her name, image, likeness, or unique, indisputable aspects of one's personality. Image rights include the right to keep one's image and likeness from commercial exploitation without permission or contractual compensation (Blackshaw & Siekmann, 2005).

The sports industry in Kenya is commercially active; sports persons accumulate personality attributes with marketable value. Yet, there is no legislation that provides a distinct property right in the image of sports persons to enable them to stop others from unjustly gaining from the commercial exploitation of their image (Mikinyango, 2017). Many jurisdictions recognize and protect the right to an image. Notably, the United States is a significant contributor to the development and protection of image rights. The right held by an individual to its *persona* is known in different jurisdictions by a variety of names, including "rights of publicity" (U.S.), "rights of privacy" (the United Kingdom), and "rights of personality" (continental Europe). They can be collectively referred to as image rights (Synodinou, 2014). This established legal right must be created in Kenya to enable sports persons from preventing unscrupulous parties from commercially exploiting their image.

This author argues that Kenya's existing laws regulating sports and intellectual property do not (and cannot) sufficiently protect the patrimonial and extra-patrimonial duality of sports image rights. Therefore, the author calls for the creation of a new intellectual property right termed "the right to image." This will prevent the unauthorized commercial exploitation of sports image rights because all advertisers, as well as merchandisers, will be required to seek consent before exploiting sports image rights.

Prevailing Corruption

The development of sports from a leisurely pastime to a commercially enriching industry has raised new challenges. One challenge is the corruption in sports. Kenyans are disappointed by the increases in doping, match fixing, and rampant corruption.

According to a report released by Transparency International Kenya (n.d.), corruption in Kenyan sports includes match fixing, buying of delegates, doping, and age. In Kenya, corruption matters are handled by the Anti-Corruption and Economic Crimes Act (2003). The Act is administered by the Kenya Anti-Corruption Commission. Under Section 2, corruption is defined as an act that consists of bribery, fraud, embezzlement, or misappropriation of public funds, abuse of office, breach of trust, an offence involving dishonesty, in connection with any tax, rate or impost levied under any act or under any written law relating to the elections of persons to public office.

The author believes that the current law on corruption does not deal with the unique corrupt acts in sports. There is a need to either amend the current anticorruption law to include corruption in sports governance, sports events, and other related sports activities or create a new law to combat and prevent corruption in sports. The government has responded to doping issues by creating an act specifically addressing doping. However, other activities also threaten the integrity of Kenyan sports.

The author believes that the government must take extreme measures to deter corruption to save Kenya's reputation and safeguard sports integrity. This can be approached through the promotion of good governance, transparency, and participation of the industry's stakeholders. Stakeholders include the government, sports persons, clubs, federations, and business partners interested in sponsorship and commercially related parties.

Betting and Sports

Historically, betting in Kenya has been in existence as an acceptable activity for decades. The first legislation regulating betting in Kenya was the Betting, Lotteries and Gaming Act Chapter 131 Laws of Kenya which was passed by parliament in 1966. Gambling is therefore legal in Kenya. However, this first law was not very effective in controlling the growing gambling industry as the growth brought a lot of unanticipated issues (Mutuku, 2013). As a result, several amendments have been made over time, in a bid to deal with gaps in betting law and policies.

The latest amendment was in 2016 and it sought to create more strict regulation of betting by giving more control to the Betting Control and Licensing Board, the authority in charge, by increasing its scope of functions and giving it more autonomy from interference politically and financially. The Act also increases the betting tax in Kenya and makes it an offence for persons under the age of 18 betting (Betting, Lotteries and Gaming Act, 2016). While this legalization of gabling has its advantages, the main one being it has been a generator of income for many, including the government through taxes, it has disadvantages as well. The lure of easy money has reportedly led to gambling addiction, depression and even suicides in Kenya and other East African countries (Koigi, 2016).

Other than these social ills caused by gambling, there is another issue born of gambling that is threatening the integrity of sports in Kenya. This is the issue of match fixing in sports encouraged by sports betting. There are several betting firms in Kenya primarily focused on betting in sports operating online and this is evidence of the exponential growth of gambling in sports (BetMoran, 2017).

This growth has brought along claims of match fixing in Kenya. There have been accusations of such unethical acts by groups or even players betting against themselves, even when players are forbidden to place such bets (Korir, 2017). Attention was drawn to match fixing in the matter between Maurice Odumbe, a cricket player and the Kenya Cricket Association (KCA) as a representative of the International Cricket Council (ICC). Odumbe was accused of match fixing based on his association with a bookmarker and a tribunal was established to investigate him. His trial was guided by rules established by ICC, not Kenyan National laws. He was found guilty and as a consequence, banned from the sport for 5 years (Akech, 2008). He moved to the High Court of Kenya to challenge the decision but the Court held that judicial review only applies to public entities engaged in public matters and his matter was dismissed because ICC and the KCA were not public entities (Republic v Kenya Cricket Association & 2 others, 2016; Kenya Law Reports).

This case illustrates that there are no national laws in Kenya dealing with such unethical consequences of sports betting, which is an emerging issue globally.

There is need for expeditious consideration of this if integrity and fairness are to be maintained in Kenyan sports.

CONCLUSION AND RECOMMENDATIONS

There has been a positive growth of sports into an influential industry in Kenya, especially economically. However, this development has its downsides. Negative issues and disputes are the result of the professionalization and commercialization of sports. Law is needed to maintain order and uphold the integrity of sports.

Sport is a fundamental part of the Kenyan society. Therefore, there is a need to regulate the conduct of sport and business to control the interests of all parties involved. This includes fundamental issues of public interest. Sports law is needed to maintain sport for its economic, social, and cultural relevance to society (both locally and internationally).

In Kenya, several issues arose with the professionalization and commercialization of sports. This prompted the government to intervene through sports legislation. This law needs further development to effectively counter prevailing and upcoming challenges.

Sports fall under the Ministry of Sports, Culture, and the Arts, which is tasked with its development. It is recommended that the cabinet secretary spearhead reform in existing employment structures and dispute resolutions. There is a need for sports employment rules and policies on terms and conditions. These guidelines can be created through the consultation and participation of all stakeholders.

In regards to gender inequality, it is recommended that the Ministry oversee the implementation of affirmative action policies in governance. The Ministry should also manage employment to ensure equitable representation of all genders in sport and administrative positions.

Further, there is need for documentation and reporting of a sports disputes resolution. Sports organizations have their own internal dispute resolution mechanisms. When the parties are dissatisfied, they have the right to appeal to the Tribunal or higher court. There is also the option of appealing to the CAS if an agreement exists between the parties. Publishing such information will assist in research development and jurisprudence of sports law in Kenya. There is limited accessible information on sports governance and regulation of sport in Kenya. Therefore, it is a challenge to implement the law.

In relation to corruption challenges, current law on combating corruption faces substantial constraints in investigating cases linked to corruption due to the unique nature of sports events and activities. Existing law must be amended to factor in this inadequacy. There is also a need for synchronization and co-operation between stakeholders, including sports governing bodies, government agencies, and legal experts. These groups should develop policies and standards to combat and prevent corruption.

In addition, awareness and compliance with international standards is key to promoting governance and preventing sports corruption. The United Nations Corruption and Economic Crime Branch Division for Treaty Affairs, for instance, has published several documents to guide nations in combating corruption in competitions and related fields of sports). Although Kenya is a party to the United Nations Convention against Corruption, there is still a need to focus on corruption in sports as a specific sector.

REFERENCES

Akech, M. (2008, December 21). *The Maurice Odumbe Investigation and Judicial Review of the Power of International Sports Organizations*. Retrieved December 22, 2017, from https://www.entsportslawjournal.com/articles/10.16997/eslj.58/print/

Aketch, B. (n.d.). *Public Regulation of Sport in Kenya*. Retrieved from https://www.academia.edu/6649922/Public_Regulation_of_Sports_in_Kenya?auto=download

Anti-Corruption and Economic Crimes Act, 2003.(2003).

Anti-Doping Act, No. 5 of 2016.(2016).

BetMoran. (2017, December 11). *List of All Registered Sports Betting Companies in Kenya*. Retrieved December 22, 2017, from https://betmoran.co.ke/list-all-registered-sports-betting-companies-kenya/

Betting, Lotteries and Gaming Act Chapter 131 Laws of Kenya (revised edition, 2016).

Blackshaw, I. S., & Siekmann, R. C. R. (Eds.). (2005). *Sports image rights in Europe*. The Hague, The Netherlands: T.M.C. Asser Press. doi:10.1007/978-90-6704-541-4

Chebet, S. (2014). *Evaluation of knowledge, attitudes and practices of doping among elite middle and long distance runners in Kenya* (Doctoral dissertation). Kenyatta University, Nairobi, Kenya.

Elias, N. (1971). The genesis of sport as a sociological problem. In E. Dunning (Ed.), *The sociology of sport: A selection of readings* (pp. 88–115). London, UK: CASS.

Government of the Republic of Kenya. (2013). *Sector plan for gender youth and vulnerable groups 2013-2017.* Retrieved from http://www.mtp3.go.ke/portal/data/apis/uploads/site/downloads/SECTOR%20PLAN%20FOR%20GENDER%20 YOUTH%20AND%20VULNERABLE%20GROUPS%202013-2017.pdf

Kamenju, J. W., Ritaungu, E. G., & Mwangi, F. M. (2016, December). Development of physical education and sports in Kenya in the 21stcentury: An early appraisal. *The Russian Journal of Physical Education and Sport (Pedagogical-Psychological and Medico-Biological Problems of Physical Culture and Sports, 11*(4). Retrieved from https://www.researchgate.net/publication/312222192_DEVELOPMENT_OF_PHYSICAL_EDUCATION_AND_SPORTS_IN_KENYA_IN_THE_21ST_CENTURY_AN_EARLY_

Kanyi, M. W. (2017). *Kenya women's journey in their quest for affirmative action.* Retrieved from https://ke.boell.org/sites/default/files/uploads/2016/06/gender_briefs_-_wambui_kanyi.pdf

Kenya Law Reports. (2007). *Employment Act.* National Council for Law Reporting.

Kenya Law Reports. (2010). *Constitution of Kenya.* National Council for Law Reporting.

Kenya National Bureau of Statistics. (2011). *Kenya facts 2011.* Retrieved from https://www.knbs.or.ke/download/kenya-facts-2011/

Koigi, B. (2016, October 14). *Kenya's betting craze leaves trail of destruction.* Retrieved December 22, 2017, from https://www.google.co.ke/search?source=hp&ei=BKU8WoqZLMSasAfdiZX4Cw&q=betting%2Bin%2Bsports%2Bpros%2Band%2Bcons&oq=BETTING%2BIN%2BSPORTS&gs_l=psy-ab.1.7.0l3j0i22i30k1l7.171091.175159.0.180494.18.12.0.0.0.0.665.1575.0j1j1j0j1j1.4.0....0...1c.1.64.psy-ab.14.4.1573.0...0.WuMOvrTAu30

Korir, P. (2017, February 08). *FIFPRO Report exposes the good and bad side of Kenyan football.* Retrieved December 22, 2017, from http://www.soka.co.ke/news/item/fifpro-report-exposes-the-good-and-bad-side-of-kenyan-football

Korir, W. (2015). Impact of Sports on Economic Development in Kenya. *International Journal of Advanced Research, 3*(5). Retrieved from http://www.journalijar.com/uploads/441_IJAR-5804.pdf

Majani, E. (2013, November 8). *Termination of a player contract in football with 'just cause' and 'sporting just cause'*. Retrieved from http://superfoota.co.ke/termination-of-a-player-contract-in-football-with-just-cause-and-sporting-just-cause/

Mikinyango, A. (2017). *Sports image rights in Kenya* (Unpublished master's thesis). University of Nairobi, Nairobi, Kenya.

Mukul, M. (2011). *Law & Sports in India*. Haryana, India: LexisNexis.

Mutuku, F. M. (2013). *The Regulatory Regime Governing the Casino Industry in Kenya: A Need for Reforms* (Unpublished master's thesis). University of Nairobi.

Mwisukha, A., Njororai, W. W. S., & Onywera, V. (2003). Contributions of sports towards national development in Kenya. *East African Journal of Physical Education*, *1*(2), 71–83. Retrieved from http://humansciences.ku.ac.ke/images/stories/2016/contribution%20of%20sports%20towards%20national%20development.pdf

Mwisukha, A., & Ritangu, E. G. (2013). Insights into the under representation of women in sports leadership in Kenya. *International Journal of Applied Sociology*, *3*(5), 102. doi:10.5923/j.ijas.20130305.02

Ndege, P. O. (2009). *Colonialism and its legacies in Kenya*. Lecture presented at the Fulbright–Hays Group Project Abroad Program, Moi University Main Campus, Kenya. Retrieved from http://africanphilanthropy.issuelab.org/resources/19699/19699.pdf

Noll, R. G. (2003). The organization of sports leagues. *Oxford Review of Economic Policy*, *19*(4), 530–551. doi:10.1093/oxrep/19.4.530

Nteere, J. S. (n.d.). *The structure and organisation of sport in Kenya and Malawi: A comparative analysis*. Retrieved from http://erepository.uonbi.ac.ke:8080/bitstream/handle/11295/32574/Nteere_The%20structure%20and%20organisation%20of%20sport%20%20in%20Kenya%20and%20Malawi.pdf?sequence=1&isAllowed=y

Obonyo, M. O. (2013). Financing sports in Kenya: A case of Kenya basketball federation. *Prime Journals, 3*(8), 1161-1170. Retrieved from https://www.primejournal.org/BAM/pdf/2013/aug/Mark.pdf

Onsongo, J. (2009). Affirmative action, gender equity and university admissions – Kenya, Uganda and Tanzania. *London Review of Education*, *7*(1), 71–81. doi:10.1080/14748460802700710

PricewaterhouseCoopers Limited (PWC). (2013). *Kenyan entertainment and media outlook: 2013-2017*. Retrieved from https://www.pwc.com/ke/en/assets/pdf/entertainment-and-media-outlook.pdf

Republic v Kenya Cricket Association & 2 others (HIGH COURT OF KENYA May 25, 2006) (EKLR, Dist. file).

Rintaugu, E. G., Mwisukha, A., & Munayi, S. (2011). *Sports: On the right track*. Retrieved from http://irlibrary.ku.ac.ke/bitstream/handle/123456789/13539/sports%20on%20the%20right%20track.pdf?sequence=1&isAllowed=y

Sports Act 2013. (2013).

Synodinou, T. (2014). Image right and copyright law in Europe: Divergences and convergences. *Laws*, *3*(2), 181–207. doi:10.3390/laws3020181

The National Olympic Committee Kenya. (2017, August 29). *The Organisation*. Retrieved December 22, 2017, from https://www.olympic.org/about-ioc-institution

Transparency International Kenya. (2016). *Global corruption report: Sport* (Issue 160). Retrieved from https://tikenya.org/wp-content/uploads/2017/06/adili-issue-160_corruption-in-sport.pdf

United Nations. (2007, December). Women, gender equality and sports. *Women 2000 and Beyond.* Retrieved from http://www.un.org/womenwatch/daw/public/Women%20and%20Sport.pdf

Wamaitha, J. K. (2015). *Gender representation in sports participation and leadership in teacher training colleges in the eastern zone-Kenya* (Master's thesis). Kenyatta University, Nairobi, Kenya.

Wekesa, M. (2010). *Regulation of doping in sports: Implications for Kenya (Doctoral dissertation)*. Nairobi, Kenya: University of Nairobi. Retrieved from http://erepository.uonbi.ac.ke

KEY TERMS AND DEFINITIONS

Bookmarker: A person who receives or negotiates bets on behalf of others.

Contract: A binding agreement between two or more parties that is enforceable by courts.

Corruption: Impairment of integrity, values and morals in performance of office functions.

Gender Inequality: Unequal treatment of women due to their gender.

Sports: Types of physical activity for leisure or competitive participation.

Sports Betting: Predicting sports results and placing a bet on the outcome to win money.

Sports Image Rights: Sports person's right to exclusively commercialization of their name and personal attributes.

Sports Law: Laws, regulations, regulations, policies, and rules that govern sports and sports persons.

Compilation of References

Aarseth, E. (2007). Doors and Perception: Fiction vs. Simulation in Games. *Intermédialités*, *9*, 35–44.

Ahdar, R., & Leigh, I. (2013). *Religious Freedom in the Liberal State* (2nd ed.). Oxford, UK: Oxford University Press.

Akech, M. (2008, December 21). *The Maurice Odumbe Investigation and Judicial Review of the Power of International Sports Organizations*. Retrieved December 22, 2017, from https://www.entsportslawjournal.com/articles/10.16997/eslj.58/print/

Aketch, B. (n.d.). *Public Regulation of Sport in Kenya*. Retrieved from https://www.academia.edu/6649922/Public_Regulation_of_Sports_in_Kenya?auto=download

Alekseev, S. (2002). Legal regulation of sports sponsorship. *Sports: Economics, Law, Management, 4*.

Almond, L. (2000). Physical Education and Primary Schools. In R. Bailey & T. Macfadyen (Eds.), Teaching Physical Education 5-11 (pp. 3-13). London: Continuum.

American Needle, Inc. vs. National Football League, 560 U.S. 183 (2010).

American Psychological Association. (2011, August 29). *Playing highly competitive video games may lead to aggressive behavior*. Retrieved March 1, 2018 from www.sciencedaily.com/releases/2011/08/110829114714.htm

Anastasopoulos, A. (2018, February 5). *German Coalition Parties to Recognize Esports as Sports*. Retrieved March 01, 2018, from https://esportsobserver.com/german-parties-recognize-esports/

Andrews, D. L., & Grainger, A. D. (2007). Sport and globalization. In G. Ritzer (Ed.), *The Blackwell companion to globalization* (pp. 478–497). Malden, MA: Blackwell Publishing.

Anti-Corruption and Economic Crimes Act, 2003.(2003).

Anti-Doping Act, No. 5 of 2016.(2016).

Antinori, P., & Blackman, R. J. (2017, July 25). Contextualization of a shifting perspective regarding the steroid era. *The Sport Journal*. Retrieved from: http://thesportjournal. org/article/contextualization-of-a-shifting-perspective-regarding-the-steroid-era/

Archer, C. (2001). *International Organizations* (3rd ed.). London: Routledge. doi:10.4324/9780203192276

ARD Broadcaster informed about new doping violations in the Russian sport. (n.d.). Retrieved March 21, 2016, from http://www.newsru.com/sport/07

Armstrong, K., Chinese, V., & Brown, S. R. (2012, December 3). Jovan Belcher leaves grisly car evidence of mayhem that preceded his shocking suicide. *New York Daily News*. Retrieved from http://www.nydailynews.com/news/national/jovan-belcher-death-car-article-1.1212182

Associated Press. (2009, November 18). Survey: Concussions inevitable. *Associated Press*. Retrieved from http://sports.espn.go.com/nfl/news/story?id=4668106

Associated Press. (2015, January 28). Youth concussion laws lack bite. *Associated Press*. Retrieved from http://www.espn.com/nfl/story/_/id/12242612/youth-concussion-laws-pushed-nfl-lack-bite-according-associated-press-analysis

Asthma and Sport. Out speak about sport. (n.d.). Retrieved December 20, 2013, from http://stop-asthma.ru/astma-i-sport

Auxent, A. (2016, February 09). *Mega Gamer Brasil and other tournaments that fail to pay out prizes are dragging esports down*. Retrieved March 01, 2018, from https://esportsobserver.com/dragging-esports-down/

Badalov, D., Vasilenkova, I., Kartashov, N., Kotov, S., & Nikitina, I. (2011). *Commentaries to the Federal Law of 13.03.2006 number 38-FZ "On Advertising"*. Retrieved April 29, 2016, from http://fas.gov.ru/documents/documentdetails.html?id=998

Badenhausen, K. (2015, October 11). The NFL players who make the most from endorsements. *Forbes*. Retrieved from https://www.forbes.com/sites/kurtbadenhausen/2015/10/11/the-nfl-players-who-make-the-most-from-endorsements/#7f98a2f26277

Badenhausen, K. (2016, September 14). The NFL's highest-paid players 2016. *Forbes*. Retrieved from https://www.forbes.com/sites/kurtbadenhausen/2016/09/14/the-nfls-highest-paid-players-2016/#4fad780a3642

Bannon, J. J., & Bannon, L. B. (1987). The insurance crisis: A dilemma for parks and recreation. In J. J. Bannon (Ed.), *Current issues in leisure services: Looking ahead in a time of transition*. Washington, DC: International City Management.

Barber, G. (2005). *Getting Started in Track and Field Athletics: Advice & Ideas for Children, Parents and Teachers*. Victoria, BC: Trafford Publishing.

Battaglio, S., & James, M. (2017, February 6). Super Bowl's TV ratings slip for the second straight year. *Los Angeles Times*. Retrieved from http://www.latimes.com/business/hollywood/la-fi-ct-super-bowl-ratings-20170206-story.html

Berr, J. (2016, September 8). Are you ready to make some moola? NFL remains a financial powerhouse. *Moneywatch*. Retrieved from https://www.cbsnews.com/news/the-nfls-financial-juggernaut-is-decades-in-the-making/

Berr, J. (2017). Sliding NFL ratings could throw networks for a loss. *Moneywatch*. Retrieved from https://www.cbsnews.com/news/sliding-nfl-ratings-could-throw-networks-for-a-loss/

Berthaud, G., Brohm, J.-M., Gantheret, F., & Laguillaumie, P. (1972). *Sport, Sport, Culture et Répression*. Paris: Libraire François Maspero.

BetMoran. (2017, December 11). *List of All Registered Sports Betting Companies in Kenya*. Retrieved December 22, 2017, from https://betmoran.co.ke/list-all-registered-sports-betting-companies-kenya/

Betting, Lotteries and Gaming Act Chapter 131 Laws of Kenya (revised edition, 2016).

Bevir, M. (2009). *Key Concepts in Governance*. London: SAGE Publications Ltd.

Bianco, J. (1994). The dawn of a new standard? Assumption of risk doctrine in a post- Knight California. *Whittier Law Review*, (15), 1155–1192.

Blackman, R. (2002). *Ethics and the historical development of comparative fault tort reform as applied in reported sports and recreation cases* (Unpublished doctoral dissertation). Indiana University.

Blackshaw, I. S., & Siekmann, R. C. R. (Eds.). (2005). *Sports image rights in Europe*. The Hague, The Netherlands: T.M.C. Asser Press. doi:10.1007/978-90-6704-541-4

Blanchard, K. (1995). *The Anthropology of Sport: An Introduction*. Westport, CT: Greenwood Publishing Group.

Bloomberg News. (2015). Nike makes the most of its NFL gear with sales to fans. *Bloomberg News*. Retrieved from http://www.oregonlive.com/playbooks-profits/index.ssf/2015/12/post_87.html

Bombela, I. (2008). *Anabolic steroids: elimination of illiteracy 2*. Retrieved February 21, 2012 from http://steroid.su/anabolicheskie-steroidy-likvidaciya-negramotnosti-2

Boorman, P. (1996). The Contributions of Physical Activity to Development in the Early Years. In G. M. Blenkin & A. V. Kelly (Eds.), *Early Childhood Education: A Developmental Curriculum* (2nd ed.; pp. 218–235). London: Paul Chapman Publishing Ltd.

Borisova, T., & Morozov, G. (2011). *Unfair Games*. Retrieved November 12, 2014, from http://rormistr2011.foxibiz.com

Boston University CTE Center. (2017). *VA-BU-CLF Brain Bank: Case studies*. Retrieved from https://www.bu.edu/cte/our-research/brain-bank/

Bourg, J.-F. (2004). Les sports collectifs professionnels en Europe: Quel modèle économique? In J.-J. Gouguet (Ed.), *Le sport professionnel après l'arrêt Bosman: Une analyse économique internationale* (pp. 43–60). Limoges, France: Presses Universitaires de Limoges.

Bowra, C. M. (1971). *Pindar* (2nd ed.). Oxford, UK: Clarendon.

Boyd, J. (2017, January 17). Who are the highest paid NFL head coaches & what are their salaries. *BoydsBets.com*. Retrieved from https://www.boydsbets.com/highest-paid-coaches-nfl/

Brautigam, T. (2016, November 11). *Esports needs to face its injury problem*. Retrieved March 01, 2018, from http://esportsobserver.com/esports-needs-face-injury-problem/

Brautigam, T. (2017). *Esports comes to the second largest multi-sports event in the world*. Retrieved 28 October, 2017 from https://dotesports.com/business/esports-asian-games-14151

Bray, J. (2016, August 15). *ESports Is Getting Big, And Here's The Scandals To Prove It*. Retrieved March 01, 2018, from https://supernerdland.com/article/esports-getting-big-heres-scandals-prove/

Bremmer, R. H. (Ed.). (1974). Children & Youth in America: A Documentary History, Volume III: 1933-1973, Parts 5-7. Cambridge, MA: Harvard University Press.

Breslow, J. M. (2013, October 6). The autopsy that changed football. *PBS.org*. Retrieved from http://www.pbs.org/wgbh/frontline/article/the-autopsy-that-changed-football/

Brief doping history in sport. (n.d.). Retrieved March 2, 2014, from http://zmix.ru/food/chemistry/articles-doping/item

Brooks, B. (2011, August 10). How practice changes could negatively impact NFL games. *NFL.com*. Retrieved from http://www.nfl.com/trainingcamp/story/09000d5d8215c8ab/article/how-practice-changes-could-negatively-impact-nfl-games

Brown, D. L. (2017). *They didn't #TakeTheKnee: The Black Power protest salute that shook the world in 1968*. Retrieved 26 October, 2017 from www.washingtonpost.com/news/retropolis/wp/2017/09/24/they-didnt-takeaknee-the-black-power-protest-salute-that-shook-the-world-in-1968/?utm_term=.1cc199b070c6

Brusnikina, O., & Peskov A. (2014). The causes and conditions that facilitate the spread of doping in professional sports. *Law and the State: Theory and Practice, 10*(118).

Brusnikina, O., & Peskov A., (2014). Legal problems of the fight against doping in professional sports. *Law and the State: Theory and Practice, 9*(117).

Brusnikina, O., & Peskov A., (2014). The practice of doping. *National interests priorities and safety, 31.*

Brustein, J., & Novy-Williams, E. (2016). *Virtual weapons are turning teen gamers into serious gamblers*. Retrieved March 01, 2018, from https://www.bloomberg.com/features/2016-virtual-guns-counterstrike-gambling/

Brysk, A. (2002). Introduction. In A. Brysk (Ed.), *Globalization and Human Rights* (pp. 1–16). Berkley, CA: University of California Press.

Buckley v. Tutty [1971] HCA 71; (1971) 125 CLR, 353.

Burk, D. L. (2013). Owning E-sports: Proprietary Rights in Professional Computer Gaming. *University of Pennsylvania Law Review, 161*, 1535–1578.

Butler, G. D. (1976). *Introduction to community recreation* (5th ed.). New York, NY: McGraw-Hill.

Byers, T., Slack, T., & Parent, M. (2012). *Key Concepts in Sport Management*. Thousand Oaks, CA: SAGE Publications. doi:10.4135/9781473914599

Caillois, R. (1961). *Man, Play, and Games* (M. Barash, Trans.). Chicago, IL: University of Illinois Press.

Calleja, G. (2011). *In-game: From Immersion to Incorporation*. Cambridge, MA: The MIT Press.

Calleja, G. (2012). Erasing the Magic Circle. *Philosophy of Engineering and Technology*, *7*, 77–91. doi:10.1007/978-94-007-4249-9_6

Carpenter, L. (2007, June 20). Compromise reigns at summit on concussions. *Washington Post*. Retrieved from http://www.washingtonpost.com/wp-dyn/content/article/2007/06/19/AR2007061902157.html

Carr, D. (1998). What Moral Educational Significance has Physical Education? A Question in need of Disambiguation. In M. J. McNamee & S. J. Parry (Eds.), Ethics & Sport. London: E & FN Spon.

Case C-519/04P David Meca Medina and Igor Majcen v. Commission (2006) ECR I-6991.

Chapman, B. (2016). Rio 2016: The Richest Games in 120 Years of Olympic History. *Independent*. Retrieved January 22, 2018 from http://www.independent.co.uk/news/business/analysis-and-features/rio-2016-olympic-games-richest-ever-usain-bolt-mo-farah-a7171811.html

Chapple, J. (2012). *International Olympic Committee and Olympic system. Management of world sport*. Moscow: Publishing House Rid Media.

Chatzigianni, E. (2014). Pluralism and Corporatism in Sport Interest Representation. *International Journal of Sport Policy and Politics*, *6*(1), 19–36. doi:10.1080/19406940.2012.694114

Chatzigianni, E. (2017). Global Sport Governance: Globalizing the Globalized. *Sport in Society*, 1–29. doi:10.1080/17430437.2017.1390566

Chatzigianni, E. (2018). *Sport Governance. Globalization, International Organization, Politics*. Athens: Sideris. (in Greek)

Chebet, S. (2014). *Evaluation of knowledge, attitudes and practices of doping among elite middle and long distance runners in Kenya* (Doctoral dissertation). Kenyatta University, Nairobi, Kenya.

Chryssafis, J. E. (1930). Aristotle on Physical Education. *The Journal of Health and Physical Education*, *7*, 3–19.

Closius, P. J. (1985). Professional Sports and Antitrust Laws: The Ground Rules of Immunity, Exemption, and Liability. In A. T. Johnson & J. H. Frey (Eds.), *Government and Sport: The Public Policy Issues* (pp. 140–161). Totowa, NJ: Rowman & Allanheld.

Comité national olympique et sportif français. (2006). *Les incidences du droit communautaire sur le sport. Brochure d'information*. Retrieved April 29, 2016, from http://centre.franceolympique.com/centre/fichiers/File/brochure_impact_ue_sport_2005.pdf

Commission of the European Communities. (1999). *Report from the Commission of the European Communities to the European Council with a view to safeguarding current sports structures and maintaining the social function of sport within the Community framework Nº COM (1999) 644 final of 10.12.1999*. Retrieved April 29, 2016, from http://eur-lex.europa.eu/LexUriServ/LexUriServ.do?uri=COM:1999:0644:FIN:EN:PDF

Commission on Global Governance (Report). (1995). *Our Global Neighborhood. Report on Global Governance*. Retrieved 10 January, 2018 from http://www.gdrc.org/u-gov/global-neighbourhood/chap1.htm

Committee of Ministers of the Council of Europe. (2001). *Recommendation Nº R (92) 14 REV of the Committee of Ministers to member states on the revised Code of sports ethics (adopted by the Committee of Ministers on 24 September 1992 at the 480th meeting of the Ministers' Deputies and revised at their 752nd meeting on 16 May 2001)*. Retrieved April 29, 2016, from https://search.coe.int/cm/Pages/result_details.aspx?ObjectID=09000016804cf400

Competition and Consumer Act (2010). Retrieved from https://www.comlaw.gov.au/Details/C2015C00327

Concussion Legacy Foundation. (2015, September 3). Sports Legacy Institute announces rebrand to Concussion Legacy Foundation. *Concussion Legacy Foundation*. Retrieved from https://concussionfoundation.org/about/media/press-releases/sports-legacy-institute-announces-rebrand-concussion-legacy-foundation

Conditt, J. (2017, July 6). *How League of Legends can shape the future of esports*. Retrieved March 01, 2018, from https://www.engadget.com/2017/07/04/league-legends-esports-lcs-changes-dignitas-liquid-immortals/

Consolidated versions of the Treaty on European Union and the Treaty on the Functioning of the European Union. (2012). *Official Journal, C 326*, 0001 – 0390. Retrieved April 29, 2016, from http://eur-lex.europa.eu/legal-content/en/TXT/?uri=CELEX:12012E/TXT

Cosgrove, B. (2014). *The Black Power Salute That Rocked the 1968 Olympics.* Retrieved 28 October, 2017 from http://time.com/3880999/black-power-salute-tommie-smith-and-john-carlos-at-the-1968-olympics/

Cotten, D. J. (2013). Liability of sports participants, sports instructors, and sports officials. In D. J. Cotten & J. T. Wolohan (Eds.), *Law for recreation and sport managers* (6th ed.). Dubuque, IA: Kendall-Hunt.

Council of Europe. (1989). *European Convention on Transfrontier Television, Strasbourg, 05.V.1989*. Retrieved April 29, 2016, from http://www.coe.int/ru/web/conventions/full-list/-/conventions/rms/090000168007b0d8, https://rm.coe.int/CoERMPublicCommonSearchServices/DisplayDCTMContent?documentId=090000168007b0fa

Council of Europe. (2001). *Recommendation No. R (92) 13 REV of the Committee of Ministers to Member States on the Revised European Sports Chapter.* Retrieved January 21, 2018 from https://search.coe.int/cm/Pages/result_details.aspx?ObjectID=09000016804c9dbb

Cousens, L., & Bradish, C. (2012). Sport and Sponsorship. In L. Trenberth & D. Hassan (Eds.), *Managing Sport Business: An Introduction* (pp. 264–284). London: Routledge.

Cousens, L., & Slack, T. (2005). Field-level change: The case of North American major league professional sport. *Journal of Sport Management, 19*(1), 13–42. doi:10.1123/jsm.19.1.13

Crawn v. Campo, 136 N.J. 494 A.2d 600 (1994).

Dailey, R. A. (2006, January 30). Steel Curtain seeks heavenly help. *Pittsburgh Post-Gazette*. Retrieved from http://www.post-gazette.com/ruth-ann-dailey/2006/01/30/Steel-Curtain-seeks-heavenly-help/stories/200601300146

Darcy, K. (2017, July 6). *Why the Associated Press Stylebook went with esports, not eSports*. Retrieved March 01, 2018, from http://www.espn.com/esports/story/_/id/19860473/why-associated-press-stylebook-went-esports-not-esports

Davis, D. (2008). *Olympic Athletes Who Took a Stand.* Retrieved 27 October, 2017 from www.smithsonianmag.com/articles/olympic-athletes-who-took-a-stand-593920/

Davis, T. (2001). What is Sports Law? *Marquette Sports Law Review, 11*, 211–244.

Delsohn, S. (2014, September 30). OTL: Belcher's brain had CTE signs. *ESPN.com*. Retrieved from http://www.espn.com/espn/otl/story/_/id/11612386/jovan-belcher-brain-showed-signs-cte-doctor-says-report

Derevoidov, A. (2012). Fight against doping: innovative approaches to testing planning. *Bulletin of RMOU, 2*.

Dichter, H., & Kidd, B. (Eds.). (2012). *Olympic Reform Ten Years Later*. London: Routledge.

Dingwerth, K. & Pattberg, P. (2006). Global Governance as a Perspective on World Politics. *Global Governance: A Review of Multilateralism and International Organizations, 12*(2), 185-203.

Dombrowski, D. A. (1979). Plato and Athletics. *Journal of the Philosophy of Sport, VI*(1), 29–38. doi:10.1080/00948705.1979.10654148

Donati, A. (2007). *World Traffic in Doping Substances*. Montreal: WADA.

Donchenko, Y. (2016, December 14). *Which countries have just recognized eSports list*. Retrieved March 01, 2018, from https://cybbet.com/news/2973-Which-countries-have-just-recognized-eSports-List

Donovan, T. (2010). *Replay: The History of Video Games*. East Sussex, UK: Yellow Ant.

Drenon, T. (2013, October 8). Mike Webster autopsy 'one of the most significant moments in the history of sports.' *Behind the Steel Curtain*. Retrieved from https://www.behindthesteelcurtain.com/2013/10/8/4814434/concussion-suit-mike-webster-thing

Dzhusoyti, A. (2001). *Oh, sport, you are the syringe. The informal Doping World Cup continues*. Retrieved May 8, 2012, from http://www.compromat.ru/page_24442.htm

Eckhardt, J. (2015). *Business Lobbying and Trade Governance, The Case of EU - China Relations*. Houndmills, UK: Palgrave MacMillan. doi:10.1057/9781137325440

ECtHR Dogru vs. France, application no. 27058/05.

ECtHR Folgero and Others vs. Norway, application no. 15472/02.

ECtHR Hasan and Claush vs. Bulgaria, application no. 30985/96.

ECtHR Kervanci vs. France, application no. 31645/04. ECtHR Kjeldsen, Busk Madsen and Pedersen vs. Denmark, application no. 5095/71, 5920/72, 5926/72.

ECtHR Kokkinakis vs. Greece, application no. 14307/88.

ECtHR Osmanoglu and Kocabas vs. Switzerland, application no. 29086/12.

Efimova, I. (2014). *Preparation with dope is my mistake*. Retrieved from May 20, 2014, from http://summer.sport-express.ru/aquatics/reviewrs/44482

Ehrmann, J., Lewis, C., & Lewis, P. (1968). Homo Ludens Revisited (C. Lewis & P. Lewis, Trans.). *Yale French Studies*, *41*(41), 31–57. doi:10.2307/2929664

Elden, S. (2004). *Understanding Henri Lefebvre: Theory and the Possible*. New York: Continuum.

Elias, N. (1971). The genesis of sport as a sociological problem. In E. Dunning (Ed.), *The sociology of sport: A selection of readings* (pp. 88–115). London, UK: CASS.

Engber, D. (2012, May 9). The concussion panic. Why are we so convinced that football head injuries lead to suicide? *Slate*. Retrieved from http://www.slate.com/articles/health_and_science/science/2012/05/junior_seau_s_suicide_are_concussions_responsible_.html

Entertainment Newsweekly (2008). *The Sports Network extends global reach in alliance with Contec Innovations, 18, 11 August*. Author.

Epifanov, V. (Ed.). (2006). *Sports medicine: study guide*. Moscow: TEOTAR-Media.

ESPN.com news services (2012, May 3). Junior Seau dies at 43. *ESPN.com*. Retrieved from http://www.espn.com/nfl/story/_/id/7882750/junior-seau-former-san-diego-charger-found-dead-cops-probe-suicide

ESPN.com News Services. (2007, January 19). Pathologist says Waters' brain tissue had deteriorated. *ESPN.com*. Retrieved from http://www.espn.com/nfl/news/story?id=2734941

ESports Heaven. (n.d.). *Twitch, AdBlock, and the Tragedy of the Commons*. Retrieved March 01, 2018, from http://www.esportsheaven.com/articles/view/5207/twitch-adblock-and-the-tragedy-of-the-commons

EU4Sports Cluster Alliance. (2014). *Guide on EU funding for sports industry.* Retrieved November 15, 2017 from https://www.clustercollaboration.eu/sites/default/files/profile-article/guide_on_eu_funding_for_sports_industry_2014_-2020_.pdf

European Commission. (2008). *Definition of Sport (Vilnius Definition 2.0 – Version 2) according to CPA 2008.* Retrieved December 2, 2017 from http://ec.europa.eu/eurostat/documents/6921402/0/Vilnius+Definition+Sport+CPA2008+official+2013_09_19.pdf/30838d11-01ea-431f-8112-50786e187c1c

European Parliament. (2007). *Resolution of 13 November 2007 on the Role of Sports in Education.* Retrieved January 10, 2018, from http://www.europarl.europa.eu/sides/getDoc.do?type=TA&language=EN&reference=P6-TA-2007-503

Executive Committee and Board of Founders of WADA are going to present the final version of Code 2015. (n.d.). Retrieved January 1, 2016, from http://www.rusada.ru/print/5269

Ezell, L. (2013, October 8). Timeline: The NFL's concussion crisis. *Frontline.* Retrieved from http://www.pbs.org/wgbh/pages/frontline/sports/league-of-denial/timeline-the-nfls-concussion-crisis/

Fainaru, S., & Fainaru-Wada, M. (2013, January 11, 2013). In brawl for Seau brain, a proxy war over concussion science. *PBS.* Retrieved from http://www.pbs.org/wgbh/frontline/article/in-brawl-for-seau-brain-a-proxy-war-over-concussion-science/

Fainaru-Wada, M., Avila, J., & Steve Fainaru, S. (2013, January 11). Doctors: Junior Seau's brain had CTE. *ESPN.* Retrieved from http://www.espn.com/espn/otl/story/_/id/8830344/study-junior-seau-brain-shows-chronic-brain-damage-found-other-nfl-football-players

Fairs, J. R. (1968). The Influence of Plato and Platonism on the Development of Physical Education in Western Culture. *Quest, 11*(1), 14–22. doi:10.1080/00336297.1968.10519652

Farina, A. M. (1973). Legal aspects of recreation. In D. Gray & A. Pelegrino (Eds.), *Reflections on the recreation and park movement* (pp. 283–287). Long Beach, CA: William C. Brown Company.

Farzin, L. (2015). On the Antitrust Exemption for Professional Sports in the United States and Europe. *Jeffrey S. Moorad Sports Law Journal, 22*(1), 75–108.

Federal Baseball Club v. National League, 259 U.S. 200 (1922).

Fink, E. (2016). *Play as Symbol of the World and Other Writings* (I. A. Moore & C. Turner, Trans.). Bloomington, IN: Indiana University Press.

Finley, M. I., & Pleket, H. W. (1976). *The Olympic Games. The First Thousand Years*. London: Dover Publications.

Fitzgerald, G. B. (1948). *Community organization for recreation*. New York, NY: A.S. Barnes and Company.

Flood v. Kuhn, 407 U.S. 258 (1972).

Florio, M. (2017, March 6). NFL will reach $14 billion in 2017 revenue. *Pro Football Talk*. Retrieved from http://profootballtalk.nbcsports.com/2017/03/06/nfl-will-reach-14-billion-in-2017-revenue/

Forbes. (n.d.). Tom Brady: Profile. *Forbes*. Retrieved from https://www.forbes.com/profile/tom-brady/

Fortin, J. (2009). *Children's Rights and the Developing Law* (3rd ed.). Cambridge, UK: Cambridge University Press. doi:10.1017/CBO9781139168625

Foxx, C. (2016). *Video game Olympics announced for Rio*. Retrieved 28 October, 2017 from www.bbc.com/news/technology-35987839

Frasca, G. (2003). Simulation vs. Narrative: Introduction to Ludology. In M. Wolf & B. Perron (Eds.), *The Video Game Theory Reader* (pp. 221–234). New York: Routledge.

Frontier Torts Project. (2013). NFL concussions: The current situation and policy implications. *Frontier Torts Project, Harvard Law School*. Retrieved from http://learning.law.harvard.edu/frontiertorts/wp-content/uploads/2013/04/NFL-Concussions-White-Paper-2.pdf

Ganeev, T. (2015, December). The defendant in doping case got the same job in the USA. *Izvestia*, 28.

Gardiner, E. N. (1980). *Athletics of the Ancient World*. Chicago: Ares. (Original work published 1930)

Gardner, A., Iverson, G. L., & McCrory, P. (2014). Chronic traumatic encephalopathy in sport: A systematic review. *British Journal of Sports Medicine*, *48*(2), 84–90. doi:10.1136/bjsports-2013-092646 PMID:23803602

Garner, M. P., & Shuman, P. J. (1988). Sponsorships and small businesses: Conceptual, strategic, and tactical issues. *Journal of Small Business Management*, *26*(4), 44–52.

Gavett, B. E., Stern, R. A., & McKee, A. C. (2011). Chronic traumatic encephalopathy: A potential late effect of sport-related concussive and subconcussive head trauma. *Clinics in Sports Medicine*, *30*(1), 179–xi. doi:10.1016/j.csm.2010.09.007 PMID:21074091

Gavrilova, E. (2011). *Sudden death in sport*. Moscow: Soviet Sport.

German athletes will be paid for use of doping. (*2006*). Retrieved November 7, 2012, from http://lenta.ru/news/2006/12/13/doping

Gerrity v. Beatty, 373 N. E. 2d 1323 (1978 Ill.).

Glass, B. D., Maddox, W. T., & Love, B. C. (2013). Real-Time Strategy Game Training: Emergence of a Cognitive Flexibility Trait. *PLoS One*, *8*(8), e70350. doi:10.1371/journal.pone.0070350 PMID:23950921

Goggaki, K. (2002). The Wreath of Athletic Victory and Its moral Symbolism. *International Journal of Physical Education (Muzaffarnagar)*, *39*(4), 32–38.

Goggaki, K. (2004). The Athletic Victory as a Value in the Pindaric Odes. *Nikephoros*, *17*, 123–134.

Gongaki, K. (2003b). Opportunities for, and sentiments associated with, physical education and sports activities among the primary and secondary pupils population in Attica Prefecture. University of Athens study. *Antitetradia tis Ekpaidefsis, 67*, 42-48. (in Greek)

Gongaki, K. (2003a). *The Conceptions of Ancient Greeks concerning Athletics*. Athens: Typothito - G. Dardanos. (in Greek)

Gordon, M. (2003). Before 'Concussion': An inside glimpse of NFL player Mike Webster's utterly tragic final days. *Reader's Digest*. Retrieved from https://www.rd.com/health/conditions/mike-webster-brain-injury/

Gorodov, O. (2011). On legal protection of Olympic symbols. *Competition Law, 2*.

Government of thc Rcpublic of Kcnya. (2013). *Sector plan for gender youth and vulnerable groups 2013-2017*. Retrieved from http://www.mtp3.go.ke/portal/data/apis/uploads/site/downloads/SECTOR%20PLAN%20FOR%20GENDER%20YOUTH%20AND%20VULNERABLE%20GROUPS%202013-2017.pdf

Graham, B. A. (2017). *ESports to be a medal event at 2022 Asian Games*. Retrieved 24 October, 2017 from www.theguardian.com/sport/2017/apr/18/esports-to-be-medal-sport-at-2022-asian-games

Graham, B. A. (2017a, April 18). *ESports to be a medal event at 2022 Asian Games*. Retrieved March 01, 2018, from https://www.theguardian.com/sport/2017/apr/18/esports-to-be-medal-sport-at-2022-asian-games

Graham, B. A. (2017b, August 9). *ESports could be medal event at 2024 Olympics, Paris bid team says*. Retrieved March 01, 2018, from https://www.theguardian.com/sport/2017/aug/09/esports-2024-olympics-medal-event-paris-bid-committee

Grasinger, C. (2015, August 27). Meet the Mobile Virtual Player, a robotic practice dummy created to make football safer. *Mashable*. Retrieved from http://mashable.com/2015/08/27/football-mobile-virtual-player/?utm_cid=mash-com-yt-desc-link#RA1tIihUSGqg

Greene, D. [Host], & Trotter, J. [Guest] (2015, December 22). Seau's suicide helped to make concussions in football a national issue. *NPR Morning Edition* [Radio podcast]. Retrieved from http://www.npr.org/2015/12/22/460656805/junior-seaus-suicide-helped-to-make-concussions-in-football-a-national-issue

Gregory P. Neeld v. National Hockey League, 594 F.2d 1297 (9th Cir. 1979).

Grow, N. (2015). Regulating professional sports leagues. *Washington and Lee Law Review*, *72*(58), 14.

Hackbart v. Cincinnati Bengals, Inc. 444 U.S. 931 (S. Ct. 1979).

Hanna, J. M. (2012, October). Concussions may prove to be a major headache for the NFL. *New York State Bar Association (NYSBA) Journal*. Retrieved from http://www.goldbergsegalla.com/sites/default/files/uploads/JMH_ConcussionsNYSBAJournal_Oct2012.pdf

Hardy, S. (1977). Politicians, Promoters and the Rise of Sport: The Case of Ancient Greece and Rome. *Canadian Journal of History of Sport and Physical Education*, *8*(1), 1–15. doi:10.1123/cjhspe.8.1.1

Hattenstone, S. (2017, June 16). *The rise of eSports: are addiction and corruption the price of its success?* Retrieved March 01, 2018, from https://www.theguardian.com/sport/2017/jun/16/top-addiction-young-people-gaming-esports

Haywood, K. M. (1991). The Role of Physical Education in the Development of Active Lifestyles. *Research Quarterly for Exercise and Sport*, *62*(2), 151–156. doi:10.1080/02701367.1991.10608705 PMID:1925038

Hecox, M. G. (2007). Strategic Alliances in the Sport Industry: A Case Review of Reebok International and the NFL. In B. G. Pitts (Ed.), *Sport Marketing in the New Millennium: Selected Papers from the Third Annual Conference of the Sport Marketing Association*. Morgantown, WV: Fitness Information Technology.

Heitner, D. (2015). *Sports Industry to reach $73.5 billion by 2019.* Retrieved November 30, 2017 from https://www.forbes.com/sites/darrenheitner/2015/10/19/sports-industry-to-reach-73-5-billion-by-2019/#33823291b4b9

Heitner, D. (2017). This week in sports law: NFL concussion lawyers ask $112M, Under Armour sued, Darrelle Revis robbery. *Forbes*. Retrieved from https://www.forbes.com/sites/darrenheitner/2017/02/19/this-week-in-sports-law-nfl-concussion-lawyers-want-112m-under-armour-sued-dykstras-firm-demand/#5b55837758c7

Henderson, B. W. (1903). *The Life and Principate of the Emperor Nero*. London: Methuen.

Henricks, T. S. (2010). Caillois's Man, Play, and Games: An Appreciation and Evaluation. *American Journal of Play*, 157–185.

Hicks, R. D. (Ed.). (1972). Diogenes Laertius. *Lives of Eminent Philosophers*. Retrieved January 2, 2018, from http://www.perseus.tufts.edu/hopper/text?doc=Perseus%3Atext%3A1999.01.0258%3Abook%3D1%3Achapter%3D1

History. (n.d.). Retrieved 28 October, 2017 from www.olympic.org/ancient-olympic-games/history

Hoosier Mountain Bike Association, Inc. City of Indianapolis, and Indy Parks and Recreation, Appellants-Defendants, v. Richard Kaler, March 23, 2017. Court of Appeals Case No. 49A04-1604-CT-865. (n.d.). Retrieved from https://www.in.gov/judiciary/opinions/pdf/ 03231701par.pdf

How to hide administration of steroids and prohibited preparations. (n.d.). Retrieved November 7, 2012, from http://sportswiki.ru

Huber, P. W. (1990). *Liability: The legal revolution and its consequences*. New York, NY: Basic Books.

Huizinga, J. (1995). The Nature of Play. In W. J. Morgan & K.V. Meier (Eds.), Philosophic Inquiry in Sport (2nd ed.). Champaign, IL: Human Kinetics Publishers. (Original work published 1950)

Huizinga, J. (1949). *Homo Ludens: A Study of the Play-Element in Culture*. London: Routledge and Kegan Paul.

International Olympic Committee. (2016). *IOC makes doping results management and sanctioning independent.* Press Release IOC. 01 March 2016.

IOC makes doping results management and sanctioning independent. (2016, March 1). Press Release IOC.

Jane Doe v. United States Youth Soccer Association, Inc., et al. H040688 February 22, 2017. (Santa Clara County Super Ct. No. CV 238994).

Jemson, T. J. (2013). *For the Love of Money, Football, and Competition Law: An analysis of whether UEFA's Financial Fair Play Regulations breach European competition law* (Dissertation submitted in partial fulfilment of the degree of Bachelor of Laws). University of Otago, Dunedin, New Zealand. Retrieved April 29, 2016, from http://www.otago.ac.nz/law/research/journals/otago065279.pdf

Jensen, C. R. (1977). *Leisure and recreation: Introduction and overview*. Philadelphia, PA: Lea & Febiger.

Johnson, E. (2015). *Video Games on ESPN? It's Time to Stop Pretending eSports Are 'Real' Sports.* Retrieved 28 October, 2017 from www.recode.net/2015/4/27/11561916/video-games-on-espn-its-time-to-stop-pretending-esports-are-real

Johnson, J. (2009, January 7). Restraint of Trade Law in Sport. *Sports Law eJournal*.

Joy, O. (2013). Manchester United pen new multi-million dollar deal. *CNN Sport*. Retrieved July 30, 2017 from http://edition.cnn.com/2013/04/08/business/manchester-united-aon-deal/index.html

Judge, A. J. N. (1978). International Institutions: Diversity, Borderline Case, Functional Substitutes and Possible Alternatives. In P. Taylor & A. J. Groom (Eds.), *International Organization* (pp. 28–83). London: Frances Pinter.

Judges, D. P. (1993). Of rocks and hard places: The value of risk choice. *Emory Law Journal*, (42): 1–142.

Kabanov A., (2014, April 12). Doping is supported in Russia at the state level. *Commersant.*

Kamenju, J. W., Ritaungu, E. G., & Mwangi, F. M. (2016, December). Development of physical education and sports in Kenya in the 21[st]century: An early appraisal. *The Russian Journal of Physical Education and Sport (Pedagogical-Psychological and Medico-Biological Problems of Physical Culture and Sports, 11*(4). Retrieved from https://www.researchgate.net/publication/312222192_DEVELOPMENT_OF_PHYSICAL_EDUCATION_AND_SPORTS_IN_KENYA_IN_THE_21ST_CENTURY_AN_EARLY_

Kane, D., & Spradley, B. (2017). Recognizing ESports as a Sport. *The Sport Journal*, 19.

Kanyi, M. W. (2017). *Kenya women's journey in their quest for affirmative action.* Retrieved from https://ke.boell.org/sites/default/files/uploads/2016/06/gender_briefs_-_wambui_kanyi.pdf

Kaplan, D. (2017). Payouts from NFL concussion deal approved; League settles with insurance companies *SportsBusiness Daily*. Retrieved from https://www.sportsbusinessdaily.com/Daily/Issues/2017/08/07/Leagues-and-Governing-Bodies/NFL-CTE-Settlement.aspx

Katz, D. R. (1995). *Just Do It. The Nike Spirit in the Corporate World.* Adams Media Corporation - Random House, Inc.

Keeton, W. P., Dobbs, D. B., Keeton, R. E., & Owens, D. G. (1984). *Prosser and Keeton on the law of torts* (5th ed.). St. Paul, MN: West Publishing.

Kelnerand, M., Harrisand, N., & Stewart, W. (2013, November 16). Victory in our fight for Russian doping justice: Drugs, bribery and cheating no more investigation triggers official probe. *The Mail on Sunday.*

Kelso, C. (n.d.). *The Importance of Physical Education.* Retrieved January 12, 2018, from http://www.veanea.org/home/1000.htm

Kenya Law Reports. (2007). *Employment Act.* National Council for Law Reporting.

Kenya Law Reports. (2010). *Constitution of Kenya.* National Council for Law Reporting.

Kenya National Bureau of Statistics. (2011). *Kenya facts 2011.* Retrieved from https://www.knbs.or.ke/download/kenya-facts-2011/

Khachadourian v. State Of New York, 2015-039-440, New York State Court of Claims, Claim No. 121855. (n.d.). Retrieved from http://vertumnus.courts.state.ny.us/claims/html/2015-039-440.html

Khemani, R. S. (2002). *Application of competition law: exemptions and exceptions*. Geneva, Switzerland: United Nations.

Kirk, M., Gilmore, J., & Wiser, M. [Producers], Kirk, M., [Director], Jim Gilmore, J., Fainaru, S., & Fainaru-Wada, M. [Reporters]. (2013, October 8). League of denial: The NFL's concussion crisis. *PBS Frontline* [Television series]. Retrieved from http://www.pbs.org/wgbh/frontline/film/league-of-denial/

Knight v. Jewett, 11 Cal. Rptr. 2d 2 (1992b).

Knight v. Jewett, 834 P. 2d 696 (1992a).

Knobel, B. (2013). Switzerland and Religious Minorities: Legal, Political and Educational Responses. In D. M. Kirkham (Ed.), State Responses to Minority Religions (pp. 137-150). Farnham, UK: Ashgate Publishers.

Koigi, B. (2016, October 14). *Kenya's betting craze leaves trail of destruction*. Retrieved December 22, 2017, from https://www.google.co.ke/search?source=hp&ei=BKU8WoqZLMSasAfdiZX4Cw&q=betting%2Bin%2Bsports%2Bpros%2Band%2Bcons&oq=BETTING%2BIN%2BSPORTS&gs_l=psy-ab.1.7.0l3j0i22i30k1l7.171091.175159.0.180494.18.12.0.0.0.0.665.1575.0j1j1j0j1j1.4.0....0...1c.1.64.psy-ab.14.4.1573.0...0.WuMOvrTAu30

Korir, P. (2017, February 08). *FIFPRO Report exposes the good and bad side of Kenyan football*. Retrieved December 22, 2017, from http://www.soka.co.ke/news/item/fifpro-report-exposes-the-good-and-bad-side-of-kenyan-football

Korir, W. (2015). Impact of Sports on Economic Development in Kenya. *International Journal of Advanced Research, 3*(5). Retrieved from http://www.journalijar.com/uploads/441_IJAR-5804.pdf

Korngold, C., Farrell, H. M., & Fozdar, M. (2013). The National Football League and chronic traumatic encephalopathy: Legal implications. *The Journal of the American Academy of Psychiatry and the Law*, *41*, 430–436. PMID:24051597

Koslowski, J. (2017, July). Law review: Crash on challenging mountain bike trail. *Parks and Recreation Magazine*.

Kotenko, V. (2013). High performance medicine and sport. *Who is who in medicine, 5.*

Kounang, N., & Smith, S. (2014, September 30). Doctor: NFL player who killed girlfriend, self likely had CTE. *CNN*. Retrieved from http://www.cnn.com/2014/09/29/health/jovan-belcher-cte/index.html

Kouroupaki, G. (2016). *Yelena Isinbayeva: The last jump and rueful goodbye of the pole vault tsarina.* Retrieved 28 October, 2017 from www.cnn.gr/news/sports/story/43413/gelena-isinmpageva-teleytaio-alma-kai-pikro-antio-apo-tin-tsarina-ton-aitheron [in Greek].

Kowalski, K. (2015). *The rights to TV broadcast of sport events* (Master Thesis). University of Lapland, Rovaniemi, Finland. Retrieved April 29, 2016, from https://lauda.ulapland.fi/bitstream/handle/10024/62155/Kowalski.%20Karol.pdf?sequence=2

Kozmik, V. (2014). Recent marketing trends of sport in the world and in Russia. The rise of the sports industry in Russia - a consequence of the major sporting events or growth economic environment? *Naukovedenie, 4.*

Kurinoi, I. (2010). Games acceptable before Heaven. Astrel, AST.

Kuzma, J., & Shanklin, W. (1994). Corporate Sponsorship: A framework for Analysis. In P. J. Graham (Ed.), *Sport Business: Operational and Theoretical Aspects*. Madison, WI: Brown and Benchmark.

Laker, A. (2000). *Beyond the Boundaries of Physical Education: Educating Young People for Citizenship and Social Responsibility*. Oxford, UK: Routledge.

Lance or cheater. Sports hero of America was a doping king. (2012). *Lenta.ru*. Retrieved January 5, 2013, from: http://lenta.ru/articles/2012/10/16/armstrong

Lauletta, T. (2017, September 20). Another NFL receiver is publicly asking defenders to stop hitting so low. *Business Insider*. Retrieved from http://www.businessinsider.com/terrelle-pryor-dont-hit-his-knees-2017-9

Layden, T. (2003). Caught in the net. *Sports Illustrated, 98*, 46–50.

Lefebvre, H. (1991). *The Production of Space* (D. Nicholson-Smith, Trans.). Oxford, UK: Blackwell.

Legal Issues Relating to Football Head Injuries (Part I & II). Hearings before the House Judiciary Committee, Senate, 111th Cong. 111–82 (2009 & 2010).

Leino, O. T. (2012). Death Loop as a Feature. *Game Studies, 12*(2).

Lévy, P. (1998). *Becoming Virtual: Reality in the Digital Age* (R. Bononno, Trans.). New York: Plenum Trade.

Lien, T. (2014, July 31). *Number of eSports tournaments in North America set to boom this year*. Retrieved March 01, 2018, from https://www.polygon.com/2014/7/31/5953611/esports-tournaments-2014-numbers

Lindström-Rossi, L., De Waele, S., & Vaigauskaite, D. (2005, Autumn). Application of EC antitrust rules in the sport sector: An update. *Competition Policy Newsletter*, *3*, 72–77.

Liquipedia. (n.d.). *2015 Match-Fixing Scandal*. Retrieved March 01, 2018, from http://liquipedia.net/starcraft2/2015_Match-Fixing_Scandal

Litsky, F. (September 25, 2002). Mike Webster, 50, dies; Troubled football Hall of Famer. *The New York Times*. Retrieved from https://www.nytimes.com/2002/09/25/sports/mike-webster-50-dies-troubled-football-hall-of-famer.html

Longley, S. (2017, November 20). *Loot Boxes Are The New Skin Betting Battlefront In Esports*. Retrieved March 01, 2018, from https://www.esportsbettingreport.com/loot-boxes-new-skins-battlefront-esports/

Lovchev's dope: politics or shame? (n.d.). Retrieved January 25, 2016, from http:www.sport-express.ru

Lumb, D. (2015, July 31). *Anti-Doping Regulations Come To Esports: A Q&A With Electronic Sports League's Michal Blicharz*. Retrieved March 01, 2018, from https://www.fastcompany.com/3049041/anti-doping-regulations-come-to-esports-a-qa-with-electronic-sports-leagues-michal-blicha

Lumpkin, A. (2017). *Modern Sport Ethics: A Reference Handbook* (2nd ed.). Santa Barbara, CA: ABC-CLIO.

Maguire, J. A. (1999). *Global sport: Identities, societies, civilizations*. Cambridge, UK: Polity Press.

Majani, E. (2013, November 8). *Termination of a player contract in football with 'just cause' and 'sporting just cause'*. Retrieved from http://superfoota.co.ke/termination-of-a-player-contract-in-football-with-just-cause-and-sporting-just-cause/

Malinovskaya, E. (2012). *The Biological Passport of Athlete – Results and Prospects*. Collection of materials of II Russian scientific and practical conference "Doping in sport: risks, counteraction, and prevention". Moscow: RUSADA.

Mandell, R. (1984). *Sport. A Cultural History*. New York, NY: Columbia University Press.

Mannix, R., Iverson, G. L., Maxwell, B., Atkins, J. E., Zafonte, R., & Berkner, P. D. (2014). Multiple prior concussions are associated with symptoms in high school athletes. *Annals of Clinical and Translational Neurology*, *1*(6), 433–438. doi:10.1002/acn3.70 PMID:25356413

Marcuse, H. (1964). *One-Dimensional Man: Studies in the Ideology of Advanced Industrial Society*. Boston, MA: Beacon.

Martinez-Torron, J. (2012). Freedom of Religion in the European Convention on Human Rights under the Influence of Different European Traditions. In H. Zacher & M. A. Glendon (Eds.), *Universal Rights in a World of Diversity: The Case of Religious Freedom* (pp. 329-355). Vatican City: Pontifical Academy of Social Sciences.

Martland, H. S. (1928). Punch drunk. *Journal of the American Medical Association*, *91*(15), 1103–1107. doi:10.1001/jama.1928.02700150029009

Mashable News. (2015, August 27). Meet the Mobile Virtual Player, a robotic practice dummy. *Mashable News*. Retrieved from https://www.youtube.com/watch?v=Cy4Xtfe3s14

Mauco, G. (1993). *Psychanalyse et Education*. Paris: Flammarion.

Mavromati, D., & Reeb, M. (2015). *The Code of the Court of Arbitration for Sport: Commentary, Cases and Materials*. Alphen aan den Rijn: Kluwer Law International.

May, C. (2015). Who's in charge? Corporations as Institutions of Global Governance. *Palgrave Communications, 1*.

McDonald, E. (2017, April 20). *The Global Games Market Will Reach $108.9 Billion in 2017 With Mobile Taking 42%*. Retrieved March 01, 2018, from https://newzoo.com/insights/articles/the-global-games-market-will-reach-108-9-billion-in-2017-with-mobile-taking-42/

McGodrick, D. (2009). Muslim Veiling Controversies in Europe. In J. S. Nielsen (Ed.), *Yearbook of Muslims in Europe* (Vol. 1, pp. 427–474). Boston, MA: Brill. doi:10.1163/ej.9789004175051.i-562.60

McIntyre, D. A. (2017, February 6). Brady's endorsements of Under Armour and UGGs big Super Bowl winners. *24/7 Wall St.* Retrieved from http://247wallst.com/media/2017/02/06/bradys-endorsements-of-under-armour-and-uggs-big-super-bowl-winners/

Mellinger, S. (2014, September 29). Jovan Belcher's brain showed signs of CTE, according to post-mortem exam. *The Kansas City Star*. Retrieved from http://www.kansascity.com/sports/nfl/kansas-city-chiefs/article2296030.html

Melnik, T. (2012). *Legal liability and modern approaches to fight against doping* Collection of materials of II Russian scientific and practical conference "Doping in sport: risks, counteraction, and prevention". Moscow: RUSADA.

Merkacheva, E. (2013, December 10). Victory gene. MK has found out what scientific developments are used by athletes at the Olympic Games in Sochi. *Moscow Komsomol.*

Mia, E., & Garcia, B. (2013). *Fundamentals of Olympism*. Moscow: Rid Media.

Mid-South Grizzlies v. National Football League, 550 F. Supp. 558 (E.D. Pa. 1982).

Migala, D. (2000). Remember these 5 Cs to make your content shine. *Sport Business Daily Global Journal.* Retrieved January 9, 2018 from http://www.sportsbusinessdaily.com/Journal/Issues/2000/07/20000717/No-Topic-Name/Remember-These-5-C146s-To-Make-Your-Content-Shine.aspx

Mikinyango, A. (2017). *Sports image rights in Kenya* (Unpublished master's thesis). University of Nairobi, Nairobi, Kenya.

Mildronate became doping upon an initiative of the Americans. (n.d.). Retrieved December 14, 2016, from http://www.ntv.ru/novosti/1612376/

Miller, S. G. (1991). *Arete. Greek Sports from Ancient Sources* (2nd ed.). Berkeley, CA: University of California Press.

Miller, T., Lawrence, G., McKay, J., & Rowe, D. (2001). *Globalization and Sport: Playing the World.* London: SAGE.

Ministry of Sport of Russia made statement to WADA's accusations. (in press). *Sport-Express.*

Mkrtchian, V. (2012). *Doping: history and facts.* Retrieved January 29, 2014, from http://www.yerkramas.org/2012/07/05/doping-istoriya-i-fakty

Monti, M. (2001). *Competition and Sport the Rules of the game.* Speech presented at Conference on Governance in Sport, Brussels, Belgium. Retrieved April 29, 2016, from http://europa.eu/rapid/press-release_SPEECH-01-84_en.doc

Moosa, T. (2017). *Esports are real sports. It's time for the Olympic Video Games.* Retrieved 24 October, 2017 from www.theguardian.com/commentisfree/2017/aug/11/esports-olympic-video-games-ioc-gaming

Moriarty, M. (2017, May 2). At $11M, Nick Saban might be America's highest-paid sports coach in 2017. *SB Nation*. Retrieved from https://www.sbnation.com/college-football/2017/5/2/15515544/nick-saban-11-million-salary-highest-paid-sports-coach-2017

Morrow, G. (1960). *Plato's Cretan City. A Historical Interpretation of the Laws*. Princeton, NJ: Princeton University Press.

Moscow Arbitration Court. (2014). *Decision on the case number A40-184735*. Retrieved April 29, 2016, from http://solutions.fas.gov.ru/to/moskovskoe-oblastnoe-ufas-rossii/05-21-65-14

Mukul, M. (2011). *Law & Sports in India*. Haryana, India: LexisNexis.

Mull, R. F., Bayless, K. G., & Ross, C. M. (1983). *Recreational sports programming*. Palm Beach, FL: The Athletic Institution.

München, O. L. G. Urteil v. 15.01.2015 – U 1110/14. (n.d.). Retrieved April 29, 2016, from http://www.gesetze-bayern.de/Content/Document/Y-300-Z-BECKRS-B-2015-N-02086?hl=true&AspxAutoDetectCookieSupport=1

Mutuku, F. M. (2013). *The Regulatory Regime Governing the Casino Industry in Kenya: A Need for Reforms* (Unpublished master's thesis). University of Nairobi.

Mwisukha, A., Njororai, W. W. S., & Onywera, V. (2003). Contributions of sports towards national development in Kenya. *East African Journal of Physical Education*, *1*(2), 71–83. Retrieved from http://humansciences.ku.ac.ke/images/stories/2016/contribution%20of%20sports%20towards%20national%20development.pdf

Mwisukha, A., & Ritangu, E. G. (2013). Insights into the under representation of women in sports leadership in Kenya. *International Journal of Applied Sociology*, *3*(5), 102. doi:10.5923/j.ijas.20130305.02

Mykles, C. (2016, July 28). *Riot's Renegades Investigation*. Retrieved March 01, 2018, from https://www.youtube.com/watch?v=HXIcwyTutno

Nabozny v. Barnhill, 334 N. E.2d 258. (Ill. App. Ct. 1975).

Nathan, A. (2017, May 19). Tom Brady signs Aston Martin endorsement deal. *Bleacher Report*. Retrieved from http://bleacherreport.com/articles/2710577-tom-brady-signs-aston-martin-endorsement-deal

National Football Players' Concussion Injury Litigation. (2012). Plaintiff's Master Admin. Long-Form Complaint at 65, In re Nat'l Football Players' Concussion Injury Litig., No. 2:12-md-02323-AB (E.D. Pa. June 7, 2012).

Ndege, P. O. (2009). *Colonialism and its legacies in Kenya*. Lecture presented at the Fulbright–Hays Group Project Abroad Program, Moi University Main Campus, Kenya. Retrieved from http://africanphilanthropy.issuelab.org/resources/19699/19699.pdf

NEWSru.com. (2016). *ARD Broadcaster informed about new doping violations in the Russian sport*. Retrieved March 21, 2016, from http://www.newsru.com/sport/07

NFL Collective Bargaining Agreement. (2006). *NFL Collective Bargaining Agreement*. Appendix C, § 9 at 251.

NFL Collective Bargaining Agreement. (2006). *NFL Collective Bargaining Agreement*. Article XLVIII-D 88 Benefit.

Nielsen. (2017, August 17). *Nielsen Launches New Esports Business to Help Define and Quantify Value for the Competitive Gaming Market*. Retrieved March 01, 2018, from http://www.nielsen.com/eu/en/press-room/2017/nielsen-launches-new-esports-business-to-help-define-and-quantify-competitive-gaming.html

Niemcyzk v. Burleson, 538 S.W.2d 737, 740 (Mo. Ct. App. 1976).

Nintendo. (2006). *Olympic Truce*. Retrieved 28 October, 2017 from www.olympic.org/olympic-truce

Noll, R. G. (2003). The organization of sports leagues. *Oxford Review of Economic Policy*, *19*(4), 530–551. doi:10.1093/oxrep/19.4.530

North American Soccer League et al. v. National Football League, 670 F.2d 1249 (2d Cir. 1982).

North American Soccer League v. NFL, 670 F.2d 1249, 1252 (2d Cir. 1982).

Novy-Williams, E. (2015, July 20). NFL teams split $7.3 billion in revenue, Packers numbers revealed. *Bloomberg*. Retrieved from https://www.bloomberg.com/news/articles/2015-07-20/nfl-teams-split-7-3-billion-in-revenue-packers-numbers-reveal

Nteere, J. S. (n.d.). *The structure and organisation of sport in Kenya and Malawi: A comparative analysis*. Retrieved from http://erepository.uonbi.ac.ke:8080/bitstream/handle/11295/32574/Nteere_The%20structure%20and%20organisation%20of%20sport%20%20in%20Kenya%20and%20Malawi.pdf?sequence=1&isAllowed=y

NTV.ru. (2016). *Mildronate became doping upon an initiative of the Americans.* Retrieved December 14, 2016, from http://www.ntv.ru/novosti/1612376/

O' Beirne, C. (2012). Information and Communications Technology and its Use in Sport Business. In L. Trenberth & D. Hassan (Eds.), *Managing Sport Business: An Introduction* (pp. 338–349). London: Routledge.

Obonyo, M. O. (2013). Financing sports in Kenya: A case of Kenya basketball federation. *Prime Journals, 3*(8), 1161-1170. Retrieved from https://www.primejournal.org/BAM/pdf/2013/aug/Mark.pdf

Office of the Federal Antimonopoly Service in Moscow. (2016). *Resolution on administrative punishment in the case of administrative violation Nº 4-14.33-191 / 77-15.* Retrieved April 29, 2016, from http://solutions.fas.gov.ru/to/moskovskoe-ufas-rossii / 4-14-33-191-77-15

Olympic favorites starve for medals. (n.d.). Retrieved March 7, 2012, from http://sport.rbc.ru/news/5755320b9a7947102987b73d

Olympic review. All gender scandals in sports world. (n.d.). Retrieved December 2, 2015, from: http://olimpiadalife.ru/interesnye-fakty/vse-gendernye-skandaly-iz-mira-sporta.html

Olympic review. Modern doping drugs. (n.d.). Retrieved December 2, 2015, from http://olimpiadalife.ru/doping/sovremennye-dopingovye-preparaty.html

Omalu, B. I., Bailes, J., Hammers, J. L., & Fitzsimmons, R. P. (2010). Chronic traumatic encephalopathy, suicides and parasuicides in professional American athletes: The role of the forensic pathologist. *The American Journal of Forensic Medicine and Pathology, 31*(2), 130–132. doi:10.1097/PAF.0b013e3181ca7f35 PMID:20032774

Omalu, B. I., Hamilton, R. L., Kamboh, M. I., DeKosky, S. T., & Bailes, J. (2010). Chronic traumatic encephalopathy (CTE) in a National Football League Player: Case report and emerging medicolegal practice questions. *Journal of Forensic Nursing, 6*(1), 40–46. doi:10.1111/j.1939-3938.2009.01064.x PMID:20201914

Onsongo, J. (2009). Affirmative action, gender equity and university admissions – Kenya, Uganda and Tanzania. *London Review of Education, 7*(1), 71–81. doi:10.1080/14748460802700710

Opinion of Advocate General Szpunar, C-90/16 The English Bridge Union Limited v Commissioners for Her Majesty's Revenue & Customs.

Origin Systems. (1997). *Ultima Online*. Microsoft Windows.

Ourand, J. (2017, June 26). Taking the pulse of ESPN: The sports media giant is on the defensive about declining subscriber base, layoffs, and executive changes. What happened? And, what's the plan for the future? *Sport Business Journal.*

Ozanian, M. (2016, September 14). The NFL's most valuable teams 2016. *Forbes*. Retrieved from https://www.forbes.com/sites/mikeozanian/2016/09/14/the-nfls-most-valuable-teams-2016/#115df7363068

Paivinen, T. (2015, April 4). *The Fastest Growing Spectator Sport You're Not Watching*. Retrieved March 01, 2018, from https://medium.com/the-oddshot-loop/the-fastest-growing-spectator-sport-you-re-not-watching-e3fdae27b6bd

Palmer, S. (2006). *Toxic Childhood: How the Modern World Is Damaging Our Children and What We Can Do About It*. London: Orion.

Papanicolau D. (2011). Fight against doping in France. *Sport: economy, law, management, 4*.

Parlour, R. R., & Jones, L. R. (1980). Theories of psychiatric defense in workmen's compensation cases. *The Bulletin of the American Academy of Psychiatry and the Law*, *8*, 445–455. PMID:6456785

Patridge, J. (2014, June 18). *Mind game: How eSports psychology can help you win.* Retrieved March 01, 2018, from http://www.redbull.com/en/esports/stories/1331659424363/mind-game-how-esports-psychology-can-help-you-win

Pearson, D. (2016, July 6). *Prominent YouTubers revealed as owners of controversial CS:GO gambling site*. Retrieved March 01, 2018, from https://www.gamesindustry.biz/articles/2016-07-04-cs-go-gambling-scandal-deepens-as-prominent-youtubers-revealed-as-site-owners

Pervitin is a weapon of the Third Reich. (n.d.). Retrieved December 18, 2013, from http://ynik.info/2008/07/30/pervitin

Petrov, A. (in press). The former chief of RUSADA Nikita Kamaev died. *Commersant*.

Pfeijffer, I. L. (1999). *Three Aeginetan Odes of Pindar. A Commentary on Nemean V, Nemean III, and Pythian VIII*. Leiden: Brill.

Pharmacological products and other substances prohibited in sport. (n.d.). Retrieved April 21, 2012, from http://sportswiki.ru

Phillip Adamson and Others v. New South Wales Rugby League Limited and Others [1991] FCA 425; (1991) 13 Atpr 41-141; 103 ALR 319 (1991) 31 FCR 242 (1991) 38 IR 427.

Pilger, S. (2014). Why the Premier League is the most powerful league in the World. *Bleacher Report Football*. Retrieved March 2, 2018 from http://bleacherreport.com/articles/1948434-why-the-premier-league-is-the-most-powerful-league-in-the-world

Pilipenko, D. (2007). *Crime in sport*. Moscow: Geleos.

Pitts, B. G., Fielding, L. W., & Miller, L. K. (1991, June). *Sport Product-markets: A Conceptual Model*. Paper presented at the Conference of the North American Society for Sport Management, Ottawa, Canada.

Pitts, B. G., Fielding, L. W., & Miller, L. K. (1994). Industry Segmentation Theory and the Sport Industry: Developing a Sport Industry Segment Model. *Sport Marketing Quarterly*, *3*(1), 15–24.

Pleket, H. W. (1975). Games, Prizes, Athletes and Ideology. Some Aspects of the History of Sport in the Greco-Roman World. *Stadion*, *1*, 49–89.

Ponkin, I. (2013). On the question of the definition of "sport". In D. I. Rogachev, & O. A Shevchenko (Eds.), *Proceedings of the seventh International scientific-practical conference "Globalization of sport: the Olympic Games and international competitions"* (pp. 136-142). Moscow, Russia: Academic Press.

Ponkina, A. (2013). *Public administration and the autonomous institutionalization in the field of sports*. Moscow, Russia: Sports Law Commission of the Association of Lawyers of Russia, National Association of Sports Lawyers of the Russian Federation.

Ponkin, I., & Ponkina, A. (2014). Limits of State Intervention and Non-Intervention in the Sports Field. *Kutafin University Law Review*, *1*, 92–105.

Ponkin, I., & Ponkina, A. (2014a). Limits of State Intervention and Non-Intervention inthe Sports Field. *Kutafin University Law Review*, *1*, 92–105.

Ponkin, I., & Ponkina, A. (2014b). To a question about the content of the concept of "professional sport". *Laws of Russia: Experience, Analysis, and Practice*, *9*, 24–28.

Porter, M. E. (1985). *Competitive Advantage: Creating and Sustaining Superior Performance*. New York, NY: The Free Press.

President LFP knew about purchase of doping. (n.d.). Retrieved November 15, 2014, from http://rsport.ru/football/20130205/643454533.html

PricewaterhouseCoopers Limited (PWC). (2013). *Kenyan entertainment and media outlook: 2013-2017*. Retrieved from https://www.pwc.com/ke/en/assets/pdf/entertainment-and-media-outlook.pdf

Pro Football Reference. (2017). Junior Seau profile. *Pro Football Reference*. Retrieved from https://www.pro-football-reference.com/players/S/SeauJu00.htm

Prosser, W. L. (1964). *Law of torts* (3rd ed.). St. Paul, MN: West Group.

Putin against doping scandal has invoked to protect athletes from administration of the forbidden drugs. (n.d.). Retrieved January 17, 2016, from http://www.newsru.com/russia/11nov2015/putinolimp.html

Rabadi, M. H., & Jordan, B. D. (2001). The cumulative effect of repetitive concussion in sports. *Clinical Journal of Sport Medicine*, *11*(3), 194–198. doi:10.1097/00042752-200107000-00011 PMID:11495325

Radovich v. National Football League (NFL), 352 U.S. 445 (1957).

RBK Daily. (2013). *China was accused of production of doping*. Author.

Renucci, J.-F. (2005). *Article 9 of the European Convention on Human Rights: Freedom of Thought, Conscience and Religion*. Strasbourg: Council of Europe Publishing.

Report of the chief of FMBA of Russia V. V. Uiba on enlarged session of board of FMBA as of July 23, 2013. (n.d.). Retrieved November 19, 2014, from http://www.gcgie.ru/Kollegia-FMBA2013/Doklad-Kol.pdf

Report on RUSADA business in 2012. (n.d.). Retrieved November 19, 2014, from http://www.rusada.ru/about/annual_reports

Republic v Kenya Cricket Association & 2 others (HIGH COURT OF KENYA May 25, 2006) (EKLR, Dist. file).

Restatement, Second, Torts: Negligence. (1965). Restatement (Second) of Torts § 314 (1965). *American Law Institute*. Retrieved from https://www.ali.org/publications/show/torts/

Restatement, Third, Torts: Liability for Physical and Emotional Harm. (2002). Restatement (Third) of Torts § 26 (2002). *American Law Institute*. Retrieved from https://www.ali.org/publications/show/torts-liability-physical-and-emotional-harm/

Reztsova, A. (2009). *In modern sport, it is impossible without doping. That is the modern life*. Retrieved from http://www.skisport.ru/news/index.php?news=8539

Rintaugu, E. G., Mwisukha, A., & Munayi, S. (2011). *Sports: On the right track*. Retrieved from http://irlibrary.ku.ac.ke/bitstream/handle/123456789/13539/sports%20on%20the%20right%20track.pdf?sequence=1&isAllowed=y

Rizzo, F. (2001). *Le droit de la concurrence au service de la specificité sportive*. Retrieved April 29, 2016, from http://www.revuegeneraledudroit.eu/wp-content/uploads/aj20011219rizzof1.pdf

Rocca, G. (2005, Septembre). L'application des règles antitrust aux règles sportives. *L'Observateur de Bruxelles, 62*.

Role of the World Anti-Doping Agency in control of doping in sport. (n.d.). Retrieved May 17, 2014, from http://sportswiki.ru

Rothstein, M. (2017, August 29). Lions QB Matthew Stafford to become highest-paid NFL player. *ESPN*. Retrieved from http://www.espn.com/nfl/story/_/id/20491086/matthew-stafford-detroit-lions-agree-historic-5-year-deal

Rowe, D. (2009). Media and Sport: The Cultural Dynamics of Global Games. *Sociology Compass*, *3*(4), 543–558. doi:10.1111/j.1751-9020.2009.00225.x

Rozelle, W. M. (2016, May 9). *Competitive Ruling: Renegades and TDK*. Retrieved March 01, 2018, from https://www.lolesports.com/en_US/articles/competitive-ruling-renegades-and-tdk

Rudd, N. (1991). *Juvenal: The Satires*. Oxford, UK: Oxford University Press.

Rusada. (2015). *Executive Committee and Board of Founders of WADA are going to present the final version of Code 2015*. Retrieved January 1, 2016, from http://www.rusada.ru/print/5269

Russ, J. (1995). *L'Aventure de la Pensée Européenne. Une Histoire des Idées Occidentales*. Paris: Armand Colin éditeur.

Russell, B. (1973). *On Education Especially in Early Childhood.* London: George Allen and Unwin.

Russia may be disqualified from athletics competitions. (n.d.). Retrieved from http://www.newsru.com/sport/09nov2015/wada.html

Russia Novosibirsk, O. F. A. S. (2015). *Decision of the Commission on the case number 06-01-02-14-15 against "Stolica".* Retrieved April 29, 2016, from http://solutions.fas.gov.ru/to/novosibirskoe-ufas-rossii/bn-2c53b7c6- c887-41b8-b217-1042605f249c

Russia spent 27 mln EUR for two laboratories. (in press). *Sport-Express.*

Russian Football Union. (2012). *Regulation of the Russian Football Union on Ethics.* Retrieved April 29, 2016, from http://www.rfs.ru/rfs/documents/strategies/

Sargent Robinson, R. (1980). *Sources for the History of Greek Athletics.* Chicago: Ares. (Original work published 1955)

Satriano, D. (2012, December 18). Chiefs' Belcher texted secret girlfriend with Perkins threat: Report. *New York Post.* Retrieved from http://nypost.com/2012/12/18/chiefs-belcher-texted-secret-girlfriend-with-perkins-threat-report/

Sawyer v. State of New York, 485 N.Y.S. 2d 695 (1985).

Schatz, P., Moser, R. S., Covassin, T., & Karpf, R. (2011). Early indicators of enduring symptoms in high school athletes with multiple previous concussions. *Neurosurgery, 68*(6), 1562–1567. doi:10.1227/NEU.0b013e31820e382e PMID:21258259

Schaub, A. (2002). Sports and Competition: Broadcasting Rights of Sports Events. *Jornada dìa de la competencia.* Retrieved April 29, 2016, from http://ec.europa.eu/competition/speeches/text/sp2002_008_en.pdf

Schiavenza, M. (2015, August 9). The tragic legacy of Junior Seau. *The Atlantic.* Retrieved from https://www.theatlantic.com/entertainment/archive/2015/08/the-tragic-legacy-of-junior-seau/400856/

Schofield, D., & Criddle, C. (2015, 24 June). Brexit wins: How will British sport be affected? *The Telegraph.* Retrieved on March,2 from https://www.telegraph.co.uk/sport/.../how-would-british-sport-be-affected-by-a-brexit/

Scholte, J. A. (2004). Civil Society and Democratically Accountable Global Governance. *Government and Opposition*, *39*(2), 211–233. doi:10.1111/j.1477-7053.2004.00121.x

Schrotenboer, B. (2016, April 30). Ex-NFL doctor accused of gross negligence in treatment of Junior Seau. *USA Today Sports*. Retrieved from https://www.usatoday.com/story/sports/nfl/2016/04/30/chargers-doctor-david-chao-accused-gros-engligence-treatment-junior-seau/83777186/

Schuck, P. H. (1994). Rethinking informed consent. *Faculty Scholarship Series*. Paper 2765. Retrieved from http://digitalcommons.law.yale.edu/fss_papers/2765

Schütz, M. (2016). *Science shows that eSports professionals are real athletes.* Retrieved 23 October, 2017 from www.dw.com/en/science-shows-that-esports-professionals-are-real-athletes/a-19084993

Scott, R., Facio, G., Wolthoff, D., Shuman, L., & Cantillon, E. [Producers] & Landesman, P. [Director]. (2015). *Concussion* [Motion picture]. Retrieved from http://www.sonypictures.com/movies/concussion/

Sells, B. L. (1994). *The soul of the law*. Rockport, MA: Element, Inc.

Seven national teams were suspected of doping in Sochi Games. (n.d.). Retrieved February 2016, from http://www.newsru.com/sport/14may2014/wada .html

Seven Network Limited v News Limited [2009] FCAFC, 166.

Shapiro, L., & Maske, M. (2005, April 19). 'Monday Night Football' changes the channel after 35 years on ABC. *Washington Post*. Retrieved from http://www.washingtonpost.com/wp-dyn/articles/A63538-2005Apr18.html

Sherman Act, 15 U.S.C. §§ 1.

Shevchenko, O. (2015). *The legal doctrine of regulation of work in the sphere of professional sport and ways of realization in Russia*. Moscow: Prospect.

Shevchenko, O., & Ponkin, I. (2014). On development of legal doctrine in the field of sport. *Teoriya i Praktika Fizicheskoy Kultury*, *6*, 32–34.

Shore, C. E. (1990). Antitrust & Professional Sports' Eligibility Rules: The Past, the Present, and the Future. *Fordham Intellectual Property. Media and Entertainment Law Journal*, *1*(1), 65–89.

Shuman, P. J. (1986). *The Power of Perceptual Marketing: An Analysis of Sponsorships*. New York: Burson-Marsteller.

Sicilianos, L.-A. (Ed.). (2017). *European Convention on Human Rights: Commentary by Article* (2nd ed.). Athens: Nomiki Bibliothiki. (in Greek)

Siekmann, R., Parrish, R., Verhoogt, P., Martins, R. B., & Olfers, M. (2005). *Professional sport in the internal market (Project Nº IP/A/IMCO/ST/2005-004)*. Retrieved April 29, 2016, from http://www.asser.nl/media/2171/cms_sports_65_1_professional-sport.pdf

Silver, J. D. (2014, October 17). A life off-center: Mike Webster's battles. *Pittsburgh Post-Gazette*. Retrieved from http://www.post-gazette.com/ae/movies/2014/10/17/A-life-off-center-Mike-Webster-s-battles/stories/201410090319

Skvortsov, A. (2006). *Infliction of harm of life and health in sport. Problems of criminal and legal qualification.* Wolters Kluwer.

Slack, T. (Ed.). (2003). *The Globalization of Sport*. London: Frank Cass.

Slack, T., & Annis, J. (2004). Money for Nothing and your Cheques for Free? In T. Slack (Ed.), *The Commercialization of Sport*. New York, NY: Routledge.

Smiles, S. (1838). Physical Education or the Nature and Management of Children Founded on the Study of their Nature and Constitution. Edinburgh, UK: Oliver & Boyd, Tweeddale Court and London: Simpkin, Marshall & Co.

Smith, C. (2015, September 14). The NFL's richest owners. *Forbes*. Retrieved from https://www.forbes.com/sites/chrissmith/2015/09/14/the-nfls-richest-owners/#7ef5079d94ba

Smith, I. (2016, April). *ESIC Threat Assessment*. Retrieved March 01, 2018, from http://www.esportsintegrity.com/wpcontent/uploads/2016/04/ESIC_Threat-Assessment_Apr-2016.pdf

Soloviev, A., & Ponkin, I. V. I., (2010). Sports code of France. Reglamentarny part – Decrees. Books I and II.//Actual problems of the sports law. Version 5. Moscow: Commission of the Sports Law of Association of Lawyers of Russia.

Soloviev, A. (2010). *Brazilian Sports Codes//Actual problems of the sports law. Version 4*. Moscow: Commission of the Sports Law of Association of Lawyers of Russia.

Soloviev, A. (2011). *Doping liability according to the Sports code of France*. Moscow: Commission of the Sports Law of Association of Lawyers of Russia.

Soloviev, A. I. V., Ponkin, I., & Ponkina, A. (2013). *Legal regulation of sport in Switzerland//Actual problems of the sports law. Version 18*. Moscow: Commission of the Sports Law of Association of Lawyers of Russia.

Soper, J. C., den Dulk, K. R., & Monsma, S. V. (2017). *The Challenge of Pluralism: Church and State Relations in Six Democracies* (3rd ed.). London: Rowman & Littlefield.

Sport-Express. (2015). *Lovchev's dope: politics or shame?* Retrieved January 25, 2016, from http:www.sport-express.ru

Sport-Express. (2015, November). Ministry of Sport of Russia made statement to WADA's accusations. *Sport-Express*, 10.

Sports Act 2013. (2013).

SportWiki. (2015). *How to hide administration of steroids and prohibited preparations*. Retrieved November 7, 2012, from http://sportswiki.ru

Statista. (2017). *Average playing career length in the National Football League (in years)*. Retrieved from https://www.statista.com/statistics/240102/average-player-career-length-in-the-national-football-league/

Statista. (2017). *Global Sports Market - Total Revenue from 2005 to 2017 (in billion U.S. dollars)*. Retrieved December 3, 2017, from https://www.statista.com/statistics/370560/worldwide-sports-market-revenue/

Stead, D. (2008). Sport and the Media. In B. Houlihan (Ed.), *Sport and Society* (pp. 328–347). London: Sage Publications.

Steinbach, V. (2008). *Reverse of the medal*. Moscow: Chelovek.

Stop-astma.ru. (2013). *Asthma and Sport. Out speak about sport*. Retrieved December 20, 2013, from http://stop-asthma.ru/astma-i-sport

Stubbs, M. (2017, December 2). *Are Esports A Real Sport? Riot Games Wades Into The Debate With 'League Of Legends' Video*. Retrieved March 01, 2018, from https://www.forbes.com/sites/mikestubbs/2017/12/02/are-esports-a-real-sport-riot-games-wades-into-the-debate-with-league-of-legends-video/#4b7b69552486

Substances, which the Russian athletes used in Sochi are stated as doping. (n.d.). Retrieved June 15, 2014, from http://www.newsru.com/sport/20may2014/xenon.html

Synodinou, T. (2014). Image right and copyright law in Europe: Divergences and convergences. *Laws*, *3*(2), 181–207. doi:10.3390/laws3020181

Szymanski, S. (2015, July). *The economic arguments supporting a competition law challenge to the transfer system*. Retrieved April 29, 2016, from https://www.fifpro.org/attachments/article/6241/Embargoed%20Stefan%20Szymanski%20Transfer%20System%20Analysis.pdf

Szymanski, S. (2006). The Economic Evolution of Sport and Broadcasting. *The Australian Economic Review*, *39*(4), 428–434. doi:10.1111/j.1467-8462.2006.00432.x

Talha, M., & Subramaniam, M. (2003). Role of e-Commerce in Economic Growth. *Journal of Internet Marketing*, *4*(1), 1–7.

Tanier, M. (2016, November 15). Growth of gambling across US is helping to pull NFL wagering out of the whadows. *Bleacher Report*. Retrieved from http://bleacherreport.com/articles/2664047-growth-of-gambling-across-us-is-helping-pull-nfl-wagering-out-of-the-shadows

Taylor, T. L. (2012). *Raising the Stakes: E-Sports and the Professionalization of Computer Gaming*. Cambridge, MA: MIT Press.

Taymazov, E. (2012). Evaluating the effectiveness of public-private partnerships in the sports sponsorship. *Proceedings of the St. Petersburg University of Economics and Finance, 6*, 153-157.

Te, Z. (2016, January 5). *Valve Issues Life Bans to CS: GO Players Who Participated in Match-Fixing*. Retrieved March 01, 2018, from https://www.gamespot.com/articles/valve-issues-life-bans-to-cs-go-players-who-partic/1100-6433549/

The Guardian. (2014). *Sepp Baltter Bemoans a Storm against FIFA over Qatar World Cup*. Retrieved January 7, 2018 from https://www.theguardian.com/football/2014/jun/09/sepp-blatter-storm-fifa-qatar

The Guardian. (2015). *Sepp Blatter re-elected as FIFA President for the fifth time*. Retrieved on January 8, 2018 from https://www.theguardian.com/football/2015/may/29/sepp-blatter-reelected-fifa-president-fifth-term

The National Olympic Committee Kenya. (2017, August 29). *The Organisation.* Retrieved December 22, 2017, from https://www.olympic.org/about-ioc-institution

The Next Level. (2016, November 23). *France Is On All In On eSports.* Retrieved March 01, 2018, from http://tnl.media/esportsproteams/2016/11/21/france-is-on-all-in-on-esports

The Next Level. (2017, March 9). *Time To Kill The "eSports Beats Sports Viewers" Stat.* Retrieved March 01, 2018, from http://tnl.media/esportsnews/2017/3/8/time-to-kill-the-esports-beats-sports-viewers-stat

Thibault, J. (2009). Globalization of Sport: An Inconvenient Truth. *Journal of Sport Management, 23*(1), 1–20. doi:10.1123/jsm.23.1.1

Thibault, L. (2012). Delivering Sport in the Global Context. In L. Trenberth & D. Hassan (Eds.), *Managing Sport Business* (pp. 231–257). London: Routledge.

Thorne, D., Berns Wright, L., & Jones, S. A. (2001, Spring). The Impact of Sports Marketing Relationships and Antitrust Issues in the United States. *Journal of Public Policy & Marketing, 20*(1), 73–83. doi:10.1509/jppm.20.1.73.17279

Tiberius, M. (1996). *When they were demolishing the walls.* Retrieved 28 October, 2017 from www.tovima.gr/opinions/article/?aid=81574 (in Greek)

Tomjanovich v. California Sports, Inc., No. H-78-243 (S.D. Texas Aug. 17, 1979).

Top-5 athletes, who ruined career with drugs. (2014). *Bigmirnet.* Retrieved February 21, 2014, from http://sport.bigmir.net/football/other/1558149-TOP-5-sportsmenov--pogubivshih-kar-eru-narkotikami

Tran, K. (2017). *Esports in consideration for 2024 Olympics.* Retrieved 28 October, 2017 from www.businessinsider.com/esports-in-consideration-for-2024-olympics-2017-8

Transgender athletes will be allowed to participate in OG without gender reassignment surgery. (n.d.). Retrieved February 15, 2016, from http://lenta.ru/comments/news/2016/01/25/transgenderathletes/

Transparency International Kenya. (2016). *Global corruption report: Sport* (Issue 160). Retrieved from https://tikenya.org/wp-content/uploads/2017/06/adili-issue-160_corruption-in-sport.pdf

United Nations. (2007, December). Women, gender equality and sports. *Women 2000 and Beyond.* Retrieved from http://www.un.org/womenwatch/daw/public/Women%20and%20Sport.pdf

US Department of Justice. (2015). *Nine FIFA Officials and Five Corporate Executives Indicted for Racketeering Conspiracy and Corruption*. Retrieved January 23, 2018 from https://www.justice.gov/opa/pr/nine-fifa-officials-and-five-corporate-executives-indicted-racketeering-conspiracy-and

USA Today sports. (2012, December 4). Belcher's girlfriend shot in chest, neck, abdomen, according to audio. *USA Today*. Retrieved from https://www.usatoday.com/story/sports/nfl/2012/12/04/jovan-belcher-audio-first-responders/1746603/

Van Miert, K. (1997, November 27). *Sport et concurrence: Développements récents et action de la Commission*. Speech presented at Forum européen du Sport, Luxembourg, Luxembourg. Retrieved April 29, 2016, from http://ec.europa.eu/competition/speeches/text/sp1997_069_fr.html

Vdovin, A., & Vdovin, D. (2014). *Everyone take doping. Only poor are caught.* Retrieved May 14, 2014, L: http://www.shooting-ua.com/books/book_18.3.htm

Vendel, C. (2012, December 4). Exclusive: Police reports detail Belcher, Perkins' last hours. *The Kansas City Star*. Retrieved from http://www.kansascity.com/news/local/article311755.html

Vernant, J.-P. (1991). *Mortals and Immortals*. Princeton, NJ: Princeton University Press.

Voros, G. (2007). *Egyptian Temple Architecture: 100 Years of Hungarian Excavations in Egypt, 1907 -2007*. Cairo: The American University in Cairo Press.

Wachtmeister, A.-M. (1998, June). Broadcasting of sports events and competition law. *Competition Policy Newsletter, 2*. Retrieved April 29, 2016, from http://ec.europa.eu/competition/speeches/text/sp1998_037_en.html

Wacke, A. (1977). Unfälle bei Sport und Spiel nach römischem und geltendem Recht. *Stadion, 3*, 4–43. PMID:11633297

WADA Anti-Doping Testing Figures Report . (2012). Retrieved February 2, 2014, from http://www.wada-ama.org/en

WADA: two Moscow laboratories eliminated doping tests. (n.d.). Retrieved May 19, 2016, from http://ria.ru/sport/20151109/1317524622.html

Wamaitha, J. K. (2015). *Gender representation in sports participation and leadership in teacher training colleges in the eastern zone-Kenya* (Master's thesis). Kenyatta University, Nairobi, Kenya.

Warman, P. (2017, February 14). *Esports revenues will reach $696M in 2017 and $1.5Bn by 2020.* Retrieved March 01, 2018, from https://newzoo.com/insights/articles/esports-revenues-will-reach-696-million-in-2017/

Weiss, T. G. (2000). Governance, Good Governance and Global Governance. *Third World Quarterly*, *21*(5), 795–814. doi:10.1080/713701075

Wekesa, M. (2010). *Regulation of doping in sports: Implications for Kenya (Doctoral dissertation)*. Nairobi, Kenya: University of Nairobi. Retrieved from http://erepository.uonbi.ac.ke

Wells, L. J. (1971). The Multinational Business Enterprise: What Kind of International Organization? In R. O. Keohane & J. S. Nye (Eds.), *Transnational Relations and World Politics* (pp. 97–114). Cambridge, MA: Harvard University Press. doi:10.1017/S0020818300026254

Westerbeek, H. (Ed.). (2011). *Global Sport Business: Community Impacts of Commercial Sport*. London: Routledge.

Wiborg, S. (2009). *Education and Social Integration: Comprehensive Schooling in Europe*. New York, NY: Palgrave Macmillan. doi:10.1057/9780230622937

Wickert, G. (2017). *Contributory negligence/comparative fault in all 50 States.* Work product of Mathiesen, Wickert, and Lehrer, SC. Retrieved from https://www.mwl-law.com/ wp-content/uploads/2013/03/contributory-negligence-comparative-fault-laws-in-all-50-states.pdf

Wikipedia. (2006). *Methamphetamine.* Retrieved December 7, 2015, from http://ru.wikipedia.org/wiki

Wikipedia. (2015). *Chegin, Viktor Mikhailovich.* Retrieved February 2, 2016 from https://ru.wikipedia.org

Williamson, B. (2015, July). Premiership Rugby Union: Through the Antitrust Looking Glass. *The Competition Law Review*, *11*(1), 41–60.

Wilson, R. (2015, April 22). Judge approves concussion settlement, could cost NFL $1 billion. *CBS Sports*. Retrieved from https://www.cbssports.com/nfl/news/judge-approves-concussion-settlement-could-cost-nfl-1-billion/

Wolfe, R., Meenaghan, T., & O' Sullivan, P. (2002). The Sports Network: Insights into the Shifting Balance of Power. *Journal of Business Research*, *55*(7), 611–622. doi:10.1016/S0148-2963(00)00191-0

World Anti-Doping Code 2015. (2016). Moscow: RUSADA.

World Intellectual Property Organization. (1981). *Nairobi Treaty on the Protection of the Olympic Symbol / Adopted in Nairobi 26.09.1981*. Retrieved April 29, 2016, from http://www.rupto.ru/docs/interdocs/nayrobi?starblind=100

World Intellectual Property Organization. (n.d.). *Broadcasting & Media Rights in Sport*. Retrieved April 29, 2016, from http://www.wipo.int/ip-sport/en/broadcasting.html

Wussow v Commercial Mechanisms, Inc., 90 Wis. 2d 136 (1979).

Wussow v. Commercial Mechanisms, Inc., 293 N. W. 2d 897 (1980).

Young, H. (2016, May 31). *ESports: Is pro video gaming a sport?* Retrieved March 01, 2018, from https://edition.cnn.com/2016/05/31/sport/esports-is-professional-gaming-a-sport/index.html

Zaitsev, Y. (2010). The right to coverage of sporting events in the Russian Federation. *Sports: Economics, Law, Management, 4*.

Zhang, Z. (2006). What Is Lived Space? *Ephemera: Theory & Politics in Organization, 6*(2), 219-223.

ZMIX.RU. (2008). *Brief doping history in sport*. Retrieved March 2, 2014, from http://zmix.ru/food/chemistry/articles-doping/item

Zubareva, A., (2012). Sporting wheels. *RBK (Business Magazine),* 9.

Zucker, J. (2017, August 7). NFL settles with 6 insurance companies over concussion lawsuit expenses. *Bleacher Report*. Retrieved from http://bleacherreport.com/articles/2726106-nfl-settles-with-6-insurance-companies-over-concussion-lawsuit-expenses

About the Contributors

Konstantinos Margaritis is an adjunct lecturer at the Department of Political Science, University of Crete. He holds a PhD in Law from the National and Kapodistrian University of Athens and an LLM in International and European Public Law from Tilburg University. He has published extensively in the fields of European Law and Comparative Public Law and Human Rights.

***

Rodney Blackman is in his second year as a member of the Resident Faculty at the United States Sports Academy and Chair of Recreation Management program. Prior to the Academy, he has worked in a range of professional settings, including academia, where he has taught at the university level since 1997. Blackman also has work experience in non-academic, public, and private sector positions. Collectively, Blackman's education and professional experience have been primarily in the areas of leadership, management, marketing, programming, operations management, and administration – all in the context of sports, recreation, tourism, and leisure services delivery systems. In addition, his foremost area of expertise is in the legal aspects of sports, recreation, and leisure services. Blackman has lived and worked in a number of different environments, including internationally, in Japan, Germany, and Russia. Also on the international scene, Blackman has spent several summers in Ireland, where he has led study abroad troupes and conducted research and development with the Gaelic Athletic Association (GAA). Blackman earned his Bachelor's Degree in Theology from The Master's College in Los Angeles, Calif., and his Master's Degree in Leisure Services Program Management from the University of Northern Iowa in Cedar Falls, Iowa. In addition, Dr. Blackman has the equivalent of a Master of Legal Studies (MLS) from Indiana University School of Law, Bloomington – and, he earned his Doctorate in Recreation from Indiana University, in Bloomington, Ind.

Efthalia Chatzigianni is Assistant Professor of International Organizations and other forms of cooperation in the field of sport, Sport Management Department, University of Peloponnese, Greece. She holds a BA in Sociology, PhD in International and European Studies (Panteion University of Social & Political Sciences, Athens), and an MA in International Politics (Université Libre de Bruxelles). She is author of two books: *Sport Governance. Globalization International Organization and Politics* (2018, Athens: Sideris) and *Lobbying: Interest Promotion Mechanisms* (2007, Athens: Papazissis). She has published numerous articles and book chapters in English, Greek, and German. She has participated in many conferences as well as in the organization of various sport events, including three Olympic Games (1996, 2002, 2004). She is currently a Visiting Scholar and Instructor at the Sport Management Department, Brock University, Canada (2017-2018) and was Visiting Professor at CERES, Munk School of Global Affairs, and the Faculty of Kinesiology and Physical Education, University of Toronto, Canada (2013 & 2014).

Konstantina Gongaki is Assistant Professor, Philosophy of Sport, National and Kapodistrian University of Athens.

Asha Mikinyango is a practising advocate of the High Court of Kenya and a certified professional mediator (MTI). She holds an LLM from the University of Nairobi and is also a member of the Law Society of Kenya. Her areas of expertise include intellectual property law, commercial law and sports law. She also teaches law at Mount Kenya University, School of Law, in Nairobi Kenya.

Reyhan Mir previously trained and gained experience at the law firm of Pintó Ruiz & Del Valle, Barcelona, followed by working at the law firm of Ruiz Huerta & Crespo Sports Lawyers, Valencia. Mr. Reyhan Mir is an international sports law consultant based in Valencia with a specialisation in eSports.

Renata Ntelia is a PhD researcher at the Institute of Digital Games, University of Malta. Her academic interests include Comparative Narratology, Philosophy of Games, and Thanatology.

Anatoly Peskov holds Academic and professional positions: Developer of the Training Course “Sport and Security”, Lector of the Russian International Olympic University Advocate of the Moscow Region Chamber of Advocates Member of the Sports Law Commission of the Russian Association of Lawyers. Member of the Board of Directors of the International Association of Spots Law (IASL) Member of the editorial board “Sport: economics, law, management” Professional experience Work in the field of security for 40 years. Retired colonel of police. Main areas of research. Criminological research in the sphere of crime and corruption, youth crime, violations of legality among police. Author of scientific articles devoted to combating match-fixing, criminal fanaticism, doping, money laundering, terrorism, extremism, racism, corruption and organized crime in professional sports. Social activities. Legal expertise of draft legislation on problems of combating offenses in professional sports. Speeches at the committees of State Duma on problems of combating offenses in professional sports. Published more 60 scientific works.

Igor Ponkin is a Doctor of Science (Law), Professor of the chair of sports law of the Kutafin Moscow State Law University, State Professor, Professor of Russian Presidential Academy of National Economy and Public Administration under the President of the Russian Federation.

Alena Redkina is a Lawyer, PhD (Law), lecturer of the chair of sports law of the Kutafin Moscow State Law University.

Olga Shevchenko is a Doctor of science (Law) Kutafin Moscow State Law University, International Association of Sports Law Arbiter of Arbitration for Sport at the CCI of the Russia Vice Chair - Legal Committee of the FISU Executive Secretary of the Committee of the Sports Law of the Association of Lawyers of Russia Executive Secretary of the Legal Committee of the Russian Football Union Legal Consultant in the field of basketball, football, hockey, dance sport. Author of more than 80 academic and methodical works, including those in English and Spanish. She had an internship at the International Labour Organization (ILO) in Geneva, Switzerland (2013). INEFC Lleida University, Barcelona, Spain (2014). At the invitation of the Ministry of Sports of Indonesia participated in an international high-level meeting in Jakarta (Indonesia) on international cooperation and the prospects for positive regulation of the Russian experience of physical culture and sports in foreign legislation (2013). Has long and varied experience of research, preparation of legal opinions, including on issues of employment and sports law. Is the chief editor of the peer-reviewed international scientific journal “e-Lex Sportiva Journal (L.Sp.J)” and the executive editor of the Kutafin University Law Review in English. Research interests include a wide range of scientific problems of international law, labor law and social security law, in cooperation with other branches of law - civil, administrative, et al., as well as sports and health law in accordance with national, foreign and international aspects.

Dino Sossi produced media for AOL, CBS's "60 Minutes," CNN, the New York Times, the United Nations and Viacom's vh1. His documentary films have screened at festivals in New York and Los Angeles, universities like Berkeley, Cambridge, Columbia, Harvard, Oxford and Pennsylvania, as well as the United Nations headquarters in New York. Dino's work has been broadcast on CBC, CTV, Discovery USA, Globe & Mail, IFC, Life, MTV Canada, MuchMoreMusic, One, Pridevision and PrimeTV. His digital storytelling has been exhibited at the San Francisco Museum of Modern Art. Dino taught and was a digital media consultant at Columbia. He also taught digital storytelling at Adelphi. Dino has performed storytelling at the Moth StorySLAM in New York. Dino earned his doctorate in Instructional Technology & Media at Columbia. He earned first class honors for his Master of Philosophy thesis at Cambridge where he also performed with the Footlights comedy troupe. Dino studied at Columbia Law School's School Law Institute and the Oxford Internet Institute Summer Doctoral Programme. He was also a fellow at the Berkman Klein Center for Internet and Society at Harvard.

Index

A

Activision 102
ADAMS 213, 232
ancient Greece 129, 157-158
ancient Olympia 159
Anti-Doping technologies 203, 222-224
assumption of risk 4-9, 13-14, 17, 21, 63
autonomy of sports 23, 26, 41

B

balance 2-3, 6, 28, 32, 34-35, 149
biological passport 205, 223
Blizzard 102, 109, 113, 115
Body culture 157-158, 161
Bookmarker 256, 261
brain injury 60, 65, 71
brain trauma 63, 70, 72-74

C

Caillois 126-130, 133-134, 136-138, 140
Chronic Traumatic Encephalopathy (CTE) 54-55, 57-69, 72-75
Commercial Competition in the Field of Professional Sports 23, 25
community interests 2-3, 21
Competitiveness in the Sport 23, 25
concussion protocols 71, 75
contract 56, 64, 66, 72, 189-190, 229, 252-253, 261
contributory negligence 3-5, 8-9, 12-14, 16-17, 21, 64
corruption 116, 164, 202, 220, 246, 255, 258, 261
cultural elements 157, 159

E

eBusiness 92
education 18, 71, 144-145, 147-153, 157-159, 161-166, 245, 249, 253-254
Employment Issues 246, 252
esports 101-119, 124-125, 128, 133-140
ethical implications 54-55, 58, 65
ethics 2, 4, 16, 91, 166, 169, 196, 198-199, 215, 226, 246, 249-251, 254

F

foreign students 149-150
fragmented treatment 158, 162
freedom of religion 144-146, 152

G

Gender Inequality 253-254, 257, 261
global sport governance 83, 86-87, 89, 91-93

H

head trauma 64-65, 67-68, 70
Human Rights 144-145

I

ice hockey, 54, 60, 62, 68
illicit trafficking of doping 230, 232

individual rights 2-3, 5, 16, 21
intelligence-based testing 232
international organization 83, 86-87, 93
IOC 91, 95, 106-108, 112, 115, 118-119, 124-125, 206, 208, 211-212, 214, 217

J

jurisdiction 2, 66, 109, 111-112, 115-116, 225, 248, 253

K

Kenya 241-258

M

martial arts 54, 61-62, 68, 128, 243
media 16, 35, 66, 75, 83-84, 86-87, 89-91, 105, 180-181, 183-184, 218, 221, 244

N

negligence 3-6, 8-9, 11-17, 21, 63-64, 191, 209
neurocognitive degeneration 67-68
NFL players 56, 58, 61-65, 72, 74
North American 48-49, 55-56, 59, 63, 116

O

Olympic athlete 138, 157-159

P

philosophical convictions 151, 153
Physical education 144-145, 147-153, 157-159, 161-163, 165
play 5-6, 21, 37, 42-43, 48, 57, 64, 67, 69-70, 74, 84, 86, 91-92, 102, 109-111, 126-130, 134-138, 140, 160, 162, 164-165, 198, 202, 219, 249
production 30, 33, 46, 55, 90, 124-125, 130-136, 138-139, 184, 189, 211, 226-229
professional athlete 169, 217, 219
professional sports 23-30, 32, 34-36, 38-42, 44-45, 47-50, 54-55, 57, 60, 62, 65-68, 169-170, 173, 180, 194, 196, 198-199, 202-203, 206, 234, 243, 248, 251
prohibited substances 203, 209-210, 212-215, 226-227, 231-232, 246
publishers 102, 104, 109-115, 117-119

R

recovery 3-4, 6, 10-12, 21, 212
recreation 7-9, 14, 17-18, 21, 88, 160, 245
religious freedom 144-149, 152
retired players 66-67, 69
right to education 147, 151-152

S

shift 3-5, 9-11, 13, 16, 18, 21, 136
societal consciousness 2-3, 21
space 75, 84, 107, 124-126, 128-132, 135-140, 169, 199
spatiality 124, 128
sponsorship 83, 87, 89-91, 95, 183, 192-193, 251, 255
sport business 83-84, 86-87, 89-90, 92-95
Sport Monopoly 26
Sport Monopsony 26
Sport Oligopoly 26
sporting competition 158
sports betting 244, 256, 262
sports corruption 258
sports entertainment product 33, 169, 184
sports ethics 169, 196, 198, 215, 226, 251, 254
sports governance 250, 255, 257
sports image rights 248, 254-255, 262
sports industry 1, 4, 7-8, 18, 23, 169-170, 172-175, 177, 179-180, 184, 192, 196, 241, 243-247, 249-250, 252-254
sports law 42, 133, 170, 209, 226, 241-242, 244, 246, 251-253, 257, 262
sports medicine 197, 202-203, 211, 223-226, 229, 232

sports product 26, 36, 169, 174
Super Bowl 5, 55, 57, 103
supervision 4, 22, 26, 211, 233
swimming classes 148, 150-152

T

tragic deaths 58, 69, 75
traumatic blows 54, 60, 62

V

vicarious liability 8, 17, 22
virtuality 124, 137

W

Western Europe 157-158, 162
World Anti-Doping Code 203, 209, 214, 222, 225, 234

www.ingramcontent.com/pod-product-compliance
Lightning Source LLC
LaVergne TN
LVHW061545290926
849162LV00004B/910